Contents

List of Figures, Charts, and Vignettes   xi

Preface   xiii

Acknowledgments   xviii

About the Author   xxi

Introduction to the Guide   1

Why the Culturally Courageous
    Leadership Paradigm Is Needed   2
Cultural Hegemony vs. Cultural Democracy   3
Institutional Obstacles   6
Popular Reasons for Major Achievement Disparities   6
Preview of Each Section in the Guide   7

SECTION I: LEADERSHIP FOR EQUITABLE
OUTCOMES—IT TAKES AN ENTIRE COMMUNITY   11

1. Identity, Teaching, and Learning   12
KWL Exercise   12
Influences on Identity Development   12
Student Identity and Achievement   15
Race and Personal Identity   17
The Hidden Curriculum   21
The Role of Culturally Courageous Leaders
    in Addressing Identity/Conflict Issues   25

2. The Absence of Cultural Democracy   27
KWL Exercise   27
Cultural Democracy   28
The "Dynamics of Difference"   29
So What?   31
The Impact of Little Cultural Democracy   32
The Impact of School Organizational Culture   35
The Role of Culturally Courageous Leaders in
    Addressing the Absence of Cultural Democracy   42

3. Grim Continuities   **44**

The Gaps in No Child Left Behind   44

KWL Exercise   46

Four Conditions in School Communities

     That May Contribute to Inequitable Student Outcomes   46

     Instruction, Hegemony, and Identity   46

     Deficiencies in Teacher/Administrator Preparation and

         Professional Development Programs   48

     Cultural Politics   51

     Human Fears   53

The Potential Role of Culturally Courageous

     Leaders in Addressing Grim Continuities   57

4. Rhetoric vs. Reality   **58**

KWL Exercise   58

What Is Done Compared

     With What Is Needed for Real Equity   60

Ten Observations   62

The Potential Role of Culturally Courageous

     Leaders in Reducing Gaps Between Rhetoric and Reality   68

5. Biases   **70**

KWL Exercise   70

Institutional Biases   70

     Curricula and Scheduling   73

     Personnel Selection and Professional Development   76

     Supervision/Evaluation   80

     Student Low Socioeconomic Status   83

     Student's Primary Discourse   86

     Involvement of Parents and Guardians   88

The Role of Culturally Courageous Leaders Related to

     Institutional Biases in School Settings   90

6. Barriers   **91**

KWL Exercise   91

Some Barriers to Equitable Outcomes   95

     Weak Instructional Leadership   95

     Insufficient Support for Instructional Staff   95

     Teaching Problems   96

     Toxic School and School Community Climate   97

     Limited Accountability   98

Relationship Between Personal Identities and Barriers   99

Relationship Between Racial/Cultural Conflicts
and Barriers   100
Relationship Between the Lack of Cultural Democracy
and Barriers   101
Relationship of Personal Biases and Norms in School
Settings to Barriers   102
The Role of Culturally Courageous Leaders in
Addressing Barriers to High Achievement   107

SECTION II: CULTURALLY COURAGEOUS LEADERSHIP—
A PARADIGM FOR CONTEMPORARY REALITIES   **109**

7. A New Paradigm for the 21st Century   **110**
KWL Exercise   110
"Major Actions Needed" by Culturally Courageous Leaders   111
The Culturally Courageous Leadership (CCL) Paradigm   116
First Component of CCL: Collaborative Leadership by
All School Community Stakeholders   117

8. Seven Principles   **121**
KWL Exercise   121
Second Component of CCL: Seven Principles/Characteristics   122
Committed Caregivers   122
Cultural Consumers   123
Consummate Conciliators   124
Conscientious Coaches   125
Courageous Change Masters   127
Community Organizers   128
Communication Gurus   129

9. Transformation and Politics   **132**
KWL Exercise   132
How Transformation and Politics Go Hand in Hand   132
Third and Fourth Components of CCL: Achieving
Personal and Organizational Transformation by
Adeptly Navigating the Politics of Implementation (POI)   134
First Dimension of POI: Engage in Problem
Definition and Analysis   134
Second Dimension of POI: Be Sensitive to the
Psychology of Equity Transformation   137
Third Dimension of POI: Focus on Standards
Categories Receiving Low Priority   138

Fourth Dimension of POI: Use Personal or Others' Observations
    Based on Implementation of Equity Initiatives   139
Fifth Dimension of POI: Reduce Some Key Barriers
    to Achievement at High Levels by All Students   140
Sixth Dimension of POI: Prevent "Equity Hustlers"
    From Compromising Equity Efforts   146

10. Stakeholder Practices   **149**
    KWL Exercise   149
    Examples of CCL Practices by All Stakeholder Groups   150
    Major Strands in CCL Practices Across
        All Stakeholder Groups   157

11. Promising Departures   **159**
    KWL Exercise   159
    Characteristics of Schools That Have Eliminated the Gap   160
        Prerequisites   161
        Conditions: The "5 A's"   163
    Answers to Questions You Might Want to Ask   177

12. Two Leadership Profiles   **179**
    KWL Exercise   179
    Consequences for a Charter School
        Committed to the "5 A's"   180
    District-Level Actions Helping School
        Sites Embrace the "5 A's"   183
    Similarities and Differences   187

SECTION III: MAKING IT REAL   **189**

13. Defusing the Political Land Mines   **190**
    KWL Exercise   191
    What Is Meant by the "Politics" of Equity Transformation?   191
    How Definitions Apply to the Term
        "Politics of Implementation"   192
    Political Savvy   193
    Equity Transformation vs. Equity Reform   194
    An Attempt at Equity Transformation—
        The Mount Vernon School District   195
    Factors Contributing to the Politics Associated With the
        Equity Transformation Effort   197
        Engage in Problem Definition and Analysis   197

    Be Sensitive to the Psychology of Equity Transformation   198
    Focus on Standards Categories Receiving Low Priority   201
  An Attempt at Equity Reform—Pierson Academy for Leadership (PAL)   203
  Factors Contributing to the Politics Associated
    With the Equity Reform Effort   205
    Learn From Observations During Other Equity Initiatives   205
    Reduce Some Key Barriers to Achievement at High Levels   209
    Prevent "Equity Hustlers" From Compromising
      Equity Efforts   213
  What Was Happening in the Vignettes   214
  Political Strategy Reminders   215

14. Three Equity Warriors   **217**
  KWL Exercise   217
  Leading by Making the Invisible Visible:
    Jean Richardson, Principal   218
  Demonstrating Leadership by Coaching and Facilitation:
    Kathryn Haywood, Principal   226
  Mentoring for Social Justice:
    Robert Montoya, University Professor   234
  Similarities in the Three Equity Warriors   239

15. Practicing the "Equity Walk"   **242**
  Setting the Stage: Introduction to Two Culturally
    Courageous Leadership Diagnostic Questionnaires   242
  KWL Exercise   243
  Introduction to the Role-Playing Exercise   243
  Background Information on the Harbor View
    Unified School District   244
  Directions for the Role-Play   245
  Brief History of Bethune-Chavez High School (BCHS)   247
  Salient Facts Related to the "Problem" at BCHS   247
  School Climate and Learning Environment at BCHS   247
  Additional Background Information on the "Problem" at BCHS   248
  In-Basket Items of Area Superintendent Related to BCHS   249
    Directions for Responding to In-Basket Items and
      Sixteen Questions   249
  Some Suggested Responses to Each In-Basket Item   255
  Questions to Be Considered in Draft Action Plan for
    Working With BCHS as the New Area Superintendent   259
  How the Sixteen Questions Relate to the
    Culturally Courageous Leadership Paradigm   260

16. The Time Is Here, the Time Is Now   **269**
    KWL Exercise   270
    Additional Issues You *Must* Consider   270
    Do's and Don'ts   277
    Debunking Lame Excuses   283
    What Next?   285

Appendix 1: Facilitator Notes for Chapters 1 Through 15 **287**

Appendix 2: Culturally Courageous Leadership
Diagnostic Questionnaire for Individuals   **337**

Culturally Courageous Leadership Diagnostic Questionnaire:
School Learning Environment   **351**

References   **363**

Index   **379**

List of Figures, Charts, and Vignettes

Figures and Charts

Figure 1a: Graphic Illustration of Interrelated Educational Conditions 4

Chart 1a: Factors That May Influence Personal Identity 22

Chart 2a: Proposed Actions and Potential Results Regarding
Intergroup and Interpersonal Relations 37

Chart 5a: Five Categories of Standards 72

Chart 5b: Major Players and Issues in Vignette 5–2 81

Chart 6a: Some Barriers to Equitable Outcomes 94

Chart 6b: Relationship Between Biases and Barriers 103

Figure 7a: The Culturally Courageous Leadership Paradigm 116

Chart 11a: Some Variables, Needs, and Prerequisites of
High-Achieving Schools 160

Chart 11b: Attitude 163

Chart 11c: Access 169

Chart 11d: Assessment 171

Chart 11e: Adaptation 173

Chart 11f: Accountability 175

Chart 12a: Examples of the 5 A's in CLAS 181

Chart 12b: Examples of the 5 A's Modeled by a District Administrator 185

Chart 15a: CCL Actions Response Sheet for In-Basket Activity 256

Vignettes

Vignette 1–1: Introduction to Jimmy   20

Vignette 2–1: Jimmy in Elementary School   33

Vignette 2–2: Description of Jimmy's Middle School   35

Vignette 2–3: Bullying in Pilgrim K–8 School   39

Vignette 2–4: Introduction to Thurgood Marshall High School   40

Vignette 3–1: Jimmy's and Josephina's Experience in Olentangy Middle School   46

Vignette 3–2: School/Community Conflict in Olentangy Middle School   54

Vignette 4–1: The Continuing Saga at Olentangy Middle School   59

Vignette 5–1: Jimmy's Experience of "Tracking"   75

Vignette 5–2: Proposed Professional Development Programs in the
    McClelland District—Causes and Reactions   79

Vignette 5–3: State Department of Education Meetings to
    Elicit Regional Input   85

Vignette 5–4: Large School District's Response to English Literacy Needs   87

Vignette 6–1: Jimmy's and His Mother's Attitudes About the
    High School He Should Attend   91

Vignette 7–1: Collaborative Efforts to Address Teacher Disciplinary Referrals 118

Vignette 9–1: Oak Canyon District—Systemic Approach
    to Equity Transformation   145

Vignette 13–1: An Attempt at Equity Transformation—
    The Mount Vernon School District   195

Vignette 13–2: An Attempt at Equity Reform—Pierson Academy
    for Leadership (PAL)   203

Preface

Long before my teaching, administrative, and consultant career, I was drawn to discovering or figuring out the back stories that help provide answers to the *what* and *why* of human behavior. Even before I began to develop awareness of how injustice, oppression, and racism permeate the fabric of society in the United States, and before I even had such words to describe it, I was consumed by the need to figure out the plot, so to speak, that would help to explain the variables and dynamics contributing to what I was observing, experiencing, and intuiting. Thus the term *back story* is one I am attracted to using when describing what may be some of the reasons or conditions contributing to the continuation of cultural hegemony. This fascination probably led to my embracing the study of history, and more particularly historiography, during my high school and undergraduate years. But it was always for the purpose of helping me make more sense out of what Myrdal called the "American Dilemma" and DuBois called the "problem of the color-line" in the United States. After all, I was a civil rights baby, coming to maturity during the height of the movement and deeply involved as a participant on many levels. Years later, I have reflected on how important it was for me to become exposed to information about my cultural heritage early in life. I grew up in a church led by a civil rights political activist whose dear wife gave me some books that opened my eyes to the Black experience and the rich legacy of excellence from my cultural and ethnic ancestors, both in this country and the motherland. I was also blessed with a family on both sides that had a history of being trailblazers, surviving and thriving despite all the odds. All of this made a tremendous difference because the school curriculum was totally devoid of any in-depth or even cosmetic attention to such content. Unfortunately, decades later, not much has changed in that regard.

I tried to incorporate, albeit sometimes surreptitiously, what are now called multicultural and culturally responsive approaches into my humanities and social science teaching. I knew before I got my feet wet teaching that graduate school was going to be absolutely essential and an advanced degree my goal, but not just from anywhere. From being blessed with an advisor for my undergraduate major who was an exemplar of what I now call culturally courageous leadership, I saw firsthand the politics he endured from such personal commitments and core values and therefore wanted to pursue advanced studies in an academic environment where they *walked the talk*.

How naïve I was! Nevertheless, I prevailed with a lot of help and having to dig deeper than I ever had before. After an initial foray for several years into attempts to facilitate a mix of curriculum/human relations/organizational reform, I morphed into giving in-depth attention to assisting and providing instructional leadership for total school and district transformation. My agenda was always equity based, regardless of position. My personal lessons were many, as much on what not to do as what to do. I have become first and foremost a student of the politics involved when planning and implementing equity transformation. And I am still drawn to discovering and figuring out the back stories behind what does or doesn't happen in my life, my professional endeavors, and in the schooling enterprise within the United States of America. I believe you must inspect what you expect, constantly! I am intrigued by how some of the major work on organizational, leadership, and teacher effectiveness, as well as on how to make schools work for all students, is not used in the least by those who are ostensibly leaders in school communities committed to eliminating disparities in educational outcomes. But I have not seen nearly as much energy given to eliminating the enormous disparities in educational inputs. To paraphrase what Ron Edmonds said decades ago before his untimely death—we already know what we need to know, the question is whether we have the will to do it. To exercise the will, we must first "wake up" as our esteemed elder scholar Asa Hilliard III often said. This guide uses many back stories to further our work in getting those school community stakeholders dedicated to social justice to first wake up and then develop the will and savvy that are so necessary.

This guide has been written because of my desire to increase the knowledge and effectiveness of school district and school site leaders, including teacher leaders, those aspiring to such positions, and other school community stakeholders. The guide has the purpose of expanding the problem-solving dialogue on how to provide collaborative leadership among all school community stakeholders that contributes to the following:

- Culturally democratic learning environments within school and classroom settings
- Sustained improvement in the educational inputs and outcomes experienced by students who are and have been on the lower end of the achievement continuum and what is called by some the racial achievement gap, which is really more of a racial opportunity gap

Two major assumptions are that the two outcomes above are some of the necessary ingredients for social justice to be significantly improved in the United States, and that equitable inputs and outcomes are reflections of social justice.

It is hoped this guide will help increase the consciousness, willingness, and political savvy of all adult school community stakeholders to successfully implement equity initiatives that result in both equity and excellence for the historically underserved in the United States. The guide is meant for stakeholders in all school communities, whether schools are in large or small urban areas, suburban areas, or rural areas. Even in schools populated almost entirely or entirely by students from the same racial, primary language, or socioeconomic background, this guide has the aim of increasing leaders' capacity to improve cultural democracy and equitable student outcomes in these settings. Many examples of cultural democracy in educational settings will be provided in the guide. However, a concise definition of the term is when schools and teachers are responsive to the cultural backgrounds and characteristics of all learners and their families as reflected in curriculum, instruction, and assessment programs as well as reflected in all other areas. Equitable student outcomes refers to eliminating the current racial achievement disparity that exists in most schools between historically underserved students of color and other students as well as ensuring that all student demographic groups receive equitable treatment in a variety of areas. Educational areas where equity is important include the percentages of each demographic group that are

- enrolled in higher level courses and programs,
- receiving additional tutoring when needed,
- assigned to special education,
- referred for disciplinary action, suspended, or expelled,
- taught by highly qualified culturally responsive teachers in all classes,
- graduating from high school, and
- subsequently enrolling in and successfully graduating from community colleges, universities, or career technical programs.

It is also hoped this guide will provoke greater consideration of the collaborative role that students and community persons should play. Community persons include university faculty in teacher and administrative preparation programs. Secondary students and community persons should have more input and responsibility for helping implement equity initiatives at the school-site level. They could help educators increase outside of the box thinking about what is necessary to achieve the goals of whatever equity initiative is undertaken.

Another critical variable to which this guide gives considerable attention is the need to redefine what has traditionally been called personal and organizational transformation in preschool through undergraduate degree university programs. This guide can be used to help individuals and organizations engage in processes that may result in adoption of the values, beliefs, attitudes, and skills needed to improve cultural democracy, which can be an outcome of personal and organizational transformation.

In some school communities, there has been a concerted avoidance of direct conversation about how race, culture, language, and socioeconomic status issues, when interfaced with community/district/school site organizational culture characteristics, have a negative influence on student outcomes. Such problem-solving discussions should be part of comprehensive systemic change efforts. However, such discussions have the potential to be volatile and should not be undertaken without considerable attention to the collaborative leadership needed when trying to achieve equity. Such collaboration must occur across all stakeholder groups, not just among teachers.

Since the beginning of the 21st century, government at the federal and state levels has tried to dramatically increase accountability for the academic outcomes of all students, as exemplified by education legislation and funding mandates. One result has been major reforms in the preparation and professional development of educational leaders. Nevertheless, the disparities in student educational outcomes persist despite changes in funding priorities and school/leadership reforms. There is a great need for new leadership paradigms and practices for current educational goals to be met. This guide can also be used to assist school community stakeholders in both program improvement schools and all schools to more effectively make changes in the scope, characteristics, and quality of educational leadership, including the changes needed in education policy at state and federal levels.

Much has been articulated in the education literature about the why and what of culturally responsive instruction, culturally relevant curriculum, and antiracist education, among other topics related to student diversity and academic achievement. This guide focuses more on things to consider when attempting to cultivate transformation in such areas. More attention is needed on why the things we purportedly know how to do have either not been attempted, or when being attempted, have been done in a piecemeal fashion or otherwise failed. For example, the *politics of implementation* related to equity issues does not receive much attention in administrator and teacher preparation programs or on-the-job professional development. Throughout much of this guide, the politics of implementing culturally courageous leadership is repeatedly addressed in a variety of ways.

This guide provides a detailed treatment of how culturally courageous leadership is related to walking the equity talk. A case is made for how the kind of leadership needed at the school district, school community, and school-site levels is qualitatively different from the way leadership may be conceptualized by school districts and institutions of higher education. The narrative includes the use of specific examples, vignettes, scenarios, leadership profiles, and experiential problem-solving exercises. The figures, vignettes, charts, leadership profiles, role-play, culturally courageous leadership diagnostic questionnaires, "Make It Personal" questions throughout the text, and facilitator notes based on some of the "Make It Personal" questions are meant to make the content more accessible and realistic for the reader and to illustrate some of the realities/conditions experienced by historically underserved students of color in school communities. Vignettes are based on real problematic situations and conditions in schools whose identity has been kept confidential where I worked as an administrator, education consultant, or external evaluator.

I rely primarily upon sources from the literature on theory, research, and practice in the areas of multicultural education/cultural proficiency, educational inputs and outcomes, transformational/instructional leadership, critical race theory in education, and planning/implementing change. This guide focuses on current manifestations of inequity in urban schools, particularly inequities experienced by historically underserved students of color in urban school settings. Although I identify some past and present conditions contributing to these conditions, such as racial identity development and woefully inadequate preparation programs for teachers and administrators when it comes to institutional racism, the guide gives as much attention to a leadership paradigm that is similar to but goes beyond most of the current dialogue about achieving social justice, equity, and excellence for all.

Although the guide applies directly to practices of school leaders, primarily district and school site administrators, it also applies to teacher leaders and other school community stakeholders. There have been many initiatives undertaken to personalize education and reduce disparities in educational outcomes. However, most historically underserved students of color, especially at the secondary level, are still not being adequately prepared to meet their needs and those of their communities in the 21st century. This guide helps those preparing to be teachers or education administrators as well as current school district and school site teacher, parent, and administrative leaders to rethink what must be done *collaboratively* to ramp up their social justice efforts to achieve equitable outcomes for all students. This guide is a resource for building more leadership capacity among all stakeholder groups, including students, in the creation of culturally democratic learning environments that foster the development of 21st century skills by all student subgroups. This guide for culturally courageous leadership can also be used to assist schools in developing more reality and data based comprehensive plans for equity transformation. When analyzing why benchmark indicators have not been achieved in school improvement plans, the guide can stimulate alternative ways of thinking and acting needed for equitable inputs and outcomes to be realized.

—*John R. Browne*

Acknowledgments

This manuscript could not have been completed without the encouragement, emotional support, help, and assistance of many friends, extended family members, colleagues, and close associates. Much thanks to the following persons who have shown in so many ways their love, support, and encouragement: Kikanza J. Nuri-Robins, Muriel Kathleen Rollins, Louise Kora Dunbar, Debra Watkins, Billie Haynes, Andrew Ahman Johnson, Ron Gibson, Shadidi Sia-Maat, Maurice W. Smallwood, Glenn A. Ray, Brenda E. Taylor, Michele and Woody Merrill, my goddaughter Mya Merrill, Ray Brown, my uncle Wendell O. Brown, Dianne, Diedtress, and Deonte Jackson, Kpakpundu Ezeze, and Sheila Williams.

In addition, special thanks must be extended to those who have given valuable critical friend suggestions, insights, input, and encouragement during development and editing earlier drafts of my work: Kikanza J. Nuri-Robins, Tawni Taylor, Geniese Ligon, and Dan Alpert, my acquisitions editor at Corwin, whose assistance and support has been invaluable; and the two review panels selected by Corwin. There are additional family, friends, colleagues, advisors, or mentors in my personal or professional life who have facilitated my growth and vision in innumerable ways and supported me more than they ever know. My godmother, many aunts, uncles, and cousins have been a true blessing. Friends, academic advisors, colleagues, scholars whose work has been especially helpful, and mentors I want to mention by name are Betty Grace Cupoli, Geneva Gay, James A. Banks, Joseph F. Johnson, Beryle Banfield, Barbara Addison Reid, Joyce E. King, Gloria Ladson-Billings, Christine Sleeter, Gail Thompson, Gary Howard, Rudy Crew, Timothy Miller, Kathryn Girard, Ples Griffin, Hazel W. Mahone, Roy P. Fairfield, Robert L. Sinclair, Thomas E. Hutchinson, Ann Lieberman, Elizabeth Norwood, Pedro Noguera, Katie Klumpp, Ward Ghory, Helen Roberts, Thomasyne Lightfoote Wilson, Charles C. D. Hamilton, Na'im Akbar, Jeffrey Duncan-Andrade, C. P. Gause, Frank Holmes, Antwi Akom, Fannie Dawson Spain, Mutiu Fagbayi, Manny Barbara, Sonia Nieto, Bobbie Brooks, Bernadine Hawthorne, Tim Allen, Catherine Pope, Myrion Doakes, Gwen Gholsen Driver, Barney Green, Richard Owen, Shirley Weber, Pastor Timothy Winters, Pastor Curtis Mitchell, Larry Hendricks as well as the late Danny Lyon Scarborough, Jacquelyn Mitchell, Aisha Amiji, Asa Hilliard III, Jack Kimbrough, Cornelius Page, Kevin Wood, Reuben Burton, Rev. Phale D. Hale, Esther Johnson, Edythe Moore

Hendricks, Norma Jean Anderson, Ron Hockwalt, James Deslonde Sr., John Palmore Jr., Phillip Williams, Ray Corn, Jack J. R. Porter, and Charles Briggs.

Finally, sincere appreciation and thanks is extended to those whose friendship and willingness to undertake this journey with me have been of inestimable value. They have so generously participated in assisting completion of this work, through what they model as exemplary educators, through sharing their stories, providing invaluable feedback, suggesting additional sources, and through their technical assistance in the final editing. They are Kathy McDonaugh, whose research assistance was extremely helpful, Christine Lim, Jan Nuno, Lillie McMillan, Ken Magdaleno, Sharroky Hollie, Tony Lamair Burks II, and the editorial staff at Corwin. The innumerable insights and shared experiences of my students at San Diego State University and the University of San Diego over the last decade have also been a significant source of inspiration and determination. The same goes for all of my students during my teaching at the secondary level, and all of the aspiring and practicing school administrators, teachers, and other educators with whom I have interacted in various work settings or professional development activities. I learned so much from all of them and deeply appreciate their sharing who they were and/or wanted to be.

Publisher's Acknowledgments

Dr. Marine Avagyan
Coordinator, Curriculum & Professional Development
Glendale Unified SD
Glendale, CA

Donna Cooper
Teacher leader, Mathematics
Stebbins High School
Mad River Local School District
Riverside, OH

Sandra L. Fernandez-Bergersen
Coordinator of National Origin
Midwest Equity Assistance Center
Kansas State University
Manhattan, KS

Geneva Gay
Professor
Curriculum & Instruction
College of Education, University of Washington
Seattle, WA

Dorothy Kelly
Student Teacher Supervisor
Fontbonne University
St. Louis, MO

Cathy Milligan
Superintendent
Fairfield City School District
Fairfield, OH

Sonia Nieto
Professor Emerita
University of Massachusetts, Amherst
School of Education
Language, Literacy, and Culture Concentration
Amherst, MA

Marsha Tappan
Principal
Niemann Elementary School
Michigan City, IN

Jennifer Yazawa
Read 180 Resource Teacher
Office of Professional Development
Albuquerque Public Schools
Albuquerque, NM

About the Author

 **John Robert Browne II** is an education consultant and executive coach who specializes in developing culturally courageous systems and collaborative leadership for achieving equity and excellence. Dr. Browne has conducted training on instructional leadership or multicultural education for four state departments of education and was the national lead consultant and trainer on effective school reform for the Bureau of Indian Affairs. He was the recipient of a Ford Foundation fellowship to complete his doctorate in education at the University of Massachusetts in Amherst, specializing in curriculum and organization studies. He was a participant in the Washington Internships in Education program, where he served as a staff associate for the National Council for the Social Studies and traveled the country studying the interface between federal, state, and local policy on desegregation and educational innovations.

Dr. Browne taught at the junior or senior high level in Columbus, Ohio (his home town), Hartford, Connecticut, and Huntington, New York. He was an education administrator for 23 years, with administrative responsibility for curriculum, integration, school choice, and leadership development programs. His work included administrative assignments in the San Diego County Office of Education and in San Diego Unified, and he was also the assistant superintendent for instruction at the Grant Joint Union High School District in Sacramento, California. More recently, he served as an external evaluator and consultant for several state-designated low-performing schools throughout California. Browne has also been an adjunct lecturer in teacher education, multicultural education, organizational and leadership effectiveness, and Africana studies at five universities in southern California at the undergraduate, master's, and doctorate levels. For more than a decade, his work and research have focused primarily on the politics of urban education.

Introduction
to the Guide

Educators and families with children of school age in the 21st century are witnessing a sea shift, equivalent to a tsunami, in the challenges and changes being implemented or on the horizon that will fundamentally and permanently impact the nature of the teaching and learning process. We must make sure that none are left behind during this cataclysm. The contemporary experiences of teachers and school site administrators, especially those in culturally diverse low-income urban settings, give new meaning to the phrase "being on the firing line."

Everyone seems to have an opinion about what is wrong with the schools and what needs to be done differently, many of them using data to buttress their point of view. The mass media and the government at all levels keep a high-powered microscope on the turn of events in the schooling process, influencing, and being influenced by each other, and parents are somewhere in the middle, trying to figure out what is in the best interest of their children. In an economic era of shrinking resources causing massive social dislocation, there are many competing constituencies for different courses of action.

It is not the first time the United States has been forced to weather a crisis of immense, even unfathomable, proportions that affects the entire population in one way or another. It also isn't the first time that those on the firing line, in the trenches, so to speak, have been the recipients of much scrutiny, second guessing, and criticism. On first blush, this guide for "walking the equity talk" via culturally courageous leadership may appear to be taking another swing at those trying to do their best on a daily basis for the families they serve, given the resources available. That is not the intent. Much attention will be given to examining the system by providing a frame of reference shaped by my professional experiences and delineating contemporary realities as experienced by the historically underserved. Those in this category are struggling to survive and thrive in what sometimes is a very contentious and adversarial environment because of how the system and each of us individually may define ourselves in relationship to others.

Any leadership committed to the social good will inherently have to be courageous. However, the guide implicitly and explicitly focuses on the *next* level of leadership for more deep seated cultural realignment of how we think and act. We must wake up and be more than just courageous. If such leadership is embraced by persons with various cultural perspectives and coming from all levels of the educational enterprise, we have a better chance of increasing our collective capacity to work smart as well as work hard to achieve a future we think our progeny are worthy of experiencing. We can then lay the foundation for moving beyond the talk to the walk of living the values and principles of social justice we may espouse.

This is not a destination but a journey that is advocated, including what to expect along the way, and how to master the prevailing winds of doubt, dysfunction, and resistance to critical self-examination as well as organizational reflection and transformation. Readers are encouraged to be very conscious of and analyze any defensiveness that may rise in their heart and mind based on what is being read. The main focus is the system and what is needed to collectively confront and change any antidemocratic processes and products without losing our own humanity and discarding democratic values.

ॐ∽⁙

WHY THE CULTURALLY COURAGEOUS LEADERSHIP PARADIGM IS NEEDED

More and more historically underserved students of color have become alienated despite new reform efforts, partnerships, funding, and legislation (Lipman, 1998). The sobering realities in many 21st century urban schools are reflected in the educational statistics on achievement levels and dropout rates of the urban poor (Lewis, Simon, Uzzell, Horwitz, & Casserly, 2010). This guide initially explores how educational outcomes, including achievement on high-stakes tests of historically underserved students, particularly students of African and Latino/a American descent in the United States, are largely a reflection of the relationship between

- personal identities, including racial identity development,
- race and cultural conflict, also referred to as the *dynamics of difference* in school communities, and
- the presence of cultural hegemony and absence of cultural democracy in educational environments.

Too little attention has been given to how persons in various school community stakeholder groups need to collaboratively intervene to keep the relationship between these variables from negatively impacting educational inputs and educational outcomes, especially those experienced by historically underserved students of color.

ॐ∽⁙

CULTURAL HEGEMONY VS. CULTURAL DEMOCRACY

Cultural hegemony, the opposite of cultural democracy, includes societal conditions where particular racial, cultural, or socioeconomic classes have inordinate influence and dominance over all others. This occurs through economic, political, educational, and cultural influence, largely through the mass media and economic resources brought to bear, to perpetuate policy decisions favoring the privileged classes (Artz & Murphy, 2000). Although frequent mention is made of the need to change power, authority, and control relationships in school communities, there has been little done about it. There are culturally hegemonic practices throughout the educational enterprise from preschool through advanced graduate school degree programs. These practices are reflected in research conducted, knowledge constructed, policies ostensibly based on such research and knowledge, curricula taught, and the differential instruction provided to students based on their demographic characteristics. The operating principle in almost all schooling within the United States, despite the equity rhetoric that may be used, is to maintain and extend the influence, priorities, and benefits accrued primarily by middle or higher socioeconomic classes of White Americans. Equitable resources, or inputs, are hardly the norm anywhere in the country.

Historically underserved students of color is a term frequently used in this guide and refers to those of diverse racial/ethnic backgrounds who have throughout the history of the United States been victimized by prejudice and discrimination in educational policy and practice. Although most of these students in urban school settings at this time may be of African and Latino/a descent, there are also Appalachian Whites, Native American, Southeast Asian, Pacific Islander, and East Asian students, among others, who experience government sanctioned bias in such areas as curriculum, instruction, and educational funding.

Figure 1a illustrates the framework in section one (Chapters 1 through 6) of this guide. All of these educational conditions are interrelated and influence each other. No hierarchy is suggested or intended in this circle continuum.

Before viewing Figure 1a and reading Chapter 1, you are encouraged to mentally answer the following three questions for the purpose of identifying a little of what you already know related to the content of the guide, what you want to know, and what you have learned from prior experience or reading of the guide (KWL) when it comes to the issue of leadership within school communities for improving cultural democracy and achieving equitable educational outcomes. A KWL exercise will be provided at the beginning of each chapter.

1. What are three major causes of low student achievement and other educational outcomes experienced by African and Latino/a American students?

2. What would you like to know about the relationship between the identities, including racial identities of students and teachers and dissonance between teachers and students?

3. What are three major insights you have, based on your life or professional experiences, about what causes students to have a negative self-concept or lack self-confidence in any area of academic performance?

Culturally courageous leadership (CCL) is a leadership paradigm for all schools in the United States. It involves joint efforts by persons from all stakeholder groups in school communities who want to achieve social justice as manifested in equitable inputs and student outcomes. The stakeholder groups are school board members, administrators, teachers, support staff, parents, community members, including university faculty in teacher and administrator preparation programs, and students. The paradigm is based on the postulate that achieving equitable student outcomes can be facilitated by cultural democracy in school communities. Cultural democracy is a form of social justice, and improving it requires changing attitudes/behaviors and school organization norms that demonstrate a lack of respect for the cultural heritage, norms, beliefs, and customs of certain groups.

Ramirez and Castaneda define cultural democracy as "a philosophical precept which recognizes that the way a person communicates, relates to others, seeks support and recognition from his environment . . . and thinks and learns . . . is a product of the

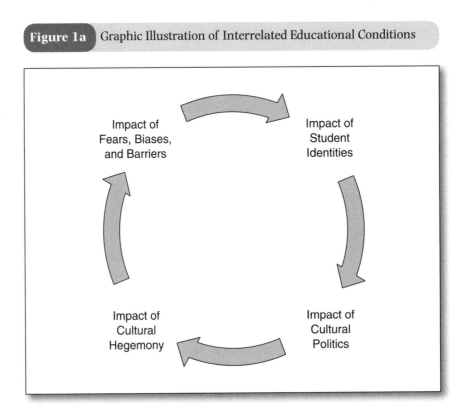

Figure 1a Graphic Illustration of Interrelated Educational Conditions

Impact of Fears, Biases, and Barriers

Impact of Student Identities

Impact of Cultural Hegemony

Impact of Cultural Politics

value system of his home and community" (1974, p. 23). They also refer to the Civil Rights Act of 1964, which states that "educational environments or policies that do not recognize the individual's right to remain identified with the culture and language of his cultural group are culturally undemocratic" (p. 23). Ramirez and Castaneda go on to say that culturally democratic learning environments are settings where students can acquire knowledge about their own culture and the dominant culture (p. 24). Finally, they assert the goal of such environments "is to help children learn to function competently and effectively in, as well as to contribute to, more than one cultural world" (p. 24). This view counteracts the Anglo conformity view of acculturation and assimilation, which continues well into the 21st century and has caused considerable cultural conflict for those who have not assimilated into the mainstream as easily as others (Dicker, 2008).

Attempting to change personal and institutional bias is part of being a culturally courageous leader. However, success in such change efforts doesn't usually occur without collaboration occurring among like-minded others across stakeholder groups to change the nature of the problem-solving dialogue and decision making in schools.

Those seeking educational transformation must recognize and help others recognize that historically, education in all societies is designed to maintain the current societal order, including the social, economic, political, and educational inequities that exist (Noguera & Wing, 2006). Some examples of such inequities are laws and norms that favor certain demographic groups over others. It is not a leap to conclude that most students at the bottom of the achievement continuum do not receive equitable opportunities and resources when examining disaggregated statistics of the following:

- School dropouts (Cataldi & Kewal Ramani, 2009; Gordon, Piana, & Keleher, 2000), suspensions, and expulsions (Gregory, Skiba, & Noguera, 2010)
- Special education designations ("Achieving Equity in Special Education," n.d.; Ferri & Connor, 2005; Harry & Klingner, 2006; Johnson, Lessem, Bergquist, Carmichael, & Whitten, 2000; van Keulen, Weddington, & DuBose, 1998).
- The numbers of so-called high-quality teachers in schools (Haycock & Hanushek, 2010; Knaus, 2007)
- The access to and quality of educational technology as well as the instructional use of technology with varying student groups (*Education Week*, 2001)
- Student enrollment in gifted or advanced placement classes/educational programs based entirely on prior academic performance, teacher recommendation, or course completion (Rubin & Noguera, 2004)
- High school graduation rates, especially graduates who have completed the requisite courses qualifying them to be accepted into 4-year universities (Balfanz, 2009; Greene & Winters, 2006)

క్రాౖ

INSTITUTIONAL OBSTACLES

Given the statistics referred to above, some of the most intractable institutional obstacles are the double standards in discipline experienced by most Black and Latino male students, the pattern of significantly fewer Latino/a and Black students enrolled in higher level courses, and the much lower academic expectations some teachers and counselors have for historically underserved students of color.

Many schools are not designed, structurally or culturally, to maximize the potential of all students. Examples of structural bias are the curriculum content, the way time is spent in many schools, and student access to teaching at high levels (i.e., scheduling practices). Examples of cultural bias are teachers' low expectations as manifested in instructional practices, educators' beliefs about the innate abilities of diverse students, as well as beliefs about the educational values of their parents. Structural and cultural features of a school may result in a waste of students' minds and inequitable educational outcomes.

Equitable student outcomes are those where students in all demographic groups experience comparable educational outcomes. An example of equitable outcomes would be if 70% of the highest achieving student group successfully complete high-level courses or score at proficient or higher levels on high-stakes tests, then a comparable percentage (usually within 10%) of all other groups would experience the same outcomes. When it comes to what is needed to achieve equitable educational outcomes, equitable resources are needed, which is not the same as having access to equal resources. Equitable resources would mean having access to what is needed rather than having the same access provided to others. Equal opportunity for those not on a level playing field is not equitable.

The term *school community* refers to all of the interactions, events, situations, conditions, and persons associated with a particular school that impact what happens in that school. One characteristic of such a school community may be a geographical area, determined to a great extent by the school's residential boundaries, but some school communities not having residential boundaries cannot be defined in that manner. The stakeholders in a school community include students, parents, and community persons (including higher education faculty who teach in teacher or administrator preparation programs, conduct research in school districts/schools, and/or provide professional development) as well as teachers, support staff, and administrators.

☙❧

POPULAR REASONS FOR MAJOR ACHIEVEMENT DISPARITIES

Some of the more popular reasons for major achievement disparities among racial/ethnic groups have included the following:

- Low socioeconomic status of student families
- The lack of adequate parent support and involvement

- The genetic inferiority of students
- The English language development levels of students
- Whether teachers are "highly qualified"
- Inadequate educational funding from all levels of government, with all mandates being fully funded

This guide stresses other reasons that may have a major impact on student educational outcomes. The lack of cultural democracy in school community settings is one such factor, because cultural democracy in school environments contributes to students of all backgrounds feeling respected, expected to do well, and supported in making efforts to achieve at high levels. Students who feel their teachers care about and have high expectations for them are more likely to do well in school (Valenzuela, 1999). When the beliefs, attitudes, and behaviors of culturally diverse persons are positive, students are more likely to feel affirmed and accepted, which may result in greater motivation to do well in school. When both individual and organizational norms affirm human differences, regardless of students' racial/cultural background and academic readiness level, students may be more open to collaboratively participating in leadership efforts that improve the quality of education for all (Mitra, 2008). The reality is that the extent of cultural democracy in a school is likely different for various socioeconomic and racial groups. Socioeconomic status and perceived racial group affiliation help determine student cultural and social capital in a school community as well as the amount of power, authority, and control they have in the larger society (Noguera & Wing, 2006). Institutional and cultural racism is alive and well in the United States.

Major concepts discussed in the book include the following: identity constructs, dynamics of difference, cultural dissonance, cultural democracy, culturally democratic learning environments, cultural politics, cultural hegemony, culturally courageous leadership by all school community stakeholders, personal and organizational transformation, and the politics of implementation. They are accompanied by illustrations and examples, are incorporated in the situations, problems, and analyses receiving attention, and are based on my experience and related research.

ॐॐ

PREVIEW OF EACH SECTION IN THE GUIDE

Section I provides the reader with information on some individual and institutional dynamics contributing to under achievement. Chapter 1, "Identity, Teaching, and Learning," discusses many of the influences on identity development, the relationships between student identity and achievement, and between race and personal identity. Personal identity is influenced by many idiosyncratic variables, including racial and cultural dynamics. The chapter concludes with a discussion of the hidden curriculum and the role of culturally courageous leaders in addressing identity issues.

Chapter 2 ties the interface of identity development and racial/cultural conflict with the absence of cultural democracy in the United States and urban schools in particular. Several examples are provided of how little cultural democracy there is in urban schools. The impact on interpersonal and intergroup relations is also discussed.

Chapter 3, "Grim Continuities," gives attention to four topics that illustrate some of the continuities between the late 20th century and the first decade of the 21st century when it comes to negative impact on the education of historically underserved students. Chapter 4, "Rhetoric vs. Reality," continues with a discussion of my observations based on providing technical assistance as a consultant or district administrative leadership to multicultural education and effective school programs. This discussion is meant to assist understanding of why a new leadership paradigm is needed. I conclude this chapter with a brief explanation of why 21st century school community leadership must include an aggressive social justice agenda.

Chapter 5, "Biases," and Chapter 6, "Barriers," build on the earlier discussion of continuities between 20th and 21st century resistance to equity reform initiatives. The biases are reflected in six policies, practices, or norms within school districts and schools that directly or indirectly contribute to cultural hegemony, the lack of cultural democracy, and disparities in educational outcomes. Chapter 6 provides concrete examples of how these biases were manifested in 10 barriers to achievement at high levels by historically underserved students in a select group of low-performing schools where I worked as an external evaluator.

Each of the six chapters in Section I concludes with introductory comments on the role of culturally courageous leaders in addressing the issues discussed in that chapter.

All of the vignettes in this guide are based on the conditions and dynamics in real schools where I have had personal experience, and most of them are from low-income, low-performing schools where I served as an external evaluator and school consultant. The entire guide is largely influenced by professional experiences and conclusions based on my career in a variety of leadership capacities. I invite readers to research my conclusions and generalizations to which they take exception. A major purpose of the guide is to stimulate readers to critically reflect on what is happening in their own work context and school communities. Not all of the "Make It Personal" questions are related to the vignette or content preceding them. In some cases, there are questions requesting the reader to reflect upon other issues or challenges discussed before the vignette or to their own lives. In addition, some of the "Make It Personal" questions are accompanied by facilitator notes at the end of the book to help those who may wish to use the guide in study groups or professional learning communities.

Section II begins with an in-depth discussion of the culturally courageous leadership paradigm in Chapters 7 through 10. Chapter 7 reviews some major actions needed based on what was discussed in Section I. This is followed by a rationale for the importance of collaborative leadership by all school community stakeholders, which is the first component of the paradigm. Chapter 8 focuses on the second component of the CCL paradigm by describing the seven principles of CCL. They are presented as essential characteristics that all school stakeholders must strive to emulate. Chapter 9 discusses how personal and organizational transformation, the third component, cannot be achieved without attention to the fourth component of the paradigm, which is adeptly navigating the politics of implementation associated with any equity initiative. Chapter 10 provides some examples of what attitudes, dispositions, and actions would be taken by members of each stakeholder group. In Chapter 11, some detail is provided on major conditions in a growing number of schools throughout the United States that have eliminated the achievement gap, while Chapter 12 provides an illustration of how the "5 A's" discussed in Chapter 11 are exemplified by two educational leaders. These leaders illustrate the vision, creativity, tenacity, and courage that are needed to help underachieving student groups. These profiles in Chapter 12 provide details about the context that stimulated specific instances of CCL at a school and district level.

Section III builds on the discussion in Section II about the nature of CCL. Chapters 13 and 14 focus on strategies and priorities that should be considered when trying to navigate the politics associated with attempting to successfully implement equity transformation or equity reform. Six dimensions associated with the politics of implementing equity initiatives are applied to specific schooling situations. A detailed description of three "equity warriors" is then provided, including their personal work conditions, leadership practices related to the politics they navigate, their equity priorities, and challenges.

Chapter 15 continues in this vein by engaging the reader interactively in a role-playing exercise that provides an opportunity to practice the equity walk and to receive feedback on completed tasks. Chapter 16 identifies other issues that require attention by those aspiring to be culturally courageous leaders as well as some do's and don'ts. For those who may hesitate to embrace the paradigm, some excuses for not doing so are debunked. The guide closes with a statement expressing faith in the ability of empowered students to keep equity efforts more honest than they may be otherwise. There is, after all, a lot of talk about equity, but few who consistently and persistently walk the equity talk.

SECTION I

Leadership for Equitable Outcomes— It Takes an Entire Community

Questions to keep in mind when reading Section I of this guide:

1. How does the leadership in your school community impact the racial identity development of educators, students, and community persons, as well as positively or negatively impact racial/cultural conflict in schools?

2. What are the perceptions of teachers with whom you are familiar regarding their sense of responsibility for influencing students' positive perceptions about school and academic effort?

3. What changes in policies, practices, politics, and identities of administrators, teachers, and students are needed to improve educational opportunity and equitable outcomes?

4. What leadership strategies by teachers and administrators can be used to positively influence the academic motivation of Jimmy, who is discussed in several vignettes?

Identity, Teaching, and Learning

1

Our self-identity has a lot to do with how we are perceived and treated by both significant and nonsignificant others.

Our identity is the very core of who we are as human beings. From birth, we are subject to how we are thought about, treated, and cared for by the significant persons in our lives as well as by others in multiple environments. Our ideas about self are largely a reflection of others' ideas about us, good and bad or in between. Schools have an enormous influence on how we come to see ourselves, the hopes and dreams we acquire, and our achievement motivation.

KWL EXERCISE

1. Based on your earliest memories as a young child and then as a student in your first 3 years of school, how would you describe your sense of self then and the things that influenced you most during that time?

2. What would be most helpful for you to know about factors influencing one's personal identity and how identity relates to school success?

3. Draw several symbols or pictures that capture some of the major ways your time in K–12 schools has impacted how you define yourself today.

INFLUENCES ON IDENTITY DEVELOPMENT

Prejudice and institutional racism are common factors influencing the personal identities of both those who have benefited from White privilege as well as those who have been historically underserved in the United States. Although the concept of race is not an accepted anthropological or biological concept, it is a very powerful cultural and political concept throughout the world. Given the history of race relations and a very mixed record of social justice in this country (Marable, 1997; National Advisory Commission on Civil Disorders, 1968), this guide begins by focusing on the relationship between school community stakeholders' racial identities and student educational outcomes.

What are the stages persons of diverse ethnicities and races might go through during the process of developing their racial identity in the United States? What are the schooling conditions influencing such development for different people and groups? These are only two of the relevant questions when trying to figure out what is behind the way educators (most of whom are White) and historically underserved students of color perceive and think about themselves compared to the way they perceive and think about those they define as racially different. Racial attitudes and experiences in the larger society and in specific school environments impact the racial identities of racially/culturally/linguistically diverse students *and* teachers in the United States.

One's identity has a major influence on how they perceive others, their self-esteem, self-confidence, aspirations, motivation, and effort expended in various aspects of their life (Smith, Walker, Fields, Brookins, & Seay, 1999). When schools don't aggressively try to facilitate positive identities by all their students, including their racial identity, there are consequences. A growing number of immigrants from all over the world who are students in our public schools, in addition to many diverse native-born students of color, are subject to stereotypes and low teacher expectations. Such bias increases student concerns about social acceptance and increases their feelings of inadequacy when it comes to academic performance (Altschul, Oysterman, & Bybee, 2008, 2006; Jackson, 2011). Identity development, especially among minority students with complex beliefs about ethnic identity, can influence the nature and depth of conflicts with diverse others, and also how well they do in school (Glenn, 2003). The personal strengths individuals develop or expand, as well as their degree of resilience when facing difficulties, may strongly influence their personal identity or be the result of their personal identity. The choices and priorities students embrace, as well as their perception of personal life chances and potential, are to some extent a reflection of the factors making up their racial/ethnic identity (McHatton, Shaunnsey, Hughes, Brice, & Ratliff, 2007; Noguera & Akom, 2000).

In many schools, there has been a major shift in student demographics over the last two decades, with a drop in the numbers of White middle class students and an increase in the numbers of limited English proficient (LEP) students from families with low socioeconomic status. LEP students are often very diverse first-generation residents in the United States, having come from southeast Asia, Central and South America, Mexico, northeast Africa, Slavic countries, and the Caribbean. They are of diverse nationalities and have diverse racial, ethnic, and language backgrounds.

Some are not literate in their home language, and some are totally new to formal schooling as implemented in the United States. Some are in war refugee families, and even more are in split families that have moved to the United States, with some family members still in the home country.

It is very important for teachers to improve their understanding of issues causing interethnic tension and conflict, especially among secondary students, and there are resources available to assist teachers in this regard (Jorgensen & Brown, 1992; Ponterotto, Utsey, & Pedersen, 2006). Students of all cultural/racial backgrounds in the United States seek greater opportunities than those their parents may have experienced. These aspirations result in even greater tension when the American economy is undergoing major adjustments and shifts causing massive unemployment and underemployment. The family characteristics and domestic realities of immigrant and native-born students help illustrate how global events and conditions worldwide impact the dynamics of difference in a growing number of American schools.

Some global events that have contributed to major waves of immigration and domestic cultural conflict are the Spanish/American War, both World Wars, the Korean War, the Vietnam conflict, the Cold War, and the more recent wars in Iraq and Afghanistan. Social, political, and economic conditions around the world have also led to immigration to the United States. Immigration has historically been a source of domestic racial/ethnic conflict in the United States, but over time some immigrants have assimilated more easily than others (Vigdor, 2008). The negative and often discriminatory reactions to war refugees who come as immigrants, as well as the reactions to other immigrants who are seeking a better life than that in their native land, may heavily influence students' personal identity (Mosselson, 2006). Some relatively new immigrants do well in school, but have very low self-esteem, and some students whose families have been in the United States have high self-esteem and do very poorly (Bankston & Zhou, 2002).

There are racial, ethnic, cultural, and socioeconomic differences that some schools are not prepared for, financially, psychologically, or programmatically. Schools historically facilitate students' socialization process and help perpetuate cultural biases of dominant groups as well as a nation's social and political order (Spring, 2009). Cultural conflict within and across diverse racial/ethnic groups continues to a large extent. Those who experience the most prejudice and discrimination in many schools continue to include persons of color. In the 19th century and first half of the 20th century, persons of Irish, Italian, Polish, Jewish, Chinese, Japanese, and German ethnicities, to name a few, were also the targets of much discrimination, but over time, most of European background were able to assimilate into mainstream culture, one of the reasons being their skin color (Aguirre & Turner, 2003).

The following questions will help you personalize the influences on identity development in the past as well as in the present and stimulate your thinking about the role schools should play in addressing the biases that may influence student identity.

MAKE IT PERSONAL

1. What are your honest reactions and/or feelings about what is said in this chapter about factors influencing and manifestations of personal identities, including racial identity development?

2. What are your opinions about how student and teacher identities impact student performance in the classroom?

3. Talk with family members, friends, or other persons aged 70 or older to identify what kinds of conflicts occurred between students and between students and adults when they were in school between kindergarten and the 12th grade.

4. What names or epithets were used by people to refer to "different" others?

5. Which of the following behaviors or conditions experienced by many limited English proficient immigrant students and native nonmainstream English-speaking students in schools within the United States have also been experienced by persons you talked to when they were in school: stereotypes, social rejection, low academic expectations, feelings of inadequacy, and dominant group biases?

6. Based on your experience, what racial slurs or epithets referring to "different" others are *currently* being used by people in the larger society and in schools?

7. What are the similarities and differences between what people thought and said about "different others" before 1950 and what people think and say about "different others" now?

8. How do the Internet and mass media influence stereotyping and cultural biases in the 21st century?

9. In your opinion, what should be done in schools to counteract such biases?

಄಄

STUDENT IDENTITY AND ACHIEVEMENT

Historically underserved students' identity and achievement performance are inextricably intertwined. This relationship may be confounded by the extent to which significant others, including educators, help students negotiate race, culture, and social surroundings when developing their identities. Akbar (1998) says the first function of education is to provide identity, which lays the foundation for what people will be able to do and what they must learn. He makes the case that education in all societies provides a foundation in one's cultural identity. He further concludes that education has the responsibility to transmit the legacy of competence and acquired immunities learned by earlier generations due to a variety of intellectual and social diseases. Institutional and cultural racism are such diseases. But some ethnic groups do not leave it up to public schools to help their children develop a positive ethnic/cultural identity, knowledge of their cultural heritage, and "immunity" to social diseases.

Murrell (2008) asserts that achievement success is mediated both by beliefs in one's capability as well as by the quality of school experiences and social interactions. His situated-mediated identity theory gives in-depth attention to how identity is related to achievement. He identifies what educators and other responsible adults should know about identity processes and the social environments in schools that promote identity development and achievement. Murrell's core proposition is that identity is based on action in specific contexts, and who we are is a matter of what we choose to do and how we choose to invest in what we do. He argues that historically underserved students fall into three broad categories: those who persist in enduring schooling even though it has ceased to make sense to them; those who eventually check out of schooling activity; and those who persist because they find meaning, purpose, and academic identity.

In his situated identity model, Murrell calls these three categories *positionalities*, as they represent the actions and decisions that students make, and how others, such as teachers and college student volunteers, respond to them as a result. Murrell suggests that educators tend to write off those students they conclude do not try hard or want to learn. Such historically underserved students are not helped to develop achievement identities.

Our identity may be more influenced by what others believe about us, their impressions of us, and how they react to our actions. Students need to both feel smart and *be* smart, according to Murrell. The ways students express their identities can sometimes undermine their achievement and goals. For example, some adolescents give high priority to being popular among their peers more than they value high grades. During the course of grappling with this dilemma related to what Murrell calls being a street kid versus a school kid, some students may make life-changing choices. Educators are also making choices when they decide whether or how to help historically underserved students they label as not valuing education.

Many students of color are victimized by educators' adherence to what Murrell calls a color-blind ideology, which he also characterizes as the "new racism, cultural racism." Race may never be mentioned when educators discuss the challenges involved when trying to help all students learn at grade level or beyond. But the subtext is that certain "differences" or "cultural characteristics" are perceived as inferior and others as superior. Equal treatment of students who come to school with major differences in life experience, customs, academic readiness, and strengths is a part of this color blind ideology. Equality is very different from equity and may be a step toward achieving equity, but it is not the same or as essential, even though a mantra of many teachers is the proclamation they proudly state: "I treat all students the same." Teacher–student communication in many low-income urban schools throughout the United States reinforces who is privileged and who is believed to be inferior, and the discourse is sometimes subtle, but often unself-consciously blatant. Most educators are socialized in preservice preparation and on-the-job activities to embrace the "color blind," "equality," or meritocracy belief system. The results are students being the ones blamed for their so-called failures without any scrutiny of the structural and cultural aspects of schooling that perpetuate disparities in outcomes (Murrell, 2008).

&-<

RACE AND PERSONAL IDENTITY

Diverse school community stakeholders' identities are reflected in their attitudes, behaviors, and comfort with both self and other racial groups. Racial identity is an important part of one's overall identity. According to Ponterotto et al. (2006), the White racial identity development process involves coming to terms with one's own unearned privilege in society. Sue (2003) asserts coming to terms with unearned privilege must be followed by an honest self-examination of one's role, active or passive, in maintaining the racist status quo. In any given school community, there may be major resistance to spotlighting the need for greater self-awareness of one's racial identity and the possible relationship to educational opportunities and outcomes. The White racial identity model (WRIM) of Helms and Cook (1999) has seven levels, the lowest four of which include personal characteristics such as denying or being oblivious to White privilege, avoiding discussions about racism, and not analyzing what personal responsibility they might have related to their own racism. The opposite end of the Helms and Cook WRIM is called "autonomy," characterized by an avoidance of participation in racial oppression, the relinquishment in some cases of White privilege, and involvement in activism against many forms of oppression. Helms (1990) suggests Whites can overcome a history of ignorance and superiority by abandoning individual racism as well as recognizing and opposing institutional and cultural racism.

Similarly, Howard (1999) has developed a model of White identity with three distinct orientations: fundamentalist, integrationist, and transformationist, each having thinking, feeling, and acting as the modalities of growth. A central theme of his work, as in *Pedagogy of the Oppressed* by Paulo Freire (1970), is that White dominance has historically and continues to be a powerful presence in the educational process. For example, Howard's fundamentalist orientation is similar to the lower levels of Helms WRIM, regarding the denial and avoidance when it comes to dealing with racism, the belief in White superiority, the Eurocentric teaching approaches, the color blind ideology, and the commitment to assimilation. Powerful experiential catalysts are required to dislodge individuals from a fundamentalist orientation, according to Howard. The integrationist orientation described by Howard includes such characteristics as an acknowledgement of White dominance but acceptance of it, see injustice as the victim's problem, don't question Western hegemony or the need for major shifts in White consciousness, and don't grasp the systemic nature of social inequality. White educators may need help in critically assessing whether they subscribe to any of these beliefs, and if so, what implications their beliefs have for the education of historically underserved students of color. Those who manifest the transformationist orientation in Howard's model are described as able to acknowledge White complicity in dominance and oppression. They have abandoned the idea of White supremacy, are not threatened by differences, are guided by respect for racial and cultural others, and are both self-reflective and antiracist. White educators with this orientation may need to be legitimized and empowered to take a more visible role of shared leadership in their school communities and also supported in their work with peers at the other end of the WRIM.

Both Helms and Howard point out there is evidence some Whites skip some of the stages they describe. Nevertheless, the reader should consider whether there is sufficient attention given to the phenomenon and centrality of racial identity to the achievement of equitable educational outcomes. If educators knowingly or unconsciously manifest many symptoms of racial identity that are inimical to facilitating equitable educational opportunities and outcomes, it is imperative that cultural courageousness as discussed in this guide be embraced to help address such a dilemma. One's level of racial identity can either facilitate or hinder "walking the equity talk" in the interest of achieving both cultural democracy and social justice for all. This guide will document some of the institutional biases and barriers to high achievement that may unwittingly be perpetuated by those whose racial identity makes it very difficult if not impossible to support cultural democracy and actively oppose cultural hegemony.

It is equally important to consider the levels of racial identity manifested by persons of African and Latino/a descent (as well as those in other historically underserved groups). Just as Helms is one who has done some seminal research in the area of White racial identity, Cross and Vandiver (2001) have done likewise in the area of Black racial identity in the United States, with the creation and refinement of Cross's nigrescence theory and measurement. The current version of his model, originally developed in 1971, has eight levels, three of which are variations of the pre-encounter stage. The first variation of this stage includes assimilationist values, with little emphasis on group identity; the next variation of pre-encounter is characterized by miseducation during which there is acceptance of inaccurate and stereotypical information about Black people and a continuing hesitancy to engage Black culture; the third iteration of the pre-encounter stage is labeled by Cross as racial self-hatred, with self-loathing regarding being Black. At the other end of the cross-racial identity continuum are three levels labeled as "internalization," from nationalist to biculturalist to multiculturalist. Persons in any of these three levels give weight to being

Black. However, the biculturalist also gives weight to being American, the multiculturalist fuses three or more personal identities, and the latter two engage in mainstream culture as well as issues related to all of their personal identities. The preK through graduate school teaching and learning process should play a major role in helping Black educators, students, parents, and community persons develop identities that help them both embrace their ethnic roots and successfully negotiate any forces of cultural hegemony they may experience. All educators should be provided more support in developing identities that enhance their efforts to facilitate achievement at high levels by all students.

The Latino/a racial identity model by Ruiz (1990) has levels similar to those of Cross. Latino/a's identified by Ruiz as being at the causal and cognitive levels of his model may experience trauma related to ethnic identity and do not identify with their ethnic culture. They have an inclination to associate group membership with prejudice and poverty. There is a tendency to equate assimilation with life success, and therefore they seek assimilation into White society to escape from prejudice and poverty. At the other end of Ruiz's racial identity model, persons highly accept their culture and ethnicity and have increased self-esteem, after experiencing extreme stress over ethnic conflict and disillusionment with assimilation. They then become disposed to reclaim their culture of origin and increase their ethnic consciousness.

In both Cross's and Ruiz's models, it is important to studiously avoid stereotyping all persons of African or Latino/a descent as reflecting one or more of the racial identity levels in the model of each researcher. Many persons may not neatly fit into any of their described levels of racial identity, especially if their background is multiracial or they are involved in multiracial relationships. What may be more important for those aspiring to be culturally courageous leaders is the willingness to take into consideration the probability that race and/or ethnicity play a major role in the personal identity of many if not most persons in the United States.

Furthermore, there might be a strong relationship between the White and Black/Latino/a racial identity levels described in this section. In other words, White educators having a racial identity at the fundamentalist or integrationist orientation as described by Howard may have attitudes and values that contribute to Black or Latino/a students developing racial identities at the pre-encounter stage or causal stage as defined by Cross or Ruiz. In addition, there are likely many schools that have White educators at both the lower levels and at the autonomy racial identity level in the Helms and Cook model, affecting their ability to work together. Teachers of African and Latino/a descent may also be very diversified in terms of their racial identity levels as defined by Cross and Ruiz. Research is needed on whether racial identity level affects the disposition of all teachers, regardless of racial background, toward meaningful collaboration in achieving equitable outcomes.

Conflicts between educators with vastly different racial identity levels may contribute to insidious covert and overt educational practices in the 21st century that help perpetuate the alienation of students of color and perpetuate White privilege in society and schools. Just as historically underserved students' identity and achievement performance are inextricably intertwined, the same is likely true for the connection between educators' racial identity and whether they give priority to providing equitable learning opportunities. Student *and* teacher identities can have major impact on interpersonal and intergroup dynamics as well as on student motivation to achieve (Zirkel, 2008). Historically underserved students who are not helped to develop positive racial identities may be much less motivated to make their best effort in school or to see a relationship between what happens in school and their daily lives, especially when they are not empowered to fight the conditions keeping them in subservient roles.

VIGNETTE 1–1: INTRODUCTION TO JIMMY

Jimmy is a 14-year-old Black male about to enter the ninth grade. He lives in a low- to moderate-income area in one of the largest cities in his state. He is the oldest of four children living with his single mother, and has many family responsibilities. As a result, he seldom studies at home. Although he has managed to please his mother most of the time in meeting his home responsibilities, she is worried about his attitude toward school. He doesn't look forward to entering the ninth grade for a variety of reasons, including the effort he will have to put into his studies in order to be eligible for seeking a spot on the track team. He likes science and Black history but doesn't care for the "White" history he is expected to learn, and struggles with his writing. Because of his writing, he tends to not like English classes, mainly because his vocabulary and comprehension skills aren't as good as they should be, even though his fluency and decoding skills are at grade level. He also doesn't think his English and math teachers really care about whether he and his friends learn or not.

Jimmy is always trying to figure out how to make some money and is frustrated that he can't get a regular job until he turns 16. He has resisted staying after school for extra help in his studies, because of his home responsibilities, his not liking the teachers, and wanting to be available for occasional odd jobs he finds in his neighborhood. He also knows he could do better if he applied himself but doesn't want to stand out from his homeboys.

Jimmy is at a critical crossroads. The personal decisions he makes in the next year are likely to have major impact on his life circumstances. Underachieving Black male students in the ninth grade are statistically in an extremely vulnerable position since many drop out of school by the end of the 10th grade. Like most adolescents, Jimmy's decisions are very influenced by the opinions of his peers and by his home responsibilities. His attitude about school and efforts to do well in his courses are also influenced by what he thinks about his teachers.

Jimmy is dealing with a lot in his young life. He has developed certain attitudes about school and conclusions about some of his teachers. His priorities may already seem set in stone. He is self-confident about some of his personal characteristics and skills, but he has very little faith that doing better in school will improve his life. Jimmy seems to have an increased consciousness of how prejudice and racism impact his life in his community and in his school, which may have caused him to feel that many Whites do not view him as an equal. He also appears to be most interested in exploring aspects of his own history and culture. Jimmy's racial identity development may be in direct conflict with the identity of his White teachers and with the policies and practices of his school/school district.

Chart 1a lists some factors that influence personal identity. Some of these items apply to Jimmy. Which items or parts of items apply to you? Develop two prioritized lists based on the items below, with your first list identifying the five factors that most influenced your identity in the eighth grade, and your second list identifying the five factors that most influence your identity at the present time. You may want to add factors not on the list.

The factors are by no means all inclusive, but suggest the range of variables that may influence each individual's self-identity. What is important to remember is that self-identity may be dynamic and ever-changing, just as life circumstances. Some life experiences or significant others have major impact on a person's identity that last a lifetime. How other persons perceive us impacts our personal identity (Kirk & Okazawa-Rey, 2004). The teacher/student relationship is one of the critical influences on student identity and is one of the major factors influencing student effort and student performance (Banks et al., 2001; Ladson-Billings, 1995; Zirkel, 2008).

ॐঔ

THE HIDDEN CURRICULUM

The teacher/student relationship is also a major part of the hidden curriculum in schools that influences students' beliefs about self. The hidden curriculum also has a pervasive influence on how school staff work together and whether students are motivated to do their best (Eisner, 1994). Characteristics of the hidden curriculum (Holcomb-McCoy, 2005; Jackson, 1990) include the following:

- Stated and unstated teacher expectations
- Discipline practices
- Communication, collaboration, problem-solving, and conflict-management norms among students and among teachers and students
- Human relationships between teachers and students, because how people think about and treat others is part of what students learn in school
- How people initiate contact, interact with, and react to each other

Chart 1a Factors That May Influence Personal Identity

	Factor	Check the five factors that most influenced your identity in the eighth grade	Check the five factors that most influence your identity at the present time
1.	Race/ethnicity/nationality, and perception of respect received based on race/ethnicity/etc.		
2.	Socioeconomic circumstances (e.g., income level of family or self, job occupations, and social status in the community)		
3.	Physical/mental/emotional disabilities, or perceptions by others of there being a disability		
4.	How the mass media portray persons of particular groups, and also how the groups are portrayed		
5.	The influence of past schooling experiences, including how teachers react to particular human differences, and how instructional materials portray particular human differences		
6.	Personal experience of and reaction to biases (e.g., biases that reflect racism, sexism, or classism), based on one's race, gender, socioeconomic background, age, sexual orientation, physical size, or any disability		
7.	Information from one's family, guardians, and significant others about the experience of persons in one's primary reference group(s) in the United States, particularly in its educational systems		
8.	Personal home life, including family relationships and personal interests		
9.	Personal phenotype characteristics, such as body type, skin color, facial features, height, weight, and hair length/texture		
10.	Primary language and/or dialect, and fluency in academic English		
11.	Geographic location of primary residence within the United States		
12.	Religious beliefs/practices		
13.	Personal perception of what significant others, the general society, and/or peers think about you		
14.	What family, friends, and teachers expect of you and how they treat you		
15.	OTHER:		

All of the above variables have enormous influence on the dynamics of difference in school communities. For example, teacher ideas about how they should be treated by students and parents, combined with the major factors influencing their personal identity, may have influence on how they react to student attitudes, behaviors, and learner characteristics, including student motivation and readiness to learn at grade level (Noguera & Wing, 2006). Similarly, students' racial identity, life experiences, and past schooling experience may influence how they perceive some of their teachers, especially those of different racial backgrounds.

MAKE IT PERSONAL

FN1–1 (SEE FACILITATOR NOTES IN APPENDIX 1)

1. What are some ways your personal identity, including race, ethnicity, religion, gender, primary language, occupation, socioeconomic status,and sexual orientation, has been a major influence in your life? For example, have you made choices or developed life priorities based on your personal identity/identities?

2. How has your self-identity influenced what you think about your life chances or potential, and what you think about others with identities very different than your own?

3. In what contexts (e.g., playing a specific sport, as a student, singing, performing, or public speaking) do you feel very confident and in what contexts do you have less confidence?

4. Name some examples of contemporary cultural bias/prejudice against immigrant groups that are held by various native-born economic and cultural groups or individuals in the United States and influence what happens in your schools.

5. What do you think you should be doing, if anything, to counteract the cultural biases you thought of in response to #4?

Race and culture have long had a major impact on schooling in America. Schools often reflect the attitudes and biases of the various subgroups from which their students come, especially those of the dominant socioeconomic classes in society (Bowles & Gintus, 1976). Conflicts within and across student groups, between adults and students, and between communities and schools are often influenced or fueled by different racial and cultural perspectives. Race relations and institutional racism in the United States continue to help shape identities, conflicts, and educational experiences, including day-to-day teaching and learning, in most school communities (Zirkel, 2008). The scenarios that follow further illustrate diverse identities and how status, power, and authority might be sought or fought over by various school stakeholders, thus impacting the conflicts, that is, dynamics of difference, in school settings.

SCENARIO ONE

A new charter school principal, appointed 2 weeks before the school year began, decided to request her predecessor remain on the job for the first month of the school year, but has not sought information from her predecessor about any of the financial, academic, or achievement challenges being experienced by the school. She is new to the district, has never been a principal before, and has no work experience in an elementary school. Some of the teachers who were told by the previous principal about her concerns related to their job performance are those who are currying favor with the new principal to get changes in the academic program and discipline policies. Enrollment is down from the previous year and some parents of Asian and White backgrounds have pulled their children out of the school because of concerns about the lack of rigor in the Grades 2–5 academic program and loss of a balanced curriculum in Grades K–8, for which the school used to be known.

SCENARIO TWO

A majority of the school board in a large school district, after hearing the concerns of many White middle to upper middle class parents and reviewing select research consistent with the parents' point of view, does not approve their superintendent's proposal for including attention to racial/cultural issues in the district's comprehensive effort to reduce achievement disparities, because they feel under achievement is caused by socioeconomic factors and not issues related to race and the quality of instruction for diverse populations.

SCENARIO THREE

An assistant principal overheard and chose to ignore very disparaging remarks of some teachers about other teachers in their school who relate well to students of color, handle all of their discipline problems, hold all students to high academic expectations, work beyond the school day with students as needed, and have more students experiencing high educational outcomes.

SCENARIO FOUR

Limited English proficient (LEP) students from one ethnic background brutally tease and stereotype LEP students from other ethnic backgrounds who are new to the elementary school.

MAKE IT PERSONAL

FN1–2 (SEE FACILITATOR NOTES IN APPENDIX 1)

1. At the end of each scenario above, identify what you think are the major influences on the identities of persons described in the situation.

2. Identify the conflicts (i.e., dynamics of difference) and reasons for the conflict in each of the four scenarios in this chapter; describe how you think each scenario could contribute to inequitable student outcomes.

3. What could be done to minimize the conflicts in each situation?

4. What does the personal identity, including the racial identity, of students and educators have to do with student educational outcomes?

⁊⁊⁊

THE ROLE OF CULTURALLY COURAGEOUS LEADERS IN ADDRESSING IDENTITY/CONFLICT ISSUES

1. Culturally courageous district and school site administrative leaders would engage in recruiting and cultivating support from all stakeholder groups in the school community for a vision of what the district and school could be. They would seek and incorporate input on their new vision from such groups after making a convincing case for educational institutions playing a much more comprehensive role in healing wounds and confronting unstated needs of the larger community. They would exemplify personal and professional identities that reflect the courage to build trust, mediate conflict, and genuinely collaborate. They would carefully plan how to engage all adult stakeholder groups in critically examining how racial identity levels may negatively impact student achievement.

2. Culturally courageous teacher leaders would incorporate more attention to addressing the learning and status needs of historically underserved students, regardless of their background. They would display genuine concern for the welfare of all students, and aggressively seek new knowledge/skills that would help them jump-start their own personal transformation. They would also display a no-excuses philosophy beginning with how they relate to peers and other school community stakeholders, especially historically underserved students and parents. They would not practice "aversive racism" where they explicitly support egalitarian principles and believe themselves to be nonprejudiced but harbor negative feelings and beliefs about Blacks and other historically disadvantaged groups (Gaertner & Dovidio, 1986).

REVIEW OF CHAPTER 1

- A new leadership paradigm is needed that includes the courage to critically examine the relationship between how schools influence identity development and student educational outcomes; such leadership must come from leaders in all stakeholder groups in school communities, including students, parents, community persons, university faculty involved in teacher and administrative preparation programs, and support staff as well as teachers and administrators.

- There are many culturally based environmental factors that influence how persons define themselves and create their unique identity construct, including their level of racial identity development, which impacts student educational outcomes.

- One's personal identity and level of racial identity development influences how they perceive and interact with persons considered different and may also have great impact on conflicts with such persons.

- The history of racial and cultural bias in the United States, including past and contemporary responses to immigration, continues to influence the dynamics in many schools as well as student educational outcomes.

The Absence of Cultural Democracy

2

Most schools in the United States influence their students' perception
of who is entitled and has special privileges in our society, through
curricula and instructional practices.

Without there being any explicit directives verbally or in writing, educators may unwittingly communicate through what they do and don't do whether every child is equally valued. What happens between kindergarten and the fourth or fifth grade that causes the historically underserved student who had unbridled enthusiasm for learning when they were 5 years old to become self-doubtful and alienated in school 4 years later? Certainly there are many out-of-school factors, such as medical care and insurance, food security, pollutants, child abuse, and neighborhood norms, that greatly impact student school success (Berlinger, 2009). What schools do to ameliorate the negative impact of such conditions is critical.

KWL EXERCISE

1. Based on your understanding of what is meant by the term *cultural democracy*, as discussed in the introduction to this guide, what are two or three examples of how cultural democracy is practiced or not practiced in your school or school district?

2. What is your major question or concern about the relationship of cultural democracy to the educational outcomes of historically underserved students?

3. In 50 words or fewer, describe what you think is the relationship between personal racial identity, racial/cultural conflict, and the lack of cultural democracy.

∂∾∾

CULTURAL DEMOCRACY

In this guide, *the term racial/cultural conflict* is used interchangeably with the term *dynamics of difference*. To further elaborate on the discussion about cultural democracy in the introduction to the guide, the term is referring to in-depth ongoing equity transformation in three areas:

- Culturally relevant curriculum that includes content that builds on students' prior learning and life experiences.
- Culturally responsive instruction that includes high expectations for all students and responds to learner characteristics, including their strengths, preferred ways of learning, *situated identities* and *positionalities*, as defined by Murrell (2008).
- Equitable conditions in schools that include more democratic participation in the decision-making process by all adult stakeholder groups. Such groups include parents, teachers, community persons, and higher education faculty who work with schools or help prepare future teachers and administrators.

Cultural democracy should help facilitate equitable educational opportunities and outcomes by all disaggregated student groups. In this guide, cultural democracy, though not a prerequisite, is considered of critical importance when attempting to achieve equitable student outcomes, but sometimes such democracy will cause discord because of negative reactions by any teachers, parents, or students who by nature of their cultural, social, and economic capital have favored status. Favored status can be exemplified by being very resistant to creating equitable learning conditions in schools for the historically underserved, which diminish the effects of an uneven playing field in society.

There is a strong relationship between a very toxic school environment and very little if any cultural democracy. For example, sometimes students of color, students whose primary language is other than English, and students of low socioeconomic backgrounds are in schools where the structure and culture strongly mitigate against equitable quality education. This may be exemplified in discriminatory staff assignments (i.e., which teachers get which classes and the student makeup of those classes), discriminatory class assignments (i.e., which students get scheduled in classes at a certain academic level and the quality of their teachers), curriculum/program offerings, teacher–teacher working relationships, funding, and the quality of leadership by persons in all stakeholder groups (Noguera & Wing, 2006).

In many schools that have a major gap in the educational outcomes experienced by most of their students of African and Latino/a descent compared with most of their White students, there is an abundance of racial segregation within higher level courses and programs preparing students for college or a career path. In addition, many students of color, regardless of their academic level, likely experience curriculum and instruction that is full of omissions and distortions related to their background (Ladson-Billings, 2003; Lowen, 2007; Martinez, 1998). For example, there may be little if any substantial information about the diversity within their group, or how persons of their specific cultural heritage have contributed to humanity. What students do learn from experience in school is how many more Black students are suspended due to differentially applied school discipline policies that reflect a lot of prejudice and discrimination (Zehr, 2010). Such conditions are the antithesis of cultural democracy, but teachers may strongly resent the notion that they should give explicit attention to such issues as prejudice and discrimination, and some have told me they fear doing so will cause more of the same.

Cultural democracy includes but is not limited to opportunities for students of all cultural/ethnic/racial backgrounds in a school community to learn about themselves, including their ancestry, cultural heritage, and contributions to humanity, as well as the ways they as a people have survived adversity. Such opportunities are almost nonexistent in most public schools within the United States, even those populated primarily by students of African and Latino/a descent when they constitute the overwhelming majority.

Cultural democracy also includes the opportunity for school staff in all teaching and instructional support roles to have meaningful input into the school's decision-making process. This should be able to occur without intimidation from their peers or supervisors. All parents and caregivers, as well, should have opportunities to be meaningfully involved in a partnership with the school to maximize their children's potential and educational experience. In some low-performing schools where I assisted the implementation of effective schools reform, a significant percentage of all staff and parents indicated in interviews or on assessments of effective school correlates that they didn't feel their input on school decisions was sufficiently solicited and not seriously considered when provided.

Many students of diverse ethnic minority backgrounds experience the reality of lower status and social influence in their daily lives, but it is not part of what they study or talk about in school. Within the regular curriculum, students may not be taught about social justice efforts of the past or present, those still needed in the United States, and what they can do to increase social justice. But ignorance isn't bliss. Students may still act on perceived injustices or slights and develop resentments against others which grow, fester, and explode because schools do not always provide students with positive ways to address their resentments or the many contextual factors, struggles, and forces affecting their identity (Sadowski, 2008).

෨൙

THE "DYNAMICS OF DIFFERENCE"

The *dynamics of difference* in a school setting includes how racially, ethnically, and culturally diverse persons with various personalities, interests, strengths, and perceived status communicate and get along with each other. The attitudes and feelings such persons have about each other, including any stereotypes, prejudices, and actions toward others, are all a part of intergroup relations, a subset of the dynamics of difference. Intergroup relations and interpersonal communication in a school are to some extent a reflection of the prevalent attitudes about human differences in the larger community and society.

Intrapersonal (internal conflict), interpersonal (conflicts with specific individuals), and intergroup conflict are a salient feature of the dynamics of difference in all kinds of schools. For example, during their K–12 schooling, all students are in the process of developing an identity (e.g., deciding how they "see" and "define" themselves compared to others as well as their beliefs, values, and goals). This process is often influenced by how other persons relate to and treat them as well as their family environment. Adolescent mental health is posited as a function of ethnic identity and family functioning among African American adolescents (Street, Harris-Britt, & Walker-Barnes, 2009).

Teachers and counselors need to access diverse funds of knowledge about ethnic identities to assist them in understanding student attitudes and behaviors. Students are often struggling internally, trying to figure out who they are, their likes, dislikes, friends, goals, and priorities. When changing their minds about any of the above, they may struggle to reconcile new choices (e.g., friends or priorities) with those discarded. Students often experience all of this inner turmoil without much help from adults, which can result in conflicts with peers perceived as "different," as well as with persons in authority positions, such as parents and teachers.

This process may be complicated by students' perception of how others respond to their personal characteristics (such as skin color, speech patterns, body type, facial and hair characteristics). Student A may develop stereotypes and biases toward student B (and vice versa) based on inaccurate notions influenced by student A's and student B's physical characteristics or personality. In some cases, what students perceive another's racial identity to be is not the same as how that student defines him- or herself. The process of forming a racial identity may be even more complex if students don't like the perceived consequences of their choices, because of conflict with other identities they are developing.

These internal struggles with identity as well as overt racially and culturally based conflicts take a lot of energy and can compromise student academic improvement (Jackson, 2011). In addition, many adults in school communities of all ages and backgrounds are also going through their own identity crises, internal struggles, and overt conflicts. This may be especially true when the ways teachers have been socialized to define themselves and define others are inconsistent with their lived realities and/or ways they prefer to be (Duncan-Andrade, 2007).

The interaction between individuals within and between groups, as well as the kinds of communication or conflict among persons of similar or diverse ages, cultural, racial, ethnic, socioeconomic, educational, and language backgrounds, are all a part of the dynamics of difference. Personal experience, negative or positive, has enormous influence on the behaviors of persons toward others.

MAKE IT PERSONAL

FN2-1 (SEE FACILITATOR NOTES IN APPENDIX 1)

1. Given the definition of cultural democracy in this guide, describe specific ways that one of the schools with which you are familiar is *not* culturally democratic.

2. What is your opinion about the quantity and nature of conflicts in very culturally diverse schools?

3. In schools you know well, what is done to minimize any racial/cultural conflicts?

4. How do you react to the statement that "adults' and students' perceptions of each other are both a result and a cause of their behaviors toward each other"?

5. What is one example of how your lived realities cause conflict between the way you prefer to be as a teacher or administrator versus how you feel compelled to be?

కళ⋘

SO WHAT?

What should or can be done to eliminate any negative consequences of the interpersonal and intergroup dynamics discussed in this chapter? Some teachers and administrators might not accept any responsibility for how they may unwittingly contribute to students' negative sense of self, group conflicts, or low educational outcomes. I have personally found many teachers of low-performing students do not feel it appropriate to be held accountable for facilitating equitable educational outcomes.

So what if how students think of themselves and how they get along impact what benefits they accrue from school? It is asking too much of teachers and administrators to be responsible for trying to improve the social ills of society, or so some educators believe—even when they acknowledge the need for schools to more directly address social justice issues. Again, I have found that a considerable number of teachers who work in low-performing schools don't see themselves being able to do anything more than what they have already done about the problems. In addition, some of these same teachers feel their time is more wisely used in directly preparing students, without attention to cultural issues, for doing well on high-stakes testing. Cultural responsiveness is not at the top of their list in most cases. This attitude prevails despite the negative reaction of many African American and Latino/a students to a curriculum that includes little if any attention to the contributions and experiences of marginalized groups, except during Black History Month and Cinco de Mayo (Thompson, 2007).

కళ⋘

THE IMPACT OF LITTLE CULTURAL DEMOCRACY

One possible reason for little cultural responsiveness by teachers may be the cultural conditioning and socialization of many educators throughout their lives and professional preparation, during which they may have been subjected to covert and overt efforts for them to give highest priority to embracing and perpetuating the common culture in the United States and its Eurocentric origins. It is the common culture that is overwhelmingly reflected in many states' literature and social science content standards (i.e., what students should know or be able to do), textbooks, and classroom instruction.

In a very large school district where I was a district administrator, all administrators within the entire district office were convened for the purpose of securing consensus that all students can learn at high levels. When some proposed the following amendment to the belief that all students can learn at high levels "if they are provided with the requisite teaching, support systems, and materials," the overwhelming majority refused to agree to such an amended statement. The reason for balking at the amendment may have been the result of not wanting to be held accountable for doing what was necessary to ensure that all children did indeed learn at high levels. However, I also think the personal or professional identity of the administrators was such that they did not view themselves as having the responsibility for doing whatever was necessary to ensure all students learn at high levels, especially if doing so meant some political pushback and increased accountability they would have to assume for results. The meeting might have been a publicity gimmick in the first place, so the district could include a statement that all children can learn at high levels in the district mission statement. This is the kind of duplicitous political correctness that prevails in many low-performing schools and districts. Another example of such subterfuge is when school district leaders acknowledge the need for their teachers and administrators to increase their effectiveness in facilitating achievement at high levels by historically underserved students, but never solicit input from various stakeholder groups, followed by issuing specific directives and/or creating policies that require a change in school practices and participation by the staff in such ongoing professional development. The public posturing is not accompanied by meaningful follow-through.

American citizens are very diverse and all have ethnic roots. Regardless of racial/ethnic or language background, socioeconomic status or geographic location, all human beings are influenced to a greater or lesser extent by such variables as the belief systems, customs, prevalent attitudes, and taboos within the larger society of which we are a part. Although these variables are also part of our "common culture," they may not be taught. Individuals may also be heavily influenced by several cultural groups to which they belong and with which they strongly identify. Examples are racial/ethnic groups, religious groups, groups based on primary language, socioeconomic status, education status, occupation, age, gender, sexual orientation, political beliefs, and so on. By nature of their shared experiences in the past and present, such groups have some prevalent beliefs, customs, and heroes/sheroes that are part of their cultural heritage.

MAKE IT PERSONAL

FN2–2 (SEE FACILITATOR NOTES IN APPENDIX 1)

1. To what extent are the cultural groups to which you strongly relate a major influence on your personal identity and perceptions of others?

2. What is your opinion about the relationship between cultural background, cultural conditioning, and cultural biases?

3. What can *you* do to challenge the cultural biases of persons with whom you work who oppose one or more equity initiatives in your schools?

છે∽જી

In vignette 2–1, Jimmy's opinions about the attitude of his English and math teachers, as well as his concern about the opinion his homeboys have of him, are probably influenced by the interactions he has with them and the importance he attaches to their opinions. There are some other experiences that may have some bearing on Jimmy's self-identity and attitude about school.

VIGNETTE 2–1: JIMMY IN ELEMENTARY SCHOOL

When Jimmy was in elementary school, there were several grade levels when he learned about various cultural groups, or when students were encouraged to engage in show and tell, such as sharing things about their families and culture. In none of these instances did the instructional materials include much information about the culture or contributions of Africans or African Americans. The teacher guidelines for student sharing did not suggest sharing information about one's cultural heritage or contributions to humanity, such as inventions. Jimmy's teachers would suggest he bring some object from home to talk about or talk about family activities. Whenever he shared in class, some of the kids would make fun of him afterwards, without teacher intervention.

It is possible to infer from the above vignette that Jimmy's attitudes about school have been developing for a long time. Although he openly expresses his opinion that two of his middle school teachers didn't care about him, he may have felt the same way about the elementary teacher in the classroom where he was teased by students after participating in show-and-tell activities. Although we don't know why he feels the way he does about his eighth-grade math and English teachers, we do know he struggles with his writing, often fails to do his math homework, and doesn't come after school to get extra help. Jimmy's writing problems are not atypical for many middle school historically underserved students. In addition, many of these same students may demonstrate problems with fundamental math skills as early as the second grade, which are essential for success in algebra. The statewide end-of-year test scores received by many Black and Latino/a students who take algebra signal major problems with what has and has not transpired as a part of the teaching and learning process during elementary school. Jimmy was one of those who needed greater mastery of his fundamental skills (e.g., addition, subtraction, multiplication, and division) before taking algebra.

In a large school district, African and Latino/a families sent their children to magnet and other voluntary enrollment programs with the hope of a better education being received. Some of these students had the opposite experience. Many Black and Latino/a adolescents, males in particular, weren't doing well in school, had a lot of disciplinary referrals and suspensions, and felt alienated before reaching the ninth grade. They saw school as a hostile environment where some teachers were scared of them and didn't seem to care whether they learned at high levels as long as they didn't make trouble. This was true both in their home schools and schools across town where they enrolled. The irony was that the schools across town in which the students of color enrolled needed them because of not having sufficient enrollment from their own neighborhoods to stay open as a school and keep their existing staff. The state funding received by the school based on average daily attendance was needed, but the attitude toward the students by some staff and resident parents was not welcoming.

When Latino/a and African American parent complaints about the teachers were investigated, there were school teachers who did seem to have double standards in academics and discipline. Many of these teachers in the receiving schools decried the poor readiness level of their bussed students for grade-level work. Perhaps low achievement was due in part to the district's expectation that pacing schedules be strictly maintained, even though such pacing focused on exposure as opposed to mastery.

Another factor is that some secondary students of African and Latino/a descent with academic problems have high truancy rates and do not consistently go to all of their classes. This is obvious when examining the period-by-period attendance records of many large urban low-performing high schools. If walking the campus of these same schools, making sure to visit the restrooms or other hideaways of truant students, some can easily be found. Some of this truancy is the result of a conflict between student learning styles, teacher expectations, and instructional strategies. Some students prefer to be truant when they don't feel they can maintain the pace of the class. This results in low student motivation and effort. In other cases, when these same students do come to class, teachers allow them to sleep or otherwise not be engaged in the teaching and learning process as long as they "don't cause trouble for the teacher."

Some teachers think they have done everything they can do to help students succeed, even though the students may feel some resentment and resistance to being asked to do what they call "dumbed down" work that includes a lot of worksheet and drill activities. Corbett (2002) discusses six characteristics identified by urban students as good teaching, and one of these is that students want to be held to high expectations. Teachers may feel they have been sensitive to their students' challenging life circumstances outside of the school, when actually what they or their school may have done is pass students with substandard performance on to the next grade if they do minimum work and don't disrupt the class. The overall system of public education reinforces low teacher expectations by not including adequate attention to how social promotion is occurring (social promotion includes passing on students who do significantly below-grade-level work), or not providing adequate professional development or mentoring, which helps teachers correct the problem. This phenomenon continues to occur in some classes despite the No Child Left Behind (NCLB) Act. School districts seem to be responding to the pressure to keep historically underserved students moving through the system if they met minimum expectations, despite the cumulative effect of so doing.

There are no easy solutions to the dilemmas of teachers and students. The identity constructs of each group are instrumental in helping shape how they relate to each other and whether there are substantial improvements in educational outcomes. In addition, schools may make few efforts or have little success in trying to involve parents or other caregivers in determining how best to meet their children's educational needs. In many cases, when prior efforts to involve parents don't work, educators conclude that parents aren't interested or don't strongly value education (Corbett, Wilson, & Williams, 2002).

ॐॐ

THE IMPACT OF SCHOOL ORGANIZATIONAL CULTURE

The organizational culture of individual schools includes the beliefs, norms, taboos, traditions, routines, ceremonies, and celebrations within the school (Deal & Peterson, 2009). Organizational cultures can have enormous influence over the behavior of individuals within them. Equity transformation cannot be successful without counteracting cultural biases, either personal or organizational. In vignette 2–2, you can get a glimpse of some cultural characteristics in Jimmy's middle school. As you read it, think about what kind of leadership is needed to positively impact the current school culture as reflected in the conditions and practices described.

VIGNETTE 2–2: DESCRIPTION OF JIMMY'S MIDDLE SCHOOL

Olentangy middle school serves a growing number of working class students, many of whom are recent immigrants of Latino/a, Asian, and African backgrounds, as well as a shrinking number of lower middle class students of African and White American descent. As the middle class students of all ethnicities have transferred out, the school has become more culturally diverse and achievement scores have declined. More than 50% of the staff are veteran teachers who have been in the school more than 20 years, and there are philosophical differences between many of them and newer teachers. When most of the veteran teachers came to the school the majority or plurality of students were White. Staff divisions have contributed to an inability to reach consensus on a school vision or mission. This impasse has negatively impacted the school improvement plan. The school is in the second year of NCLB program improvement . The current principal has been in the school for 1 year and is perceived by most veteran teachers as insensitive to their concerns. The rate of mobility for all students and staff has greatly increased in the last 3 years. Some of the veteran teachers are struggling to meet the needs of the present student population, which is not as homogeneous as the students they have taught most of their careers. Several resist and resent pressures for them to seek transfers, and have sought support from their teacher's union, because of feeling the district is not providing adequate financial support for program improvements and reduced class sizes. Some organizations in the Black and Latino/a communities have accused the school of bias, because of the increase in disciplinary referrals, instruction that is not perceived as responsive to the diversity in the school community, and limited school/home communication. A recent district parent survey revealed the percentage of unsatisfied Olentangy parents has increased by 20% in the last 2 years. Most teachers do not feel parents support the school or value education as much as they should, based on parent participation rates at school functions and no response to letters sent home. This was the middle school attended by Jimmy before he recently graduated.

Teachers, with good intentions, may try interventions with students they label as at risk, which may not work for some students of color. But there are specific actions not often tried that might lessen the conflicts between persons within and across teacher/parent/community groups.

For example, in chart 2a are examples of actions and results that I have initiated and had various degrees of success with when working as a human relations consultant to schools or as a district administrator. There is no guarantee these actions by themselves will improve the dynamics of difference in school settings or result in equitable student outcomes, but they will contribute to building the kind of school environment that lays a foundation for more collaborative efforts by all school stakeholders to improve the school climate and make it more conducive to achievement at high levels by all.

Readers should compare any actions they have taken to improve intergroup and interpersonal relations (i.e., part of the dynamics of difference) with actions listed in the table.

Chart 2a	Proposed Actions and Potential Results Regarding Intergroup and Interpersonal Relations

Actions That Can Be Taken Within a School Community	Place an "n" or "c" if this or a similar action has been taken nominally or consistently on an ongoing basis	Describe what was done in detail	Describe what results and barriers were experienced when taking the actions described
After providing an orientation to what is meant by intergroup and interpersonal relations, engage all teachers on a site-by-site basis with culturally and racially diverse parent, community, and student representatives in identifying their concerns related to communication problems within school community groups, between groups, and between individual persons. Follow up by engaging all parties in identifying two or three of the problems identified to use for problem-solving discussions and participation in problem-solving hands-on exercises. If appropriate, transition to involvement of some or all parties in team and trust-building activities.			
Create a safe environment, including agreement on ground rules for behavior, where persons of various ages, races, and cultures are comfortable in openly exchanging ideas from their diverse perspectives, and by making "I" statements.			
Over time, facilitate candid group discussions about their "self-talk" when confronted with differences in ideas, opinions, and priorities of others, and when promoting appreciation for diversity, where differences are not treated as sources of conflict.			

Chart 2a (Continued)

Help all participants recognize their own beliefs and assumptions, then accept the benefits of changing negative attitudes and resistance into cooperation.			
Engage participants in a "re-education" process during which they discover the origins of their stereotypes and prejudicial norms, including the role of culture in forming perceptions.			
Provide chances for all participants to engage in small group activities which enable them to practice how to have respectful dialogue with and about people different from self.			
Results That Have Been Achieved From Implementing the Above Actions	**Place an "n" or "c" if this result was nominally or consistently experienced on an ongoing basis**	**Describe in detail the specific results experienced**	**Describe any new challenges related to the dynamics of difference that have arisen due to this result**
A shift in thinking that creates a greater comfort level with diversity.			
Assuming more responsibility for respectful communication.			
Developing and practicing a personal "tool box" of effective communication styles that foster teamwork.			
Increase in self-confidence to identify and implement more culturally sensitive communication behaviors toward culturally/racially diverse others.			

In the absence of the enumerated actions in chart 2a that can be taken within a school community, there is a greater chance the items listed under results will not occur. The following is an example of where such actions *did not* take place.

VIGNETTE 2–3: BULLYING IN PILGRIM K–8 SCHOOL

Pilgrim K–8 school is having a growing problem with student bullying, as are many other schools in the Delta Rivers school district. This is occurring both among boys within Latino/a and African American student groups and across racial groups and is usually physical in nature. Girls engage in a different kind of bullying, which is more verbal and between social cliques. In both cases, the individual or group of students initiating such actions are seeking more status among their peers, even at the risk of disciplinary action. When teachers or principals discuss the problem in their meetings, they tend to studiously avoid exploring whether there are any biases, physical and emotional violence students are mimicking from their homes, or emotional violence from adults in the school setting. The possible relationship between how adults talk about and treat others they perceive as different and the behavior of students in school is almost a taboo subject.

Student bullying is a national phenomenon (UCLA School Mental Health Project, Center for Mental Health in Schools, 2011). In the mid-1970s, it was more commonly referred to as scapegoating behavior. At that time, in a suburban school district on the East coast where I served as a consultant, there was a lot of within-as well as cross-racial scapegoating, and the students who initiated scapegoating and those who were the recipients of such behavior were both considered problematic. Classroom and counseling activities were often initiated to influence change in student behavior, but there was resistance to focusing on how adults in the school community setting might be unwitting contributors to the problem.

Then and now, when students manifest attitudes or behaviors considered dysfunctional, hurtful, and distracting from a focus on academic performance, the attitudes and behaviors of adults in the school community may not be the subject of inquiry. Although some of the adults were open to a more holistic approach to dealing with the problem, some were not, and the impasse resulted in a limited approach being used because focusing on adults was considered very threatening. In both the vignette about Pilgrim elementary and the additional example of a school focusing on what was called scapegoating decades ago, there was a hands-off approach to adult self-examination of what personal changes needed to be considered.

Not all bullying occurs amongst students. Koenig and Daniels (2011) identify two types of teacher bullies, in their article titled *Bully at the Blackboard*. Those who have been identified as either a power-dominant bully or a power-lax bully have taught for more than 5 years and usually were bullied themselves as children. When there aren't safe school environments conducive to the willingness of school staff to engage in self-examination, the result may be the use of cosmetic approaches to change dysfunctional norms related to culture and race in school settings.

Cultural democracy in schools should include attention to the development of social and emotional competence by both students of all backgrounds and staff, since the lack of such emphasis has major impact on school success, specifically academic achievement. Unless there is priority given to developing capacity in recognizing and managing emotions, handling challenging situations, solving problems effectively, and establishing positive relationships with others, then student and adult resilience is greatly compromised (Elbertson, Brackett, & Weissberg, 2010; Zins & Elias, 2006).

Furthermore, when no attempts are made to improve cultural democracy in schools, there is greater likelihood that race and cultural differences will result in more conflict. Another way the absence of cultural democracy in schools is manifested is when many school stakeholders, students, parents, teachers, or support staff have no influence over or meaningful input into what happens in the school. Such schooling conditions can be one of the major factors influencing the academic outcomes of most historically underserved students of color, because when adults are so busy fighting among themselves or are angry and alienated in their work environment, they may be giving inadequate attention to the needs of students. When some of the staff don't feel valued or respected, it may be very difficult for them to value or empower students with perceived lower status.

Vignette 2–4 exemplifies many of the major issues and conceptual relationships discussed in this chapter.

VIGNETTE 2–4: INTRODUCTION
TO THURGOOD MARSHALL HIGH SCHOOL

Thurgood Marshall High School is overwhelmingly populated by students of African and Latino/a American descent, and 80% of the students qualify for free or reduced-price lunch. However, a majority of the students in college preparatory or advanced placement classes are of White or Asian descent who collectively constitute only 30% of the student body. The parent community groups who are protesting the makeup of higher level classes claim that students of African and Latino/a descent are not held to high academic expectations nor do they experience a culturally inclusive curriculum. Limited-English-speaking students are mostly at the intermediate or beginning English language development levels, with approximately 25% at the upper intermediate or advanced levels of English language development. The percentage of English language learners who have been redesignated as fluent speakers in the last 5 years is very low. Many students of African and Latino/a descent at the school appear to have strongly embraced select aspects of their racial/ethnic heritage, and an overwhelming majority of all students self-segregate most of the time. The exceptions to self-segregation are some students in Music, Drama, career paths (i.e., also called vocational education classes in some places), college preparatory classes, and students in some athletic programs. Gang-related conflicts off campus between a few African, Hispanic, and Southeast Asian males spill over onto the high school campus and occasionally result in school fights.

There is also very little collaboration among teachers within three of six academic departments (including ESL), and outright enmity among faculty subgroups in the math and ESL departments. A high rate of teacher absenteeism is compounded by an inability to get substitutes, and in most cases, substitutes are not qualified to teach the classes they are assigned to teach.

The Marshall formative assessments and year-end state standardized test scores are in the lowest three out of five performance levels for most African and Latino/a students (i.e., students score no more than 30% of the items correct), thus indicating most of these students are performing well below the level of proficiency. These results are interpreted very differently by teachers as a whole compared with parents and community groups. Students don't seem to care one way or another. Most teachers feel the results reflect factors over which they have no control and also blame the district and site administration for not providing stronger leadership and programmatic support for the school. They would like the administration to reassign approximately 15% of the students to off-site continuation or independent study programs, because some of them are highly disruptive, are truant approximately half of the time, are functioning at least 3 to 5 years below grade level, and keep others from being able to learn. Parents of these students label this request as blatantly racist and threaten to close down the school with protests and civil unrest if it is enacted. Some of Jimmy's homeboys are in this group of students.

Two officers of the district teacher's union work at this school and are part of a group of teachers (approximately 30% of all faculty) who have been teaching at the school for most of their teaching careers. Most veteran teachers at the school have taught large numbers of Black and Brown students for most of their careers and derisively dismiss Black and Latino/a community claims that they are racist. They feel they know best how to teach students of color and just need more support from the district administration, school board, and the community. These same teachers resist and resent efforts to require their participation in professional development programs that focus on conversations about race and cultural responsiveness in the classroom.

Vignette 2–4 illustrates diverse personal identities by different stakeholders, the impact of diverse racial/cultural perspectives on the dynamics of difference, the perceived absence of cultural democracy in educational environments, and some of the educational outcomes of historically underserved students of color in a poor urban high school. For example, in the vignette many teachers don't seem to respect each other or have any inclination to collaborate with each other. Whether all of the variables in the above vignette are related depends on who is asked the question. However, the characteristics of Thurgood Marshall High School are not fabricated and may exist in many schools with similar educational outcomes for historically underserved students.

A large number of educational theorists and research studies have addressed the problem of widely disparate achievement by students of diverse ethnic and socioeconomic backgrounds in the United States. The culture and organizational structure of schools are major factors influencing such achievement outcomes, and whether or how the issue of race is addressed is part of the school culture.

Many students' self-perception of their academic prowess as well as whether they have the motivation to do their best is influenced by how educators and others of all backgrounds relate to them, as well as by whether they can relate to the curriculum and instruction experienced. That was the case in the vignette about Jimmy in his middle school and is likely to be the case in Thurgood Marshall High School where he is about to matriculate. Students' academic self-perception and attitudes toward school are often a reflection of the interface between life circumstances over which they feel they have no control, how others view them, and how they view themselves, with their peers having a major influence.

❧⚮❧

THE ROLE OF CULTURALLY COURAGEOUS LEADERS IN ADDRESSING THE ABSENCE OF CULTURAL DEMOCRACY

1. Culturally courageous community leaders, including higher education faculty, would be more active listeners and partners in the schooling enterprise, such as developing and sharing their voice to help build greater intergroup understanding and coalition building, with no self-serving personal agendas. They would consciously represent the third rail and dimension of school reform, engaging community stakeholders in expanding their awareness of what is meant by *cultural democracy*, and identifying ways that stakeholders would like to see an improvement in cultural democracy within the district and school environment.

2. Culturally courageous leaders from stakeholder groups within school settings would do the same as community leaders, but with representatives of the student body and all instructional staff. They would make sure to help participants reach understandings of how cultural democracy could influence all school programs and operations. Conditions that could be positively impacted include student identity development, staff professional development, student and teacher bullying, school/home communication, and collaboration. Cultural democracy in schools can contribute to improved teacher collaboration and involvement in the decision-making process, culturally responsive counseling and guidance, intergroup relations, and conflict management. In addition, attention to cultural democracy is needed in curriculum and instruction that reflects both the common culture in the United States as well as specific cultures in the school and community.

Chapter 2 has provided several ideas about some of the school community dynamics influencing the educational outcomes of historically underserved students. Readers should answer the questions below based on their own experience and based on ideas from the chapter with which they agree.

MAKE IT PERSONAL

FN2–3 (SEE FACILITATOR NOTES IN APPENDIX 1)

1. Why does racial/cultural bias continue unabated in many school communities (or in your school community)?

2. What needs to happen so that implementation of changes proposed in this chapter will indeed result in meaningful societal change for the "have nots"?

REVIEW OF CHAPTER 2

- The social and educational environments in schools are significantly impacted by the dynamics of difference and degree of cultural democracy practiced in these settings.

- School organizational cultures, including intergroup and interpersonal functioning, need to be critically examined and new norms established that reflect respect for all "differences" and greater collaboration that focuses on empowering all students.

- Cultural democracy includes the extent to which the learning styles and cultural heritage of all students are used during the teaching and learning process. In addition, there is a concerted and persistent effort to solicit and use the input of all stakeholder groups in the decision-making process.

అంఈ

Grim Continuities   3

The more things change, the more they stay the same.

THE GAPS IN NO CHILD LEFT BEHIND

The grim continuities between educational policy and practice in the late 20th century and early 21st century are a continuation of racial/cultural bias, consciously or unwittingly, at all levels of public schooling. The U.S. elementary and secondary education act was first passed in 1965, and last renewed in 2001 when it was titled the No Child Left Behind (NCLB) Act. The NCLB legislation has several sections to address equity issues, including Title I for economically disadvantaged students; Title II for preparing, training, and recruiting high-quality teachers and administrators; and Title III for language instruction of limited English proficient and immigrant students. These sections of NCLB all ostensibly have the intent of improving educational equity (NCLB, 2002).

Despite the relatively recent initiatives in the NCLB legislative development process that focus on creating more equal educational opportunity and eliminating achievement disparities, success remains elusive, especially in secondary schools throughout the country (Knaus, 2007). NCLB has also been faulted by Smith (2012), who identifies five problematic areas: (1) unfunded mandates, making it difficult or impossible to purchase textbooks or implement policies required by NCLB; (2) standardized tests that are set state by state, allowing manipulation; (3) tests that are thought to have cultural and linguistic biases, including testing in English non-English-speaking students who are recent immigrants; (4) punitive sanctions for schools designated as failing, because they don't meet all of their achievement targets but are improving; and (5) requirements for corrective action that are too restrictive, such as reconstituting or restructuring schools that include firing school staff and management. These criticisms are echoed by many members of the U.S. Congress, state politicians, and educational practitioners. A research-based critique by Mathis (2005) on how NCLB had been underfunded up to that time is comprehensive in its analysis. Corrections in the legislation related to some of these criticisms are being proposed during congressional negotiations on renewal of NCLB.

However, there are no proposed changes in NCLB that would require the incorporation of information in the curriculum about cultural/ethnic groups of color *from the perspective of the cultural groups.* Such information is also called *cultural funds of knowledge* since it is knowledge created by participants of each culture (Moll, Amanti, Neff, & Gonzalez, 1992). In addition, no changes are being proposed related to the NCLB requirements for schools to have highly qualified teachers, even though such requirements do not include any reference to teachers needing to learn content and skills for effectively teaching culturally and racially diverse students. This absence implicitly and explicitly conveys the message that such funds of knowledge are insignificant and inconsequential when it comes to achieving equitable student outcomes.

For example, differential teacher expectations based on student gender, racial, linguistic, and socioeconomic characteristics and historically inaccurate/incomplete instructional materials continue to be commonplace throughout the country. There are many different interpretations of why this is the case, and some might deny that such conditions as those stated above have anything to do with federal initiatives to increase equal opportunity. It is possible that the above continuities between the 20th and 21st century reflect the beliefs of decision makers that reforms related to culturally relevant curriculum do not merit high priority in order to improve student academic outcomes. Who are these decision makers? They include classroom teachers, textbook authors and editors, district curriculum administrators/writers, and boards of education at the state and local levels.

The content standards approved by many state boards of education, which in some subject areas are now the common core standards developed nationally, drive what is included in hard copy or electronic textbooks and do not specify the need for in-depth information about cultural/racial oppression in the United States. Major publishers of history, reading, and literature textbooks do not include such content. Nevertheless, fledging efforts have been made by some publishers to make textbooks more honest about the lived realities of many historically underserved groups. However, this information is not being used by most teachers to help students critically analyze political, economic, and cultural forces that perpetuate inequities, nor are teachers including instruction in most cases on how students can engage in social justice efforts to change inequities. The excuse for such omissions may be the absence of any content standards on causes of inequities or ways to attempt changing such causes. Such omissions in content standards reflect an unstated policy commitment to perpetuating the ideology of dominance discussed in Chapter 2.

This chapter builds upon what was discussed in Chapters 1 and 2 about the relationship between identities, conflicts, and the lack of cultural democracy, by providing information about four conditions in school communities that contribute to inequitable student outcomes.

અ∙જ

KWL EXERCISE

1. In your opinion, to what extent, if at all, do students of various ethnic/cultural/language backgrounds, age, and achievement levels need cultural democracy in order to thrive and achieve at high levels?

2. What assistance do you need in order to more effectively help underserved students who are operating on the margins when it comes to school success?

3. What have you learned from the guide so far that peaked your interest about what you can do to positively impact student identities?

⪼⪻

FOUR CONDITIONS IN SCHOOL COMMUNITIES THAT MAY CONTRIBUTE TO INEQUITABLE STUDENT OUTCOMES

- **Instruction, hegemony, identity:** How instruction is influenced by and reflects cultural hegemony in the United States, and how hegemony negatively impacts students' personal identities as well as their motivation and effort to succeed in school
- **Deficiencies in teacher/administrator preparation and professional development programs:** How most preparation and professional development programs do not adequately help teachers and administrators recognize or effectively deal with the impact of covert and overt institutionalized racism or cultural conflicts in schools
- **Cultural politics:** How cultural politics is manifested in school communities, and some of the consequences experienced related to student outcomes
- **Human fears:** How attitudes and behaviors associated with human fears may influence cultural conflicts and organizational cultures in school communities, negatively impacting student educational outcomes

Instruction, Hegemony, and Identity

The continued dominance in schools of Eurocentric instructional materials and instructional practices

VIGNETTE 3–1: JIMMY'S AND JOSEPHINA'S EXPERIENCE IN OLENTANGY MIDDLE SCHOOL

Jimmy attended Olentangy middle school with his friend Josephina; they both graduated at the same time and are going to the same high school. Josie tried to help Jimmy with his writing assignments in eighth-grade English, but he didn't put his best effort into it, so her help didn't work. They often talked about how turned off they were by most of the assigned readings in their eighth-grade English class. They both felt there

> were few stories of interest to them and wondered why what they were reading was mostly about the White experience when most students in the school were from cultural backgrounds of color.

What Jimmy and Josephina perceived happening in their English class at Olentangy Middle School was a reflection of curriculum, instructional material selection, and pedagogical decisions. From all appearances, these decisions didn't seem to take into consideration the realities of students like Jimmy and Josephina, who are of African American and Puerto Rican American heritage. Students from historically underserved groups may become alienated when they think what they are being taught omits significant information about their past and present reality. Conversely, if the same students constitute a very small minority in a given classroom, sometimes being the only student of their ethnic group, they may feel more uncomfortable when such teaching occurs because they are unfairly signaled out by the teacher or subject to racial/cultural slurs from other students.

The personal identities of all students are influenced in part by whether they can relate to what is taught in school. Vignette 3–1 describes a mismatch between curriculum content and students' cultural background. Jimmy and Josephina think their English class is grossly insensitive to who they are and also feel their school only teaches about White cultural experiences. In other words, they think their English and social studies textbooks and teacher instruction make White middle class people the favored group.

To the extent that students of historically underserved groups across the United States feel the same way about some of their classes, this perception has the potential of significantly contributing to turning students off and fostering resentments about what the school is teaching.

When there is dominance of one cultural group over other groups in such areas as economic, social, and educational policy, the result has been characterized as cultural hegemony (Ladson-Billings, 2003). Ethnic groups of color in America have been systematically objectified and stereotyped in the media and by some scholars who believe in the intellectual and cultural superiority of White Americans.

When curriculum and instruction in a school is focused primarily on one cultural group to the exclusion of others represented in the student or national population, how does that impact the educational outcomes of students whose groups are left out? Such educational practices can be construed as examples of cultural hegemony, defined as a condition where the cultural experiences and priorities of one cultural or socioeconomic group are given priority over the beliefs, experiences, and interests of other groups in a culturally diverse educational setting (Gause, 2011).

This is a common condition in many school communities regardless of their demographic makeup. Students not seeing themselves reflected in the curriculum may impact their effort, motivation, and on-task behaviors, which can then negatively impact educational outcomes, especially in the absence of other support systems being in place (Noguera, 2008).

MAKE IT PERSONAL

FN3-1 (SEE FACILITATOR NOTES IN APPENDIX 1)

1. In your opinion, what is the responsibility of teachers to build on students' life experiences to teach about prejudice and discrimination, including the oppression experienced by persons of diverse cultural/racial/ethnic backgrounds?

2. What are some of the consequences when students of all backgrounds don't learn about how much the political and economic fabric of society in the United States has been influenced by historical and contemporary discrimination, such as racism, ethnocentrism, sexism, classism, and homophobia?

3. If you were the teacher in the eighth-grade English classroom of Jimmy and Josephina and were aware of their attitudes about what is taught in the class, how would you respond?

4. Describe an example of where the customs, history, or common culture in the United States is being taught in your elementary or secondary school with very little if any attention to inclusion of the positive contributions of various historically underserved students' cultures/races/religions represented in the school.

5. Hypothetically, if all or most students attending a school in your community were from Asian, Black, Latino/a, and Native American cultural groups, how might English language arts and history/social studies curriculum/instruction be different or the same as in schools where Whites are in the majority? OR

   Briefly describe what your English language arts and history/social studies curriculum would include if you were teaching in a school where a majority of students were from African and Latino/a American backgrounds, and whether it would be any different if your class included all major racial/ethnic groups.

Deficiencies in Teacher/Administrator Preparation and Professional Development Programs

The continuation of major omissions in teacher and administrator training

Based on accreditation criteria, teacher and administrator preparation programs are not likely preparing future and current teachers and administrators to recognize and change institutionalized racism that impacts all students, particularly historically underserved students of color. The National Council for accreditation of teacher education (NCATE), the University Council for Educational Administration (UCEA), and the Interstate School Leaders Licensure Consortium (ISLLC) all fail to include any explicit attention to the need for culturally responsive/relevant curriculum and instruction, or what corrective measures are needed to eliminate covert and overt discrimination in school functioning. Institutional and cultural racism are not explicitly addressed.

The consequence is that most university teacher and administrator preparation programs do not include attention to such topics in their programs. As a result, future and current teachers and administrators may not be equipped to plan and implement culturally democratic professional development programs or transformation initiatives fostering equitable educational outcomes. This may be due to what has been called "White institutional presence," which includes the attributes of monoculturalism and White blindness (Gusa, 2010). Lin, Lake, and Rice (2008) report that many teachers currently in the classroom say they feel inadequate to teach multicultural or anti-bias curriculum. They go on to say that teachers' attitudes about and sense of efficacy in addressing cultural diversity influence and affect their teaching practices, and may become barriers that prevent the integration of anti-biased curricula. There is little attention in teacher and administrative preparation programs on how to identify and deal with institutional racism and cultural hegemony at all levels, preK through graduate school. Depending on your perspective, it could seem like a major avoidance of acknowledging the elephant on the ceiling, so to speak.

Nevertheless, there are exceptions to the avoidance syndrome. Murrell discusses a model that helps teachers develop cultural competence in actual work contexts. It is called "Circles of Co-practice" and involves urban school-university-neighborhood collaboratives to improve urban education (Murrell, 2006). Irizarry reports on practices identified as culturally responsive by Latino/a students in an urban, multiethnic/racial context. The concept of "cultural connectedness" is discussed as a dynamic approach that acknowledges the hybrid nature of culture and identity (Irizarry, 2007). The National Urban Alliance for Effective Education engages school communities by building relationships with educators, students, parents, and community stakeholders and currently has partnerships in 26 school systems in 8 cities across the United States. The goal is to reverse effects of institutional racism and work with districts to close the achievement gap (Doubek & Cooper, 2007). Staples (2010) examines some of the literature on the identities of most teacher candidates in the United States and posits a corollary between their inexperience with historically underserved students and their conceptions about language in relationship to racism and sexism. She also provides examples of how demeaning words used by "privileged" persons alienate and oppress "others," thus having implications for how to improve pedagogical practices among teacher candidates who can counter wounding words and assist students' reaction to them.

I advise some caution when touting reforms in teacher education, which may actually help teachers learn racism rather than equipping teachers with the skills necessary to effectively address many invisible forms of racism, power, and Whiteness (Cross, 2005), with the result being a continuation of the "same ole oppression."

Bottom line, there is little that happens during teacher preparation or during on-the-job professional development within most schools and school districts to help new or veteran teachers and administrators become culturally proficient and capable of countering institutional racism (Knight & Wiseman, 2005). Even when such learning opportunities occur in school districts, administrators and teachers need capacity building on how to deal with both internal and external forces that cause a lot of anxiety about or resistance to school reform initiatives that involve teaching for social justice and unlearning racism (Cochran-Smith, 2004; Hynds, 2010). Such teacher development is not a priority in most school districts. Even though there has been considerable criticism of school administrative preparation programs (Levine, 2005), these criticisms don't mention the above inadequacies.

One reason preservice programs may give only scant attention to helping teacher candidates develop cultural proficiency is the belief (or excuse) there is no research to support the relationship between such training and increased academic outcomes, despite evidence to the contrary (Gay, 2010; King & Hollins, 1997; Lee, 2007; Montecel & Cortez, 2002; Stroder, 2008; Zirkel, 2008). More research is still needed on the connection between preservice education or cultural proficiency professional development and teacher practice. Political resistance occurs when trying to conduct such research or when trying to give ongoing emphasis to cultural issues during preservice programs and school district professional development.

In addition, some schools where staff members have experienced training on cultural proficiency or culturally responsive teaching are very uncomfortable with research on the extent of implementation. In these cases, there may have been very little if any follow-up support given to teachers after the training. The quality of the initial professional development on the above topics may have been at an awareness or cosmetic level. Schools are not walking the equity talk when they schedule cursory superficial on-the-job training with little or no subsequent support to assist implementation. At best, they are simply checking off an item on a laundry list of things to do in order to give the impression of commitments they don't have.

In university preservice teacher preparation programs, faculty teaching the same course may have very different definitions of and teaching strategies for building capacity in cultural proficiency and culturally responsive teaching, resulting in no agreement among them on core principles or elements associated with the terms. This was the case when I was a lecturer in teacher education at a large state university. Some students were resistant to a focus on such topics, and faculty may have been influenced by this resistance as well as by their own discomfort.

District office administrators and school board members may also studiously avoid such topics because of feeling it is not politically expedient to do so. For example, they may anticipate strong resistance/push back from some dominant group members in their communities who have more social, political, economic, and cultural capital, and will politically retaliate if priority is given to such policy development and capacity building.

MAKE IT PERSONAL

FN3-2 (SEE FACILITATOR NOTES IN APPENDIX 1)

1. Based on your experience, what are some examples of how cultural hegemony is being practiced in schools or in teacher/administrator preparation programs with which you are familiar?

2. What is your opinion of whether schools should help teachers and students learn about and collectively combat institutionalized racism?

3. To ensure that such instruction occurs, what support is needed by teachers and school site administrators?

Cultural Politics

The manifestation of competing racial/cultural attitudes attempting to influence educational policy and practice

Cultural politics, also known as identity politics, revolves around diverse perspectives and priorities when it comes to which group or groups will maintain political and economic domination in the United States. Power and power relations between people are at the center of cultural politics (Jordan & Weedon, 1995).

Racial conflict is both a cause and possible by-product of such politics. Dominant cultural values and practices that function in the schooling process help to marginalize and silence the voices of African American, Latino/a American, Asian American, Native American, and other historically underserved students in the United States. A result may be that teachers don't attempt to empower their students or legitimize student voice. For example, personal perceptions of such concepts as beauty, intelligence, dangerous, and qualified depend on the background and life experience of the person defining the terms. Stereotypes abound, largely influenced by significant others, the mass media, and prevalent societal attitudes (Gay, 2010; Omi & Winant, 1994). Attitudes about and behaviors toward persons of particular groups, sometimes caused by or made worse by the mass media, are all a part of the cultural politics in any given setting. A manifestation of such politics is cultural dissonance, which is an uncomfortable sense of discord, disharmony, confusion, or conflict between culturally diverse persons, usually in the midst of change. Angus and Jhally (1989) provide multiple perspectives on cultural politics in the United States that document how pervasive and destructive it can be.

Some principals and teachers in low-performing schools or schools with underperforming historically underserved students resist professional development on culturally responsive pedagogy. Teachers use many different excuses to justify their lack of receptivity, including the impact on their emotional well-being, the irrelevance of the training to their instructional effectiveness, and the ineffectiveness of the trainers. Sometimes, they also deny any discomfort or conflict in values, that is, cultural dissonance, between themselves and some of their historically underserved students, despite repeated referrals of these students to the office for frivolous reasons. On-the-job professional development programs seldom, if ever, provide support for teachers, new or veteran, that attempts to help reduce cultural dissonance with students and/or parents in their schools. Thompson (2007) reports on the resistance from educators to professional development on culturally relevant education, particularly, but not exclusively, White educators.

Cultural politics in school communities includes competing ideas of what is in the best interests of the society and the children, based on the perspectives of those making the decisions, which often reflect priorities of the dominant groups in society. The persons with competing views include those who may seek equitable cultural relationships and a greater share of power, influence, and control within their school communities or may want their current power and control to be even more entrenched than at the present time.

There are also many competing demands within American society for how major structural elements in any school should be implemented. These structural elements have tremendous impact on the teaching and learning process. They include the curriculum content, instructional practices, how students are assigned to particular classes, and the school schedule. Curriculum and instruction are ostensibly based on what students should know or be able to do, driven by state content and performance standards. How time is allocated is commonly called the school schedule, which includes the sorting, that is, tracking, of students and distribution of time for different events and subjects. Curriculum and instruction, sorting of students, and time allocations are school structures often insensitive to the needs of all students (Oakes, Wells, Datnow, & Jones, 1997).

Eurocentric curricula marginalize and minimize the cultural existence of African and Latino/a Americans as well as other historically underserved students. The American White identity is characterized as the cultural norm, with other cultural experiences reduced to being given scant if any attention. Most textbooks tend to marginalize content about racial/ethnic groups. Also, my experience is that most teachers with whom I have worked do not engage historically underserved students of color in knowledge construction activities related to their cultural heritage or background. In addition, how the media characterize persons of color can represent powerful forms of discrimination, whether it is in the news, movies, or other forms of entertainment (Bell-Jordan, 2008; Omi, 1989).

Some people, including scholars, may unwittingly support the privileged status held by the dominant cultural group in the United States, even when they reject the notion that they personally benefit from "White privilege" (Johnson, 2006). Having had responsibility for facilitating the process that resulted in several history/social science textbook adoptions, I have witnessed how cultural politics in the textbook industry influences *how* knowledge is created, *what* knowledge is created, and what knowledge/data is perceived as *legitimate/worthy of publication.* The cultural politics in state governments and local school districts influence what knowledge is *taught* and what knowledge/skills are *assessed* (King, 2005).

When state content standards have been revised to give the appearance of being more culturally responsive, they do not include attention to the kinds of critical media literacy students should be taught, which would help them learn about and counter the subversive way that the media help perpetuate the continuing American legacy of racism, ethnocentrism, sexism, classism, and homophobia (Kellner & Share, 2007) as well as the perpetuation of destructive cultural politics. Such curriculum inclusion would enable students to avoid being unwittingly seduced into supporting the power, control, and influence of the dominant group. Finally, the negative impact of cultural politics is also reflected in state assessment practices, which don't include assessment of cultural content or movements to improve social justice and end institutional racism. The implicit message is that such content is not essential enough to be included, and if included, even superficially, not essential enough to be assessed.

MAKE IT PERSONAL

1. Describe two examples of how cultural politics is practiced in your work setting, for example, between school board members, school board members and administrators, administrators and teachers, teachers and parents, parents and parents.

2. How would you like the cultural politics to be changed in your school or district so there is more concerted effort by all stakeholders to improve student educational outcomes?

3. In your opinion, how is what is taught in schools a result of the cultural politics in a state, school district, and school?

Human Fears

The prevalence of fears that drive and exacerbate racial/cultural conflict

There are also human fears that contribute to the dynamics of difference in schools and school communities. These fears cause biases that may result in toxic organizational cultures in districts and schools that contribute to low educational outcomes. An important characteristic of an organization's culture is the formal and informal leadership: those who have an inordinate influence on the thinking and behavior of others within a school setting (Deal & Peterson, 2009).

Human fears that may influence organizational cultures include the following:

- Fears based on lack of open and honest personal experience with and personal ignorance about diverse others
- Teacher fears of some students and/or parents
- Prevalent societal attitudes about certain human differences
- Perceived threats to the maintenance of one's status or privileges within the organization

Vignette 3–2 provides examples of the above fears.

VIGNETTE 3–2: SCHOOL/COMMUNITY CONFLICT IN OLENTANGY MIDDLE SCHOOL

At Olentangy middle school, as major changes occurred over the last few years in the student population, some teachers became uncomfortable with the new influx of Muslim families as well as immigrant students with no formal schooling experience in their native countries. Teachers are frustrated by students who don't come close to having the entry-level skills expected in their class and require a lot of individualized or small group instruction. Demands from some school community organizations for more in-depth culturally responsive instruction at the school were agreed to by the board of education. Most Olentangy teachers were enraged by the board agreement. They resented the money that would be spent on materials and professional development to implement the decision, and some thought the decision would make teaching of diverse students more challenging, especially given the limited amount of time they had to prepare students for high-stakes testing. There was no acknowledgement by teachers and administrators of other factors causing their resistance to culturally responsive teaching, such as cultural biases and fears that time spent on being culturally responsive would increase discipline problems and embolden "problem" students and parents. Problem students and parents are defined as those who in the minds of the teachers are always looking for racial bias in classroom discipline, materials used, or teacher actions. There is very little trust between these parents and the teacher.

Some preservice students in my university classes and teachers in professional development I have conducted have protested they cannot and should not be expected to learn about all of the cultural backgrounds represented in their classrooms. They think it is an impossible task. They further claim there isn't sufficient time to teach about all of these backgrounds, given the standards they are expected to make sure students master before high stakes testing. These last two excuses can be a convenient rationale for teachers not having to learn about their students of color and for students of color not needing to learn about themselves and their historical/contemporary realities. However, if the overwhelming majority of what White students were required to learn about cultural groups was about historically disenfranchised cultural groups in the United States, and not about their own (i.e., White) customs and contributions, there would likely be an even greater exodus from public schools. Nevertheless, that is exactly what cultural groups of color in the United States are expected to accept, without objection.

MAKE IT PERSONAL

FN3–3 (SEE FACILITATOR NOTES IN APPENDIX 1)

1. What are some of the cultural politics practiced in your school community or school district?

2. To what extent is cultural hegemony a cause and/or consequence of the cultural politics you described in response to the above question?

3. What would be the reaction of culturally diverse students and school communities where you live if all students were required to learn about how oppression has been experienced by many groups in the United States, and also learn how discrimination against some groups continues to the present day?

4. How do school organizational cultures with which you are familiar influence whether teachers include instruction about societal biases toward some cultural/ethnic groups?

5. In your opinion, what are some of the prerequisites that must be met for improving the response to new students in a school community when the new students seem very different from the majority?

6. What are some of the human fears in a school community that may inhibit equitable treatment and equitable outcomes?

As articulated by Covey (1990), many persons have a scarcity mentality or worldview, including the idea that when some advance or get more (such as getting more equitable treatment in the curriculum), they will lose. Although not usually articulated in this manner, there is a major fear in many communities that equal attention in the curriculum and equal respect for all major cultural/ethnic groups within school communities will lead to less attention/priority given to what is called the American culture, that is, White people, thus resulting in a loss of power, authority, and influence over what is taught (Smith & Smith, 2009).

I have also had a few teachers in my classes or professional development sessions strongly imply that attempting to implement a curriculum that gives attention to all cultural groups within a given school is very impractical and almost anti-American. When explicit reference is made to the history and pervasiveness of racial/cultural bias in the United States, the reaction is even more volatile. In my discussions with teachers or preservice students, this belief and fear has been most strongly articulated by those who consciously or unconsciously have certain entitlements and privileges and may claim to not have any ethnic identity other than being an "American."

There is an indirect but powerful relationship between human fears, cultural politics, and inequitable educational outcomes:

- When teachers, students, or parents have diverse perspectives/priorities and may have had little or no positive shared experiences with culturally diverse persons (e.g., teachers with students or vice versa, parents with teachers or vice versa, students with students), they are vulnerable to embracing stereotypes and prejudices about these same persons. When the additional variable of perceived threats or attacks to one's status or dignity is added, a palpable fear and anger can be stimulated.

- This fear or anger influences the nature of the cultural politics practiced, which under the best of circumstances involves competing worldviews, values, cultural mores, and interpretations of events by diverse persons with widely varying cultural orientations. The fears, threats, and politics can combine to cause major barriers to providing opportunities for achievement at high levels by historically underserved students. If they aren't declared as unqualified due to not meeting the biased criteria established for access to such classes or teaching, then when they are exposed to such instruction, they may not be given the support necessary for success. Such barriers often result in inequitable educational outcomes, because students may not be considered worthy of certain opportunities, and not perceived as having the requisite attitudes, readiness, or skills. In return, the affected students may perceive teachers as not respecting them, or they may internalize the negative perceptions others have of them. Teachers may not be perceived as respecting parents or vice versa, and students may not be perceived as respecting other students. These perceptions, however misguided they may be, have inordinate influence on the social and academic climate. In 21st century schools, most students do not make their best effort or do their best work when perceiving the school climate as uncaring or disrespectful. The same is true of teachers not doing their best work if they perceive disrespect or lack of support.

૭૦૦૬

THE POTENTIAL ROLE OF CULTURALLY COURAGEOUS LEADERS IN ADDRESSING GRIM CONTINUITIES

1. Culturally courageous leaders would lobby for major improvements in NCLB, based on the documented criticisms of the legislation, including full funding of programs in successor legislation to NCLB.

2. Culturally courageous leaders would take local actions related to the grim continuities, such as stopping culturally and linguistically biased testing, implementing capacity building activities for all instructional staff on culturally responsive teaching based on their input, helping create district-based administrative credential programs so they can make sure there is an emphasis on leadership for equity, negotiating with regional teacher preparation programs to make sure their courses focus on district priorities related to equity, and attempting to democratize district power relations, so no group has a built-in advantage during the competition between staff for status and privilege.

3. Culturally courageous leaders would attempt to create a task force with representatives from all stakeholder groups to investigate the extent to which there are gaps between district or school site vision and mission statements about equity, and the actions of boards of education and all educational practitioners.

REVIEW OF CHAPTER 3

- Three sections of federal NCLB legislation give woefully inadequate attention to equity issues, in the areas of support for economically disadvantaged students, training for teachers and administrators, and policies related to curriculum and instruction for limited English speaking students. In addition, there are at least five criticisms of current NCLB legislation that aren't addressed in proposals for renewal of NCLB, such as unfunded mandates, no consistency in state standardized tests, culturally and linguistically biased testing, unfair punitive sanctions for schools not meeting all targets, and restrictive corrective actions for failing schools.

- There are grim continuities in four major areas of educational policy and practice between the late 20th and early 21st century that are interrelated and reinforce cultural/racial bias. The continuities are the impact of cultural hegemony on students' personal identities, motivation, and effort; deficiencies in teacher and administrator preparation; cultural politics; and human fears.

Rhetoric vs. Reality　　4

There is a yawning gap between the rhetoric and reality of equity initiatives.

Most of the research on what works when attempting to achieve both equity and excellence is accompanied by acknowledgement that this research is not being used or implemented in most schools (Gay, 2010). There is a gap between theory and practice that I have personally witnessed throughout my career in various roles and places. Five examples of equity initiatives over the last 40 years are as follows: (1) integration of multicultural content and culturally relevant/responsive instruction into teaching and learning; (2) incorporating diverse cultural perspectives into educational materials, plans, and decision-making processes; (3) restructuring schools and reducing class sizes as an aid to eliminating achievement disparities; (4) providing historically underserved students greater access to lessons, courses, and programs taught at high academic levels; and (5) reducing disproportionate disciplinary referrals, suspensions, expulsions, drop outs, and assignments to special education of historically underserved students. The theory underlying the advocacy for such initiatives has been that they would lead to equitable educational outcomes and a society where there is greater cultural democracy in the distribution of power, authority, and control. Many school districts in the United States have not meaningfully attempted most of the initiatives mentioned, and even when they have, there is reason to doubt that the desired outcomes have occurred or been sustained over time.

KWL EXERCISE

1. Describe one or two examples of major differences between equity goals in schools with which you are familiar and what actually happened.

2. What questions do you have about the differences between what was attempted and what happened in the equity efforts already described?

3. Based on the first three chapters in this guide, what have you learned about possible causes of differences between equity initiative goals and equity initiative results?

The vignette below introduces some of the issues that may emerge when trying to implement what has been called "education that is multicultural." This approach to multicultural education is rarely found in practice, because of the cultural politics already discussed (Ladson-Billings, 1995; Lee, 2005; Noguera & Wing, 2006; Zirkel, 2008). The issues in vignette 4–1 illustrate some attitudes and practices of various educators in a school when they have been directed to implement culturally responsive teaching.

VIGNETTE 4–1: THE CONTINUING
SAGA AT OLENTANGY MIDDLE SCHOOL

As a result of the Board of Education's response to the social protests and demands of community organizations, the Olentangy school site plan was amended to include explicit reference to being culturally responsive in all instruction and school programs, including school community relations. A modest budget was also provided for securing supplementary instructional materials that focused on the cultural heritage of various racial, ethnic, and cultural groups represented in the school population, including the new influx of Muslim students. What was conspicuously absent in the school plan was any reference to teacher accountability for utilizing such materials, or any professional development for staff on how to implement at least four approaches to multicultural education. In addition, site administrators in Jimmy's school do not make note of whether there is any implementation of multicultural approaches during instructional observations. At staff meetings, they also don't explain why multicultural content is important to include in the instructional program for all students, not just students of color. When conducting feedback sessions with teachers after classroom observations, Jimmy's principal and assistant principal never referred to instances where they observed lower teacher expectations toward students of African American, Muslim, and Latino/a background. Also, administrators don't ascertain whether teachers monitor the academic progress of all students, based on academic benchmark targets required for each student subgroup. Jimmy and his neighborhood friends of African American, Muslim, and Latino/a backgrounds talk about how their teachers think they are "dumb" and don't think they can do the work. Based on their insights, some of these students don't try to perform to the best of their ability. Even when some of their teachers seem to have high expectations for all students, that isn't enough to motivate most of Jimmy's friends in his classes because they think the majority of their teachers don't care about them. Many feel their classes are boring and unrelated to their life experiences.

MAKE IT PERSONAL

FN4-1 (SEE FACILITATOR NOTES IN APPENDIX 1)

1. In your opinion, what instructional supervision strategies should be used by school administrators when working with teachers in the school attended by Jimmy?

2. If you were a teacher or administrator in the middle school attended by Jimmy, how would you attempt to improve the personal motivation and academic success of Jimmy and his school friends?

3. Identify some examples, if any, of how education administrators with whom you are familiar are not holding staff accountable for taking actions related to equity objectives in school site improvement plans, and describe the role you are playing to foster collaborative efforts to improve accountability for equity.

❧❧

WHAT IS DONE COMPARED WITH WHAT IS NEEDED FOR REAL EQUITY

In most schools with which I am familiar, there have been gradualist efforts when implementing multicultural education or effective school equity initiatives. School districts seem to prefer implementing a sanitized version of either initiative because it allows the school or district to implement so called equity activities without even discussing, much less challenging, the status quo relationships of power, privilege, and control that characterize public schools.

Duncan-Andrade (2004) has reported on the use of teacher inquiry groups he led which have focused on urban teacher retention, professional support, and development, which are critical to move beyond and around minimalist efforts sanctioned by decision makers. Nieto (2003) also writes eloquently about using the same kind of intervention to support teachers staying the course in spite of everything. This kind of professional support is essential for teachers to both survive and thrive with little site or district support during equity initiatives, and also signals the kind of preparation faculty in teacher preparation programs need to provide to future teachers and/or teacher leaders.

I encourage the reader to investigate whether there has been any sustained professional development in your district that included in-depth attention to race and culture and contributed to achieving equitable educational outcomes. Such investigations should also include a critical examination of whether there has been any significant change in the relationship of power, privilege, and control that characterize public schools. An example of how that relationship could possibly be altered is when boards of education (without court orders to do so) create permanent community-based advisory committees and provide staff support for their work, which focuses on investigating and recommending change in current policies and practices related to equitable educational opportunities and outcomes. That would be an example of institutionalizing advocacy for making a school district more accountable for providing equity. Such committees should include but not be limited to representatives from advocacy and civil rights groups like the Education Trust, student and parent organizations, university ethnic studies departments, and local or statewide ethnically based alliances of Black and Latino/a educators. I also encourage similar investigations of university preparation programs for teachers and administrators to ascertain if they are committed to preparing future teachers and leaders for the equity walk.

Although there is some rhetoric in most large and/or culturally diverse school districts about the need for social justice initiatives to be undertaken, there often isn't the leadership expertise or support to do so. What is done is often more "feel good" oriented, and cosmetic in nature. Nevertheless, there seem to be laudable efforts in some places to teach multicultural education critical pedagogy in teacher preservice programs that includes attention to social realities and issues of oppression (Sleeter, Torres, & Laughlin, 2004).

As stated earlier, my contention is that the cultural politics associated with equity transformation can be a major stumbling block unless the critical consciousness and mobilization of various school stakeholders is markedly increased. Two examples are provided to buttress this assertion. A 5-year study of six schools during the 1970s revealed that schools and communities often unwittingly reproduced racial inequality by maintaining White privilege within desegregated schools. Yet students and educators crossed the color line in ways never done before or since (Wells, Revilla, Holme, & Atanda, 2004). More than 20 years after this study, I personally witnessed the maintenance of White privilege in desegregated schools when serving as a district administrator. When challenging this situation, I was shut down by executive-level district administrators who didn't want to rock the boat. Almost 40 years after the study mentioned, there are still middle and upper middle class parent constituencies, mostly White, who will aggressively fight any threats to their privileged status, as reflected in programs or student sorting they perceive in their child's best interest. This may be seen in districts where there are upper middle class families living in the "hills," versus more culturally diverse low- to moderate-income families living in the flatlands.

Privileged status is defined as including access to achieving mastery in 21st century skills, high level curriculum content, higher level classes, and the most experienced teachers whose students have done well. In schools that are desegregated on the surface but segregated within classrooms, those children who have privileged status are in families with the most social, cultural, and economic capital (Noguera & Wing, 2006). There is no level playing field when it comes to all students having the opportunity to learn.

Unfortunately, many historically underserved parents do not have the time or resources to organize and lobby nearly as much for what they think is best for their children. However, there are a few beacons of light, where resources and direction are being provided to empower parents and advance social justice (Oakes, Rogers, & Lipton, 2006). Culturally courageous leadership in school communities is needed to expand these efforts.

For the most part, equity initiatives have not tried to fundamentally change the purpose of schooling. Boards of education and school district superintendents, as well as all other adult stakeholder groups, must be willing to collaboratively confront and change practices that help perpetuate glaring inequities in the quality of education and educational outcomes of historically underserved students.

Change is needed at systemwide (macro) and classroom (micro) levels that can only occur if transformation is the goal, not reform. There is a big difference between "reforms," usually more public relations oriented and structural in nature that focus on what I call "tweaking," that is, improving existing systems, and "transformation," which focuses on developing an entirely new educational enterprise that will develop the capacity to apply new knowledge on an ongoing basis. Transformation is much broader and deeper (Futrell, 2010).

For equitable educational outcomes, transformation must encompass more deep-seated fundamental change in how individuals and organizations interpret their reality, define themselves, evolve, grow, and problem-solve. The dimensions or correlates associated with multicultural education and effective schools reform are only a few examples of what on occasion have been effective in helping to reduce educational disparities in districts where in-depth sustained efforts were undertaken. There is an enormous difference between the equity rhetoric (i.e., what should be done that we know works) and the sobering reality of what is actually done when some reform or transformation initiatives have been implemented. The gap between the rhetoric and reality on a mass scale can only be lessened through such efforts as culturally courageous leadership by all school community stakeholders.

᪥

TEN OBSERVATIONS

Many schools with underachieving students of color have a lot of unexamined assumptions, beliefs, and practices that constitute "business of usual" and "the way things are done around here." They are accepted as just the way it is. In some cases, students, parents, and staff get categorized as being a certain way with immutable characteristics that will never change. Some aren't seriously challenged to "walk the equity talk" by their leaders or peers. Superintendents, school board majorities, and Deans of Education at universities set the tone. If they don't consistently articulate a vision of social justice and then demonstrate they mean what they say, then assistant superintendents, principals, directors, university faculty members, teacher leaders, department or grade level chairs, and parent and student leaders might talk it but not walk it.

When there is acceptance of the status quo regarding equity efforts, such decisions usually fit into the indigenous cultural and organizational norms of the university, school district, and individual school communities. The thesis of this guide is that culturally courageous leadership by all stakeholders working collaboratively is a prerequisite for changing such norms. My experience providing consultant assistance or district leadership to multicultural education and effective schools equity initiatives as well as my work as an external evaluator in low-performing schools greatly influenced each of the following 10 observations.

1. There is an absence of school district board policies and school district administrative practices, including staff selection, staff assignments, and allocation of resources, that focus on institutionalizing a commitment to equitable inputs and outcomes for all students.

Many factors can contribute to board policies and practices that are counterproductive to equitable inputs and student outcomes, such as employee contracts that limit a school district's ability to reassign teachers where it has been determined there would be a greater fit between student needs at particular schools and teacher competencies. Employee contracts might also limit the district's ability to evaluate teacher and administrative performance based in part on how employee professionalism is defined and whether there are student educational outcomes being sought that go beyond scores on high stakes tests. School board adoption of particular curricular materials that are culturally biased via omission or distortion can also be counterproductive. Finally, school board budgetary decisions and district priorities have enormous impact on whether equitable inputs and outcomes are possible. Board members must set the tone for practicing what they preach.

2. There is dysfunctional cultural dissonance within each stakeholder group and within and between stakeholder groups.

Stakeholder groups in school communities include teachers, students, support staff, parents, administrators, community persons, and higher education faculty. When there are major misunderstandings or conflicts within or between any of the above-mentioned groups, then engaging in collaboration to achieve mutually agreed upon desired ends is almost impossible. Many parents or caregivers of students of color often perceive a lack of interest and support from professional educators, who may feel likewise toward them.

3. There are few teacher and administrator preparation programs that walk the talk of being culturally responsive as well as school district

reality-based on-the-job professional development related to the effective education of historically underserved students of color.

Although some university school of education faculty have working relationships with urban schools, assisting teacher development and program implementation, in most cases they are pursuing their own research interests, which do not include attention to providing help for those who have completed credential programs at their university. They do not get their hands dirty in getting immersed with school districts grappling with how to improve teacher capacity so equitable student outcomes can be achieved. If they have research interests even remotely related to this area, it doesn't usually include spending much time in school classrooms except to collect data for their research. Furthermore, despite their protestations to the contrary, most university faculty have not specialized in improving achievement or other educational outcomes of historically underserved students of color. Most Deans of Education in universities preparing teachers and administrators do not give priority to involving their entire college faculty in the transformation of school communities with inequitable educational outcomes. Nor do most of them recruit junior or senior faculty of African or Latino/a descent who have a strong track record of having helped schools achieve social justice and equitable student outcomes. If they do, they don't fight to see that this important work is one of the major criteria used during tenure decisions for junior faculty. In addition, there is very little if any cross-curricular collaboration or joint program development at the university level focused on student equity and excellence for African and Latino/a students as well as other historically underserved student groups. Examples of joint work would be that between different ethnic studies departments or between such departments and the college of education. Their work might as well be on different planets given how often they share perspectives or engage in joint efforts.

4. Students and parents, especially those of color, are not nurtured as resources in helping to develop and implement/monitor comprehensive reform and school improvement plans.

Leadership practices in most school districts and schools reflect a very narrow paradigm of leadership. For example, students and parents of color in most places are not perceived as having an important role in helping determine the purposes, functions, and activities of schools. They are considered the customers that schools serve, not as needing to be in the group of those who decide what schools do and how they do it. Parents and students of color, who represent valuable sources of information, do not have representatives with seats at the table. Their input on some issues may be solicited, and just as quickly disregarded. This is even true for students and parents of color in some schools where they constitute the overwhelming majority of the school population. Nevertheless, they are expected to enthusiastically follow decisions made on their behalf, and if they don't, they are castigated as not valuing education, and being both "difficult" and "culturally disadvantaged," a term very popular in education circles during the early years of the multicultural education movement.

5. There is an absence of detailed accountability measures and incentives at state, district, and school-site levels for all educator groups regarding equitable treatment of and equitable outcomes by historically underserved student groups.

In this era of No Child Left Behind (NCLB), the federal elementary and secondary education act, there is the appearance of greater accountability for the educational outcomes of all student groups. However, the devil is in the details, and the so-called greater accountability is based on state standardized test results by student subgroups in several academic subject areas. There is no requirement that the subject area curricula are culturally inclusive without significant omissions and distortions or that the pedagogy for each subject area is culturally responsive and builds on the prior knowledge and strengths of all students in the classroom.

Even more problematic is that the state assessments upon which accountability is based do not include, for the most part, items requiring student knowledge about issues associated with cultural diversity and social justice in the United States. This omission conveys the message that if it isn't tested, it isn't worthy of receiving priority during the teaching and learning process. In addition, the planning and performance rubrics given to Title I or NCLB program improvement schools do not include requirements for implementing academically rigorous culturally responsive/relevant curricula and instruction, much less teacher training on high expectations and cross cultural communication.

The consequence is the absence of true accountability for teachers, administrators, and other educators, despite the evidence that such instruction and training can lead to improved educational outcomes. In addition, few if any incentives or supports are offered at all levels of education for schools to implement research-based equity reforms, such as transformative and social-action-oriented multicultural education/culturally responsive teaching.

6. There are many games played, where dichotomies are used as a rationalization for why greater priority cannot be given to planning, implementing, and holding staff accountable for equity transformation.

False dichotomies are when claims are made that either "a" or "b" can be done but not "a" and "b." One such claim is that teachers can spend more time teaching students about their cultural heritage and that of others or more time can be spent on helping students develop grade-level competencies in core academic subjects. The inference is that there isn't time to do both, as if they are mutually exclusive when they are not.

Another false dichotomy is the claim related to how limited funds should be spent. For example, some claim achievement disparities between various student racial/socioeconomic subgroup populations can be more easily ameliorated through additional funding for teachers to spend more time with needy students. Others claim underachievement will be significantly reduced through more money being spent on structural changes, such as smaller secondary schools and class sizes. The argument is that money cannot be spent on both more instructional time and smaller schools/classes, as if these choices are mutually exclusive.

Both examples above are false dichotomies, but all of the choices mentioned do not adequately address the issue of holding teachers and school districts accountable for engaging in equity transformation to achieve equitable student outcomes. Such efforts require changes of the heart as well as fiscal, cultural, and structural change. Changes of the heart, of beliefs, of will and determination, of self identities, including racial identity, are cultural in nature and inherently political.

7. There is too little political mobilization (i.e., community organizing on a large scale by all stakeholders working collaboratively) to lobby for greater support at the school, district, and statewide levels, when it comes to equity transformation. Most of the lobbying for more funds is not related to deep-seated equity practices.

Major equity transformation initiatives are perceived by the dominant social and economic classes as major threats to the status quo in terms of the cultural, political, and economic hegemony existing in the United States. For example, equity initiatives are seen as focused on the needs of minority or poor students at the expense of what is needed for the continuation and increase of programs for students currently being taught at high academic levels. In addition, policymakers and educational institutions help perpetuate such hegemony through their decisions about personnel, curriculum, scheduling, evaluation, and support programs.

Community, civil rights, and other social advocacy or professional organizations, some of whom are issue and/or ethnic specific in focus or membership, rarely, if ever, engage in joint efforts to change problem identification and decision-making processes in school districts.

8. There are very few instances where the agendas and priorities of diverse ethnic, cultural, school, community, and professional groups are harmonized, sometimes resulting in sabotage of district equity initiatives.

Groups of color at all age, income, and educational levels in the United States often experience the same kinds of injustice and inequitable treatment. However, they work at cross purposes, instead of collaborating to influence the political and economic norms reflecting various forms of discrimination. Their inability to work together is influenced by many factors, including past history, significant others, level of racial identity development, the media, and their cultural institutions. In addition, within some schools or school systems, if an equity proposal doesn't seem to have direct benefits for a particular racial/ethnic interest group, they will lobby against it. The reform might be perceived as requiring attention and giving greater priority to certain groups or tasks that persons don't value, or it could be perceived as threatening to current privileges held by some. All ethnic communities display this attitude and behavior.

Persons may mobilize to fight certain equity initiatives because they are perceived as an affront to their identities, sense of self and values, and above all, they may resent the greater accountability that would be expected should the initiative be successful.

9. There is far too little political will and savvy to undertake meaningful equity transformation that is sustained over time.

For more than 50 years, major efforts to improve both educational inputs and outcomes for historically underserved students of color have had mixed results. Despite many equity efforts, the achievement disparities and dropout rates are higher than ever.

In some cases, the political will to initiate and/or sustain systemic transformation hasn't been present or if so hasn't been strong enough. In other cases, the will has been consistently strong, but there has been almost a total lack of political savvy about what to do and how to do it in the face of unrelenting opposition and mischaracterization of what is intended. The short shelf life of those who are the major force behind equity efforts is also a major problem. It is very demanding work that requires 24/7 effort, and some people burn out after a few years. Others only stay involved as long as it serves their purposes, and then they choose to move on.

10. There is a lot of resistance to participation in ongoing trust building, communication, and collaboration by various school community stakeholders and cultural groups with diverse identities and backgrounds.

All stakeholders with diverse perspectives in the same school communities must engage in focused and disciplined team building, within their groups and across groups, if they are truly serious about wanting to achieve social justice, equity, and excellence. This is not common within and across stakeholder groups, not even among educators or community members with the same racial, ethnic, socioeconomic, language, and professional background. One of the most salient characteristics of low-performing schools where I served as an external evaluator was a major lack of team and trust building, especially when attempting to address sensitive issues related to race, culture, language, and socioeconomic background.

Competing agendas and priorities of diverse ethnic/cultural groups discourage and even threaten the growth of political will and savvy among various stakeholders to work together. They don't attempt to increase their trust and collaboration with each other, sometimes because they fear rejection and retaliation from peers. This can result in teachers and students, teachers and teachers, teachers and administrators, administrators and administrators, and parents/community members working at cross purposes. If the preceding picture of reality is real to the reader in your sphere of influence, then you will probably agree that our children pay the price for this dysfunction.

MAKE IT PERSONAL

FN4–2 (SEE FACILITATOR NOTES IN APPENDIX 1)

1. What three items from the list of ten observations require top priority in your work context?

2. Explain the extent to which the statement "There is a yawning gap between the rhetoric and reality of equity initiatives" is consistent or inconsistent with your personal experience.

ळ०ॐ

THE POTENTIAL ROLE OF CULTURALLY COURAGEOUS LEADERS IN REDUCING GAPS BETWEEN RHETORIC AND REALITY

1. Culturally courageous leaders would not only lobby for implementation of a particular equity initiative in the classroom, they would learn how to do it, and then model with children for other adults to observe, followed by soliciting critical friend feedback and discussion of what was done.

2. Culturally courageous leaders would examine major studies on the limitations and failures of past equity initiatives in such areas as cultural and structural reform, and make efforts to learn from the causes of previous gaps between the rhetoric and reality.

3. Culturally courageous leaders would give major attention to reducing the divisions both within and between different ethnic and socioeconomic groups, as well as other subgroup populations, so they can achieve greater understanding of and respect for the interests and needs of each other as well as the ability to work together.

4. Culturally courageous leaders rise above the societal pressures to think and act in ways that are divisive and counterproductive to improving social justice for all. They don't let petty ego issues between adults get in the way of achieving meaningful equity transformation.

REVIEW OF CHAPTER 4

- Although there is some rhetoric in most large and/or culturally diverse school districts about the need for social justice initiatives to be undertaken, there often isn't the leadership expertise to do so.

- Change is needed at systemwide (macro) and classroom (micro) levels that can only occur if transformation is the goal, not reform, where transformation includes a focus on more deep-seated fundamental change in how individuals and organizations interpret their reality, define themselves, evolve, grow, and problem-solve.

- Ten observations based on the author's experience as a consultant or district administrator leading multicultural education or effective school reform initiatives include the absence of needed school board policies and priorities, dysfunctional cultural dissonance between and within stakeholder groups, and inadequate political mobilization in support of equity transformation.

Biases

5

The history of public school equity initiatives in the United States
is in large measure the history of race relations and social justice efforts
in the larger society throughout the United States.

The biases discussed in this chapter are closely intertwined with the grim continuities and 10 observations already discussed. All of these conditions were either experienced as a participant observer or based on my direct work in a variety of roles to assist elimination of the obstacles to cultural democracy and improved student achievement in districts, schools, and classrooms. During this time I worked collaboratively with instructional staff and administrators to create and implement plans, programs, and capacity-building experiences that would positively impact educational outcomes of historically underserved youth.

KWL EXERCISE

1. How do you think it feels when teachers, parents, or historically underserved students experience the consequences of cultural hegemony, cultural politics, or human fears, as previously defined?
2. What would you like to know about institutional biases that may be negatively impacting achievement at high levels by historically underserved students in your district?
3. Share two personal observations about actions that are necessary in order to improve cultural democracy and student educational outcomes.

INSTITUTIONAL BIASES

Policies, practices, or norms within school districts and schools may directly or indirectly have a negative impact on personal identities, cause racial/cultural conflicts, and result in historically underserved groups having little power, control, and influence over what happens in their school communities. When this occurs, these policies, practices, and norms are construed within this guide as institutional biases that can have a deleterious effect on student educational outcomes.

Examples of institutional biases are the norms related to:

- *curricula and scheduling* (i.e., the content in courses offered and how class assignments are made for teachers and students);
- *personnel selection and professional development* (i.e., the processes used to make decisions about staff selection as well as topics and design of training to enhance knowledge, skills, and attitudes) provided or not provided for district and school staff;
- *supervision/evaluation* (i.e., accountability for job performance and student outcomes);
- *student low-socioeconomic status;*
- *student's primary discourse;* and
- *involvement of parents and guardians.*

In my experience working with schools not serving historically underserved students well, there was evidence of several institutional biases as discussed in this chapter. In all cases, these schools were giving scant attention to delivery, opportunity to learn, and professional development standards as described in chart 5a. Chart 5a briefly describes all five categories of standards as well as the relationship between categories.

MAKE IT PERSONAL

1. Based on the description of each standards category, what is your district doing to implement opportunity to learn, delivery, and professional development standards?

2. Describe any efforts that specifically focus on improving the opportunity to learn provided to historically underserved students.

The standards categories in chart 5a provide a much more holistic concept of what is necessary in order to achieve whatever state-specific content standards or national core standards are finalized by each state. There is a lot of controversy over whether school districts provide historically underserved students equal access to schooling where there is a commitment to standards in each category. In addition, there is a lot of tension over how the rush to standardize curriculum that is already overwhelmingly Eurocentric will be antithetical to culturally responsive teaching and culturally relevant curriculum.

Chart 5a Five Categories of Standards

Standards Category	Description of Category	Interrelationship Between Categories
Content	Knowledge and skills students are expected to know, be able to do, or develop	What students are expected to learn should drive all other standards
Performance	The level of mastery students are expected to achieve and demonstrate, regarding what they know and can do, and how they are expected to demonstrate what they have learned, as determined by the use of rubrics and exemplars	The content and performance standards, and characteristics/needs of the learners should drive the delivery and opportunity to learn standards
Delivery	The planning and pedagogical knowledge, skills, strategies, activities, and products teachers are expected to demonstrate with a wide range of culturally and academically diverse students in whole group, small group, and one-on-one learning settings, and to what extent, as determined by the use of rubrics and exemplars	Results from implementing the content, performance, and delivery standards should influence decisions about what is needed to meet the opportunity to learn standards
Opportunity to learn	The extent to which students have access to equitable funding, highly qualified culturally proficient teachers, and adequate instructional time; the extent to which the requisite instructional materials, equipment, technology, and facilities are available and appropriately used for a wide range of culturally diverse learners with different learner characteristics and learning styles. Also, the extent to which teachers have the instructional support, supervision, coaching, mentoring, and planning time needed to maximize their job performance and student outcomes	Results from using the opportunity to learn standards should influence revisions in the content and delivery standards used with particular groups of students, and revisions in the professional development standards used with teachers and instructional support staff
Professional development	Professional development that is academically rigorous, utilizes adult learning theory and state-of-the art knowledge about effective training strategies, models desired practices and attitudes, is culturally responsive, provides follow-up support in a variety of forms, and elicits ongoing participant input in design of the training	All of the above standards should drive the ongoing professional development provided, and the results of using these standards should influence any revisions in subsequent delivery and opportunity to learn standards

Content standards can be utilized to strengthen unequal power relations among diverse demographic groups as well as define the purpose of schools in a manner that perpetuates the lack of cultural democracy and social justice (Sleeter & Stillman, 2005). Leaders from all stakeholder groups in school communities must take more concerted collaborative action to erase institutional biases reflected in the norms described in this chapter. There is less chance that equitable educational opportunities will be provided or equitable educational outcomes experienced by all student subgroups if such cooperative initiatives aren't undertaken.

Curricula and Scheduling

The history/social studies content standards adopted by many states make no explicit reference to the past or present practice in the United States of institutional racism, ethnocentrism, or sexism, including its origins and consequences (Chandler & McKnight, 2009). Although several states give more attention than others in their content standards to the contributions, customs, leaders and life experiences of diverse cultural groups, there is usually little emphasis given to the contemporary distribution of power and influence. In addition, there are no state standards explicitly addressing the relationship between educational policy, practice, and widespread actions that exemplify a belief in White supremacy. Finally, there is a need for state standardized assessments to include items on what little their standards may include in these areas. When there are omissions in content or assessments, that speaks volumes about the overwhelming proclivity of states to avoid including information that explicitly addresses the contradictions between the nation's espoused values and cultural oppression in the United States, past and present.

State content standards drive textbook adoption decisions, instructional program choices, and school district curriculum adoptions. When there is superficial treatment of or no attention to social injustice in the standards, the likely result is teaching practices that are devoid of in-depth attention to the contemporary reality of historically underserved groups in the United States.

There is also a need for more attention to whether state content and performance standards set high academic expectations requiring intellectual rigor, or whether in some states, grade levels, and subjects, the criteria for mastery of the standards are a minimalist approach set to the lowest common denominator to meet federal NCLB requirements. Asa Hilliard addressed the issue of standards-based education as quality control or decoy (2003). For example, he asserted that in addition to the importance of content validity (e.g., consistency between what is meant by the content standard and what is taught, and between what is taught and what is measured), establishing standards of output without having standards of input is a travesty. A few states have been accused of setting lower performance standards so a higher percentage of their students in all subgroups are able to score at proficient performance levels that they establish.

Since the federal government sanctions schools not meeting their annual performance targets for all student subgroups, it is essential for schools to ensure all students have opportunities to learn (i.e., master) the content associated with each key standard. Not only must the content of standards be taught, it must be taught in ways that facilitate mastery by all student subgroups. The strong proclivity of most states to avoid establishing a more rigorous and culturally democratic definition of "highly qualified teacher" is a strong indication of cultural hegemony.

In addition, when content standards avoid specifying what students should learn about the challenges and progress related to eradicating racial/ethnic and cultural oppression in the United States, the omission is tantamount to supporting cultural hegemony. It is not enough for states to have history/social studies standards that focus on teaching some of the contributions, customs, and experiences of diverse ethnic/cultural groups. It is even more important for states to include standards that explicitly reference how various groups in the past and present have been and may continue to be subjected to political, economic, cultural, and social discrimination, including their treatment in public schools (Spring, 2007).

A close examination of the history/social studies standards would reveal little or no reference to the history of racial/cultural oppression in the United States, and very limited reference to social justice/social action movements that have tried to counteract such societal norms. This omission is a major point of contention by those advocating more cultural democracy in what students are expected to learn about their country. Taylor and Whittaker in *Bridging Multiple Worlds: Case Studies of Diverse Educational Communities* (2003) talk about the role of traditional school curriculum in failing to meet the needs of many culturally and linguistically diverse students. In addition, Zeichner (2003) points out that the teaching standards used as the basis for performance assessment in teacher education programs do not adequately incorporate what is known about culturally responsive teaching, and the teaching pool in teacher education programs is very culturally homogeneous, not coming even remotely close to the demographic makeup of the schools where these prospective teachers will work.

Dr. Carter G. Woodson, the father of "Negro History" in America, had his book *Mis-education of the Negro* published in 1933, and contended that education in the United States was intended purposefully to make people of African descent feel inferior and people of European descent believe in their superiority (1990). That purpose was then and still is manifested in curriculum, in instruction, in books, newspapers, broadcasting and films, and, most importantly, in public philosophy and public policy.

The National Alliance of Black School Educators (NABSE) commissioned a group of distinguished Black educators to write a document based on the inseparable linkage of academic and cultural excellence for students of African descent. NABSE issued its report *Saving the African American Child,* which was coauthored by

Dr. Asa G. Hilliard III and Dr. Barbara A. Sizemore and distributed nationwide in 1984 (Hilliard & Sizemore, 1984). *Saving the African American Child* made explicit that the process of educating African American students requires pedagogy and curriculum whose objective is the combination of academic and cultural excellence. The desired outcomes of cultural excellence are to correct and reverse the emotional, historical, and cultural damage of White supremacist distortions and untruths about students' African origins, the enslavement of their ancestors, and to renew their self-esteem.

Hollins (2008) discusses "reframing the curriculum." She asserts one purpose of curriculum is to transmit culturally valued knowledge and perpetuate cultural values and practices. Hollins says this means that public schools present a curriculum that serves the purpose of maintaining and perpetuating Euro-American culture. Picower (2009) discusses how such a curriculum is more meaningful to Euro-American students than to those who identify with other ethnic and cultural groups.

Another example of institutional bias is academic tracking and scheduling. Educational policies or practices exist in many schools that support the continuation of highly tracked standards-based college preparatory courses that deny student access based on academic criteria or teacher recommendation. Those most denied are historically underserved students of color (Loveless, 1999; Oakes, 2005). There is such status and prestige associated with both teaching and being a student in honors, advanced placement and/or college preparatory courses that both educators and parents of color will usually choose to not question the viability of such programs in terms of their impact on student ethnic consciousness, as long as they think their self-serving interests are met. In other words, teachers may acknowledge the Eurocentric nature of the course content, but not object to it, or may not even be conscious of the cultural bias. African American and Latino/a parents may be so eager for their children to be enrolled in such courses that they give lower priority to trying to change the content of such courses, or again, may not even be aware of the biased content.

Vignette 5–1 illustrates the possible impact on students of such practices.

VIGNETTE 5–1: JIMMY'S EXPERIENCE OF "TRACKING"

Jimmy first experienced "academic tracking" in elementary school, and the emotional scars he endured then are still with him, influencing some of his current priorities and choices. Both Jimmy and many of the homeboys he has known since the primary grades were in different groups, sometimes within the same classroom. Each group was taught at a different academic level. He now thinks the teachers wanted to make sure there weren't too many Black boys from his neighborhood in the same group, because of concerns about control and discipline. Jimmy did his best in school until the fourth grade when he started to rebel against being segregated from his peers.

MAKE IT PERSONAL

1. If you were Jimmy's fourth-grade teacher, what would you do to motivate Jimmy to continue trying his best?

2. If you were the site administrator supervising Jimmy's fourth-grade teacher, what would you do to help teachers identify and effectively respond when some of their historically underserved students appear to be unmotivated and are making fewer efforts to do well in school?

Personnel Selection and Professional Development

There is a need to ascertain the extent to which personnel selection practices in school districts include explicit attempts to assess applicants' knowledge about, skills in teaching/leading, or dispositions toward culturally diverse students/staff. This need may be greater in districts where there is a very Eurocentric curriculum and multicultural student population. Persons of color have been historically underrepresented among employees in many job categories within some districts.

Regardless of the need in all districts for culturally proficient educators of all backgrounds, teachers and administrators may be hired who have had little or no training or successful experience in urban culturally diverse educational settings where most students of color reside. Such hires, depending on their work assignment, may be provided little if any capacity building related to their assumptions and beliefs about culturally diverse students. Teachers may not be aided in critically reflecting on the root causes of underachievement, or in planning/implementing culturally responsive standards-based instruction (Garcia & Guerra, 2004).

It is important to determine whether teacher preservice education (or in-district on-the-job alternative teacher credential programs) gives adequate attention to cultural consciousness and responsiveness before probationary teaching credentials are issued. Even though there has been some improvement, most teacher education programs and teacher credential institutions have failed to integrate any research-based rigorous treatment of cultural diversity/cultural proficiency issues *throughout* their programs. Having a course or two does not adequately prepare future teachers for responding fully to the needs of students who have been historically underserved.

Most teachers new to the profession have not been adequately prepared for effectively dealing with the range of student needs they will confront, including the racial, cultural, ethnic, socioeconomic diversity, and life circumstances of their students (Melnick & Zeichner, 1995). Based on my work with teachers in a variety of settings, most acknowledged they were not adequately prepared to effectively teach their historically underserved students. They said their academic courses for the most part, as well as on the job professional development, were woefully inadequate in that regard. Another example comes from culturally and racially diverse teachers, some relatively new to the profession, and others who were veterans with 10 to 20 years of experience, who participated in a community-based professional development program. This was a graduate-level certificate program that focused on "effectively teaching African American students," jointly sponsored by a local association of African American educators and the college of extended studies at a local university. As the program administrator and one of the faculty, I was told by an overwhelming majority about the almost total lack of preparation they received during their teacher credential and graduate degree programs for effectively teaching racially and culturally diverse students.

A qualitatively different kind of leadership is needed in preK–16 education, for a major increase in on-the-job professional learning, preservice education, and personnel practices that result in academically rigorous culturally responsive teaching. There is a need for leaders in all stakeholder groups to be engaged in supporting systemic approaches that will contribute to achievement at high levels by all students.

For example, when districts implement professional development associated with equity transformation, such as training on teacher expectations, the training design should be conceptualized in a manner that contributes to its success. Teachers participating in such training should be accompanied by their principal, or separate training on the topic should be provided for the principal. Parent representatives should ideally be invited to the training as well. This will lessen the possibility of a disconnect between what the teachers have learned to do and the support provided once they return to their school site. Peer observations, as well as parent observations, can provide valuable feedback to the teacher once they have received the training on expectations. Students, from upper elementary grades through high school, can also be engaged in helping give the teacher feedback on the behaviors they are demonstrating during instruction. An important aspect of such training should be helping teachers get in touch with any mental baggage they are carrying which compromises their expectations (Thompson, 2007).

The equity training should be conducted in a manner that dovetails with other district training initiatives in curriculum and instruction, so teachers can easily see how to integrate their equity skills within the regular instructional program. The equity training activities and other training related to teaching and learning need to be complementary so teachers are not pulled in different directions. To the extent possible, implementation issues that teachers experience related to all training being received should be addressed collectively rather than in separate settings. For example, if training is being provided in a new math program, the use of new technology (e.g., Smart Boards) and, in culturally responsive teaching, implementation issues related to each of these areas should be done concurrently so issues related to equity implementation are not left out of the loop.

The providers of teacher training on cultural competencies, or those who will provide follow-up support, should be involved during the planning process for all other training so there is a seamless web when teachers are engaged in any capacity building. The process outlined above is rarely undertaken.

In many cases, students of African, Asian, Latino/a, Native American, and Pacific Islander descent, as well as students from low socioeconomic status families, among others, are subjected to lower teacher expectations. However, these topics are seldom given the ongoing priority needed or incorporated into other training activities. Professional development related to equity initiatives is largely a solo undertaking, totally unconnected to other kinds of professional development. This is the antithesis of a systemic approach.

Many teachers believe good instruction for some students is good for all students, regardless of student cultural characteristics (Gay, 2010). They may believe that how a student learns is not as important as the "one size fits all" instructional paradigm of some instructional programs (e.g., Success for All or Direct Instruction), which are labeled by the U.S. Department of Education as highly successful research-based programs for low-achieving students of color. These assumptions need to receive critical scrutiny during any training.

The flawed personnel and professional development practices described are further illustrated by the barriers to high student achievement identified in a sample of low-performing schools in the next chapter. Some of the barriers discussed that are related to personnel and professional development practices are toxic school and school community climate, teaching problems, and insufficient support for instructional staff.

Teachers may experience little or no ongoing support from policymakers for professional development that systematically addresses the causes (such as level of racial identity development) and consequences of educators' racial/cultural attitudes, expectations, and instructional practices. When that is the case, it is an example of institutional bias.

Another politically sensitive topic is helping teachers learn how to build on historically underserved students' prior knowledge and learner characteristics when teaching subject matter content (Hall, Strangman, & Meyer, 2011; Roschelle, 1995). From extended personal observations in dozens of classrooms, I have found many teachers don't adequately build on students' prior knowledge and a few think the learner characteristics of some students of color are disruptive to the learning of other students. Educators who do not give priority to or know how to access students' prior knowledge and do not make the effort to redirect students when they are labeled as "disruptive" will not likely seek more information about them, much less be willing to align subject matter content and instructional practices with student strengths and interests.

Some teachers need help in their cross-cultural communication skills. District office administrators may fail to give priority to such professional development, using the excuse of fiscal constraints. Often it is a matter of whether districts have the in-house capacity to do such training as well as whether decision makers perceive it can be integrated with other teacher training, without compromising what is considered "more important" professional development.

When any of the personnel and professional development inadequacies described in this section are present, there may be a dire need for culturally courageous leadership. All appropriate parties need to be involved in collectively resolving any logistical, philosophical, or political concerns.

Vignette 5–2 describes a situation where there is a major conflict over how a district should respond to a recent influx of immigrant and other low-income students. The players in the conflict are organized groups of parents on different sides of the issue, the board of education, community-based organizations, and the teachers union.

VIGNETTE 5–2: PROPOSED PROFESSIONAL DEVELOPMENT PROGRAMS IN THE MCCLELLAND DISTRICT—CAUSES AND REACTIONS

In the McClelland secondary school district, a few local leaders of community-based organizations are claiming that current conflicts and social unrest in the community are related to the recent influx of limited or non-English-speaking immigrants and disgruntled native-born students of color from low socioeconomic backgrounds. The parents of these students are accused of having American Civil Liberties Union lawyers from outside the community file lawsuits on their behalf alleging discriminatory practices in the allocation of federal funds for professional development. A result of such legal action was the court requiring the school district to reallocate federal Title I funds for district professional development based on the needs of students with the lowest academic outcomes rather than based on student per capita.

The long-term residents are primarily of European background, but also include a small and stable African American community. In the last decade, middle class Blacks in McClelland have experienced more social acceptance, educational supports, and less employment discrimination in the school district. They allege their hard-won educational supports are being threatened by the court-ordered reallocation of district funds to address the needs of new students to the district. The school board, in response to the court order, reallocated some district funds and chose a consultant firm to help develop a plan for resolving the community conflicts. The firm proposed a 3-year community development intervention that the state would help fund, including professional learning and follow-up coaching for all administrators, select teachers, and some parent representatives on "transformational strategies for reducing achievement gaps." This led to the largely White local teachers union deciding to take whatever actions necessary to block approval of the proposed program. They are trying to form an alliance with some of the more long-term economically comfortable and politically connected parents in the community who fear such training will threaten the academic rigor of the current college preparatory curriculum that their own students experience. The union wants any potential alliance they form to lobby the school board and superintendent to not approve the program proposal of the consultant firm.

Vignette 5–2 illustrates the role that various stakeholders can have. The vignette describes a situation where some school board members, the teachers' union, and more "privileged" parents of all racial backgrounds can work against equity transformation when they perceive that attempts to improve staff capacity and accountability will compromise the quality of education and outcomes of other "more privileged" students. Limited school district effectiveness in dealing with conflicts between community-based groups with opposing agendas can contaminate any efforts to find win-win solutions that benefit all students. This is even more complicated when the conflicts have a decidedly cultural/racial/socioeconomic dynamic.

Chart 5b illustrates the major players and issues at play in the preceding vignette. Fill in the third column, which requires describing the leadership you think must be provided on issues in column two.

MAKE IT PERSONAL

FN5-1 (SEE FACILITATOR NOTES IN APPENDIX 1)

1. How does your experience support or refute the claim that personnel selection practices are largely devoid of any attention to whether job candidates are knowledgeable about or have experience with culturally diverse students?

2. To what extent does your preservice teacher or administrator training and on-the-job professional development give attention to developing cultural proficiency and culturally responsive standards-based instruction?

3. In your opinion, how should preservice or on-the-job professional development needs be identified and addressed?

4. Discuss the extent to which there are conflicts in your school community that are similar to those in the McClelland secondary school district and what your school district is doing about it.

Supervision/Evaluation

Institutional biases are also demonstrated when district or school site administrators do not personally provide the level and scope of school/classroom supervision

Chart 5b	Major Players and Issues in Vignette 5–2

Major Participants	Major Issues	Leadership Needed to Address the Issue
Local leaders of community-based organizations representing long-term residents	Whether causes of current conflicts and social unrest are due to recent influx of limited English speaking and low-income native-born students of color	
Community members who initiated lawsuit	Discrimination alleged in lawsuit against district about how professional development program (PDP) funds are spent	
Long-term residents of White and Black backgrounds	Court decision requiring district to allocate PDP funds based on student academic need and not based on student per capita	
School board	Reallocation of district PDP funds and hiring of consultant firm to develop plan for resolving school community conflicts; proposed plan would result in 3 years of training for different groups on reducing achievement gaps	
Teachers union	Attempts to block superintendent and board approval of proposed plan by forming alliance with long-term politically connected residents	

and follow-up support needed. Administrative supervision and support should include one-on-one coaching and facilitation of small group problem solving on issues related to achieving equitable educational outcomes. Coaching and small group problem solving need to directly address how to improve instructional efficacy with historically underserved groups, particularly students who have been at the lower end of the achievement continuum.

When instructional supervision occurs, there may be limited ability to discern or little attention paid to biased teacher behaviors toward students of color, including the manifestation of low expectations and double standards related to discipline, student engagement, and response to special needs. For example, when visiting classrooms, does the principal make sure to notice whether all students are on task, following directions, comprehending instruction, and applying what they are learning as directed? If the teacher does not demonstrate critical instructional behaviors, such as having a clearly stated objective that all students comprehend, there is a problem. If the teacher does not display expertise in checking for understanding of all students, including males, students of color, or students at the lower end of the achievement continuum, there is an even greater problem.

If a principal doesn't address such problems with the teacher over time, that might be an example of culturally insensitive observation and supervision. When supervisors don't even notice the above problems during observation, then that is a bigger problem. Some school administrators don't recognize explicit or implicit cultural biases or don't have the political will and savvy to address what they do identify.

When differentiated instruction is employed in racially/culturally/academically diverse classrooms, those doing classroom supervision should ascertain if the approach is accompanied by lower academic expectations and less access to standards-based rigorous content for some students. In schools not serving all students well, I have observed inappropriate use of differentiated instruction in many instances, resulting in some historically underserved students learning at much lower levels than their higher performing peers. Scaffolding should not mean that students needing a different kind of teaching strategy and more time to learn the lesson objective are held to lower standards.

MAKE IT PERSONAL

FN5-2 (SEE FACILITATOR NOTES IN APPENDIX 1)

1. What changes are needed in your school community for supervision and evaluation practices to more effectively address the low achievement of historically underserved students?

2. What should be done when or if site administrators don't know how to identify explicit or implicit cultural biases during their classroom observations or don't have the political will and/or savvy to address what they do identify?

3. What successful leadership practices are being used in your school community so the above problems in #2 are minimized?

4. Describe actions taken by a school board member, district administrator, or principal in your school community who has actively and publicly been an advocate for historically underserved student groups receiving an equitable education.

Most schools may not have fully embraced the concept of cultural democracy for all subgroups and persons because it is not viewed as politically expedient. This is especially noticeable when it comes to the lack of rigorous instruction and use of inequitable discipline practices for Latino and Black males (Valles & Miller, 2010). When the leadership in a school community, including those in all stakeholder groups, allows such negligence to occur, it is an indictment of all persons in both formal and informal roles of influence.

A sobering reality I have noticed in many low-performing schools is little effort expended to improve cultural democracy, as exemplified by Eurocentric curriculum and a very hierarchical non-inclusive decision-making process. Perhaps the leadership at district and/or school site levels think the effort to improve cultural democracy would be at their peril because of next-to-no support in the wider community for cultural democracy. Most public schools consciously or unconsciously promote assimilation more than cultural pluralism, resulting in the denigration of some cultural groups by acts of omission or distortion in curriculum and instruction. As suggested earlier, schools help perpetuate the biases and privileges of the dominant group.

When parents, school board members, and district administrators do not actively, publicly, and consistently assume roles of advocacy for underserved student groups to be educated at high levels in culturally democratic learning environments, equitable educational outcomes will not likely occur or be sustained. This lack of leadership causes a void, which is filled by opponents of any change to their current privileges. Their first priority is not what is in the best interests of all children. If there is no demonstration of vigilant oversight by school community leaders when it comes to the quality of education received by historically underserved students, there may be limited monitoring by school district policymakers and school site leaders. Supervision and evaluation practices are a major tool that can be used to leverage greater social justice or prevent it from occurring.

Student Low Socioeconomic Status

For several decades, the federal Elementary and Secondary Education Act has provided funds to and stipulated requirements for school districts related to the education provided to K–12 students identified as qualified for free or reduced-price lunch. For example, funds for implementation of research-based instructional programs and materials are sometimes available to schools who have not met all of their improvement targets for several years. There have also been funds for educational technology to be enhanced and professional development provided.

Historically, funding was provided to facilitate the development and maintenance of desegregation programs. In many cases, a lot of segregation was practiced within desegregated schools as well as the provision of fewer educational opportunities.

At the present time, most students of African and Latino/a descent are in de facto seg-regated schools. In some cases, a greater percentage are in such schools than before the landmark supreme court decision of 1954 (Frankenberg, Lee, & Orfield, 2003).

The funding regulations for the professional development of teachers and other staff working with economically disadvantaged students do not require utilization of various cultural funds of knowledge. These funds of knowledge have been devel-oped by scholars with expertise on the relationship between culture and cognition of particular low-income historically underserved cultural groups and are not based on deficit thinking and paradigms. This oversight contributes to culturally biased deficit-oriented approaches being financially supported by government funds. Most students from low-income families are in historically underserved groups of color and have not been educated with adequate attention to their learn-ing styles, learner characteristics, and unique needs. These very characteristics have often been erroneously associated with cognitive, intellectual, or genetic defi-ciencies. When those racist assumptions undergird any training or program inter-ventions, it makes it even more necessary for more culturally responsive funding regulations. However, there are efforts to improve the competencies of public school teachers to teach in high-poverty, high-risk, and culturally diverse communities (Byrd-Blake, 2009).

For policy making to be more comprehensive and equity-effective, educational research and scholarly publications upon which policy is based must be more explicit and comprehensive when it comes to the required competencies of all educators and support staff related to race and culture. The federal statutory requirements related to "highly qualified teacher" do not include reference to the explicit cultural compe-tencies needed by all teachers and administrators, which would enable them to be culturally responsive to the unique needs of each student subgroup. There is much more specificity in the legislation on the skills and competences needed by teachers seeking a credential specialization in an English as a second language or a bilingual teaching credential. The same level of specificity is needed when it comes to the com-petencies needed by teachers of other historically underserved students, notably students of African descent.

The credentialing requirements of states for teachers and administrators require very little when it comes to how racial/ethnic/cultural oppression in the United States negatively impacts educational outcomes. Teachers and administrators must be supported in developing the capacity to identify and change instances of institu-tionalized racism, sexism, classism, disability bias, or homophobia.

In addition, the regional accreditation agency criteria for university teacher and administrator credential programs lack adequate specificity related to race and cultural bias. An example of the content that should be included in credential pro-grams is discussed by Yosso (2005) when she discusses the forms of "capital" or community cultural wealth that students of color bring with them from their homes and communities into the classroom. Likewise, an example of teacher learning that should be required for permanent credentials is that reported by Abbate-Vaughn, Frechon, and Wright (2010). They discuss four dimensions of urban teaching: relationships and shared authority, linking classroom content with student experience, incorporation of familiar and culturally compatible communication patterns, and development of counternarratives that challenge stereotypical conceptions of at-risk students and families.

NCLB legislation provides inadequate assistance for school districts receiving very large numbers of low-income, low-achieving students of color. These students, with the most negative outside-of-school influences (Berlinger, 2009), are migrating from urban to suburban schools with very unprepared teachers who are also not disposed to effectively teach them (Orfield, 2008).

NCLB does not spell out what constitutes discriminatory practices toward students in Title I and program improvement schools where the overwhelming number of historically underserved students go to school. Nor does the legislation stipulate professional development requirements related to discriminatory practices or issues of race, culture, and socioeconomic status in Title I schools. Roach and Elliott (2009) discuss what consultants committed to social justice can do when working with these schools to increase access and opportunity for all students.

The vignette below describes part of a process utilized by one state department of education to get input from local educational practitioners related to an equity initiative being considered.

VIGNETTE 5–3: STATE DEPARTMENT OF EDUCATION MEETINGS TO ELICIT REGIONAL INPUT

At regional focus group meetings convened by a state education department, there were several educators present in each regional meeting who have responsibility for providing instructional support, professional development, and technical assistance to Title I and program improvement schools in their school district. A topic being discussed was the need and concern of those in attendance related to the state advisory panel's recommendation that culturally relevant and responsive professional development be required for all school personnel. Many indicated the state needed to provide more specific guidance to school districts in the form of credentialing requirements for school district staff. Others countered that local boards of education were not being prohibited from taking such initiatives and that such training priorities needed to be taken at the local level, especially in program improvement schools. A few suggested the buck was being passed back and forth between local and state policymakers, because neither wanted to issue any mandates and were even less inclined to find the money necessary to fund such an undertaking. This reticence existed despite the acknowledgement of a racial achievement gap in the state and despite many local district superintendents espousing the need for improved teacher competency related to increasing the educational outcomes of economically disadvantaged students. The federal and state definition of "highly qualified teacher" (based on passing a content knowledge exam and having a degree) was also identified as one of the constraints to implementing such a recommendation. Most anticipated that teachers would resist any requirements beyond what is necessary to become a highly qualified teacher.

MAKE IT PERSONAL

FN5-3 (SEE FACILITATOR NOTES IN APPENDIX 1)

1. What would be the reaction in your No Child Left Behind program improvement schools if they were required by the state to participate in a program of culturally relevant and responsive professional development for all school staff?

2. What are the major needs in the quality of education provided to low-income students of color in your district/school, and what leadership is being exercised at all levels to correct educational disparities?

Student's Primary Discourse

When delivery, opportunity to learn, and professional development standards do not receive priority, it is very difficult to improve the literacy achievement experienced by historically underserved students. That is true for any student group, and especially for those whose primary discourse is other than standard academic English. Teachers in poor urban schools may not receive sufficient support related to delivery standards. Most school districts probably do not implement all of the opportunity to learn and professional development standards that are needed to develop and nurture highly qualified teachers for historically underserved students. But the reader must determine whether that is true in your instructional setting.

The school climate and school/home relationship are also major factors. Literacy instructional practices for students of color in most cases do not adequately build on the home language of the students. School schedules may not provide sufficient instructional time during the school day for the most academically at-risk students, especially with limited-English-speaking students and nonmainstream English native-born students.

The teacher's reaction to students' primary discourse, learned in the home, is a major influence on literacy instruction. Gee (1989) defines discourse as an "identity kit," that is, ways of *saying-writing-doing-being-valuing-believing*, and thus much more than reading and writing. Gee also defines secondary discourses as those attached to institutions or groups one might later encounter. Discourses are not equal in status; some are socially dominant—carrying with them social power and access to economic success (Delpit, 1995).

Historically underserved students, particularly those of African descent, who have a primary discourse at considerable variance from that of the teacher or from the discourse used in the schooling context (sometimes described as standard or academic English) are viewed by some teachers as having less intelligence or academic potential. Students in this category may experience lower expectations in the classroom and may be subject to a double standard when it comes to discipline practices. This is especially true when students perceived as having lower status learn differently than the way their teacher likes to teach.

Culturally democratic literacy instruction respects and builds upon the strengths of students whose primary discourse is other than standard English. Teachers providing such instruction do not assume having been reared in a home with a discourse other than the dominant discourse means the student can never master the dominant discourse (Delpit, 1995; LeMoine, 2009).

Such instruction requires persistent advocacy from community leaders, administrators and teacher leaders, and strong support from university faculty in teacher and administrator credential programs as well as graduate education programs. Multicultural interdisciplinary instruction that honors the home language of the child and uses it as a bridge to facilitate mastery of standard academic English is an example of culturally democratic literacy instruction. Vignette 5–4 illustrates the opposite of such support and instruction.

VIGNETTE 5–4: LARGE SCHOOL DISTRICT'S RESPONSE TO ENGLISH LITERACY NEEDS

In one of the 10 largest school districts in the country, more than 70% of the students have a primary language other than mainstream academic English, and a majority of these students are limited English speaking at the beginning or intermediate levels of English language development. There are students of European descent whose primary discourse is nonmainstream academic English; there are just fewer of them, percentagewise, and attention is much less riveted on their oral communication patterns. Immigrants of Latino/a, Asian, and African descent comprise the majority of nonmainstream English students. In addition, a very large percentage of students in the district who are of native-born African descent have a primary discourse other than standard English. A large percentage of all students identified above receive inadequate instructional support for achieving grade-level mastery in English literacy. In addition, there is no board policy requiring culturally and linguistically appropriate interventions to address the literacy needs of nonmainstream English students.

MAKE IT PERSONAL

FN5–4 (SEE FACILITATOR NOTES IN APPENDIX 1)

1. In your school community, to what extent are various student subgroups capable of code switching to mainstream academic English, and to what extent do they have grade-level writing skills? Do most entry-level teachers have the requisite skills to help such students code switch when appropriate to mainstream English in their speaking and writing? What is the implication for what professional development is needed by teachers as well as what success can be achieved with the students they teach if insufficient support is provided?

2. What are your ideas about how to build upon the nonmainstream English home language of all your students as a bridge to mainstream academic English?

Involvement of Parents and Guardians

Many low-performing schools have very low levels of parent involvement as traditionally defined, especially among families with historically underserved children. This may be a function of the limited range of activities in which parents are asked to participate. Parent involvement is usually defined only in terms of what happens at school, not at home or in the school community. Visitation by teachers to student homes is a rare event, even when teachers were offered a stipend in one state for making such visits. Teachers often misinterpret the affect, attitudes, and values of parents or caregivers with whom they speak (Corbett, Wilson, & Williams, 2002).

There is little reciprocity nurtured between school and the homes of students of color. Some parents/caregivers, based on their cultural background and socioeconomic status, are expected to make most of the adjustments to what the school is comfortable in communicating and when such communication takes place. The unstated expectation is that working-class parents or caregivers of historically underserved students should willingly assimilate into the school culture, follow the rules, and not ask too many questions.

Patrick Finn (2009) discusses four different types of education provided in the United States, based on the socioeconomic status of the families served. His conclusions don't even consider the additional consequences students of color might experience, regardless of socioeconomic status. Finn's study found that students of working-class background have significantly more instructional emphasis on copying notes and answering textbook questions, and little classroom discussion. They are not encouraged as much to discuss controversial issues, engage in problem-solving, or ask "why" types of questions. Acceptance of authority and following directions are expected. From these reported characteristics of the education that may be more commonly experienced by White working-class students, one can infer it may be even worse for working-class parents of color, who are also expected to follow directions and accept the authority of the school.

Based on Finn's research, cultural democracy, as defined in this guide, is not practiced in many schools, especially those with students from cultural/racial minorities or low socioeconomic backgrounds. In fact, a forthcoming article in *Teachers College Record* suggests White middle- and upper-middle-class parents who support urban public schooling may exacerbate race and class-based inequalities in public education (Posey-Maddox, 2012).

Miretzky (2004) conducted research on parent–teacher relationships and found a tendency to relegate parents to visitor roles. She argues for recognizing the importance of talk among parents and teachers to increase trust and mutual support and suggests there are some "communication requirements" for those in both groups who are committed to democratic values.

A training module of the California School Leadership Academy on "Involving Parents as Partners in Promoting Student Learning" advocated seeing parents as advocates/decision makers, supporters, teachers, and learners. I have very seldom seen most parents/caregivers given opportunities to play all of these roles in traditional school settings, and especially in schools populated primarily by historically underserved students.

The improvement of cultural democracy and culturally democratic learning environments in schools would likely result in a more level playing field, with more priority given to ongoing communication and collaboration between school and home. Culturally courageous leaders are needed among all stakeholder groups, including working- and middle/upper-middle-class parents, for cultural democracy to be increased.

MAKE IT PERSONAL

FN5–5 (SEE FACILITATOR NOTES IN APPENDIX 1)

1. Describe the difference between the school/home connection in high- and low-performing schools with which you are personally familiar. What are schools and what are parents doing differently in each type of school?

2. What do you think are some of the additional roles parents can play in the schools of their children, other than what is usually done?

3. Based on the above information about parent involvement and how schools may treat parents differently based on income level, identify the points in this section with which you strongly agree or strongly disagree.

⋙⋘

THE ROLE OF CULTURALLY COURAGEOUS LEADERS RELATED TO INSTITUTIONAL BIASES IN SCHOOL SETTINGS

1. Culturally courageous leaders would use their "equity lens" when examining the beliefs that underlie educational decisions and the norms or way things are done in their work setting. Based on their observations, they would work collaboratively with other stakeholders to develop an action plan, including political advocacy, for how to positively influence beliefs and norms they consider counterproductive to facilitating equitable educational outcomes. For example, they might try to help others develop their own equity lens. They might start small, starting with one person at a time, and phase in their plans, but they would persevere, and make sure they had a support system for sharing ideas and receiving critical friend feedback/suggestions.

2. Culturally courageous leaders would never advocate what they cannot authentically attempt to demonstrate. They would always be trying to improve their ability to walk the equity talk when it comes to any of the six institutional biases.

REVIEW OF CHAPTER 5

- Five categories of standards that must all be addressed in order to minimize institutional biases are content, performance, delivery, opportunity to learn, and professional development standards. When the latter three categories are not adequately addressed, the possibility of equitable educational outcomes is greatly compromised.

- Six institutional biases demonstrated in the norms of low-performing schools are related to curricula and scheduling, personnel selection and professional development, supervision/evaluation, student low socioeconomic status, student's primary discourse, and involvement of parents and guardians.

Barriers

6

Relationships, rigor, and relevance may help to eliminate
barriers to educational equity that are not easily overcome.

S ome or all of the institutional biases discussed in Chapter 5 were manifested in
10 barriers to high levels of achievement by historically underserved students
in a sample of low-performing schools where I served as an external evaluator. The
vignette below provides the reader with a preview of how some of the biases and
barriers converge in a specific educational setting.

KWL EXERCISE

1. Describe how institutional biases in your school district or school setting
   become actual barriers to achievement at high levels by your historically
   underserved students.

2. What do you want to know about how to respond to what teachers think are the
   barriers to achievement at high levels by the most underachieving students?

3. What have you learned from this guide so far about what is needed to begin
   removing barriers to achievement at high levels?

VIGNETTE 6–1: JIMMY'S AND HIS MOTHER'S
ATTITUDES ABOUT THE HIGH SCHOOL HE SHOULD ATTEND

*Jimmy will soon be entering the ninth grade at Thurgood Marshall High School (see
vignette 1–5 in Chapter 1 for an earlier description of Marshall), even though his
mother would like him to apply for acceptance at a high school across town for a variety of reasons. These reasons include her desires for a safer and more academic environment, her concern about the negative influence of his homeboys, and wanting her son*

to have more supportive teachers. However, even though Jimmy's eighth-grade achievement would likely keep him from being accepted, he has resisted applying to the district's school choice program because all of his friends will be going to Marshall. Like most adolescents, Jimmy wants to attend the same school where his friends will be going, even though he has heard the teachers at Marshall don't seem concerned about their Black and Brown students and have negative stereotypes about most of them. His priorities, unlike his mothers, are not whether the school has a strong academic program. Even though he is confident he can do well in school when he applies himself, Jimmy is more interested in the athletic program and is convinced the track-and-field program at Marshall is one of the best in the school district. He is afraid he would have to work harder to become academically eligible for the track team if he went anywhere else and would also experience even more racial bias. Even though Jimmy isn't in a gang, he doesn't seem worried about whether he will be pressured to join one when he goes to Marshall or about staying out of trouble when fights occur between a few of the Black and Brown males. Bottom line, Jimmy is not focused on the relationship between how he does in his classes and his future after high school. He has never had a male role model he looked up to who stressed the importance of doing your best in school or motivated him to adopt such goals.

MAKE IT PERSONAL

1. Describe how a school's response to students with Jimmy's perspective could be a barrier to improved student achievement.

2. Describe how educators you know have responded to students like Jimmy, and reflect on whether their response helped create or reduce barriers to improved achievement.

Thurgood Marshall High School has many characteristics found in low-performing schools that are populated primarily by students of color from low- to moderate-income working-class families. Schools like Marshall usually have a group of teachers relatively new to the teaching profession. They may or may not have volunteered to work in such schools and may have little if any preparation for doing so. Many teachers have students with cultural backgrounds and life experiences different than their own and have not worked in any school where equitable student outcomes for all subgroups were achieved. They are learning how to do the job while teaching, and the metaphor "flying the plane while building it" is appropriate.

My work in low-performing schools included assisting the principal and school staff in each setting to identify barriers to achievement at high levels and then develop/implement/revise multiyear action plans for comprehensive improvement.

The barriers identified in these state-designated "low-performing schools" are echoed in the research literature review on the features of ineffective schools (Sammons, 2007).

In chart 6a, there are 10 barriers in five categories found in all of the 12 schools. The barriers were determined by collecting data in each school community in six ways:

- Individual and small group interviews
- Total staff meetings
- Focus group meetings
- Classroom observations, campuswide monitoring, and shadowing the principal
- Examination of school improvement plans and student achievement data at each school
- Data from training, providing technical assistance, or coaching site administrators and teachers in some of the schools

The following words introduce in a nutshell the major areas requiring improvement in these low-performing schools:

- Leadership
- Support
- Planning
- Curriculum, instruction, and assessment
- Data utilization
- Attitudes
- Conflicts
- School climate
- Accountability

&◆&

MAKE IT PERSONAL

FN6–1 (SEE FACILITATOR NOTES IN APPENDIX 1)

1. When no meaningful support is forthcoming from the district office, what initiatives should principals take to increase the support they and their staff need in order to effectively address challenging conditions at the school site?

2. Given the limited resources available to school sites in the area of staff support, what in your opinion are some strategies site staff should consider to increase support within the building?

Chart 6a Some Barriers to Equitable Outcomes

Ten Barriers In Five Categories	
Category	**Weak Instructional Leadership**
Barriers	Principal doesn't successfully engage staff in developing consensus on school vision, mission, goals, objectives, culturally responsive standards, plans with benchmark indicators, or efforts to improve sense of efficacy regarding the achievement of equity
	Insufficient time spent on classroom observation, and few efforts to address instructional areas needing improvement, except when it is time for annual evaluations
Category	**Insufficient Support for Instructional Staff**
Barriers	District staff provide little training or assistance to school site administrators or designated teacher leaders on strategies for improving instructional performance with underachieving students of color
	Districts provide limited training or guidance for school site staff who teach special needs students (not special education) significantly below grade level, and no help to site administrators on how to improve school climate/work environment
Category	**Teaching Problems**
Barrier	Many new and veteran teachers demonstrate low expectations, their students have low time on task and student engagement; students' life experiences not tapped; even when on task, many students do not understand what they are doing, why they are doing it, or what successful efforts would look like
Category	**Toxic School and School Community Climate**
Barriers	Teacher conflicts among staff at same grade level, within same department or schoolwide, negatively impact cohesion and morale; there is a lot of within- and across-group distrust and/or fear among certificated, classified, and parent stakeholders Stakeholder strengths not adequately utilized and staff input not sought on major decisions affecting them; communication, collaboration, problem solving, and conflict management not facilitated within/across stakeholder groups
	Administrators and staff do not proactively reach out to parents on a regular basis unless their children are in trouble; parents are generally not viewed as partners, and their leadership is not nurtured
Category	**Limited Accountability**
Barriers	Few efforts by administration to increase staff's sense of urgency and commitment; many teachers have a low sense of efficacy (i.e., belief in their ability to teach all students to high levels); some teachers do not follow through on district/site initiatives or directives related to improving instruction, and experience no consequences Students' socioeconomic status, parent values, the district administration, board of education, or state politicians are frequently blamed for low student achievement, with no personal responsibility taken

SOME BARRIERS TO EQUITABLE OUTCOMES

Weak Instructional Leadership

Most principals in this small sample of low-performing schools did not attempt structural and cultural changes contributing to equity as part of their instructional leadership role, and some did not have the discretion to undertake such initiatives because of district-level micromanagement. Teacher leadership was very unevenly nurtured and utilized to help achieve school goals. Most administrators were preoccupied with just maintaining the semblance of an orderly environment. Some of the principals, because of other demands such as district meetings or directives, felt the need to delegate many instructional leadership functions, or to perform the tasks they associated with instructional leadership from their office. A few were new to the job and others were seasoned veterans. In these schools, there were some institutional biases, such as curricula, scheduling, professional development, personnel, and supervision practices. As instructional leaders, school site administrators, particularly principals, set the moral tone for their school site, in terms of what are nonnegotiable priorities, essential tasks, and no-excuse attitudes. When principals of schools with a large majority of historically underserved students don't regularly inspect what they expect, don't monitor the follow-through of those to whom they delegate some leadership tasks, don't provide support for those who need help to perform at an acceptable level, and don't constantly keep considerations of race and culture on the table in all conversations related to school improvement, then some of their staff may act in counterproductive ways. The school leaders in the sample of schools did not engage in any of these behaviors on a consistent basis. Loyalty to the principal was perceived by staff as more important than staff effectiveness in some cases. In a few cases, the same was true when it came to the relationship between principals and their district supervisors.

Insufficient Support for Instructional Staff

MAKE IT PERSONAL

FN6–2 (SEE FACILITATOR NOTES IN APPENDIX 1)

1. What additional support is needed in your school(s) in order to effectively address student, parent, and staff needs?

2. What are the common explanations given in your school(s) for why it is not possible to improve staff support?

Low-performing schools are often paralyzed and unable to make substantive progress in improving achievement because of very little if any "thinking outside the box."

Many staff in such schools are afraid to acknowledge their own areas where growth is needed and may want school transformation to occur without their having to engage in any personal transformation. In the sample of schools, those feeling differently were hesitant to express their ideas about the changes needed, due to fear of retaliation, ridicule, or being ostracized by other staff. The concept of leadership in the schools within this sample was very narrow, and the school leadership didn't attempt to reach out and more fully engage the broader community in addressing the problems.

There was no professional development support to help staff improve their cross-cultural communication skills among themselves or with parents and students. In addition, there were very few adults, either employees or community volunteers, providing extra help to underachieving students. When teachers of color, however few, were hired, they were the first to go when budget problems arose.

Excuses were often used to explain the low degree of parent/community involvement at each site, especially among historically underserved student groups, and there were no parent liaisons/volunteers who could try to increase parent involvement.

Teaching Problems

MAKE IT PERSONAL

1. To what extent are the items mentioned under teaching problems in chart 6a the same as those you have witnessed or personally experienced in low-performing schools?

2. What are the top three priorities regarding teaching problems that need to be addressed in your work setting?

3. What strategies do you utilize to build on students' life experiences and interests during the instructional process?

The characterization of some teacher behaviors as inadequate is idiosyncratic, to some extent, based in part on the particular context of the classroom, school, and school community where the teacher is working. Black and Latino/a students were a large percentage of the population in most of the low-performing schools within this sample, and the teachers were very diverse in their instructional and classroom-management skills. Some were much more competent in specific areas than other teachers. The labeling of some teacher behaviors as inadequate was not based on how they compared with other teachers or based solely on the teacher effectiveness research. The primary criteria utilized was whether what the teacher was doing in their classroom with particular students demonstrated progress toward students' development of grade-level competencies.

Some teachers spent an inordinate amount of time on classroom management, and successful time on task was universally low in almost all classrooms. For example, students might be highly engaged on teacher assigned tasks, but in some cases, they didn't know why they were doing the task or what success would look like. Such engagement was not leading to progress toward developing grade-level competencies in specific cluster skill areas within English/language arts or mathematics.

A few teachers in this sample of schools did not know the language arts or math curriculum they were teaching, staying at best only 2 days ahead of their students. This was true for veteran teachers as well if newly adopted textbooks or other new instructional materials were being used. In addition, teachers with the least experience were assigned to work with the most needy students. No professional development was tailored to the needs of these teachers. Also, these same students were usually not scheduled into small group tutoring or given access to afterschool academic support programs that provided targeted assistance in their areas of greatest need. When they were so scheduled, there was little if any articulation with what was happening in the regular classroom.

Toxic School and School Community Climate

MAKE IT PERSONAL

FN6–3 (SEE FACILITATOR NOTES IN APPENDIX 1)

1. What are some of the work conditions that most affect some of the indicators of toxic school climate mentioned in chart 6a?

2. Prioritize the three work conditions that you think have the greatest negative impact on school climate in your work setting.

Just as successful time on task was universally low in almost all classrooms, poor school climate was universally the case in all schools within the sample. Nevertheless, there were some teachers in each school who were very positive and industrious, trying hard to do a good job, but not always succeeding. Likewise, there were some students who were very positive about school, liked school, and were trying to do their best most of the time.

However, despite these beacons of light, the overall school climate was problematic in all schools within the sample. This was the case in secondary schools more than in elementary schools, and more in large schools at any grade level than in small schools. In several schools, there was considerable fear or resentment of the administration by some teachers. The lack of civility between the administration and some teachers was apparent in some schools. Where there was a lack of civility, a lack of professionalism was usually observed. In those cases, a few staff were derelict in carrying out their responsibilities, such as meaningfully engaging all students throughout the allotted time for instruction, and demonstrating "stand-up teaching" with detailed standards-based culturally responsive lesson plans. Unfortunately, in many instances, what I observed was the teaching and learning process being peripheral and held hostage to adult/adult animosities, dramas, a lack of professionalism, and personal idiosyncrasies. Some teachers were also overwhelmed with the range of student academic levels and needs in their classes.

Limited Accountability

MAKE IT PERSONAL

1. What have you found to be the major constraints to improving accountability of all stakeholders in low-performing schools, including the accountability of faculty in higher education teacher/administrator preparation programs?

2. Describe the strategies you have used or know others have used that helped improve teachers' sense of efficacy, that is, their believing they have the ability to help students of all subgroups to achieve at high levels?

Accountability of all stakeholder groups was observed to be much better in schools where the school climate was perceived as better by staff, students, and parents, or where most staff perceived the administration making serious efforts to improve school climate. Likewise, students made stronger and consistent efforts to improve their academic performance when they perceived teachers caring about them and respecting them.

However, when teachers bribed students with food, time off, class parties, or field trips based on their good citizenship, there were often short-term benefits. Student bribing was common.

In a few schools within the sample, a very small number of teachers consistently engaged in insubordination and a lack of professionalism, without suffering any negative consequences because of contract language that protected them from being held accountable. In addition, district/school site administrators or teachers who were derelict in their responsibilities were sometimes protected by their political alliances.

MAKE IT PERSONAL

FN6–4 (SEE FACILITATOR NOTES IN APPENDIX 1)

1. Of the ten barriers to high achievement in chart 6a, which three do you think most apply to schools with which you are familiar, especially low-performing schools?

2. In your opinion, which of the institutional biases discussed in Chapter 5 most contribute to the identified barriers to equitable outcomes?

3. Select any *two* of the five *barrier categories* in chart 6a and describe what administrators and/or teachers can do to lessen or eliminate these barriers.

4. Select any *one* of the *barrier categories* and describe what support staff, students, and/or community persons can do to lessen this barrier category.

5. What actions are being taken by the school board and/or higher education faculty to eliminate any of the stated barriers?

6. What are *you* personally interested in doing, or are currently trying to do, related to any of the barriers you experience that are mentioned in chart 6a?

ॐॐ

RELATIONSHIP BETWEEN PERSONAL IDENTITIES AND BARRIERS

You cannot change how people see or define themselves, or how they perceive others defining them, especially the older they get; they are who they are and we just have to live with the situation.

This statement may be believed by many, but others will have an inclination to challenge it and make constant efforts to influence the thinking and identities of those with whom they work or live. Teachers have varying degrees of comfort with helping students of color to develop healthy, well-informed self-identities based to some extent on their cultural/ethnic heritage(s), strengths, interests, life experiences, value of mutual respect, and respect for "different" others. A teacher's personal identity, including their level of racial identity development, may have an enormous impact on how they relate to and work with historically underserved students.

How people derive or change their self-image, self-concept, and self-esteem is very complex, but the results of self-image are often simple to explain. Personal identities may have a major bearing on perceptions, beliefs, intentions, and actions in every sphere of one's life (Weitzenkorn, 2010).

The personal identities of those in school communities are not just influenced by their roles and the expectations of others based on their role, but also on how they see themselves beyond their role as principal, parent, teacher, community activist, university faculty member, and so on. Most persons' sense of self-worth affects what they do or avoid, and also affects their intrapersonal and interpersonal conflicts. For example, when persons are struggling with obvious discrepancies between some of their self-proclaimed values, or between some of their beliefs and actions, these may be intrapersonal conflicts that are not observable.

Conversely, interpersonal conflicts, between two persons, are explicit and observable. One aspect of a person's personal identity is how they see themselves in the work setting. For example, if principals have a very traditional concept of leadership that includes the belief that they alone should make all of the decisions, and arbitrarily decide if, when, and from whom they will seek input, it may be a barrier to staff taking initiatives on their own to improve achievement and reduce achievement disparities.

Likewise, when university faculty in teacher preparation programs see their role as separate and not part of the schools receiving new teachers that university faculty have taught, then they may not take any responsibility for the degree of competence or incompetence demonstrated by their graduates.

In a few cases, when the principal is a person of color, of a different cultural background, or is a female in a high school or district office setting, there are some staff who will have difficulty receiving direction. They may have prejudices they aren't even aware of until being in the situation. Experiencing resistance to one's leadership may be more or less true for those who are the first from their race/ethnicity/gender occupying a position of leadership in their school community.

I have personally experienced such resistance. This dynamic can also be triggered by other human differences between the new leader and all followers. How people manifest their personal identities can ultimately contribute to or help eliminate barriers to high achievement.

The barriers in chart 6a all refer primarily to the attitudes or behaviors of various stakeholders. Barriers to high achievement are to some extent based on the personal identities of all stakeholders and how they use and further enhance their personal and position power.

∂◦⑥

RELATIONSHIP BETWEEN RACIAL/CULTURAL CONFLICTS AND BARRIERS

Conflicts between people are natural because we are all human beings with different beliefs, ideas, and ways we respond to life experiences.

There is a self-assessment diagnostic tool called the DiSC profile, available from Inspiring Solutions (http://inspiringsolutions.com/disc) that has been used for decades by more than 40 million people worldwide to improve organizational development and performance improvement. It helps people to explore behavior across four primary dimensions: dominance, interpersonal, steadiness, and conscientiousness. In addition, individuals completing the assessment can discover the extent to which they are uncomfortable with conflict. Others may discover they thrive on conflict or are not bothered by it at all. Most barriers to high achievement in low-performing schools are pregnant with multiple conflicts between students, students and adults, and adults with adults.

For example, I have found conflicts in schools may be manifested as different interpretations of the thoughts or actions of others, different beliefs, values, and priorities, and different interests, strengths, or expectations. People may resist and resent others expecting them to think or act in ways contrary to their preferred ways of being. In most of the above barriers, school community participants are upset with what they think some others are doing or not doing; they may feel slighted, not valued, and mistreated. Sometimes they will totally withdraw or react with explicit or camouflaged anger. When most conflicts are not openly addressed and managed, they may fester and get worse.

When human differences, that is, conflicts, are not addressed in positive ways, with interventions tailored to the situational context and characteristics of the persons involved, there may be negative consequences. Some people may withdraw even further, get more entrenched in their point of view, and the conflicts can get worse, resulting in more rather than less dysfunctional behavior.

A complex variable impacting accountability is whether one cultural group in the school community is able to exercise disproportionate dominance over other groups. Some schools overtly and proactively take measures to minimize or camouflage any negative fallout from human difference conflicts. They may have administrative, teacher, parent, and community leaders who work at creating the impression of win-win solutions among stakeholders who have differing perceptions, identities, and priorities. Diverse school community members all have their want lists and unique needs. I find most stakeholders in all groups need help to strengthen their culturally responsive management of conflict, which includes how they deal with conflict of any kind, especially with culturally different others.

∂∾❧

RELATIONSHIP BETWEEN THE LACK OF CULTURAL DEMOCRACY AND BARRIERS

The job of schools is to teach about American culture, not about all of the cultures students bring to school from their home; that is unrealistic, and teachers already have more than enough to do.

Cultural democracy is a very emotionally laden issue with many school stakeholders and the public at large. Many persons in diverse stakeholder groups, perhaps based on their own narrow self-interest, are very opposed to a greater democratization of the curriculum (from its current Eurocentric emphasis) or the decision-making process in schools. Many, if polled, would not support the notion that schools have a responsibility to teach all students not only about the common culture but also about how U.S. citizens and persons worldwide from all cultures and ethnicities have contributed to global humanity and to the development of the United States. Even more controversial is whether schools should include in United States history/social studies curricula any attention to the many kinds of oppression and discrimination experienced by U.S. citizens of many ethnic, racial, and cultural backgrounds, past and present.

There is some consternation over whether students should learn about how oppression has been fought, reduced, and eliminated for many in the United States, but not for all. Such teaching may be characterized as a social justice agenda, as if that is anti-American, even though the country is based on historical documents proclaiming the right to life, liberty, and pursuit of happiness by all.

For those school communities and school community leaders in all stakeholder groups who are committed to improving cultural democracy as well as achieving equitable inputs and equitable student outcomes, it should be noteworthy that in schools having eliminated achievement disparities (see Chapter 11), cultural democracy has been one of the schooling conditions significantly improved. Culturally democratic schools conscientiously avoid exclusive implementation of a Eurocentric curriculum, and each teacher avoids being overly influenced by their own cultural lens when diagnosing student needs, capacities, and potential. In the sample of schools discussed in this chapter, there was evidence that several of the barriers to equitable achievement in chart 6a were in part the result of a low priority given to cultural democracy, which includes meaningful involvement of all school stakeholder groups—especially teachers, culturally diverse community persons, and parents—in critical school decisions.

❧

RELATIONSHIP OF PERSONAL BIASES AND NORMS IN SCHOOL SETTINGS TO BARRIERS

Integral to all of the biases and barriers discussed in Chapters 5 and 6 is the resistance of many school community stakeholders to making personal changes in some of their thoughts and actions. Despite such resistance, they usually blame others for inequitable student outcomes of historically underserved students of color.

Chart 6b Relationship Between Biases and Barriers

Institutional Biases	Barrier: Weak Instructional Leadership	Barrier: Insufficient Staff Support	Barrier: Teaching Problems	Barrier: Toxic School and School Community Climate	Barrier: Limited Accountability
Curricula and scheduling practices	Lack of attention to cultural responsiveness and curriculum inclusion during instructional supervision	Few staff, volunteers to provide needed help for marginal students	No adaptation of curricula to build on students' prior knowledge, strengths, and interests	No teacher collaboration on lesson planning and problem solving that gives explicit attention to racial and cultural issues	Board of education approval of Eurocentric instructional materials; teachers not helped to adapt curricula as needed
Personnel and professional development practices	No consistent use of student data to determine staffing needs and limited efforts to expand/ develop instructional leadership team	No ongoing assistance for marginal teachers	No focused assistance for teachers on how to improve successful time on task with their diverse students	No site or district help to improve teacher collaboration	Staff selection and evaluation protocols do not include cultural proficiency, cultural responsiveness, or other equity performance criteria
Supervision/ evaluation practices	No positive modeling and follow-through on stated expectations for staff performance	Poor allocation, utilization of existing resources	Classroom instruction and classroom management not tied together	Little help to resolve staff–staff or parent–teacher conflicts	Little effort to change "pass the buck" mentality or assess teachers' cultural proficiency as well as their students' performance

(Continued)

Institutional Biases	Barrier: Weak Instructional Leadership	Barrier: Insufficient Staff Support	Barrier: Teaching Problems	Barrier: Toxic School and School Community Climate	Barrier: Limited Accountability
Practices primarily influenced by student socioeconomic status	Few systems put in place to help most needy students, and inability to get many low socioeconomic status (SES) parents and students to participate in afterschool extra support provided	Teachers who fear or are unable to relate to students, and don't believe historically underserved students can achieve at high levels	Teachers have no knowledge of students' cultural heritage and perspectives of scholars with same cultural background as their students of color	Teacher–teacher conflicts over low expectations and grade inflation practices; conflicts between ELL teachers and other teachers	Differential standards for tea. performance and professionalism in low SES schools compared with primarily middle class schools with smaller numbers of low SES students
Practices influenced by student primary discourse and vocabulary	Little adult peer pressure and no leadership taken to confront prejudices against students and parents based on their primary discourse	No staffing for in-class assistance with nonspecial-education ELL students	Teacher academic expectations and degree of instructional rigor based on culturally biased criteria	Philosophical, personality, and pedagogical differences make teacher collaboration difficult	No accountability assumed for implementing delivery, opportunity to learn, and professional development standards
Practices related to involvement of parents and guardians	No leadership to increasing involvement of and respect for Black and Brown parents, or to more broadly defining parent involvement	No use of parents to improve communication and school–home partnerships	Very little teacher home visitation or ongoing communication with student families	Conflicting perspectives by parents of color and teachers on each others commitment to do what is best for their students	No specific objectives, activities, or who is accountable for improvements in parent involvement

Barriers to high achievement include very complex conditions, with multiple causes from different sources, but they all have some common characteristics. Central to all barriers are biased beliefs (i.e., thoughts) and norms (i.e., routine actions) in school settings:

1. BIASED BELIEFS (i.e., thoughts and attitudes) include negative stereotypes of different others and a proclivity to accept unfounded hearsay and prevalent attitudes in the larger society. Biased beliefs may also be personal self-assessments of one's inability (i.e., efficacy) to improve the achievement of some students based on their demographic characteristics. Finally, biased collective beliefs can be reflected in school site plan language about subgroup academic gains to be accomplished, reflecting conservative goals and low expectations based on federal NCLB annual yearly progress targets.

2. BIASED NORMS (i.e., routines in school settings) include patterns of behavior in schools, between districts and schools, in school communities, classrooms, and on playgrounds. These norms may reflect cross-cultural, ideological, and jurisdictional conflicts and struggles over who controls what happens and who controls the reaction to what happens in schools. For example, a powerful norm in schools is whether input in the decision-making process is solicited and used from historically underserved parents and students as well as from support staff. Another norm in schools is how students in particular ethnic/cultural groups think about and treat each other on playgrounds as well as when away from school. For example, student bullying is a major national problem, but teacher bullying is given much less attention, if any.

Personal Beliefs

How people think and feel influence how they act.

Beliefs are central to all achievement barriers. Whether the barriers are weak instructional leadership, insufficient support for instructional staff, toxic school and school community climate, or teaching problems, personal beliefs play a major role in determining what is or is not done. When engaging stakeholders in identification and critical investigation of school barriers, they often reveal as much about their own way of thinking and belief systems as they do about the institutional dilemmas experienced. Many do not perceive their complicit role in the barriers identified or how their beliefs influence their actions.

For example, site administrators, especially principals, will sometimes describe the multiple and conflicting demands on their time as a major constraint to spending more time on instructional supervision. From their perspective, they don't have control of the demands on their time. However, I have found those who perceive themselves having expertise in instructional supervision/classroom observation are much less likely to find it impossible to give priority to this task. Some persons tend to spend more time doing what they perceive themselves doing well, have more experience doing, or are most comfortable doing. Others allow instructional supervision to take second priority because they don't *push back against* district office directives or meetings that are blamed for taking time away from such duties.

Likewise, teachers have shared with me a litany of reasons for why their students don't achieve proficiency of grade-level standards, from the students' academic readiness level to the students' failure to complete class assignments or pay attention in class. Teachers seem unaware of the extent to which their reasons for students' poor performance are also their beliefs about student potential, based on certain student characteristics.

Norms in School Settings

Habits, unconsciously formed, are very difficult to change.

The norms, or patterns of behavior, in school settings or in school community settings are usually very strong and help to shape personal relationships of all kinds between particular adults, particular students, and between adults and particular students. The historical politics are influenced by race, ethnic, and cultural relations within the nation as a whole, as well as within specific communities. The politics influence the communication, problem-solving, decision-making, conflict management, and collaboration norms that persist in schools.

To some extent, norms that don't contribute to sustaining high-level student outcomes for the historically underserved may be a function of no one asking the hard questions or providing the critical friend support for all stakeholders, including superintendents and boards of education. Anti-democratic norms in the schooling process may have a better chance of being changed when there is a transformation of the personal identities developed by various stakeholders, including policymakers. For example, the norm in many schools is to not explicitly discuss the thorny issues associated with shared accountability for the educational outcomes of underachieving students.

MAKE IT PERSONAL

1. Based on your experience, *prioritize* the following topics addressed in Chapters 1 through 6, regarding how much these issues contribute to perpetuation of inequitable educational outcomes:
   - Cultural hegemony
   - The personal identities, including level of racial identity development, of all school community stakeholders
   - Students' personal identities
   - Cultural conflict/cultural politics
   - Deficiencies in teacher/administrator preparation programs
   - Human fears

- Institutional biases negatively impacting equitable educational outcomes (see chart 6b)
- The five categories of barriers to achievement at high levels by historically underserved students

2. What beliefs or personal patterns of behavior in school settings do you have or persons you know have that could be construed as barriers to achievement at high levels by historically underserved students of color?

᪻

THE ROLE OF CULTURALLY COURAGEOUS LEADERS IN ADDRESSING BARRIERS TO HIGH ACHIEVEMENT

1. Culturally courageous leaders would critically examine the factors influencing their own personal identities, including level of racial identity development and educational philosophy, followed by writing their own racial autobiography, as discussed in *Courageous Conversations About Race* (Singleton & Linton, 2006). They would do this to jump-start their foray into personal ways of being that might stimulate insights into how they unwittingly help perpetuate barriers to high achievement by historically underserved students.

2. Culturally courageous leaders would continue such critical self-reflection by self-assessing their attitudes and practices related to each of the five barrier categories. They would then choose one barrier to develop a personal growth plan on what they can do to strengthen their awareness and ability to lessen that barrier to achievement at high levels in their work environment.

REVIEW OF CHAPTER 6

- In a small sample of schools, five categories of barriers to high achievement were weak instructional leadership, insufficient support for instructional staff, teaching problems, toxic school and school community climate, and limited accountability.

- There is a relationship between barriers to high achievement and personal identities, racial/cultural conflicts, and the absence of cultural democracy.

- There is a strong relationship between personal biases, school norms, and barriers to achievement at high levels.

- Culturally courageous leadership by all stakeholders includes confrontation of biases and explicit ongoing attempts by all school community stakeholders to eliminate identified barriers to all students achieving at high levels.

SECTION II

Culturally Courageous Leadership

*A Paradigm for
Contemporary Realities*

Keep the following questions in mind as you read Section II:

1. What is different about the culturally courageous leadership (CCL) paradigm when compared with other ways of thinking about the purpose, values, and essential elements associated with providing leadership for equity?

2. How can the CCL paradigm address contemporary realities in your school or district differently than how they have been addressed thus far?

3. What are the specific roadblocks or "landmines" in your school or district that might make it difficult for the CCL paradigm to be embraced?

A New Paradigm for   7
the 21st Century

Only together can we create educational institutions that facilitate all
students learning 21st century skills in culturally democratic learning environments.

Culturally courageous leadership (CCL) is already practiced to some extent by a few persons in some school community stakeholder groups. However, the practice of collaborative CCL by all school community stakeholders is a totally new concept. This chapter begins with a review of needed actions, based on what is discussed in Chapters 1 through 6. These needed actions are the basis for the CCL paradigm.

KWL EXERCISE

1. Even if you cannot personally relate to any of the previously discussed biases and barriers to achievement at high levels, what do you think has been, other than limited financial resources, the major obstacle to high achievement by "historically underserved students"?

2. What questions are you most interested in having addressed so you can be more effective when attempting equity transformation?

3. In your experience, which conditions in school communities have been the greatest barriers to achievement at high levels by historically underserved students?

ॐ৶

"MAJOR ACTIONS NEEDED" BY CULTURALLY COURAGEOUS LEADERS

One of the central ideas advanced in Chapters 1 through 6 is the critical relationship between various stakeholders' personal identities, institutional biases, barriers, and educational outcomes.

I found several commonalities in low-performing schools where I was retained to identify major barriers to achievement at high levels, but the contextual variables in each school community require serious consideration when deciding *what* combination of things need to be addressed and *how* they should be addressed. Each school community is unique in some respects, and no one size fits all.

In all of the school districts where I served as a district administrator or external evaluator, some teachers said they found it difficult to teach and model equity in the classroom when they didn't experience more equity and support in their school environment. More support for teachers was articulated as essential for them to provide equitable educational opportunities, given increased class sizes and a broader array of student readiness levels in their classes. The actions needed in all of the schools are listed. The actions reflect many of the conditions described in the guide.

1. Engage in ongoing collaborative efforts that involve persons from various school community stakeholder groups, to improve cross-cultural communication and conflict management within and between various cultural/racial groups.

These efforts should also be aimed at confronting and changing culturally destructive attitudes, behaviors, and norms. It is important to be mindful that there are major cultural differences in self-identity, worldview, values, and priorities *within* racial/cultural groups. For example, not all Blacks, Latino/a's, Asians, or Whites think alike when it comes to anything, and especially when it comes to their opinions about what if any obstacles keep them from achieving to their fullest potential and what should be done to get rid of these obstacles.

2. Change the nature of cultural politics that usually emanate from human fears.

The media play a major role in helping to perpetuate identity politics, also known as cultural politics. Such politics includes competition for scarce resources to fund curriculum or program priorities of different constituencies, all of whom are trying to achieve more support for their perceived needs being adequately addressed. For example, advocates for improvements in English language development and bilingual programs may be competing with advocates for improvements in head-start or enrollment options that used to be euphemistically called "school choice," "desegregation," or "integration" programs. Such programs in the past may have been characterized as Latino/a priorities or Black priorities. Labeling such advocacy in this manner is very divisive and counterproductive to collaborative joint efforts to achieve equitable educational outcomes.

3. Change the toxic hidden curriculum, which would involve helping teachers engage in critical self-reflection and receive helpful feedback from peer or supervisor observation.

Related needed actions are an increase in the courage and savvy of peers and supervisors to collaboratively confront and help change conditions or teaching behaviors that prevent teaching all students at high levels. Remembering that "hidden curriculum" includes attitudes, communication, collaboration, and conflict management norms as well as expectations, a "toxic hidden curriculum" reflects dysfunctional relationships between adults or between adults and students. Any school norms that are culturally insensitive may cause emotional abuse of students. Such norms work against cultural democracy and compromise any efforts to achieve equitable outcomes by student subgroups in such areas as disciplinary practices, test scores, graduation rates, successful completion of higher level courses, and referrals to special education.

4. Increase the capacity of teachers and administrators to identify and effectively confront racism, ethnocentrism, sexism, and so on in their school environments.

There is a strong relationship between deficiencies in teacher and administrative preservice preparation and on-the-job professional development programs and teachers/administrators ineffectively dealing with racism, ethnocentrism, ageism, and sexism. The "ism's" also include classism (i.e., discrimination against persons of low socioeconomic status) as well as bias based on primary language, disability, religion, phenotype characteristics such as obesity, and sexual orientation. Most teachers and administrators have probably had minimum exposure to coursework or professional development on how to identify and effectively confront both the blatant and even the most subtle but very destructive manifestations of these discriminatory practices. This includes alternative ways to confront and eliminate them when making decisions about all major educational functions in a school and district, such as facilities, business operations, personnel, instructional, administrative, and school/community and support services.

The work of Judith Warren Little (1982) on teacher collegiality and experimentation is a professional development model worthy of being used to facilitate teacher collaborative focus on identifying and eliminating the "isms" and biases in the curriculum, in schools in general, and in facilitating teacher capacity to engender achievement at high levels by students of African and Latino/a descent.

5. Increase team and trust building to reduce cultural dissonance and achieve equity.

The relationship of cultural dissonance within/across stakeholder groups to long-term failure of equity transformation efforts is not given nearly enough attention. Deep-seated equity initiatives are extremely difficult to achieve, such as offering sufficient incentives to attract many of the most experienced teachers to work in schools of the most academically needy students. Another equity initiative that might meet a firewall of resistance is requiring all staff in a district to engage in developmentally appropriate professional learning programs that focus on creating culturally responsive schools. Cultural dissonance is when there is some discord, discomfort, and disagreement between persons with very different attitudes, behaviors, and priorities that are influenced by a host of factors, such as one's socioeconomic status and perception of their life chances.

Cultural dissonance occurs between persons who have very different ways of interpreting and judging what they witness or learn. So when equity initiatives such as those mentioned above are attempted, there is the distinct possibility there will be major conflicts or dissonance within stakeholder groups, such as teachers, and also between stakeholder groups, such as teachers and parents. Such dissonance within and between groups may contribute to erosion of support for equity programs in place, and the inclination by district- or site-level decision makers to not attempt other equity initiatives. Dissonance within groups and across groups can increase when there aren't ongoing leadership efforts to improve communication and trust/team building.

Team building usually includes attention to increasing awareness of personal similarities, differences, life experiences, and strengths in a variety of areas, and engaging in group activities that enhance comfort with and respect for each other as well as the ability to effectively utilize each other's strengths on complex tasks.

Trust building will sometimes go a step further by engaging participants in completing tasks that require sharing personal values on controversial topics, appropriately sharing other aspects of one's hidden self or taking risks that may go beyond one's comfort zone. The goal of trust building is to strengthen the capacity of culturally/racially diverse groups to fully and unequivocally commit to some equity priorities. Another goal is to function effectively with high levels of trust in very stressful conflict-ridden environments where there is little control over what can happen at any given time.

6. Increase ongoing advocacy and support for in-depth equity transformation.

It is seldom acknowledged that a lack of political mobilization and community organizing for increased advocacy of particular equity initiatives can result in having no sustained support for deep-seated equity transformation of any kind. For example, if there is no ongoing effort to develop a constituency of support among parents, community persons, district office administrators, principals, teachers, or higher education faculty for professional learning related to teacher expectations, then such training is not likely to occur or be sustained over time for a critical mass of persons.

Deep-seated equity transformation is defined as when both in-depth personal and organizational transformation is being pursued simultaneously. If there are fledging efforts to improve the academic expectations that a small group of teachers has for historically underserved students, with no follow-up support, then such training is not likely to continue and few results will be observed in the classroom. The quest to engage teachers in personal transformation related to their expectations of students in the classroom must be accompanied by advocacy and support for transforming the entire district or school related to student expectations.

When there is an absence of such advocacy across stakeholder groups, with little positive results for whatever is done on a piecemeal basis, then the likelihood of generating widespread advocacy and support for more ambitious equity transformation is negligible.

Education is a very political process, meaning there are always competing agendas and interpretations or rationales of what is most needed to achieve desired results. In-depth equity transformation would include more than cosmetic changes like one-time-only professional development sessions and annual school or classroom activities during the appropriate month for celebrating the heritage and accomplishments of a particular group.

Many equity initiatives are not comprehensive and play around the edges of including cultural and structural transformation that would significantly affect the development of cultural democracy and the achievement of equitable educational outcomes. Such outcomes are not possible without unrelenting advocacy and support from a supermajority of the school board, and a superintendent willing to utilize all of the leverage at his or her disposal in implementing the board's progressive vision related to equity transformation.

Boards may need to be lobbied by the superintendent and an articulate, persistent constituency in the community for them to provide such support. Superintendents will likely need the same kind of community support and advocacy even when they have the public support of their board of education. There will be a lot of naysayers and resistance to deep-seated equity transformation from all levels in the school community. Opponents of equity transformation may think they have a lot to lose regarding the privileges held by many under the status quo.

Advocacy and support are different phenomena. Advocacy involves public lobbying by educators and community activists for particular issues or changes and the solicitation of funds as well as volunteers to help increase such advocacy. Support involves employees having both the psychological disposition and work-related skills, providing their expertise, and taking the initiative to recruit others who will assist in the successful implementation of equity policies and practices that result in achieving cultural democracy and equitable educational outcomes. "Cultural democracy" and "equitable educational outcomes" must be more than mere slogans; they must be broken down into specific policies and practices, the sequence in which they should occur, with implications for the functioning of each stakeholder group. Benchmarks are essential to use as guideposts for monitoring progress in achieving desired outcomes, coaching and use of exemplars must be used to facilitate success, and evaluation criteria must be used to determine whether the benchmark targets have been achieved. This is the outline of an accountability process that is essential for equitable educational outcomes to have a meaningful chance of being achieved.

7. Involve a representative group of stakeholders in systematic investigations of any alleged bias and in investigating how schools are run related to equity reform/transformation.

When there is any reasonable doubt of good faith on the part of educators in how schools are run for historically underserved students, appropriate accountability actions need to be proposed. There are several norms that probably need to be established for any biases to be defused, neutralized, or eliminated. These norms include the creation of new joint ventures by school districts and community organizations that result in coalitions across racial, cultural, socioeconomic, and stakeholder groups. These coalitions could expand those meaningfully participating in developing a strong political constituency for equity reform/transformation.

Community participants need to learn the educational, problem-solving, decision-making, and accountability processes within schools and districts related to equity goals. Systematically attacking biases must be based on a strong knowledge base and includes not taking on too much at once. It might be wise to start with efforts to correct one biased area where there is greater likelihood of being successful. Such a strategy can also be characterized as piloting and phasing in equity initiatives.

MAKE IT PERSONAL

1. Based on your experience attempting to reduce or eliminate any racial achievement disparities, what are the three most *needed actions* in the above list, and which are the least needed, if any?

2. What are some other problems and needed actions you feel must be addressed to achieve equitable educational outcomes?

3. Identify the needed actions you are already addressing, and rate your efforts on a scale of 1–10, with 1 meaning very little success and 10 meaning great success.

4. What else must be addressed for historically underserved students of color to experience a level playing field in their school communities?

೭ಀ৩

THE CULTURALLY
COURAGEOUS LEADERSHIP (CCL) PARADIGM

Figure 7a illustrates the components of CCL, each of which is discussed after identification of the paradigm's purpose and values. Examples are provided of how all stakeholder groups can individually and collaboratively practice CCL.

Purpose

To facilitate transformational thinking and leadership by those attempting to achieve equitable educational outcomes by all student groups

Values

- Schools have a responsibility to promote social justice.
- All students, especially those who have been historically underserved, have an equal right to cultural democracy.
- Elimination of cultural hegemony is a high priority.

Figure 7a The Culturally Courageous Leadership Paradigm

FIRST COMPONENT OF CCL:
COLLABORATIVE LEADERSHIP BY ALL
SCHOOL COMMUNITY STAKEHOLDERS

A major distinction of the CCL paradigm is inclusiveness. Persons from all major stakeholder groups in school communities must collaboratively provide leadership for equitable educational outcomes to be achieved. These groups include students, parents, and community members, as well as support staff in schools, none of whom are usually thought of as part of the leadership team for helping bring about transformational change. The community member stakeholder group must include local or regional university faculty in teacher and administrator preparation programs who are desired as resources to schools in their area(s) of expertise.

Other more traditional stakeholder groups who must be part of the collaborative leadership team for equity are teachers, board members, and district and school site administrators. Although teachers and school site administrators by nature of their job assignments have more responsibility for the direct work with students, they cannot do it alone. Fullan and Hargreaves (1996) remind us that collaboration should mean creating the vision together, not complying with what the principal says, and this may result in initial conflict, but that should be confronted and worked through because conflict is part of the collaborative process. Contrived collaboration can be worse than none at all.

The two groups who are not seen by most others or by themselves as necessary players on the leadership team for equity are students and community members, including university faculty as already described. Parents and students have token roles in many districts and schools, such as being members of advisory groups, school site councils, and governance teams. They are usually not involved at the operational level. However, students' belief in their ability to perform at high levels and their ideas about how to improve the ways they are taught are of critical importance. Likewise, parents, guardians, and community persons must be helped to increase their awareness, skills, and effectiveness in supporting and nurturing students so they make their best effort. All stakeholders must see themselves as "leaders for equity."

Culturally courageous leaders manifest the courage to challenge any beliefs or actions getting in the way of equitable educational outcomes. Beliefs and actions based on those beliefs are ingredients of any culture. So culturally courageous leaders are committed to changing cultural factors at a personal and organizational level that impede social justice for all.

Collaboration on providing leadership to equity efforts by persons in all of the groups mentioned is a rare occurrence. But the time has come for such leadership to become more widely practiced. Sabotage of equity efforts may be wittingly or unwittingly initiated by those in various stakeholder groups because they aren't totally committed to the success of all students. Boards of education and administrators need to be held accountable by all other stakeholder groups for giving high priority to achieving equitable outcomes. Regardless of how well a school is moving toward or has achieved equitable outcomes, their success is not likely to be sustained without ongoing board of education support.

Collaboration by all school community stakeholders includes the following characteristics:

- Persons work together with a high degree of trust and without any disrespectful hierarchical status dynamics among them. They build upon the strengths of each other.
- Complex tasks are completed by subgroups, with differentiated tasks assigned to each person based on their unique frame of reference and skills.
- All participants are democratically engaged in problem identification, problem analysis, priority setting, planning, monitoring, and evaluation activities.
- An ongoing norm of consensus building and culturally responsive interests-based negotiation are used as part of the decision-making and problem-solving process. Interests-based negotiation, a term more commonly used in teacher/ school district contract negotiations, includes the presentation by each side of their priority needs when trying to agree upon contract language. Culturally responsive interests-based negotiation related to equity would include the presentation by each stakeholder group of their priority needs when considering equity goals, equity practices, and expected equity outcomes.

The work of the National Center for Culturally Responsive Educational Systems (NCCRESt) strongly supports the training of diverse school community stakeholder groups to enhance their capacity in collaboratively creating equitable schools (2005). In addition, the text edited by Krovetz and Arriaza is an excellent resource for helping strengthen teacher leadership in collaboratively fostering equitable schools (2006).

An example of collaborative culturally courageous leadership will hopefully help the reader visualize and more easily understand what is meant by the term.

VIGNETTE 7–1: COLLABORATIVE EFFORTS TO ADDRESS TEACHER DISCIPLINARY REFERRALS

In a middle school populated by a very culturally, socioeconomically, and linguistically diverse student population, there were a growing number of student–student conflicts and teacher discipline referrals for what is called "willful defiance." Teachers were upset because the school administration was not implementing the kind of consequences they wanted for discipline referrals or responding in what they thought was a timely fashion to student–student conflicts within race and cross-racial groups.

The school administration was hesitant to impose a heavy hand on those students referred to the office by teachers for several reasons. An overwhelming majority of the students referred were African American, even though they constituted less than a third of the student population. For the most part, the teachers referring these students taught the classes where there was the greatest achievement gap between racially diverse groups of students. The district administration had already increased oversight of whether middle school sites were using a double standard in discipline practices, as alleged by some African American parents who had been complaining to their school board members. Board members wanted the complaints to stop and wanted the school sites to do a better job of addressing the underlying causes of disciplinary infractions, whatever they were.

When school disciplinary practices were discussed in a meeting of middle school principals with their immediate supervisor (a district office assistant superintendent), the principal of the school described above shared the challenges she faced related to discipline. Other principals described similar situations.

The assistant superintendent facilitated a problem-solving discussion on what kind of systemic intervention should be attempted. This was followed by his convening a study group that included some middle school principals, all assistant principals in middle schools, some counselor and parent representatives, and a business leader in the community who conducted training on neurolinguistic programming (NLP). This program focuses on the relationship between brain functioning and verbal/nonverbal communication behaviors. A study of NLP can help diagnose and reduce misunderstandings in communication and interpersonal conflict.

At this meeting, a selection process was developed for identifying student leaders at each school, who would, upon parent approval, be invited with their parents to meet with representatives of the study group to discuss the discipline problems. At the meeting with a very diverse group of student leaders, all students were very forthcoming in sharing their opinions about why there were so many student fights and why there were so many disciplinary referrals of African American students to the office.

After the meeting, 90% of the students (with parent permission) who had attended indicated an interest in becoming part of a new student leadership group at their school. The student group would have some responsibility for collaborating with adults at their school to work on reducing the conflicts and referrals, after receiving training by the community consultant described above. It was decided that follow-up support for the students so engaged would also be provided on a regular basis.

The assistant superintendent and principals collaboratively decided on how to fund this new program. A presentation was made to the board of education on the proposed program, and the board was requested to name a board member who would be their liaison to the program and attend future meetings when available.

The program was implemented and remained in effect for the next 3 years while the assistant superintendent remained in the district. The program was evaluated after its second year and found to have a significant impact on reducing student–student conflicts and disciplinary referrals at each school. All students involved in such incidents were first referred to a student "conflict mediator" for resolution of the problems and only then referred to an assistant principal if necessary.

Seventy-five percent of all referrals to the student mediators were resolved at their level without any necessity for direct involvement of school administrators. The program was expanded to the high school level after its first year, with the same results. Most teachers were pleased with having student mediators, but some still complained that students were not receiving sufficient consequences for their actions, especially for "willful defiance."

Concurrently, professional development was provided for all teachers in each school on "education that is multicultural" and equity pedagogy. Data on the NLP program, including data on resolution of the referrals to student mediators, were used as part of the training. Some teachers resented having to participate in the training. Nevertheless, although it was implemented in various ways depending on the school, involvement was not optional.

MAKE IT PERSONAL

FN7–1 (SEE FACILITATOR NOTES IN APPENDIX 1)

1. In your work setting, what are the major constraints working against meaningful sustained collaboration for equity by all school community stakeholders?

2. What is your experience in collaborating on achieving equity with at least two stakeholder groups other than your own?

3. What are some small victories or major defeats you have experienced when collaborating with any other stakeholder groups to achieve equity?

4. On reflection, what would you do differently in prior efforts to achieve equity reform/transformation?

REVIEW OF CHAPTER 7

- Seven major issues (introduced in Section I) related to cultural democracy and equitable educational outcomes are presented as actions that need to be taken by all stakeholders collaboratively practicing culturally courageous leadership.

- The characteristics of collaboration by all school community stakeholders, including culturally responsive interests based negotiation, were described.

- A vignette describing an example of collaborative culturally courageous leadership was presented as an example of how it might look.

Seven Principles **8**

*The acid test of whether one is practicing culturally courageous leadership
must be the extent to which he or she embraces some critical beliefs and
engages in some essential practices, even when in very adversarial circumstances.*

A commitment to achieving equitable inputs and outcomes for all students is akin to seeking change in the fundamental purpose of public schooling in the United States. Although there has been a lot of equity talk about needing to do that, especially in the last 30 years, we have not walked that talk. The seven principles of culturally courageous leadership (CCL) represent the personal characteristics needed by those wanting to exemplify such leadership. They represent a philosophy, worldview, and the drivers of a blueprint for closing the gap between equity theory and action. Equity leaders must be guided by some moral and ethical parameters that enable them to ascertain if they are "perpetrating" or are totally dedicated to fostering a more just society that honors everyone.

KWL EXERCISE

1. What are some of the personal characteristics and values of those who engage in unrelenting efforts to advance social justice and equitable educational outcomes?

2. Describe the knowledge and skills you would like to acquire in order to be a more effective equity leader.

3. Based on what you have learned so far from reading this guide, describe how you could help aspiring equity leaders.

SECOND COMPONENT OF CCL: SEVEN PRINCIPLES/CHARACTERISTICS

CCL principles (i.e., leadership characteristics) are the major guidelines, moral imperatives, and essential prerequisites for implementing this leadership paradigm. The principles must be reflected in the leadership characteristics of all persons who are attempting to achieve the goal of equitable educational outcomes. The seven principles are also characteristics of CCL. They are absolutely essential for administrator, teacher, and instructional support staff, who must help to nurture CCL by persons from other stakeholder groups. Reference to vignettes in Section I of the guide assist the reader in seeing how the principle could be manifested in problematic situations already described.

Committed Caregivers

Committed caregivers persevere in working on behalf of the most academically needy students without neglecting the needs of all other students. They make decisions about how to facilitate learning based on multiple assessments. When necessary, they attempt to convince the families of underserved students that they care even when they disagree with them or find their attitudes and behaviors unacceptable.

Committed caregivers have high expectations for all students, without reservations or excuses. They give high priority to increasing student motivation and effort without relying solely on extrinsic rewards, and nurture resilience when in or out of school circumstances negatively impact self-esteem and aspirations. Caregivers help learners feel good about positive aspects of their identities and see them as sources as well as providers of knowledge, not just passive recipients.

If necessary, they will publicly fight on behalf of students' due process rights. They have the courage to step out of their comfort zone when it would be politically expedient to not do so, including collaboration with racially/culturally diverse others in various stakeholder groups. Committed caregivers are action-oriented rather than emotion-centered, as reflected in their faith and conviction in students' abilities, and are demanding, yet supportive and encouraging (Gay, 2010).

Why Committed Caregivers Were Needed in Vignette 1–1

In vignette 1–1, Jimmy was described as an eighth-grade student about to graduate from middle school who is ambivalent about school and believes his eighth-grade English and math teachers didn't really care about whether he and his homeboys succeeded in school or not. The fact that Jimmy didn't like some of his teachers decreased his motivation to do his best, especially in subjects where he was struggling. All of the ways that caregivers are described need to be displayed by the adults in Jimmy's middle school so students like Jimmy don't give up.

Cultural Consumers

Cultural consumers maintain a lifelong quest for increasing personal knowledge about the cultural heritage, strengths, struggles, customs, and resilience of diverse people and apply these insights when functioning in whatever role they have in the school community. They consistently seek ways to improve their cultural competence through a genuine interest in the personal lives and backgrounds of others in their school community.

Cultural consumers also value learning about their own ethnic roots and cultural heritage, including how their cultural view influences the way they see the world and their students (Saifer, Edwards, Ellis, Ko, & Stuczynski, 2011). They come to understand that assessing their own culture as well as that of the school as an organization is a critical step in appreciating how diverse learners interact with instructors and with each other (Nuri Robins, Lindsey, Lindsey, & Terrell, 2002). They respect others personal and group identities by not making disparaging remarks about them.

Cultural consumers create or seek opportunities to participate in experiences that increase their comfort, empathy for and ability to effectively interact with culturally diverse others, even when making such efforts might initially be beyond their comfort zone (Lindsey, Nuri Robins, & Terrell, 2003). They are disposed to learn and understand their students' cultural and familial contexts and experiences (Ordonez & Jasis, 2011). They are also committed to utilizing intersectional knowledge about their students' background and multiple identities (e.g., race, social class, gender, and hybrid identities based on students personal lived experience) for curricular and instructional purposes (Grant & Zwier, 2011).

Finally, they take the initiative to solicit others in their stakeholder group and in other stakeholder groups to lobby for changes in Eurocentric curricula that provide little or no information about the racism experienced by those historically underserved, and they enlighten students about the heritage and contributions of all historically underserved groups in the United States.

Why Cultural Consumers Were Needed in Vignette 2–1

In vignette 2–1 about Jimmy's experience in his elementary school when being taught about cultural groups, his racial group was hardly mentioned, and when sharing about his own family activities, he felt alienated because of the way other students reacted. During these formative years, Jimmy started feeling school was not a place where he felt supported or acknowledged for who he is. All of the cultural consumer characteristics need to be displayed in Jimmy's elementary school. Jimmy's teachers did not insist on the display of respect by all students for each other, nor did his teachers model such respect themselves in their teaching practices, through their reactions when students were disrespectful to what was being shared by their peers.

MAKE IT PERSONAL

FN8-1 (SEE FACILITATOR NOTES IN APPENDIX 1)

1. What do you consider your most important personal qualities when it comes to being a committed caregiver?

2. What additional cultural knowledge do you need in order to improve student receptivity to and respect for what others share about their cultural heritage or family traditions?

Consummate Conciliators

Consummate conciliators are willing to mediate/manage conflicts that are based on different cultural perspectives among adults and/or students, or conflicts that arise from efforts to correct past wrongs. They anticipate potential conflicts that may be based on race and culture, and try to defuse them before they occur or manage them when they occur. They take the initiative to help facilitate an examination of race in the United States within the domain of democracy, including the ugly history of race, racial hierarchies, and historical injustices, for the purpose of defusing the possibility of a more fractured nation (Howard, 2010).

Consummate conciliators persistently engage in critical self-reflection on personal attitudes, assumptions, and behaviors, including their racial identity level, that may contribute to racial/cultural conflicts or the exacerbation of existing conflicts. They work to change such personal characteristics. They also persistently work to reduce discord based on racial/cultural/language differences, or alleged instances of "isms" or biases, and try to eliminate underlying factors contributing to the manifestation of any "ism" or bias.

Students and adults are helped by consummate conciliators to become more aware of any prejudicial or discriminatory reactions to people they consider different from them and then helped to develop a range of culturally proficient responses. Conciliators also attempt to change the nature of cultural politics when it is based on unstated or even subconscious fears about losing "White" privilege. They constantly attempt to increase awareness and willingness to deal with cultural dissonance within and between groups.

Finally, consummate conciliators are willing to publicly acknowledge the "elephant on the ceiling" so to speak, such as old grievances, biases, unspoken assumptions, or stereotypes of each other. After putting the issues on the table, conciliators take the initiative to work with others over the long haul in managing conflicts that are obstacles to equity and excellence.

Why Consummate Conciliators Were Needed in Vignette 2–2

In vignette 2–2, the conflicts described in the middle school where Jimmy attended are associated with a "changing student population." Middle-class flight in general, and White flight in particular, has been rampant. There are many struggles between different people who all want to control what happens in the school. Falling test scores, low staff cohesion, and increasing parent dissatisfaction are only a few of the challenges being experienced. All of the consummate conciliator behaviors mentioned are needed in this school. The relationship between conflict and low achievement was not formally addressed by all staff and representatives from other stakeholder groups. Consummate conciliators from all stakeholder groups are urgently needed to help all of the players work through their "personal stuff," differing perspectives and tensions.

MAKE IT PERSONAL

FN8–2 (SEE FACILITATOR NOTES IN APPENDIX 1)

1. What is the relationship between conflict and low achievement in your school community?

2. What are two of the conflicts experienced in your school(s) that contribute most to inequitable student outcomes?

Conscientious Coaches

Conscientious coaches are very receptive to serving as an equity coach for others in their peer group or other groups. As an integral part of coaching teachers, administrators, or instructional support staff on how to improve student academic success, they engage peers in developmentally appropriate conversations about human difference bias. In response to expressed concerns of those they coach, they ask questions and facilitate reflection on what constitutes biases of any kind in the classroom, school, and community. This is followed by helping problem solve how to deal with identified biases. They find ways to "get around" any propensity of those they are coaching to blame family poverty or other life circumstances for student underachievement. They model how to actively fight for justice through anti-racism work of some kind, and refuse to remain silent (McIntosh, 1989; Asante, 2003). By helping keep a focus on data and by facilitating as much teacher–peer observation as possible, they encourage and set the tone for dispassionate self-evaluation of professional weaknesses on an ongoing basis (Chenoweth, 2009).

They are not intimidated by the fears of those they coach that pushing social justice issues will further divide people and are patient in helping those coached to develop respect for alternative ways of thinking and being. For example, conscientious coaches have the ability to gently but unrelentingly nurture critical analysis of any prevailing beliefs that good teaching is transcendent and identical for all students and under all circumstances (Gay, 2010).

Conscientious coaches are always working on increasing their personal courage and savvy as well as that of others, to confront and change conditions preventing the teaching of all students at high levels. They work closely and collaboratively and never didactically with those they coach who want to serve the best interests of historically underserved students of color.

Finally, conscientious coaches engage in transformational coaching that has a culturally democratic philosophical bent. Such coaching includes use of strong interpersonal communication skills such as active listening, mirroring body language, perception checks, providing hypothetical scenarios requiring a quick response, modeling, and culturally responsive feedback. These skills are used to increase political savvy in nurturing a critical cultural consciousness and commitment to social justice.

Why Conscientious Coaches Are Needed in Vignettes 3–1 and 3–2

In vignettes 3–1 and 3–2, Jimmy's middle school is further discussed, first from the perspective of Jimmy and Josephina who complain about most of the readings in their English class not being of interest to African and Latino/a students, and then from the perspective of the teachers. The teachers are frustrated by the low entry level skills of many students, necessitating a lot of small group guided instruction, and are also enraged by the board of education decision that they be more culturally responsive when they are under the gun to improve state test scores. They don't see a relationship between such teaching and improved scores. Some teachers' concerns about the board decision are also fueled by their own racial identities, cultural biases, and fears related to strengthening those they label as "problem students and parents." There is a great need for conscientious coaches in this school who are able to be persistent and consistent in helping all school community stakeholders critically examine their assumptions, beliefs, biases, fears, and behaviors, especially when the going gets tough and there is a lot of push back. Such coaches need to be well along on their own transformational "journey" and able to model ways of thinking and acting that help others jump-start their becoming more culturally courageous.

MAKE IT PERSONAL

FN8–3 (SEE FACILITATOR NOTES IN APPENDIX 1)

1. What are some fears and/or prevailing beliefs in your school community that drive the resistance to changes you consider necessary for equitable educational outcomes?

2. On a scale of 1 to 5, with 1 being very low and 5 being excellent, how would you assess your effectiveness as a conscientious coach?

Courageous Change Masters

Courageous change masters help staff increase their knowledge about and ability to manage change forces in general and develop additional resources in schools that will help achieve more equitable inputs and educational outcomes. They recognize that achieving such outcomes requires that students be assisted in increasing their cultural and social capital, and others' respect for their unrecognized abilities. This is consistent with their modeling rejection of deficit theories about historically underserved students. They also demonstrate an ability to deal with both the macro and micro needs of historically underserved communities, schools, and students. An example is when they simultaneously focus on leading major improvements in preK and early childhood education as well as establishing major support systems for those middle and high school students in great danger of dropping out of school. The work by Cohen and Lotan (1995) on producing equal-status interactions in heterogeneous classrooms is an example of what change masters do to help students redefine what they are capable of achieving.

In other words, change masters recognize the urgent need to work on helping the youngest to develop strong foundations as well as work on changing the peer culture of at-risk adolescents who need different kinds of role models so they can believe in the value of pursuing different paths at critical crossroads, and that it is never too late to make qualitatively different choices (Tough, 2008).

Finally, they help school communities develop, pilot, and phase-in comprehensive systemic plans for equity transformation, including greater responsiveness to student realities and community concerns. Courageous change masters help create organizational cultures that result in a climate conducive to greater accountability for achievement at high levels by underserved students of color, based on a greater sense of urgency, responsibility, and accountability.

Why Courageous Change Masters Are Needed in Vignette 4–1

In vignette 4–1, information was provided about culturally responsive pedagogy in the school site plan of Jimmy's middle school. In addition, this vignette provided several examples of administrator inaction regarding teacher accountability for actions spelled out in the school site plan. Principals need to manifest all of the ways that courageous change masters are described in order to effectively work with their school community in achieving equitable educational outcomes. Staff in this vignette must be able to manage the change forces at play in their school and be collectively accountable for implementing equity transformation. Students need to feel better about their innate abilities, and administrators need to be courageous and thorough in their fostering collaborative partnerships to develop school plans. Fullan (1993) has been incisive in his discussion of the need for schools to be learning organizations and why moral purpose combined with skilled change agents are essential. Courageous change masters are needed to both learn from the failure of well-funded, ambitious projects that may be totally top-down instead of a mix of top down and bottom up, and to focus more on facilitating the cultural changes needed in the school organization than on structural change. True meaningful collaboration is elusive but of paramount importance.

MAKE IT PERSONAL

FN8–4 (SEE FACILITATOR NOTES IN APPENDIX 1)

1. What, if any, changes related to equity have been most difficult to implement in your district or school, and what support was provided to administrators or teachers to help them embrace the changes and implement them with fidelity?

2. Describe the role you are playing to foster courageous change efforts related to equity.

Community Organizers

Community organizers help develop and lead both ethnic specific and culturally diverse coalitions that actively lobby policymakers for changes in schools that will increase equitable educational outcomes. They organize specific or multiple stakeholder groups to collectively advocate for social justice. They also provide leadership to increasing public awareness about why cultural democracy is needed and how it is related to equitable educational outcomes in schools. They also take a leadership role in recruiting more persons from all stakeholder groups to assume the mantle of community organizers and assist their recruits to refine and further develop their community organizing skills so there is ever-increasing community support for equity transformation.

Community organizers constantly seek to increase personal knowledge and skills that will help them build broad-based coalitions for equity goals and objectives. They assist parents/students/community members of Latino/a and African American backgrounds to improve their trust and team building so they can work together for in-depth equity transformation by participating in a strong coalition for social justice. It is desirable for community organizers to not only be principals, who should spend as much time in their communities as possible to enhance their own awareness and growth, but other stakeholder groups as well, such as parents, students, community members, and teachers. Principals need to play a central role in community organizing, and help their teachers make wider contacts with the community and the professional world, to stimulate their own critical reflection, learning, and improvement (Fullan & Hargreaves, 1996).

Why Community Organizers Are Needed in Vignettes 5–1 and 5–2

In vignette 5–1, Jimmy began to rebel against being segregated in his classroom from some of his homeboys assigned to other small study groups differentiated by academic level. In vignette 5–2, there was a major conflict in a secondary school district over the formula for allocation of professional development funds. In the first case there was no community awareness of or organizing against classroom practices that alienated Jimmy. In the second case, there was considerable mobilization of support by different constituencies on the issue of how to best meet the academic needs of the most at-risk students. Each group had different perspectives based on what they thought was in their best interest. All of the descriptions of community organizers were needed in both of these vignettes. There is a need for those who mobilize community support for any educational cause to try working collaboratively with other stakeholders and with those opposing them. A more unified approach is needed when seeking equitable educational outcomes. Without more coalition building, adversarial relationships between different school community constituencies will increase and all will engage in self-serving politics that can greatly compromise any improvement in student educational outcomes. It also must be noted that often there are major differences in perspective, values, priorities, and approaches within constituent or stakeholder groups. The community organizer must not only work on cross-group differences but within-group differences or rivalries as well, which can be even more challenging to resolve or manage. Stronger coalitions are definitely needed within oppressed groups and may need to initially receive higher priority than cross-group animosities.

Communication Gurus

Communication gurus have the interpersonal competence enabling them to take risks to share more of their "hidden self" and seek feedback on their "blind self," in order to improve interpersonal communication with persons who have a variety of personal identities and racial/cultural backgrounds. Hidden self and blind self are social psychological concepts that are part of the Johari Window, created by Joseph Luft and Harry Ingham (Luft, 1969; Yen, 1999). Hidden self is what you know about your attitudes, beliefs, skills, and fears related to equity that is relevant and not known by others. Blind self is what relevant information related to equity that others know about you but you don't know. In order to build strong relationships that result in embracing the same vision for strengthening equity outcomes, all of these communication skills are very important.

Communication gurus are able to diagnose their own and others' work and communication styles because they know the behavioral indicators in the DiSC Personal Profile associated with preferred ways of being (http://inspiringsolutions.com/disc/). Gurus also apply situational leadership theory and practices when leading equity initiatives and make decisions about how to best motivate supervisees or peers, based on their job and psychological readiness (Hersey & Blanchard, 1993) in relationship to specific equity tasks they are assigned or volunteer to undertake. Examples of equity tasks requiring the use of situational leadership are working with peers on some new interdisciplinary curriculum units or reaching out to the community to solicit greater support for improving student access to higher level courses. It is of critical importance to know what the mix of attention should be when helping supervisees or peers learn how to complete specific tasks (task orientation) versus responding to the supervisees' or peers need for strong relationships (relationship orientation), or a combination of both. Situational leadership must be applied to strategies for working with persons engaged in equity transformation with as much expertise as may be applied to delegating other tasks that are not equity related.

Communication gurus facilitate a greater commitment to equity based on their sensitivity and immediate response to the primary interests, concerns, and expressed needs of those one supervises or with whom one works. Communication gurus, through their diagnostic, analytical and interpersonal skills, as well as their genuine authenticity, are able to bond with very diverse colleagues in ways that result in a mutual stretching of personal horizons and increased efficacy when trying on new attitudes and behaviors. They work well with both new and veteran teachers to improve teaching and learning of historically underserved students. They are often effective in their efforts to increase support for equity initiatives because people are attracted to their personalities and want to be a part of team efforts being undertaken by the communication guru.

Why Communication Gurus Are Needed in Vignettes 5–3 and 5–4

In vignette 5–3, there is a description of regional meetings for district- and county-level educators within a large state. The meetings focus on the relative merits and politics of a statewide proposal for all school personnel to experience professional development on culturally relevant and responsive education. Of note was the obvious difference in perspective of those who have responsibility for federal Title I and federal/state program improvement schools. In both Title I and program improvement schools, historically underserved students may exhibit much lower scores than other student groups on statewide assessments. The persons responsible for these programs in their respective districts wanted the state to give them more clout in the professional development requirements school districts had to meet in order to continue receiving funding. Other participants in the regional meetings were adverse to any new mandates.

In vignette 5–4, the issue discussed is literacy in mainstream English and how to best meet the needs of the large number of limited English proficient (LEP) students and native speakers of nonmainstream English in one of the largest school districts in the United States. There are some major challenges faced by this school district in meeting its goals related to English language proficiency. The characteristics of communication gurus are very important when working with educators at any level to secure consensus on how to proceed in achieving greater capacity and political will for accomplishing equitable educational outcomes. Those attending the regional meetings and those second language and English language arts staff in the large school district are frequently engaged in discussions about the nature of the achievement problems being experienced and what to do about them, but they have not been able to reach consensus on creative solutions that most will actively support. This may be due to poor communication and problem-solving adequacy. It may be because many teachers fear being called racist if they take on the issue of nonmainstream English being so prevalent across ethnic groups of color. The role of the communication guru is to help increase mutual understanding and motivation of people to work together on such an equity task. The guru should be able to diagnose and respond to the communication styles of those with whom they are working as well as know how to elicit and take advantage of their unique qualities (i.e., predispositions) or strengths. Individuals have different levels of achievement motivation, depending on the subject, task, or project. The communication guru must be able to discern the varying levels of achievement motivation and readiness for equity tasks, and work with adults accordingly to try improving their motivation and success just like a teacher should do in the classroom with students.

REVIEW OF CHAPTER 8

- There are seven principles/characteristics of CCL that are major guidelines, moral imperatives, and essential prerequisites for implementing the CCL paradigm. Examples of attitudes, skills, and behaviors associated with each principle provide the reader with concrete illustrations of what dispositions and savvy are required to demonstrate each CCL characteristic.

- One or more of the vignettes in Chapters 1 through 5 were used to provide examples of schooling conditions or problematic situations that required use of particular principles/characteristics of CCL.

Transformation and Politics

9

Personal and organizational transformation occur more easily with simultaneous priority to transforming the "politics" of equity transformation.

KWL EXERCISE

1. Based on your experience, what is the relationship between the intensity of conflict between those with pro and con political positions on an equity initiative, and the degree of success in the initiative contributing to equitable educational outcomes?

2. What would assist your efforts to foster school organizational changes that improved the education received by historically underserved students?

3. What aspects of cultural courageousness can positively influence the politics of equity transformation in your school or district?

৵৽

HOW TRANSFORMATION AND POLITICS GO HAND IN HAND

The collective actions and individual characteristics associated with culturally courageous leadership (CCL) are more likely to be incubated and thrive in environments where there are conscious efforts to overcome major political obstacles to personal and organizational transformation. There will always be some obstacles, regardless.

There is a lot of politics associated with trying to achieve equitable educational outcomes for historically underserved students. There will be resistance to any attempted change, especially changes of long-established norms that help perpetuate inequitable student outcomes and the existing power/control/authority dynamics.

Such norms are usually not seen as the problem, because student and parent characteristics are often labeled as the cause of student underachievement.

Personal transformation involves a change in how stakeholders see themselves and define their role in social justice efforts. Personal transformation cannot be sustained without organizational transformation, and organizational transformation cannot occur without simultaneous personal transformation.

Within most school districts, there are "sacred cows" that seem untouchable when it comes to eliminating major constraints to equity reform. Examples of sacred cows are a propensity of school board members to micromanage the schools within their jurisdiction, the requirements that accompany certain educational programs or initiatives that are funded by major foundation or government grants, and certain schools that might be populated primarily by some of the most politically and economically powerful families in the community. In all of these examples, cultural politics is at play, with certain privileges of those with a lot of formal or informal power, control, and authority being untouchable. Organizational transformation must accompany personal transformation for equity reforms to become institutionalized.

In addition, personal and organizational transformation are not likely to occur if there isn't a concurrent effort to transform the politics (i.e., social influence networks and decision-making processes) associated with seeking equitable student outcomes. If those who have always had their way continue to have their way when it comes to what happens in particular schools populated by the historically underserved, then cosmetic superficial efforts are likely to be undertaken instead of deepseated equity transformation.

When undertaking equity initiatives, it is of critical importance that the proposed equity changes in personal and organizational characteristics are made clear and that at least a majority of the target audience sees a need for change, is involved in planning for change, and is encouraged and supported in changing. The personal transformation needed for equity and excellence is largely what is needed for any organizational change to be successful: willingness, commitment, motivation, capacity, risk taking, and influence. However, given the history of race relations and oppression in the larger society and in the educational systems of the United States, there are additional norms, policies, skills, or dispositions that the school as an organization must nurture, and cultural courageousness is needed for organizations to provide such nurturing.

Personal and organizational transformation are very dependent on CCL, and such leadership makes personal and organizational transformation possible. Because politics involves some adversarial interplay and struggle between those with different philosophies, interpretations of reality, and priorities, the identity constructs/personal identities of those espousing divergent ideas are usually quite different, as are their beliefs and values. But culturally courageous leaders must be able to navigate the politics in such ways that compromises are struck with the opposition in the pursuit of a higher good. For the culturally courageous leader, buy-in to the process for achieving equity transformation is a higher good.

MAKE IT PERSONAL

FN9–1 (SEE FACILITATOR NOTES IN APPENDIX 1)

1. What are some of the "sacred cows" in your school district or school that seem impossible to change when trying to foster equity transformation?

2. Describe the current politics in your school(s) when it comes to seeking equity, including some of the landmines that must be circumvented in order to achieve equity transformation.

૭૦૯૭

THIRD AND FOURTH COMPONENTS OF CCL: ACHIEVING PERSONAL AND ORGANIZATIONAL TRANSFORMATION BY ADEPTLY NAVIGATING THE POLITICS OF IMPLEMENTATION (POI)

Six dimensions of POI are as follows:

1. Engage in problem definition and analysis.

2. Be sensitive to the psychology of equity transformation.

3. Focus on standards categories receiving inadequate priority.

4. Use personal or others' insights from trying to implement previous equity reforms.

5. Reduce some key barriers to high achievement by all students.

6. Finesse the equity hustlers, who may be "wanksters," "gangsters," and/or "riders."

First Dimension of POI:
Engage in Problem Definition and Analysis

The definition of all problems addressed by equity initiatives is inherently a political undertaking. How equity problems are identified and analyzed is of critical importance for any modicum of success in achieving greater social justice. Problem Analysis was one of several managerial skill dimensions of the original National

Association of Secondary School Principals (NASSP) Principal Assessment Center (Hersey, 1982) when I was one of the regional directors of a NASSP assessment center in the United States. The assessment center was adopted by many school districts as a vehicle to assist them in identifying individuals who had high potential for being successful school site administrators, and some districts required high scores from the assessment center for persons to be considered for administrative positions. The NASSP 21st Century Principal Assessment Center is focused on instructional leadership as reflected in the assessment of such skill areas as setting instructional direction, teamwork, sensitivity, development of others, and a results orientation (NASSP, 2004). All of these skill areas are essential if one is to adeptly navigate the politics of implementing any equity initiative. Politics includes competition and negotiation/interplay between persons with different ideas who seek the support or acquiescence of a majority. Problem definition and analysis should be based on situation-specific information from multiple perspectives that has been collected and analyzed; utilizing this skill is inherent in practicing the other skill areas mentioned. However, politics is always involved when deciding what questions to ask, what information to collect, how to analyze what is collected, and how to define problems based on the data. In addition, the information collected will likely reveal several problems. Problem analysis should reveal the relationships between these problems, the context of each identified problem, and the assumptions undergirding each problem.

For example, if a school district pursued an equity initiative to implement professional development on teacher expectations, there are several steps related to problem definition and analysis that should be undertaken during the planning and implementation process. Data from classroom observations that focused on specific teacher behaviors related to expectations should be collected beforehand. It would also be ideal to secure information from teachers on the challenges being faced in their classrooms and the instructional approaches they are utilizing to address the challenges. Whatever problems are experienced should then be identified as well as the relationships between all of the problems, the context and assumptions undergirding each problem. Problems related to teacher expectations could include incomplete instructional plans and classroom management strategies, the range of student academic readiness levels in any one class, and several students with special needs in each classroom. Without adequate problem definition and analysis, the equity initiative will be compromised.

Politics is also involved during the problem analysis process, because there are often a lot of conflicting interpretations about the relationships between problems, the context of problems and the assumptions behind them.

The culturally courageous leader must be able to facilitate civil dialogue among those with different political positions by attempting to find common ground where they can agree. This requires the personal commitment and self-discipline that enables one to not be totally bound by personal predilections and cultural norms of a school or district if they reflect cultural hegemony or antidemocratic dispositions.

For example, a major problem in some low-performing districts is the limited accountability of all stakeholder groups for the disparities in educational outcomes experienced by historically underserved students of color. Several biased assumptions and myths still prevail about the causes of these disparities, and many only point a finger at students and families.

The politics of implementing equity transformation is at play when trying to get all stakeholders to have a sense of urgency and responsibility for eliminating any educational gaps. Critical decisions are made when determining what data to collect and how to interpret the data to define problems contributing to such gaps.

Whatever data are collected should include multiple perspectives that will help clarify the context in which these gaps are occurring and the degree of accountability by all stakeholders that currently exists. There might be multiple conditions contributing to the overall problem of limited accountability, such as some deeply held beliefs about the intellectual capacity of low-performing students, and their parents/guardians' value of education. Other conditions could be the limited instructional supervision skills or limited time given to instructional supervision when it comes to fostering academically rigorous culturally responsive teaching. When these conditions exist, they exacerbate any problems associated with low teacher expectations.

Two other conditions contributing to limited accountability for teacher expectations could be the absence of board policies and board of education priorities in this area. Such absence could result in no on-the-job professional development that specifically focuses on holistic approaches to addressing the needs of historically underserved students.

Those navigating the POI must know how to handle the potentially volatile dynamics that may be present when soliciting diverse perspectives on what the problems are. Unless there are concurrent efforts to foster personal and organizational transformation, it is unlikely that problem definition and analysis will be given the priority it deserves.

MAKE IT PERSONAL

FN9–2 (SEE FACILITATOR NOTES IN APPENDIX 1)

1. Compare the process for equity problem definition and analysis utilized in your school or district with the process suggested in this chapter.

2. What are the steps in the problem analysis process which you feel are in greatest need of being implemented right away within your work setting?

Second Dimension of POI: Be Sensitive to the
Psychology of Equity Transformation

Assumptions, attitudes, feelings, beliefs, values, and behaviors associated with achieving or not achieving equitable educational outcomes are all part of the psychology of equity transformation, as well as the racial identity orientation of all players. Vignette 6–1 (see Chapter 6) describes the fears of Jimmy's mother about the high school her son is scheduled to attend, and these fears center around concerns about safety, negative peer influence, and nonsupportive teachers. Jimmy's attitudes about the same high school are very different because of his interests, priorities, and the interpersonal relationships he has or hasn't had. This vignette illustrates how psychological factors can play a major role in affecting how stakeholders view particular schools, and we can infer these perspectives affect their degree of skepticism or trust regarding the possibility of equitable opportunities.

Other psychological dynamics at play when trying to foster equity are reflected in chart 2a, which invites the reader to engage in diagnosing whether certain kinds of intergroup and interpersonal communication activities have occurred in schools with which they are familiar. These dynamics include the nature of communication and collaboration related to attitudes, beliefs, and behaviors toward human differences. Beliefs in the possibility, even likelihood, of positive change are sometimes based on one's past experience.

Navigating the POI includes the necessity to "sell" stakeholders on embracing a given equity initiative, and believing that if they do, there is a better chance of achieving equitable student outcomes, or whatever the goal. In order to "sell" stakeholders on the possibility of achieving equity initiatives, the culturally courageous leader must use high "task" and "relationship" behavior with the target audience. Stakeholders must be encouraged to believe that if they make certain efforts, the equity initiative will likely succeed. The need to suspend distrust or cynicism must be explicitly discussed. There is a high likelihood that many are very uncomfortable with acknowledging they do not believe that equity can be achieved. However, initiating a dialogue on distrust issues is an important acknowledgement that many may be having those feelings without revealing them.

The psychology of equity transformation includes the relative degree of openness and priority given to considering the "isms," such as racism, classism, and sexism, and biases based on disability, sexual orientation, primary language, and so on, when making any major decisions related to school functioning.

Individuals providing leadership to navigating the POI must weigh the comfort and skill levels of persons to explicitly deal with issues of race, culture, the "isms" and biases on an ongoing basis, so they can adjust their approaches, but not their goals. Over time, the reluctance by some to giving ongoing attention to the "isms" or biases may be overcome.

MAKE IT PERSONAL

FN9-3 (SEE FACILITATOR NOTES IN APPENDIX 1)

1. What, if any, anxiety or discomfort have you felt or know about related to explicitly discussing race, culture, and the "isms" and biases in staff meetings, professional development activities, parent forums, classroom instruction, and teacher preparation classes?

2. Describe the actions you have taken or avoided if feeling such anxiety or discomfort, and the underlying causes of your feelings.

Third Dimension of POI: Focus on Standards Categories Receiving Low Priority

Chart 5a provides a description of five standards categories and the interrelationships between each category. Only two categories are codified into law (i.e., content and performance standards) in most states. These two standards categories are based on outcome measures. Three other standards categories are in dire need of receiving greater priority for schools to have effective comprehensive systems for achieving equitable educational outcomes. The delivery, opportunity to learn, and professional development standards described in chart 5a are not being implemented at high levels in most school districts, and most certainly not in schools populated to a large extent by historically underserved students of color. These three standards categories are educational inputs, which are necessary to achieve the educational outcomes.

From an equity perspective, content standards must not only be aligned with instruction and assessment, they must also reflect the cultural pluralism inherent in the United States. They must also help students be able to successfully function in an increasingly interdependent global society that transcends historical boundaries of race, nationality, nation state, culture, class, and socioeconomic status. For this to occur, all students must have the opportunity to learn (Hilliard, n.d.). The opportunity to learn is greatly influenced by the extent to which delivery standards and professional development standards are part of the transformation agenda. Opportunity to learn is also influenced by such variables as whether there is close instructional supervision of the teaching and learning process experienced by special needs students and the degree to which these same students receive disproportionate discipline referrals, suspensions, and expulsions (Boykin & Noguera, 2011).

The POI for equity initiatives involves advocating, lobbying, and negotiating for greater implementation of these standards categories, which would have fiscal implications. For example, massive cuts in the education budgets of most states have made it easier for districts to rationalize not being able to implement professional learning programs in all areas of need. In addition, limited funds make it more difficult for school districts to provide the necessary materials, equipment, and facilities.

Being adept at navigating the politics of implementation requires taking next level steps that go beyond past practice and present fears if the neglected standards categories are to receive higher priority. It is even more critical that political advocacy be undertaken collaboratively by all school community stakeholders for these standards categories to be more fully embraced. Political advocacy must include presentations to diverse audiences. The target audiences should include boards of education, parent groups, community groups and organizations, such as churches, social organizations, and community newspapers. The electronic media should also be used to increase awareness and mobilize support. In some if not most cases, this will not be enough, and lawsuits must be considered.

MAKE IT PERSONAL

FN9-4 (SEE FACILITATOR NOTES IN APPENDIX 1)

1. Describe the extent to which delivery, opportunity to learn, and professional development standards as described in chart 5a are implemented in schools populated primarily by historically underserved students of color.

2. If you had the power to cause an instant improvement to a standards category currently receiving the lowest priority in your work setting, what would that standards category be and the improvement needed?

Fourth Dimension of POI: Use Personal or Others' Observations Based on Implementation of Equity Initiatives

Ten of my observations when helping implementation of equity initiatives are briefly described in Chapter 4. The politics of implementation was unique in each school and district. In some schools, there were situation-specific instances of cultural dissonance within and between stakeholder groups, about school and student needs as well as strategies and solutions. In all schools, there was little if any nurturing and utilization of students and parents of color as resources in helping develop and implement school improvement plans focusing on equitable educational outcomes.

An important dimension of POI is to use whatever you have learned from previous work you have done in attempting to implement equity initiatives. If you have no previous experience, seek the insights of individuals who have such familiarity.

Culturally courageous leaders utilize their own funds of knowledge from experience, study, or research when taking new equity initiatives. They also attempt to improve communication in order to reduce or eliminate dissonance within or across demographic and job-specific groups. They may foster collaboration between student, parent, and teacher leaders to improve student educational outcomes. Culturally courageous leaders give high priority to a no-excuses attitude when it comes to equitable inputs as well as outcomes.

My experience is that there is an attempt to implement many equity "reforms" (as opposed to equity transformation) in a piecemeal fashion, sometimes knowingly and sometimes unknowingly. Reforms are less invasive than transformation efforts and may involve tinkering with structural changes without giving adequate attention to influencing change in personal identities and other cultural conditions in schools that are inimical to achieving equity. Usually there is inadequate attention to being proactive in directly addressing documented constraints or barriers to high achievement. The success of equity plans may also be subject to the untimely mobility of administrative, teacher, and/or community leaders of such efforts, before any traction has been achieved in the equity initiative. In addition, political constituencies in the school community who provide strong support for such programs are subject to being highly mercurial, where their support is tenacious and unwavering one year, but tepid or nonexistent the next. Finally, the funding for such programs is also susceptible to being yanked entirely or severely reduced because of budget cuts or for support of another priority. Many policymakers may unrealistically insist on major results within a short time span, and when they don't occur, reduce funding levels.

MAKE IT PERSONAL

1. What are your observations about what happens when any equity initiative is undertaken in your school or district?

2. What happened when you sought support for an equity initiative based on your experience and observations of past efforts? What would you do differently?

Fifth Dimension of POI: Reduce Some Key Barriers to Achievement at High Levels by All Students

In Chapter 6, chart 6a identified 10 barriers, within five categories, to achievement at high levels in a sample of low-performing schools where I served as an external evaluator. Three of the most salient barriers were weak instructional leadership, toxic school and school community climate, and limited accountability.

Weak Instructional Leadership Barrier and the Politics of Implementation

Instructional leadership, as conceptualized based on considerable research (Marks & Printy, 2003; Murphy, Weil, Hallinger, & Mitman, 1982; Southwest

Educational Development Laboratory, 1992) involves a host of behavioral indicators, two of which are as follows:

1. Successful engagement of all staff in developing consensus on school vision, mission, goals, and objectives in the school improvement plan.

2. Implementing strategies to increase the sense of efficacy felt by staff and students regarding achievement at high levels.

The political complexities involved when attempting to achieve the first indicator, "Successful engagement of all staff in developing consensus on school vision, mission, goals, and objectives in the school improvement plan," include the need to reconcile very different perspectives about what the long-term goals, vision, and priorities of a school should be. This is because of different philosophies and values held by various stakeholders.

Similarly, there are political complexities when attempting to achieve the second indicator, which is "Implementing strategies to increase the sense of efficacy felt by staff and students regarding achievement at high levels." This aspect of instructional leadership has documented success when used by the Efficacy Institute, an organization with considerable success in helping schools achieve more equitable achievement outcomes among all student subgroups; their training model is built on the premise that if you don't believe you can teach certain students at high levels or don't believe the same students are capable of achieving at high levels, then these students will not likely achieve at high levels (The Efficacy Institute, 2011). The beliefs about one's ability to do "X," whatever that is, greatly affect whether you can do it. For example, many students (and teachers) don't believe they have the ability to actually learn higher level math and may have had this belief reinforced by how others taught them or what was said to them. Such a belief affects the degree of effort expended to learn or effectively teach higher level math. Personal belief systems are very important factors affecting student achievement, and instructional leaders must be capable of positively impacting the efficacy of teachers and other practitioners on the front lines, who must then be able to do the same for all students, including those historically underserved.

The POI involved when trying to improve any indicator of instructional leadership at any grade level and among any group includes creating a safe environment where the target audience can share their concerns or beliefs without fear of recrimination. Such sharing contributes to the willingness to adopt new attitudes and behaviors. Many persons may resent and resist being expected to reveal areas where they don't feel very competent or confident, because that behavior has never been part of how they engage in problem solving.

Instructional leadership includes a large number of specific behaviors and skills, all related to influencing the attitudes, knowledge, skills, and behaviors associated with providing academically rigorous instruction. Instructional leadership should not be the sole province of site and district administrators. Distributed and differentiated levels of instructional leadership are needed. Teachers and instructional support staff can serve as instructional leaders within their area of responsibility and sphere of influence, including working collaboratively with all other instructional leaders to plan and implement multifaceted action plans. Murphy (2010) makes a compelling case for much more attention to external and internal environmental causes of achievement gaps, including community, racism, out-of-school, instructional program, school culture, structure, and support issues. But there is little reference to the kind of holistic CCL needed to address these issues with any success, or the politics involved in doing so. Most preservice and on-the-job professional development programs for both administrators and teachers give scant attention if any to how to navigate the politics involved when disposed to "walk the equity talk" for historically underserved students of color.

Toxic School Climate Barrier and the Politics of Implementation

All low-performing schools where I have worked as an external evaluator had a very toxic school climate, as reflected in staff perceptions of low employee morale and cohesion, limited communication and problem-solving adequacy, inappropriate resource utilization and allocation, hierarchical decision-making processes, and no goal focus. How these dimensions of school climate were manifested was often very diverse, rather than being the same in each school. I found that these conditions in each school's work environment severely impacted the teaching and learning process as well as student educational outcomes.

Other consequences of toxic school climate in most of these schools were high staff turnover and student transiency, low staff and student efficacy related to making significant improvements in student achievement, and a lot of conflict between adults, adults and students, and between students.

The POI involved when trying to turn around such climates requires much more than negotiating school site council approval of a plan for improving school climate. There is a need to facilitate personal and organizational transformation, including changes in attitudes, self-concepts and identities, relationships, and norms, including the rituals, routines, ceremonies, and celebrations at a given school. Reversing a toxic school climate in most or all of these categories is a multiyear undertaking in most cases, requiring a mix of modeling, flexibility, consistency, perseverance, creativity, resilience, and not being driven by personal self-serving ego needs.

Limited Accountability Barrier and the Politics of Implementation

Achieving equitable educational outcomes by historically underserved students of color cannot be achieved unless there is a major shift in the degree to which all school community stakeholders are more accountable for desired outcomes. I have found very little mutually interdependent accountability by all stakeholders for those who have historically been recipients of the greatest neglect and low expectations. Mutual interdependence is an entirely different way of thinking about what leadership is and who must be engaged in practicing such leadership for success to be achieved. The context in which this goal is undertaken must receive very serious consideration in order to gain momentum in this area, because there are no cookie-cutter approaches to fostering mutual interdependence.

There are several conditions that currently exist in many schools and districts without much conscious thought about how they reflect and help perpetuate the structural and cultural inequities in American society. These conditions need more critical examination in the light of day. If not, it is not likely that accountability will be significantly expanded, and it is also not likely that expanded accountability would be any more successful than what we have at the present time.

The context in the world of school accountability for student outcomes at the present time includes 10 conditions that I have found in the low-performing schools receiving in-depth scrutiny by me. Each is very briefly described in order to draw a picture of the politics that must be maneuvered in order to remove the limited accountability barrier to achievement at high levels by those most underserved.

Some of the schooling context contributing to limited accountability:

1. CULTURAL BLINDNESS (Lindsey, Nuri Robins, & Terrell, 2003): a term applied to persons who say they do not see "color," value ignoring racial/ethnic/cultural differences, and by claiming to treat everyone the same render some invisible.

2. FEAR OF RETALIATION: a belief expressed by teachers, other staff, parents, or students based on how they think they will be treated or how they have been treated because of their cultural background, personal ethics, or what they are accused of saying, doing, or alleging that others have said/done.

3. FEAR OF STUDENTS: the feeling of some teachers about some students, based on racial stereotypes, prevalent attitudes in society, hearsay, and personal characteristics of the students in question, including the many ways students express their multiple identities.

4. EMOTIONAL AND PHYSICAL VIOLENCE: racially/culturally influenced verbal conflicts or physical fights between students, including student and teacher bullying.

5. DANCE OF THE LEMONS AND STAFFING CUTS: the administrative reassignment of teachers or other staff who have not met performance or political expectations, as well as the release of some of the most dedicated and creative teachers because they don't have the requisite seniority when budget reductions force cuts in staff.

6. MANDATES WITHOUT MONEY: state or federal requirements for compliance without the allocation of funds for carrying out the mandate; such mandates are common in special education and some curriculum reforms.

7. CLOSET SKELETONS OF "SHINING LIGHTS": persons hailed as demonstrating exemplary attitudes or behaviors related to equity, but privately exhibit prejudices, deficit thinking, low expectations, discriminatory actions, or illegally tampering with student assessment results. These private attitudes and behaviors are not commonly known and are the antithesis of accolades received; these persons might be board members, district or site administrators, teachers, parents, community residents, university faculty serving as resources to schools, and so on.

8. VICTIMOLOGY: as defined by McWhorter (2000), the silent and not so silent despair of many in historically underserved school communities or those speaking for them who feel victimized by individual and institutional racism that causes inequitable educational outcomes. Furthermore, they feel most educators do not have their best interests at heart, and accept no responsibility for the failure of historically underserved students. In some cases, I think historically underserved students and parents are justified in their conclusions about the prevalence of biases or institutional racism. However, I do not think the correct diagnosis justifies the attitude when it exists that all the fault can be attributed to educators. I reject McWhorter's insinuation that victimology in the African American community is a major factor contributing to inequitable educational outcomes. It is at least as important to examine the extent to which the victimology card is played by some educators in schools with underperforming historically underserved students who blame every toxic condition and everyone else but themselves for student underachievement.

9. CROSS-CULTURAL AND INTRACULTURAL CONFLICT DYNAMICS: the racial undertones undergirding communication between adults, adults and students, and students and students of the same or of diverse ethnic and cultural backgrounds. The dynamics are fueled by diverse life experiences, level of racial identity development, and in some cases untested assumptions about self and others; these dynamics are within racial/ethnic groups as well as across diverse groups.

10. UNCONSCIOUS INCOMPETENCE: the degree to which persons don't know what they don't know and therefore make judgments and decisions totally unaware of the negative impact they may be having on others, especially the life chances of historically underserved students. People may cause irreparable harm because of their unconscious incompetence if they aren't first helped to

become consciously incompetent on their way to becoming competent. If major efforts are undertaken to facilitate greater competence and they don't succeed within a reasonable time period, then persons may need to be counseled out of the profession. That is also an act of cultural courageousness.

Those adeptly navigating the politics of implementation must take calculated actions to confront, reduce, or eliminate the above conditions lest they cause schools to become totally dysfunctional. Such actions should include nurturing CCL among persons from various demographic and stakeholder groups. Collectively, these groups can make a substantial difference in the capacity building, political will, and savvy of their peers, leading to in-depth collaborative accountability on a much broader scale. Vignette 9-1 illustrates what one district did to successfully implement greater accountability for equity transformation.

VIGNETTE 9-1: OAK CANYON DISTRICT—
SYSTEMIC APPROACH TO EQUITY TRANSFORMATION

Oak Canyon elementary district serves a very ethnically diverse middle- to lower-middle-class population. The numbers of Asian, Black, Hispanic, and White students are almost equal in size, with a smaller population of Native and Pacific Islander students. The percentage of administrators and teachers within each of the above groups of color are within 10 percentage points of their numbers in the general population of the school district, but there are disproportionately more White teachers and administrators. The superintendent has led the district for more than 10 years and was a school psychologist in the district before becoming a district administrator. His own White ethnic background contributes to his cultural sensitivity and value of cultural diversity. His professional background has contributed to the orientation he has toward what is necessary to facilitate greater expertise in teaching ethnically/culturally diverse children at high levels. The tenure he has in his role speaks to his political acumen and ability to adapt to changing conditions.

For example, the demographic makeup of his district has dramatically changed in the last 10 years. Oak Canyon administrators are nurtured in developing cultural proficiency (Lindsey, Nuri Robins, & Terrell, 1999) under the superintendent's tutelage, and held accountable for nurturing the same in others. The superintendent has deliberately given high priority to implementing courageous conversations on race (Singleton & Linton, 2006) and requiring follow-up in policy and practices at all levels. The accountability for doing so has been both implicit and explicit. Many of the above conditions listed under schooling context that contribute to limited accountability have been openly addressed and changed. Structural and cultural inequities have also been openly addressed by staff at all levels. Potential conflicts have been anticipated and in some cases defused. There has been systematic implementation of systemic change that fosters equity. Improving the political savvy to implement accountability for equity has been a major priority. Such savvy has included strategies for making sure all district stakeholders are on board. Equity transformation has been approached as a systemwide undertaking requiring buy-in and leadership by all stakeholder groups.

MAKE IT PERSONAL

FN9–5 (SEE FACILITATOR NOTES IN APPENDIX 1)

1. Describe how limited accountability for equitable educational outcomes is currently manifested in your school or district.

2. How do you try to navigate the politics of implementation when attempting to improve accountability for equitable educational outcomes?

Sixth Dimension of POI: Prevent "Equity Hustlers" From Compromising Equity Efforts

Navigating the politics of implementation is a very complex undertaking when attempting to foster equitable educational outcomes. It is important to not depend on or inappropriately delegate important tasks to persons who are wanksters, gangsters, or riders, three terms originally conceptualized by Duncan-Andrade (2007) that I have redefined. Persons who play these roles can be of any cultural/racial background in any stakeholder group. In addition, educational or community organizations, including school districts and universities in the public or private sector, can be equity hustlers insofar as they engage in any of the same practices described in this chapter as individual behaviors. This is especially true in the *wankster* category when there are conscious efforts to convey a false impression of support for equitable educational inputs and outcomes, perhaps for "public relations" reasons, without any commitment to do what is necessary to achieve such equity. Such duplicity may even include use of equity consultants or implementation of superficial practices that do not include attention to deeply imbedded institutional policies reflecting cultural hegemony.

Wanksters are individuals who deceive, dissemble, and don't show up. They espouse cultural awareness, sensitivity, and willingness to take risks beyond their personal comfort zone but always have excuses when it is time to take action. They are cultural hypocrites who do not practice what they preach or "walk the talk." Wanksters want to be perceived as supportive of equity reforms that improve the quality of education for underserved students as long as it doesn't involve any change in power, authority, and control norms. However, when it comes time for them to follow through on any commitments made, they have a lot of excuses and provide only tepid follow-through, if any. To avoid being surprised or ambushed by "wanksters," the culturally courageous leader must provide multiple opportunities for persons who ostensibly support equity to practice "walking the talk" under their close supervision.

The teacher, administrator, board member, or parent who is attracted to giving the impression they are totally committed to social justice may only be willing to do that if they don't have to act on such claims. Or they may not want their true feelings about equity to be exposed, because of the criticism to which they would be subjected. In addition, they could also desire the personal power and popularity that might be accorded them because of being viewed erroneously as a champion of the historically underserved. However, they may have an even greater fear of strong push back from those who want to protect the privileges some have under the present system where inequitable student outcomes have been the norm.

Gangsters are individuals who steal, exploit, or act in fraudulent ways. They may align themselves with those trying to walk the talk, or form partnerships with and provide technical support to those actually walking the talk. However, their ultimate purpose is ripping off the ideas of genuine courageous leaders for their own personal gain and taking the ideas as their own. The ultimate goal of the gangster is to steal the ideas of others to strengthen their credibility or image by creating the illusion they support something they don't. It is important to determine the integrity of persons who seek to enter into partnerships with you.

Persons who seek a working relationship with someone who has expertise in facilitating equity leadership and then use what they learn for their own purposes and gain are gangsters when they take credit for what they have learned without attribution to the real source.

Riders are individuals who totally associate with the efforts of the culturally courageous leader. They use the same rhetoric and simulate walking the talk, but they ride the coattails of those genuinely involved. The riders are with the courageous leader as long as they don't have to lead the effort. They feed off of the courageous leader's passion and energy and want to be part of the "team." However, they like being in the background when it is time to walk the talk, letting someone else do all the risk taking or heavy lifting. They are like the person riding on the back of a two-person bike, with the person at the front of the bike doing all of the pedaling. Riders are incapable of working independently or leading any effort on their own. They may have the technical skills to do so, but not the psychological comfort and self-confidence, efficacy, and willingness needed. They need a lot of coaching and support.

It is important to keep "riders" under close surveillance but not avoid any contact. As with the wankster above, create situations where you can assess what persons are willing to actually do and can do well. Engage them in planning some joint leadership activity and then step back and encourage them to take on a more visible leading role, so you can see what happens.

MAKE IT PERSONAL

FN9–6 (SEE FACILITATOR NOTES IN APPENDIX 1)

1. Assume you are going to start practicing CCL by joining others leading an effort to implement a particular equity initiative. Based on your assessment of the politics in your school community when it comes to the equity initiative you are about to undertake, describe at least two actions or strategies in your work plan in each of the next three years.

2. What are your greatest fears/concerns about taking the initiative to co-lead an equity initiative, and what would you do to alleviate your concerns?

REVIEW OF CHAPTER 9

- The terms personal transformation and organizational transformation are defined, as is the relationship between the two. Personal transformation may include major changes in values, cultural lenses, assumptions, and priorities, all of which are part of one's identity, when it comes to such actions as embracing anti-racism, shedding any colorblind or assimilationist ideologies, and fighting for eliminating other forms of oppression. Organizational transformation includes attention to eradicating any policies, norms, and practices related to teaching and learning that keep historically underserved students in subservient roles.

- Examples of some sacred cows and other politics that can stymie such transformation are board member practices; some schools populated by those with the most social, political, and cultural capital; and certain programs funded by huge grants or government funds.

- The politics of adeptly navigating the implementation of any equity improvements involves addressing six dimensions: engage in problem definition and analysis, be sensitive to the psychology of equity transformation, focus on standards categories receiving inadequate priority, use personal or others' observations from trying to implement previous equity initiatives, reduce some key barriers to high achievement by all students, and gracefully eliminate any negative influence caused by "wanksters," "gangsters," and "riders."

Stakeholder
Practices

10

*Every stakeholder group has a unique role to play, but they must all be bound
by the unswerving commitment to cultural democracy and social justice for all.*

A unique feature of the culturally courageous leadership (CCL) paradigm is the
inclusiveness and respect for all stakeholder groups having a meaningful role
in collaborative efforts to achieve both equity and excellence for all students.
Although there are some unique practices each stakeholder group must be willing to
perform, the work of all must be complementary and synergistic.

Some of the behaviors and practices of each stakeholder group are similar to
what any group would do to strengthen their group functioning and effectiveness in
working well together. Some are very specific to what is required of equity advocates
in public education, and others are influenced by the history of race relations and
oppression in the United States.

KWL EXERCISE

1. What are your ideas about how each stakeholder group identified in the guide
   can practice CCL?

2. What are the questions you would like answered by a trusted colleague who
   is giving you advice on how to improve three of your behaviors you consider
   examples of CCL?

3. Identify the major understandings and concerns you have about navigating
   the politics when walking the equity talk.

EXAMPLES OF CCL PRACTICES BY
ALL STAKEHOLDER GROUPS

The CCL paradigm is a *collaborative* undertaking within and across the following diverse stakeholder groups:

- board of education members,
- district and site administrators,
- teachers,
- instructional support staff,
- parents/guardians,
- community persons,
- university faculty in teacher and administrator preparation programs, and
- students.

A stakeholder group is composed of individuals with a similar role in the educational enterprise, and all stakeholder groups should have a vested interest in the quality of education provided to all students. However, there are often conflicting perspectives within and across stakeholder groups in their interpretation of events and perceived causes, needs, problems, and solutions. Students, appropriate university faculty, parents, and other community persons must have representatives who are actively engaged in this collaborative undertaking. The voices of all stakeholder groups must be legitimized, heard, and utilized.

In this guide, a major postulate is that equitable educational outcomes cannot be achieved and sustained without greater collaboration among and new kinds of leadership by all of the above stakeholder groups. Each group must feel empowered to share their perspectives about counterproductive and constructive attitudes and behaviors of persons in their group and in other stakeholder groups. But sharing is not enough. That is only the first step. Once everyone's "voice" has been heard, and understood, the larger task is to collectively decide upon equitable educational inputs and strategies to implement that are aimed at achieving equitable educational outcomes. Every stakeholder group must have persons who are vested in working individually and collectively to make this happen. A critical mass of culturally courageous leaders from all stakeholder groups is needed to achieve and sustain social justice, but a critical mass is not necessarily a majority in each group on all occasions. However, I have found it very helpful when at least 30% in each group are "flying in sync and in the same direction" so to speak.

In a nutshell, culturally courageous leaders must be willing to critically examine and transcend the cultural influences in their own life that may have resulted in personal biases toward others that severely compromise their ability to work together in the best interests of all students. During the course of seeking equitable educational outcomes and social justice, such leadership also requires the willingness to collaboratively identify, confront, and change organizational norms and barriers, such as the "isms" and biases already discussed in this guide. Can there be a complete transformation of schools without efforts to make similar changes in the community? I think not, but major considerations are timing and readiness.

To reiterate, the modus operandi of culturally courageous leaders is to not be limited by their personal cultural influences or the culture of school organizations, when either or both are major obstacles to equity and excellence for all. People in school communities who claim to be totally committed to social justice must be culturally courageous in order to enlist others to join with them in taking anti-racist initiatives and in order to withstand the inevitable pressures to go with the flow and maintain the status quo.

Examples of practices by each stakeholder group enable the reader to have some concrete ideas of what CCL might look and feel like. These examples by no means totally describe the scope of CCL.

Board of Education Members Practicing CCL

1. Demonstrate the willingness to work on practicing the four components of CCL as appropriate in their board functioning.

2. Try to be a model of CCL for others to emulate, in both public meetings and executive sessions.

3. Secure board development (i.e., professional development for board of education members) that focuses on how boards can improve their leadership to improving cultural democracy and achieving equitable educational outcomes.

4. Initiate and agree to a vision and strategic plan for the entire district that articulates a commitment to equity and excellence for all, including goals, objectives, and activities for the board of education.

5. Make sure there is language in the superintendent's contract for how that person and his/her senior staff will be held accountable for achieving specific measurable outcomes in all categories of equitable educational outcomes.

6. Convene meetings of executive staff and a very representative community-wide advisory panel, and charge the group to conduct public hearings throughout the school district, with media coverage, on analysis of extent to which there are efforts being made to achieve equitable educational outcomes and the progress/problems being experienced.

7. Solicit advice from the advisory panel on specific policies, procedures, and practices that need to be changed because they mitigate against equitable educational outcomes.

8. Require the superintendent and senior staff to make semiannual reports on progress in achieving equitable educational outcomes based on benchmark assessments. Require simultaneous contingency planning to take place so that backup plans are in place if initial efforts don't succeed.

9. Seek technical assistance from appropriate scholars representing diverse cultural perspectives and from organizations specializing in educational equity on what provisions related to equity should be in the accountability language for the superintendent and senior staff.

10. In collaboration with the superintendent, reach out to culturally diverse officials in the public and private sectors at local, state, and national levels to develop partnerships and joint ventures that will contribute to achieving equitable educational outcomes.

11. Personally engage in advocacy of equitable inputs and educational outcomes, acknowledge the role of cultural hegemony and other ideologies that are counterproductive, report on progress toward achieving equity when visiting school sites in the district, and when meeting with/making speeches to student, parent, business, and community groups in the school district.

12. Make sure the voices of students, parents, and teachers are heard and represented in the design and implementation of equity transformation initiatives.

District and Site Administrators Practicing CCL

1. Are open to redefining their personal and learned meanings of what constitutes leadership when it comes to improving cultural democracy and achieving equitable educational inputs and outcomes, including how they will foster distributed "dense" leadership for equity among teachers and other stakeholders (Krovetz & Arriaza, 2006).

2. Take appropriate risks in being more explicit and candid when sharing their concerns and vision, and when providing feedback to others on attitudes, behaviors, and norms related to the "isms" and biases practiced in district and school functioning.

3. Elicit diverse student perspectives on how the "isms" and biases are manifested in curriculum, instruction, and school functioning.

4. Give high priority to trust and teambuilding, and being authentic during communication with and among all stakeholders in all work and school community settings.

5. Demonstrate a sense of genuine urgency and laser-like focus when identifying and eradicating obstacles to equitable educational outcomes.

6. Model the kind of visioning, conflict management, and accountability expected from other school district staff, including guidance on corrective actions needed.

7. Are unrelenting in efforts to convince staff and community of the need to be totally on board with the priority of achieving equitable educational outcomes.

8. Help each other and persons in all stakeholder groups develop capacity in their areas of need related to achieving equity.

9. Increase as well as integrate into all supervision and evaluation practices accountability language related to implementation of all five standards categories.

10. Accept no excuses for unprofessional, incompetent, or mediocre performance by self or others related to the achievement of equitable outcomes.

11. Facilitate skilled peer mentoring of all educators on challenges of practice related to diverse learners (Achinstein & Barralt, 2004).

12. Leave no stone unturned when investigating and eradicating instances of bias or discrimination in school functioning.

13. Recognize CCL as a journey, not a destination, which requires constant learning and growth in cultural awareness, cultural proficiency, culturally courageous instructional leadership, cross-cultural conflict mediation, and building transformational relationships.

14. Collaboratively engage in institutionalizing change forces which identify and weed out anything working against equitable educational outcomes, such as resource allocations, curricula and instruction, personnel selection, and professional development practices.

Teachers Practicing CCL

1. Care for students as if they are their own, helping all students feel needed, wanted, empowered, and an important member of a learning community (Corbett & Wilson, 2002).

2. Directly address examples of cultural oppression in the United States, past and present, as well as student beliefs about diversity to correct any miseducation that has occurred.

3. Engage in critical self-reflection about whether they practice aversive racism (Gaertner & Davidio, 1986), based on inconsistency between espoused support of equity and negative beliefs about Black and other students of color, and dysconscious racism (King, 1991), which is uncritical acceptance of White privilege, accompanied by a justification of inequity.

4. Resist pressure from any source to not go the extra mile for underserved students, including providing above and beyond tutorial support for those with the greatest need, or working with those providing such support to ensure there is strong articulation between tutoring and what is transpiring in the classroom.

5. Publicly challenge and seek peer support to change school norms, such as cultural hegemony, that contributes to the underachievement of those historically underserved.

6. Negotiate the political contexts of their school and district policies in appropriate legal ways so they can challenge, accommodate, and subvert the local and federal constraints of testing and scripted programs (Achinstein & Ogawa, 2006; Kavanagh, 2010).

7. Constantly seek to increase personal and peers' cultural knowledge and skills that can enhance their ability to create culturally relevant curricula and implement culturally responsive teaching that honors the multiple identities of students as well as the ways they are expressed (Gay, 2010; Murrell, 2008, 2000; Ponterotto, Utsey, & Pedersen, 2006).

8. Lobby teacher preparation programs to include more emphasis on race and culture as well as how to identify and combat any of the "isms" and biases in preK–12 educational settings.

9. Engage in collaborative leadership with other school community stakeholders, including engaging students in knowledge construction, so there is a united effort to achieve equitable educational outcomes (Krovetz & Arriaza, 2006).

10. Utilize a social action approach during the teaching and learning process which helps students develop the critical consciousness and academic skills enabling them to study and learn how to be agents of social change to improve oppressive conditions in their everyday lives and communities (Banks & Banks, 2003; Cochran-Smith, 2004; Duncan-Andrade & Morrell, 2008).

11. Improve their understanding of the life worlds of English language learners (ELLs) and build more meaningful relationships with them by bringing transnational and community literacies into the classroom curriculum to build upon students' prior knowledge and facilitate ELL youth becoming more fully engaged in language, literacy, and content area learning (Jimenez, Smith, & Teague, 2009).

12. Utilize the literature from appropriate cultural diversity scholars, and direct assistance from local university faculty in teacher preparation programs who have the expertise and commitment.

Instructional Support Staff Practicing CCL

1. Help teachers customize their instructional plans for historically underserved students, take into consideration culturally influenced learner characteristics, learning styles, and cognitive processing (how cultural background influences information processing).

2. Help teachers diagnose historically underserved students' immediate academic and personal needs, particularly those with special needs, and help customize one-on-one or small group tutorial assistance provided to the same students based on the results of such diagnoses.

3. Assist teacher efforts to build stronger reciprocal communication and problem solving between the school and home, especially with the families of historically underserved students.

Parents/Guardians Practicing CCL

1. Attempt to communicate with parents of the same or of different ethnic/cultural backgrounds, to discover mutual concerns/priorities and share ideas on how the school can improve.

2. Engage in efforts to mobilize parents and community members in support of educators who demonstrate the competence to meet the academic needs of historically underserved students.

3. Participate in coalitions and community organizing with other parents and school community stakeholders on mutually shared goals related to helping achieve equitable educational outcomes for all students.

4. Actively serve as a parent activist, making efforts to increase personal knowledge and communication skills that will help parents monitor school effectiveness, the educational progress of one's children as well as all student groups, and the teaching and learning process experienced by students of different backgrounds.

Community Persons* Practicing CCL

*Members of community-based organizations, including churches and businesses.

1. Increase their knowledge about racial achievement disparities and other inequitable educational outcomes, as well as factors contributing to these inequitable outcomes and the consequences.

2. Form coalitions with other school community stakeholders to lobby boards of education for new educational policies and practices that help increase educators' capacity and commitment to achieve equitable educational outcomes.

3. Provide diverse community perspectives to school districts on needs that must be addressed to improve the district's vision and mission related to equity, including the educational inputs and outcomes experienced by historically underserved students.

4. Seek support within their organizations for initiating or expanding such community-based programs as tutorial assistance and academic enrichment, including cultural heritage activities.

University Faculty in Teacher and Administrator Preparation Programs Who Practice CCL

1. Conduct research in collaboration with school districts and school community stakeholders that identifies schooling conditions contributing to inequitable educational outcomes, and strategies for diminishing the conditions identified.

2. Identify the most salient aspects of equity transformation efforts that contribute to equitable educational outcomes.

3. Assist school districts to implement corrective actions based on research findings.

4. Give priority attention to equity research findings, including those from scholars guided by critical race theory, when teaching future teachers or administrators.

5. Help students become adept in conducting similar research.

6. Spend time on a regular basis in schools with underperforming historically underserved students of color to increase personal knowledge and frame of reference about the schooling conditions contributing to student underachievement.

7. Use personal observations and insights to revise teacher or administrator preparation programs so future educators are better prepared to negotiate the politics associated with achieving equitable educational outcomes.

8. Engage in joint efforts and partnerships with school community stakeholders from historically underserved groups of color.

9. Expand synergistic efforts that improve preservice and on-the-job capacity building related to helping teachers and administrators become "multiculturally proficient" so they give priority to both academically rigorous cultural responsiveness and the ability to engage youth in "situated learning" outside the traditional classroom (Murrell, 2000).

10. Help prepare future teachers and administrators to develop the skills necessary to provide leadership for equity, including the ability to identify and critique attitudes and practices of self and others that perpetuate cultural hegemony in educational practice.

Students (Grades 4–12) Practicing CCL

1. Share on an ongoing basis with the principal or designee specific reasons for their likes, dislikes, concerns, and problems associated with school in order to improve the school for all students.

2. Enhance leadership skills by participating in a group of students in their school that helps resolve or manage student conflicts or other disciplinary problems and helps the school be more responsive to the needs of all students.

3. Work with adults in the school and the community to improve student attitudes about school and student motivation/effort to do their best in school.

4. Participate in experiential activities that improve respect for persons of all cultural and racial backgrounds.

5. Actively participate in learning activities that increase personal knowledge and appreciation for their own cultural/ethnic heritage and that of others in the larger society.

6. Develop the knowledge and skills necessary as well as take actions to help improve the living conditions and social justice in their own neighborhoods and school communities.

❧

MAJOR STRANDS IN CCL PRACTICES ACROSS ALL STAKEHOLDER GROUPS

CCL involves seven major strands, regardless of the stakeholder group. The strands are increased *communication* within and across racial, cultural, and same role groups; participation in *problem-solving* activities related to equity transformation; *collaboration* among stakeholders within groups and across groups; *increased knowledge* about cultural diversity; taking *leadership initiatives* to increase support for underachieving students; *helping empower* other stakeholders within their group and in other groups; and *modeling* the kind of attitudes and behaviors desired in others. These behaviors, in total, could enhance personal and organizational transformation if the politics of implementation are successfully navigated by all adult stakeholder groups working in concert with each other.

MAKE IT PERSONAL

FN10-1 (SEE FACILITATOR NOTES IN APPENDIX 1)

1. Identify those behaviors listed for your stakeholder group with which you agree, those you have implemented, and those listed for other stakeholder groups you consider most important.

2. Identify other CCL behaviors you think would be equally important for any stakeholder group.

REVIEW OF CHAPTER 10

The following topics were discussed in this chapter:

- The importance of stakeholder groups working collaboratively.

- An elaboration with specifics on what is meant by CCL, as practiced by different stakeholder groups.

- Examples of CCL that might be manifested by persons in the following eight stakeholder groups within school communities: board of education members, district and school site administrators, teachers, instructional support staff, parents/guardians, community persons, university faculty in teacher and administrator preparation programs, and students.

- Seven major strands in CCL practices across all stakeholder groups.

Promising Departures **11**

*There are qualitative differences in both the self-identity of
school communities that have sustained an elimination of achievement
disparities and in the degree to which they "walk the equity talk."*

A growing number of schools that serve historically underserved students in the United States provide all of them with educational experiences that reflect both equity and excellence in educational practices and outcomes. In these schools, there are some promising departures from the grim continuities discussed in Chapter 3 of this guide. This chapter details the findings of Joseph F. Johnson (2007, 2010) and Karin Chenoweth (2007) about schools that are "getting it done," and how such educational results are achieved. To some extent, the achieving schools they discuss are implementing the culturally courageous leadership (CCL) paradigm. The reports of Johnson and Chenoweth have been chosen because each of them did extensive on-site examinations of the conditions, attitudes, behaviors, and policies they describe in their work. They utilized a rigorous on-site process including use of rubrics, observations, interviews, and examination of data, to identify "achieving schools."

These "achieving schools" have developed environments where staff, students, parents, and community members feel respected and meaningfully involved in collaboratively making classrooms more successful places for everyone. This is occurring among very diverse students of color who have traditionally been "historically underserved." The schools are throughout the United States, and their success in eliminating the racial achievement gap is a major achievement, given from whence they started.

KWL EXERCISE

1. What are three educational practices you have used or know about that significantly contribute to eliminating achievement gaps experienced by historically underserved students?

2. Which of the following categories of strategies that have contributed to eliminating gaps in educational outcomes is of greatest interest to you: board of education/district-level strategies, instructional strategies, school environment/climate conditions, or school site leadership strategies?

3. What, if any, relationships do you see between the "5A's" discussed in this chapter and the four components of CCL discussed in Chapters 7 through 10?

ᐧᐧᐧ

CHARACTERISTICS OF SCHOOLS
THAT HAVE ELIMINATED THE GAP

The chart below introduces the variables, needs, and prerequisites that Johnson (2007) found necessary for schools to become high achieving.

Johnson feels the interplay between *relationships, curriculum,* and *instruction* are of critical importance to school success. He emphasized how they must intertwine in ways that make learning exciting and fun.

For example, relationships are greatly influenced by school climate as well as student, teacher, and parent beliefs regarding how others feel about them in the school. Such feelings and relationships may or may not contribute to a collaborative focus by teachers on academic rigor and depth, rather than superficial and shallow treatment of subject matter.

In high-performing schools, instruction is punctuated by frequent checks for understanding and connections with student interests, backgrounds, cultures, and

Chart 11a Some Variables, Needs, and Prerequisites of High-Achieving Schools

Variables	Needs	Prerequisites
Strong interpersonal and intergroup relationships	Need to believe success is likely with required effort	A sense of urgency for improvement: priority given to corrective actions and no excuses
Rigorous and relevant curriculum	Need to have great clarity about goals, objectives, strategies, benchmarks, and consistency in the efforts taken	Everyone has responsibility for improvement: high expectations for self and others
Culturally responsive instruction	Need to have support from all stakeholders	Collective efficacy regarding improvement: willing to adopt new attitudes and behaviors in concert with others

prior knowledge. The relationships among all stakeholders contribute to the formal and hidden curriculum, and vice versa. When there is open, honest, and respectful communication between all stakeholders, the high levels of trust between all groups might contribute to making curriculum and instruction more culturally relevant, more effective management of any conflict, and higher expectations of as well as support for all students.

The interface between the variables in chart 11a is also influenced by the extent to which the three needs listed in the chart are all met. These needs are prevalent whatever the equity initiative being pursued and may be more pressing when initiatives focus on correcting past injustices contributing to racial achievement disparities. I have found that all three of these needs are rarely met before most equity initiatives are undertaken.

Johnson points out that successful schools also meet certain prerequisites that enable key conditions he calls the "5 A's:" attitude, access, assessment, adaptation, and accountability. There is a strong symbiotic relationship between prerequisites and conditions. Without a sense of urgency, responsibility, and efficacy, there is not likely to be a commitment to nurturing certain attitude, accessibility, assessment, adaptability, and accountability norms.

Prerequisites

Example of "Urgency"

Valley View Junior-Senior High is the oldest secondary school in its community, and 100 years ago was attended by White students from the wealthiest families in the city. In the last 40 years, there has been a major change in the demographic makeup of the student population and the dropout rate for students of color is now almost 50%. The new principal appointed a year ago has successfully encouraged several retirements and transfers, allowing him to recruit a more diverse and skilled faculty. The school has improved communication with the home, involved parents and students with faculty in collaborative problem solving, and more faculty involvement in decision making related to scheduling, program, and professional development. The sense of urgency related to academic performance of all student subgroups has greatly increased.

Example of "Responsibility"

Hunter's Creek Elementary was losing its strongest students after the second grade because parents thought the teachers were not as responsive to student academic needs. After Hunter's Creek became a program improvement school, the administration secured staff consensus on a plan with a revised vision and mission that spelled out the responsibility of all teachers, instructional and administrative support staff, parents, and students for helping improve academic performance. Benchmark indicators were established for all stakeholder groups. For example, one benchmark indicator for parents was the expectation they engage in 5 hours of on-site school activities each semester.

Example of Efficacy

Most teachers at the small Sherman K–3 school initially became very uncomfortable with major student population changes. Fifteen years ago, Sherman students were primarily from native-born African American families. Then, as the population in the school community drastically changed, large numbers of Latino/a students enrolled in the school. Sherman now has a majority of limited English speaking students from recently arrived immigrant families of Mexican, Central American, and East African descent. When this population change occurred, most teachers had limited experience with and confidence in their ability to effectively teach the recently arrived students. A new principal was appointed the same year the school was designated a program improvement school because of low test scores. After 3 years of curriculum and instructional reform efforts and some intense professional development, there was a substantial improvement in the collective sense of efficacy. Teachers of all racial backgrounds began to believe in their ability to effectively teach all Sherman students.

As described above:

- having a sense of urgency for reduction/elimination of achievement disparities suggests giving ongoing priority to corrective actions and not accepting any excuses;
- having a sense of responsibility for equitable educational outcomes suggests the willingness of all to "walk the equity talk," including the demonstration of high expectations for self and others, and being flexible by making adjustments as needed; and
- having a collective sense of efficacy suggests all stakeholders being confident, thorough, supportive, and willing to adopt new attitudes and behaviors in concert with others in the school community.

These "prerequisites" of urgency, responsibility, and collective efficacy for successful schools make it possible, but not a certainty, for the "5 A's," a small sample of which are listed in charts 11b–f. Johnson and Chenoweth found very similar conditions in schools where the achievement gap was eliminated or significantly reduced. When Johnson refers to leaders, he is not just talking about district and school site administrators; he is also talking about other leaders in the school community, such as teachers, parents, and community members.

Conditions: The "5 A's"

Chart 11b Attitude

Johnson Found in Schools That Serve Diverse Student Groups Well:	Chenoweth Found That High-Performing Schools:
1. Educators believe they can make a difference in the lives of all children.	Have . . . constantly rising expectations for teachers, and teachers have high expectations for students. . . . Failure is not . . . an option.
2. There is a vision of academic excellence for all students and they believe they have the capacity to make the vision reality.	Believe students are capable of excellence.
3. Leaders collect information that helps them know how to improve relational issues. They identify and resolve issues promptly and professionally.	Make sure students understand what they are expected to do.
4. Respectfully, but clearly, administrators and teacher leaders speak out when others claim that goals are unattainable. Leaders use research and data to focus on opportunities to improve, not on reasons to blame.	Have teachers who believe it is their job to help all students meet high standards.
5. Leaders push beyond compliance and encourage everyone to embrace goals that will make a difference in students' lives.	[Are places where] teachers talk to students at all levels about the consequences of not getting a good education.
6. Leaders give students, parents, teachers, and support staff reasons to believe that their efforts are worthwhile.	Spend. . . . more time "leading" students, in such areas as the expression of kindness and consideration. . . . and how to disagree with someone without getting upset and fighting.
7. Frequently, leaders celebrate improvements (both formally and informally). They find elements of success worth celebrating in results others see as failure.	[Teach] . . . older students . . . to be role models for younger students.
8. Leaders create platforms for the leadership of many others who want to influence school improvement. Leaders distribute leadership opportunities in ways that build the capacity of individuals to contribute to the school's success.	[Are places where] . . . students, teachers, and parents are treated with respect.
9. School boards model leadership that builds strong climates.	

(Continued)

Chart 11b (Continued)

Johnson Found in Schools That Serve Diverse Student Groups Well:	Chenoweth Found That High-Performing Schools:
10. School boards insist upon data collection efforts that include measures of school climate and use these data in assessing improvement efforts.	
11. School boards promote training opportunities for school and district leaders that emphasize the leader's role in improving climate.	
12. School boards give special attention to improvement and growth, and maximize attention to the teams of individuals who generate growth.	
13. School boards carefully scrutinize and modify policies that might lead students, parents, and teachers to give up.	
14. Educators understand the power of mutual respect.	
15. Cultures are created in which trust is commonplace.	
16. Educators perceive that they are valued as part of an effective team.	
17. Powerful collaborations are fostered that make individuals feel supported and valued. These collaborations lead to a strong sense of efficacy: a feeling that "together, we can accomplish anything!"	
18. Educators develop programs and practices that help students learn to value each other and the diverse groups of students in their community and in the world.	
19. Educators build student leadership that reinforces acceptance of others.	

Many educators may reflect the prevalent attitude in the United States that students of color do not have the capacity to achieve excellence. However, Johnson and Chenoweth found that teachers who value working together in their efforts to help all students achieve academic excellence are changing a long-standing norm of teacher practice in American education.

An aspect of CCL is demonstrated when teachers take the risk to confront and change any personal or organizational norms getting in the way of collectively helping all students achieve at high levels. When teachers engage in joint lesson planning that includes integration of culturally responsive instructional strategies into the teaching of core academic subjects, they are likely changing both personal and organizational practices.

There is a growing trend toward the creation of teacher professional learning communities (PLCs) in schools for collaborative lesson planning and problem solving. However, more research is needed to ascertain if this practice results in more equitable educational outcomes. A popular belief is that when teachers develop shared values and vision, and when principals engage teachers in information sharing, decision making, and authority, there is a greater likelihood that equity practices will be implemented in classrooms. However, this is not necessarily the case. There are many schools with PLCs, who have shared decision making and authority, that are not exemplars of achievement at high levels by historically underserved students. In my experience, such schools studiously avoid any ongoing focused attention on the impact of race and culture. However, Jackson's study (2010) found a correlation between teacher classroom practices associated with educational equity when teachers perceived the PLCs in which they participated helped increase their shared values and vision.

Many teachers are uncomfortable discussing issues of race and culture in professional development activities, and have had little experience, prior training, or support on how to improve cultural responsiveness in their teaching (Nieto, 2007). In addition, many do not believe such strategies contribute to improved academic outcomes by students of color and do not embrace the idea that it is important for all students to experience greater integration of multiethnic content into the curriculum.

The synergistic effect of teachers building upon each other's ideas on how they can demonstrate high expectations for all and push every child to excel can be very positive. For example, frequent checking for student understanding through a variety of means might be strengthened through more teacher collaboration.

However, teachers must be receptive to participating in problem-solving discussions that explicitly focus on the relationship between race, culture, socioeconomic status, primary language, and educational outcomes experienced by historically underserved students. Such activities stretch many teachers beyond their comfort zone and may challenge some of their existing beliefs and behaviors. Personal and organizational biases will likely be surfaced, which can lead to consideration of whether institutional racism is at play. From my work with schools on these issues, I have found many teachers are very uncomfortable with participation in such discussions. In the high-performing schools studied by Johnson and Chenoweth, the attitudes of all school community stakeholders are of critical importance to their success.

Educators who create educational environments in which trust is commonplace have taken a major step in creating a collaborative culture. Successful collaboration by all school community stakeholders can only occur when there is a high degree of mutual respect and trust. This is far from being a common condition in schools where there are grossly inequitable outcomes experienced by historically underserved students. Such a condition suggests there is a need for commitment to constant work on strengthening interpersonal communication skills; soliciting the input, opinions, and concerns of others; and then incorporating their ideas and concerns into final strategies.

Having a high degree of mutual respect and trust is a monumental achievement in any work setting, but especially in schools, whether the staff is from diverse cultural, racial, and linguistic backgrounds or is more homogeneous. In either case, staff usually have varying levels of professional experience and very different life experiences. In some schools, the school climate and dynamics of difference are such that some veterans have inordinate power and influence, and the concerns and feelings of those less experienced or of "different" backgrounds are less well received, even totally discounted.

Educators who perceive being valued as part of an effective team are much more motivated and committed to each other and to achieving their goal. An indicator of personal transformation, which is part of CCL, may be occurring when individuals are willing to let go of personal agendas or pet peeves and work as a team. In many schools, a commitment by individual staff members to personal transformation is necessary for open and honest discussions on how race, culture, and institutional bias impact student achievement. In other cases, such discussions can contribute to persons making a commitment to personal transformation. However, neither personal nor organizational transformation can alone suffice for the achievement of equitable educational outcomes. Each is necessary for such outcomes to be achieved and sustained.

MAKE IT PERSONAL

1. In school communities with which you are familiar, what conditions are most toxic and compromise any efforts to build greater trust among all stakeholders, including support staff, parents, and students?

2. In your opinion, what kind of leadership is needed to build greater trust within and across all stakeholder groups?

In this guide, disagreements are defined as conflicts and reflect the "dynamics of difference," since all individuals have unique life experiences and circumstances that may influence their perspective and priorities in any given situation. However, when educators can handle any disagreements in a respectful, professional manner, that can have a very positive impact on their collective ability to solve the most challenging constraints to achievement at high levels by all students.

In many schools, low and high performing, a norm of respectful, professional conflict management is not always evident, especially when the school and the school community are populated by persons who have diverse cultural, racial, linguistic, and socioeconomic backgrounds. Gladwell (2008) discusses how one's cultural background (including race, ethnicity, gender. nationality, socioeconomic status, age, and social psychological variables) greatly contributes to "cultural legacies." One's cultural legacies can influence how one communicates when in conflict with "different" others, especially in a work context. However, Gladwell thinks training can help people to act in counterintuitive ways. He documents how communication can be contaminated and costly misunderstandings occur when the persons communicating are overly influenced, sometimes involuntarily, by the history of their different levels of social or economic status, power, and authority.

Achieving a norm of respectful communication is a daunting task, and more open, honest, and respectful responses to human differences may require a new paradigm of leadership being modeled and taught in educational settings. New ways of thinking and acting are needed by both adults and students in Grades K–12.

Collaboration is key to increasing mutual feelings of respect and support. Through collaboration in an environment of trust, people can develop a strong belief in their ability to accomplish things that heretofore haven't been accomplished. However, mutual respect, support, and collaboration can also result in a total rejection of social justice goals and cultural democracy in schools. It depends on the beliefs and values of the persons. Collaboration that leads to equitable student outcomes must include a commitment to certain key principles, discussed in Chapter 8.

MAKE IT PERSONAL

FN11-1 (SEE FACILITATOR NOTES IN APPENDIX 1)

1. As you reflect on successful collaborative efforts regarding student achievement in which you have been involved, what were some of the major conditions and/or activities that led to all participants feeling supported and valued?

2. What is your pattern of behavior when you personally experience interpersonal conflict in a work setting, whether it be in the classroom, in a staff meeting, or one-on-one with a colleague?

Within any state and within school districts, there are many competing ideas about when there is a need for integration of cultural content into curriculum and instruction. One school of thought may be based on the belief that discussing diversity is only needed when there are obvious conflicts that are causing schools or classrooms to become dysfunctional. However, the absence of major overt conflict does not mean students are being prepared to maximize their potential in the larger society or know who they really are.

Such systematic efforts should not be peripheral to the mainstream curriculum and instructional process, but an integral part of it. Both personal and organizational transformation are prerequisites for such programs and practices to become an ongoing reality, primarily because of the history of race and cultural relations between various population groups in the United States and the history of public education as well.

Positive student leadership is of critical importance in both elementary and secondary school settings. When there is a concerted effort by educators to build student leadership that values human differences of all kinds, the dynamics of difference (how people think, feel, and act toward each other) and classroom learning environments are positively impacted.

MAKE IT PERSONAL

1. What personal leadership do you provide to help your school community discard old prejudices and discriminatory practices that are part of the history of race and cultural relations between various population groups in the United States?

2. What consequences have you experienced when making such leadership efforts?

3. As you reflect on your work with students, what stands out as most noteworthy when it comes to nurturing student leadership that simultaneously increases self-acceptance, academic motivation, and valuing of others?

4. To what extent have you found that student self-acceptance significantly contributes to academic motivation and valuing of others?

One of the major frustrations of many well-meaning teachers is their perceived inability to overcome the constraints to providing all students with access to challenging academic coursework. Most students of all backgrounds are more motivated to do their best when they see a relationship between prior knowledge, life experiences, and what they are being taught; when they are challenged; and when they don't think what they are being asked to learn is "dumbed down."

All stakeholders in a school community must work together to achieve this schooling condition. When it is achieved, the dynamics of difference amongst diverse stakeholders is much more positive because they are working together to achieve a common goal. At the same time, CCL is not just an administrative practice or teacher practice, but a practice of all school community stakeholders.

Chart 11c   Access

Johnson Found in Schools That Serve Diverse Student Groups Well:	Chenoweth Found That High-Performing Schools:
1. Care is taken to ensure that all students have access to challenging academic coursework. This means, first, that educators have a clear understanding of what constitutes challenging academic coursework.	Find . . . extra time for instructional enrichment, especially for struggling students.
2. Leaders provide time and support in a manner that helps educators learn that one of their primary roles is to support the ongoing learning of their colleagues.	Organize outside mentors, volunteers, local service organizations, social service agencies, colleges, and companies for specific help.
3. Leaders help educators teach in ways that students like to learn. They encourage teachers to build upon students' interests, backgrounds, cultures, and prior knowledge. They help educators consider how they can make learning enjoyable.	Make sure that teachers have time to work together in highly structured ways so they can share responsibility for instruction.
4. Leaders help parents renew hope for their children's future.	Expand the time students—particularly struggling students—have in school.
5. Leaders help parents understand the actions that must be taken to ensure children have access to their goals.	
6. Faculties use data to identify and prioritize the key standards that must be taught exceptionally well.	
7. Cross-curricular integration is sometimes used to facilitate deeper understanding.	

MAKE IT PERSONAL

FN11–2 (SEE FACILITATOR NOTES IN APPENDIX 1)

1. What is necessary for teachers in most situations to provide all of their students with challenging academic instruction?

2. What should be done to enable more challenging academic instruction for all students to be more widespread and feasible?

There can be no higher purpose than helping parents renew hope for their children's future, because they will help instill that hope in their children as well. Parents must be recognized and nurtured as an important group of leaders in the school community that need to work collaboratively with leaders in other stakeholder groups to ensure children access their goals.

Persons from all groups need to listen to and demonstrate respect for each other. This doesn't mean they will always agree, but mutual respect will go a long way toward increasing the probability of success in achieving the goals for each student. When school leaders work closely with parents and embody a no excuses philosophy when it comes to seeking greater parental involvement, they are demonstrating an aspect of CCL.

MAKE IT PERSONAL

1. Describe what has occurred in your sphere of influence to increase communication and collaboration with parents, and with what results?

2. What have been the results of your efforts to improve school/parent communication?

Cross-curricular integration is very consistent with some of the brain research on how many students best learn, but in districts where I served as a curriculum administrator, most teachers had not been trained to develop or implement such curriculum. District funds were used to sponsor multicultural cross-curricular programs at the middle school level, which were very popular with both students and faculty who sought participation. To accomplish such integration requires both personal and organizational transformation for such efforts to be successful, including helping teachers rethink what teaching is all about, how to teach their subject(s) in ways that students best learn, the scheduling changes needed, and the protocols they should use when engaging in cross-curricular instructional planning and problem solving.

Prescriptive structural changes, such as increasing the time students have in school, are not nearly as successful over the long run as when they are collaboratively agreed upon and implemented, which can then improve the dynamics of difference among all players and the improvement of cultural democracy. It is important to facilitate the involvement of all relevant stakeholder groups in communication and problem-solving activities when planning an extended school day.

In low-performing schools where I served as an external evaluator, the extended school day was of critical importance for more attention to mastery of key content standards. As much as one half of the student body in each school needed such help, but only 30% to 40% of the Grade K–8 students most in need of such assistance participated (and even fewer in high school settings) and then not on a consistent basis. Less than full participation greatly compromised the positive impact of receiving extended instruction/afterschool tutoring. Parents did not always cooperate in allowing their children to spend the time they needed in such programs. However, little effort was made to get parents' and students' buy-in beforehand.

I have found an inclination by some teachers and administrators (as opposed to those in schools examined by Johnson and Chenoweth) in low-performing schools to resist or resent professional development activities that focus on improving cultural responsiveness and cultural competency. They may have a lot of experience working in schools heavily populated by historically underserved students of color and react

Chart 11d Assessment

Johnson Found in Schools That Serve Diverse Student Groups Well:	Chenoweth Found That High-Performing Schools:
1. Assessment results help determine professional development needs.	Use both individual student and student group assessment results to help them determine the best sources of information and training so that teachers can become better teachers, and no student falls through the cracks.
2. As professional development initiatives are implemented, assessment results are used to gauge the effectiveness of those efforts.	[Use] . . . data to examine what's not working and make changes in every area of school life.
3. School boards insist upon data collection efforts that include measures of instructional effectiveness.	
4. School boards ensure that school administrators can reasonably spend 40% to 60% percent of the school day in classrooms.	
5. School boards reconsider processes for evaluating school leaders to emphasize their role in improving instructional effectiveness.	
6. School boards encourage professional development that helps teachers minimize the use of worksheets and "busy work" and maximize student engagement in powerful learning activities.	
7. There are effective systems for promptly identifying students who are having difficulty learning key content.	
8. Assessment results lead to tailored interventions designed to ensure student progress.	

negatively to the implication they may need to improve their instructional effectiveness. Some also claim the results of high stakes assessments (statewide standards-based tests) cannot easily be tied to the need for such professional development.

A broader range of assessments is needed, including observation-based measures. However, there has to be a political willingness to acknowledge the "elephant on the ceiling" that everyone may be trying to ignore, that is, how the cultural and racial dynamics in a school community impact receptivity to professional development that focuses on culture and race. The Culturally Courageous Leadership Diagnostic Questionnaires (CCLDQ) in Appendix 2 can also be used to stimulate critical reflection and jump start substantive conversations about what is really going on in a school related to race and culture. Discussion of the CCLDQ results can also help to engage teachers in discussing why such capacity building is important. Some staff may be denying any relationship between the racial and cultural dynamics in society at large and in their school, or need to feel there will be support for addressing such issues over the long run, without it being a blame game. Administrators and instructional staff who support such capacity building should go public with their support. Sometimes, supporters of professional development on culturally responsive teaching are so intimidated by peers who feel differently that they will not acknowledge their true feelings or share student data on why there is a need for such capacity building.

MAKE IT PERSONAL

FN11–3 (SEE FACILITATOR NOTES IN APPENDIX 1)

1. What should be done to increase teacher receptivity to professional development on cultural responsiveness, cultural proficiency, and race-specific training when student assessment results consistently show a need for new instructional approaches?

2. What are some other strategies needed in order to facilitate greater teacher receptivity to professional development on cultural responsiveness, cultural proficiency, and race-specific training?

Formative assessments are utilized in most schools to monitor student progress in meeting benchmark targets during the school year in select academic subjects and grade levels. Utilizing the results of such assessments to tailor subsequent interventions is no easy task, and even though the technology software now exists to assist in analyzing the results, it still takes time for teachers to subsequently plan and implement tailored, sometimes personalized interventions that are culturally responsive.

When interventions are tailored for specific students based on the results from using a broad range of assessment measures, these interventions should take into consideration the learner characteristics, "positionalities" (see the section "Student Identity and Achievement" in Chapter 1), and learning styles of the affected students. Such practices are made somewhat easier when teachers who have the same students in their classes work collaboratively in cross-curricular collaboration during lesson planning.

MAKE IT PERSONAL

1. Given the pressures of time, with so much to teach, and in some cases with higher class sizes, how can collaboration amongst representatives from all school stakeholders help to tailor interventions designed to ensure student progress?

2. In your opinion, what are the pros and cons to consider, if any, when trying to tailor instructional interventions for historically underserved groups?

The schooling conditions in chart 11e suggest a value is placed on implementing the kinds of professional development that is more culturally responsive. Such capacity building must include joint planning, follow-up support, and open and honest communication.

All stakeholders, including students and parents, can be leaders in helping facilitate this kind of personal and organizational transformation. An example would be soliciting student feedback on what kinds of lessons or teacher behaviors are more likely to increase their understanding of what is being taught and their motivation to make a stronger effort in class. Parents can also be asked to provide teachers more ongoing information on the life circumstances, interests, and likes of their children,

Chart 11e Adaptation

Johnson Found in Schools That Serve Diverse Student Groups Well:	Chenoweth Found That High-Performing Schools:
1. Educators learn to instruct in ways that are responsive to the learning strengths, backgrounds, cultures, interests, and prior knowledge of students.	Diverge from what was learned in university teaching programs if that is the logical consequence of putting students first.
2. Leaders ensure that professional development is not "an event"; it is a culture that pervades the school. People are constantly learning to improve their craft.	Change the way they teach any subject area if the way they teach isn't getting all students to learn the content.
3. Educators evaluate intervention programs regularly to ensure they are meeting student needs. Ineffective programs are modified or eliminated.	[Have] . . . safety nets operating before school, during school, after school, on Saturdays, and/or during intersessions.

so teachers can take that into consideration. Teachers calling home or sending letters home might also yield very helpful information, but parents may need to be involved in deciding with the teacher beforehand the best ways to reach them.

MAKE IT PERSONAL

1. How can elementary and secondary students help teachers implement instruction that builds on their learning strengths, backgrounds, cultures, interests, and prior knowledge?

2. In your school community, what are the major constraints to ongoing adaptation to student characteristics and needs?

Safety nets can be a culturally responsive intervention that increases cultural democracy if the parents and students have meaningful input into deciding the options provided for helping those who need above and beyond assistance. Since parent and student cooperation is necessary for the provision of extra help to be successful, their input may help ensure active participation of students in such programs. It is critical that extra help be provided to the extent possible by students' classroom teachers, because it removes the potential problem of inadequate articulation between what is going on in the regular classroom and what occurs in afterschool tutoring.

Intervention programs don't always adequately meet student needs. This may happen more frequently when the intervention providers haven't had adequate communication with the classroom teacher. It is very important to evaluate the effectiveness of intervention programs from their inception, so effective practices can be incorporated into regular classroom instruction when possible. Evaluation data can also help identify ineffective programs, which can then be modified or eliminated.

Altering how time is spent in schools so there is a value placed on providing time for teacher collaboration is an indication of including teachers among those stakeholders needing support for developing new forms of leadership. When professional development is part of the school culture instead of being an event, there are structural changes in how time is spent, which can then contribute to the kinds of cultural changes in beliefs, values, and norms needed in the school organization.

MAKE IT PERSONAL

FN11–4 (SEE FACILITATOR NOTES IN APPENDIX 1)

1. Based on your experience, what kinds of efforts are needed in your school or district to facilitate greater leadership by students and parents?

2. What has your school or district done to ensure student safety nets are culturally responsive interventions?

Chart 11f   Accountability

Johnson Found in Schools That Serve Diverse Student Groups Well:	Chenoweth Found That High-Performing Schools:
1. Students, teachers, parents, support staff, and administrators share a sense of responsibility for generating progress in learning.	Figure out what other schools who have outperformed them do and incorporate what they find out into their own practice.
2. Leaders monitor both student performance and teacher instructional improvement regularly. Leaders spend significant time observing instruction. They know what progress is made and where attention is needed.	Pay a lot of attention to the quality of the teaching staff, especially in hiring and supervision practices.
3. Leaders visit classrooms frequently to gauge student learning. They constantly seek evidence that students are learning what their teachers are teaching. Leaders share this evidence regularly in ways that build the capacity of teachers from day to day, creating a culture of professional growth.	Give great emphasis to making sure [professional development] deepens teachers' content knowledge, understanding, and/or pedagogical skill.
	Train and acculturate new teachers . . , and retrain experienced teachers in effective instruction.
	Have principals who are a constant presence . . . in the building, walking the halls, in the classrooms, conferring with teachers and parents.
	[Are places where] . . . teachers and other administrators, parents, and community members . . . make important decisions for the school.

All of the characteristics mentioned by Johnson and Chenoweth are very impor-tant in elementary, secondary, public, private, and charter schools. When imple-mented, they are a function of leadership being nurtured among persons in most stakeholder groups within a school community. Sharing a sense of collective respon-sibility for progress in learning is accomplished by nurturing critical self-reflection and an ongoing assessment of organizational functioning related to progress in learning for all student subgroups.

For example, I have found that limited English proficient students with special needs in low-performing schools do not have timely responses to the assistance needed, and their needs are also frequently misdiagnosed because of language and cultural differences. In some smaller districts, they don't have sufficient personnel with the requisite competencies to assist schools in responding appropriately. There must be an explicit and implicit value placed on securing the competent personnel to properly address the special needs of all students and also more effort is needed to secure timely input from the families of special needs students.

Some special needs do not justify placing students in special education programs. This is especially true for Black and Latino male students, who are disproportionately assigned to special education.

A study that echoes the findings of Johnson and Chenoweth regarding schools with more equitable outcomes was conducted by Jesse, Davis, and Pokorny (2004) titled *High Achieving Middle Schools for Latino Students in Poverty*, conducted for the Center for Comprehensive School Reform and Improvement. The study investigated what practitioners are doing to create effective middle schools for Latino/a students. Important characteristics of the schools in the study were strong school leadership, teacher expertise and relationships, the organizational structure of the schools, the special training of many teachers for working with English language learner populations, the community and parent involvement, the caring about students, and high expectations. Data-driven planning activities and resource allocations, large numbers of staff participating in the development of school improvement plans, and continual evaluation and adjustment of activities were also of paramount importance.

Leaders are teachers, parents, support staff, community persons, and students as well as school site administrators. Teachers working collaboratively with administrators monitor student achievement and instructional improvement regularly. Both teacher peer observation and structured feedback from students can be very powerful components of instructional improvement and are integral parts of the new teacher performance assessment system in the Denver Public Schools (2011). Such nonevaluative monitoring/feedback can contribute to greater team efforts, shared accountability, and identification of when celebrations are appropriate for progress being made.

MAKE IT PERSONAL

FN11–5 (SEE FACILITATOR NOTES IN APPENDIX 1)

1. How do schools with which you are familiar motivate elementary and secondary students to share a sense of responsibility for eliminating the achievement gap?

2. What are some strategies you feel should be implemented to improve collective accountability for equitable educational outcomes?

ANSWERS TO QUESTIONS YOU MIGHT WANT TO ASK

1. Are the "5 A's" discussed in this chapter considered prerequisites for elimination of the achievement gap?

In Johnson and Chenoweth's work, they do not definitively claim that the presence of the above conditions related to the "5 A's" causes the elimination of the achievement gap in the schools examined. However, there is a high correlation between these conditions in the schools they closely examined and a significant reduction or elimination of the achievement gap between the lowest and highest achieving student groups.

2. Which of the "5 A's" should have the highest priority for the achievement gap to be eliminated?

Given the history of public education and racial/cultural bias in the United States, it may be critical that leadership by all stakeholders initially occur in the areas of "attitude" and "access" in order to then effectively impact the areas of "assessment," "adaptability," and "accountability." "Attitude" refers to the attitudes and commitment of all school community stakeholders regarding cultural democracy and equitable student outcomes, and "access" refers to the need for all stakeholders to have access to the professional development, teaching, training, or other supports they need and deserve.

3. How do I determine what needs to happen in my school community to secure the kind of leadership required to implement any of the above "5 A's"?

The reader should review the seven culturally courageous actions that are needed (see Chapter 7) as well as the seven principles and characteristics of CCL (see Chapter 8). This review can help you determine which of these have the most critical need in your district and school. My experience is that effective communication (i.e., communication gurus) and advocacy (i.e., community organizers) are two characteristics from the second component of the CCL paradigm of most importance in many school settings to achieve any of the 5 A's as described by Johnson and Chenoweth. These two CCL characteristics/principles also subsume to some extent three of the five remaining principles.

In addition, I have found four of the seven needed actions discussed in Chapter 7 to be of great importance in many schools where historically underserved students experience very inequitable outcomes. They are a need to change the cultural politics emanating from human fears, a need to change the toxic hidden curriculum, the need to increase capacity building regarding any of the isms or biases (e.g., racism, sexism, classism, and biases against LEP students), and the need to increase team and trust building regarding equity. All four of these needed actions are very much intertwined. It will probably be almost impossible to achieve any of the 5 A's without simultaneously working to improve culturally courageous instructional leadership and school climate while tackling these four needed actions. In the schools studied by Johnson and Chenoweth, these were some of the leadership characteristics and actions either evident or implied.

REVIEW OF CHAPTER 11

- Five charts were used to illustrate specific examples of attitude, access, assessment, adaptability, and accountability (the 5 A's), which have been identified by Johnson as conditions in schools serving diverse student groups well, where the achievement gap has been significantly reduced or eliminated. A few of the conditions and values in high-performing schools documented by Chenoweth were also listed in the same charts.

- In these schools, there were promising departures from the four conditions contributing to inequitable educational outcomes discussed in Chapter 3, my observations based on involvement in other equity initiatives discussed in Chapter 4, and the institutional biases and barriers contributing to student underachievement discussed in Chapters 5 and 6.

- A relationship was drawn between the promising departures described in this chapter and the examples of CCL by various school community stakeholders provided in Chapters 7 through 10.

Two Leadership Profiles

12

A culturally courageous leader is only worthy of the title if and when he or she unrelentingly demonstrates the propensity and passion for galvanizing divergent personalities to higher levels of collective functioning than he or she could do individually in the pursuit of equity and excellence. The 5A's are a way of "being" as well as functioning.

The 5 A's discussed in Chapter 11 represent beliefs and norms associated with personal and organizational transformation necessary for the achievement of equitable educational outcomes in many low-performing schools. The two leadership profiles in this chapter personalize the situational context these school leaders grappled with when demonstrating their beliefs and commitments related to the 5 A's. A comparison of the similarities and differences in their leadership challenges and actions helps illustrate the complexity when trying to effectively respond to the specific needs of staff, community, and students.

KWL EXERCISE

1. In your opinion, which of the schooling conditions listed as part of the "5 A's" make the most difference when attempting to eliminate any gaps in the educational outcomes of historically underserved students?

2. What is your highest priority when it comes to the capacity building you want to personally experience in order to become a culturally courageous leader?

3. As you reflect on how decisions are made and how teaching occurs in your district or school, what content in this guide is most relevant to your work context?

CONSEQUENCES FOR A
CHARTER SCHOOL COMMITTED TO THE "5 A'S"

The characteristics of gap-closing schools found throughout the United States by Johnson, Chenoweth, and many others were manifested to a large extent in the Culture and Language Academy of Success (CLAS), a K–8 charter school located in Los Angeles, California, until a major turnover in staff and students. CLAS is the entity spawned by the Center for Culturally Responsive Teaching and Learning, the brainchild of Dr. Sharroky Hollie, a faculty member in teacher education at California State University, Dominquez Hills. The Center is a nonprofit corporation cofounded in 2003 by Janis Bucknor, Sharroky Hollie, and Anthony Jackson, who also codirect the school. They are responsible for the pedagogic vision and teacher and professional development model reflected in CLAS, a school populated primarily by historically underserved African American students. Until recently, CLAS achieved end-of-year scores on statewide tests significantly above those of students from the same subgroup in the city of Los Angeles.

Characteristics of the model include embedding culturally responsive pedagogy and 21st century technological tools into instructional curricula and effective school management practices. Five pillars of the CLAS program that emphasize culturally and linguistically responsive teaching are (1) standards-based teaching using culturally relevant literature; (2) systematic teaching of situational appropriateness in language to support standard English mastery of nonstandard English learners and English learners; (3) building on cultural behaviors and tapping into personal learning styles for a positive classroom community via use of learned protocols; (4) expanding academic vocabulary through conceptually coded words; and (5) creating a validating and affirming learning environment.

CLAS is structured on the small charter schools model and is devoted to enabling successful assimilation/acculturation of its students without their having to give up their cultural identity. Quite the reverse, the school helps students become more knowledgeable about their cultural heritage and to develop a strong cultural identity. Sharroky Hollie characterizes CLAS as a school swimming upstream in that it is populated primarily by low-income African American students whose primary discourse is nonmainstream English, and whose families want them to become knowledgeable about their culture, academically proficient, and able to succeed in the mainstream. Hollie is dedicated to CLAS living up to their dreams and expectations.

While observing instruction in CLAS and interviewing two of the codirectors, Sharroky Hollie and Anthony Jackson, I learned that an overwhelming majority of the schooling conditions described by Johnson and Chenoweth in the five categories of attitude, access, assessment, adaptation, and accountability are reflected in the CLAS. For example, the following items identified by Chenoweth and Johnson that are listed in Chapter 11 are part of the bedrock of CLAS.

Chart 12a	Examples of the 5 A's in CLAS

Have constantly rising expectations for teachers, and teachers have high expectations for students. Failure is not an option.
Believe students are capable of excellence.
Leaders collect information that helps them know how to improve relational issues. They identify and resolve issues promptly and professionally.
Older students are taught to be role models for younger students.
Care is taken to ensure that all students have access to challenging academic coursework. This means, first, that educators have a clear understanding of what constitutes challenging academic coursework.
Leaders help educators teach in ways that students like to learn. They encourage teachers to build upon students' interests, backgrounds, cultures, and prior knowledge. They help educators consider how they can make learning enjoyable.
Leaders help parents understand the actions that must be taken to ensure children have access to their goals.
Cross-curricular integration is sometimes used to facilitate deeper understanding.
Assessment results help determine professional development needs.
Assessment results lead to tailored interventions designed to ensure student progress.
Leaders ensure that professional development is not "an event;" it is a culture that pervades the school. People are constantly learning to improve their craft.
Change the way they teach any subject area if the way they teach isn't getting all students to learn the content.
Data are used to examine what's not working and make changes in every area of school life.
Leaders visit classrooms frequently to gauge student learning. They constantly seek evidence that students are learning what their teachers are teaching. Leaders share this evidence regularly in ways that build the capacity of teachers from day to day, creating a culture of professional growth.
Train and acculturate new teachers, and retrain experienced teachers in effective instruction.
Students, teachers, and administrators share a sense of responsibility for generating progress in learning.

The cultural politics of an all-Black administrative team running a charter school dedicated to the utilization of culturally responsive pedagogy for a mostly Black student body meant to some third-party funders that the school is Afrocentric, when in the eyes of the codirectors it is culturally responsive. Dr. Hollie feels one of the reasons for the characterization of CLAS as Afrocentric is that the scholars whose research interests and writing are about culturally responsive teaching haven't reached consensus on what the term means. The term Afrocentric may also be utilized because of the fallacious reasoning that a school curriculum cannot be culturally responsive/pro-Black without also being anti-White. CLAS does not characterize itself as

Afrocentric in any way, but it does maintain fidelity to being culturally responsive, which means validating and celebrating the culture of the students in the school.

Some detractors have problems with the school being structured around building upon the culture and language of its African American student population. CLAS honors and explicitly utilizes the cultural heritage of its student body, including its ancient African heritage, and also involves students in drawing upon their prior knowledge and life experiences during the completion of academic assignments.

CLAS has experienced some major fiscal problems over the years, resulting in a deficit of approximately $2 million dollars. As already suggested, the school has not been successful in acquiring third-party grants and relies solely on state funding. The limited funding has affected the instructional program in that most recently there was a cessation of the use of instructional technology where every student had a laptop with curriculum lessons and assignments on their computer.

In addition, almost all of the veteran teachers left the school after funding delays due to state budget deficits, which resulted in not being able to pay staff for 6 months. However, the dedication of most veteran teachers in the program was demonstrated by their not resigning until the school year was over. At the end of the school year, CLAS had the best California standards test score results ever achieved in the school's history.

Currently, there are only three veteran teachers on staff who are each exemplary, and all remaining positions are filled by new teachers with no previous experience. They each have part-time mentors who are former CLAS teachers. The mentors work with the new teachers twice a week. The codirectors acknowledge there has been inadequate attention to fund development and marketing. However, they also feel the philanthropic community has not been receptive because of the Afrocentric allegations.

The reasoning of the codirectors is buttressed by experiences in the Los Angeles Unified School District when it came time for the school's charter to be renewed by the Board of Education. In two cases, efforts to shut down the school were not successful. In one instance, the codirectors felt the Board of Education backed down because of overwhelming lobbying on behalf of the school by school parents from all over the city who went to a Board meeting where closing the school was to be decided. In the other instance, a meeting of the codirectors with the charter school office of L.A. Unified resulted in the school being allowed to continue despite its deficit. At this meeting, the CLAS codirectors pointed out that the closing of other charter schools with larger deficits was not being recommended to the Board of Education, even though their deficits were between $4 million and $30 million.

Recently, it has been hard to get more parents involved because of huge student transiency. The year during which the school was visited, 145 out of 330 students were totally new to the school. Parents take responsibility to transport their children to the school every day from all over Los Angeles.

CLAS has done it their way, without compromise on their vision and program, having to contend with the politics within the school district. Dr. Hollie says the dilemma is aggravated by trying to run a very small school committed to both equity and excellence with a social justice mission. But its continued existence is in peril each year. The location of the school has changed 4 of the last 5 years because of the finances and the politics.

The Los Angeles school board has been lobbied to allow some of the all-Black or mostly Black schools in L.A. Unified that are in their fourth year of program improvement to contract with CLAS to run them. The California Public School Choice Act mandates that such low-performing schools be given the option to contract with charter providers. However, the L.A. Board has never contracted with a Black school provider, choosing instead to allow schools to contract with huge charter school providers such as Green Dot.

CLAS is a member of the coalition of black student equity, an advocacy group for Black students in Los Angeles. The coalition, which includes the National Association for the Advancement of Colored People and the Urban League, is hoping to get the board to allow interested low-performing Black schools to contract with CLAS. It is an uphill battle because the teacher's union is not supportive of CLAS's commitment to culturally responsive teaching. They feel threatened by this approach because they know their members at the school would have to adhere to the school's philosophy, vision, and instructional plan.

CLAS is an anomaly existing and prevailing in the second largest school district in the United States but struggling with very adversarial cultural politics. The small size of the school is another factor being used to rationalize denials of third-party funding. Other schools similar to CLAS in Detroit and Philadelphia closed because of economic problems. But the antipathy of the teacher's union is indicative of a much larger challenge to schools like CLAS because they threaten the institutional domination by teachers who are not receptive to being culturally responsive in their entire instructional program for historically underserved students of African descent.

∂∞∞

DISTRICT-LEVEL ACTIONS
HELPING SCHOOL SITES EMBRACE THE "5 A'S"

Tony Lamair Burks II was an area superintendent in the San Diego Unified School District. He was responsible for two high school clusters, which included 27 elementary, middle, or high schools. His schools were populated by some of the most culturally, socioeconomically, racially, and linguistically diverse students in the school district.

A major intervention related to the 5 A's was Dr. Burks's rolling out the Board of Education's community-based school reform model in his administrative area. A major purpose of the reform model is to organically develop and sustain strategic community engagement efforts through cluster councils. This work began with the creation of councils that include community members and parents as well as representatives from a high school and their feeder elementary and middle schools.

The overarching goal of the reform model is for each council to improve cluster communication, coordination, and development, resulting in a cohesive preK–12 environment that provides a quality education for all students.

Each cluster council decides what strategies it will employ to collectively improve or enhance the quality of education provided in cluster schools. Dr. Burks jump-started the work of his cluster councils by visiting his schools and initially talking to site administrators about what needed to change or be improved. By their own acknowledgement, principals said they were not in classrooms enough. Based on these instances of informal dialogue, Dr. Burks then distributed a comprehensive survey to all stakeholders in each cluster in their native language. The results of the survey were used by Dr. Burks to develop a shared vision for the area that included increasing the time administrators spend in classrooms, as well as coaching faculty and staff in promising practices.

A change was made in the focus of most administrative observations from evaluation to opportunities for feedback, coaching, and instructional improvement. In addition to whatever cluster councils decide to focus upon, Dr. Burks took the initiative in his area to provide The Breakthrough Coach, a professional development seminar, for all school administrators within his administrative area. Principals and their secretaries attended the 2-day seminar to learn best practices for using administrative support, organizing schools to produce break-throughs in student achievement, and observing instruction multiple times each week. He developed a master plan for follow-up support and coaching. The master plan included an ongoing focus on improving communication and problem solving within and across school sites.

Burks brought in Dr. Joseph F. Johnson, whose work was discussed in Chapter 11, to conduct interactive presentations on "teaching and leading in high performing urban schools" for all of Burks's school site administrators who brought teachers and community representatives. Dr. Burks laid a foundation for his administrators, administrative support staff, and site teacher leadership teams to develop a critical consciousness, become better organized, and have a common language. Chart 12b lists some of the conditions identified by Johnson and Chenoweth that were being modeled by Burks in preparation for more widespread cluster collaboration on achieving high-performing schools.

There were some major challenges to the goals Dr. Burks established for improving the focus on instructional leadership in his 27 school sites. One challenge was how to blunt the major impact of severe cuts in the district budget, necessitated by the state's huge deficit. He confronted some district norms related to the district being very compliance driven even when it is at the expense of what is in the best interests of students. He is very student-centered and expected his site administrators to walk that talk, inspecting what they expect, as he does. When he approved a principal's request to make adjustments in the school's time schedule, the office of pupil accounting told the principal he couldn't do it. Dr. Burks had to confront this office and others so they wouldn't continue blocking what the principal wanted to do to improve the educational outcomes of students. What he found was that all of the

| Chart 12b | Examples of the 5 A's Modeled by a District Administrator |

Visited classrooms frequently to gauge student learning. Constantly sought evidence that students are learning what their teachers are teaching.
(Used) . . . data to examine what's not working and make changes in every area . . . .
Organized outside mentors, volunteers, local service organizations, social service agencies, colleges, and companies for specific help.
Encouraged teachers to build upon students' interests, backgrounds, cultures, and prior knowledge.
Powerful collaborations were fostered that made individuals feel supported and valued. These collaborations led to a strong sense of efficacy: a feeling that "together, we can accomplish anything!"
Pushed beyond compliance and encouraged everyone to embrace goals that will make a difference in students' lives.
Collected information that helped him know how to improve relational issues. Identified and resolved issues promptly and professionally.
Used research and data to focus on opportunities to improve, not on reasons to blame.
Created platforms for the leadership of many others who want to influence school improvement.
Understood the power of mutual respect.

district fanfare about being committed to community-based school reform was more talk than walk if efforts were made to change long established district practices.

Soon after assuming his assignment as area superintendent, Dr. Burks lobbied the board of education and superintendent for differentiated financial support to his two high school clusters that were not receiving an equitable share of district funds based on student academic needs and the average daily attendance when compared with other high school clusters. He started changing other long-standing norms, engaging principals in talking about their successes and failures, and being resources to each other. After The Breakthrough Coach training, Dr. Burks served as a coach helping them to implement what they learned. He also announced to all appropriate district persons, such as cabinet members, that his principals should not be expected to attend any meetings before 1:00 p.m. so they could devote more time to being in classrooms during prime instructional hours. All parents were also sent a letter with the same message that they shouldn't expect to have access to principals during most of the school day because the first priority was principals being in classrooms.

Dr. Burks also started coaching his principals on how to engage in rigorous supervision of teachers who consistently display questionable instructional performance. His game plan was to first facilitate everyone developing a common language, followed by getting all to give high priority to getting in classrooms much more frequently, and then engaging in conversations about what needs to be different than what they observed. He also recognized the quality of professional development must dramatically improve if teachers were going to be held accountable for utilizing what they have learned.

At the same time, Dr. Burks began his process for enhancing principal instructional supervision competencies, partially through joint visits to classrooms with his principals. He also asked each principal to identify two teachers whose classroom he could visit on his own, with one being a person perceived by the principal as an effective teacher, and one whose instruction was perceived as needing major improvement. Discussions with the principal followed these observations.

Tony Burks told his principals that he envisioned them *serving* as chief executive officers of their schools; *making* decisions that are in the best interest of their students; *functioning* as experts who monitor and observe teaching and learning, *utilizing* data-differentiated decision making and decision management; *exercising* creativity and responsibility with financial resources; *engaging* parents, guardians, students, community members, and service organizations in various ways; and *capitalizing* on the gifts, talents, and experiences of fellow administrators through communication and collaboration.

In an era of drastic budget cutting, another of the challenges experienced in schools populated to a large extent by limited or non-English speakers was how to provide translation services in community meetings and how to send out information or make calls to students' homes in the appropriate language. Despite the challenge, Dr. Burks was able to secure such services through the acquisition of start-of-the-art equipment that provides translation in three languages simultaneously.

Burks also found the time to personally mentor a group of high school males of color, called the "Crew," checking up on the good things they were doing, much to the students' dismay. Many of them have at times been labeled as disengaged, disruptive, and disrespectful, but they have dispelled these mythical labels, living up to the high expectations placed upon them. Through these activities and priorities, Dr. Burks demonstrated the 5 A's in chart 12b.

In one of his high school clusters, there are a large number of students recently immigrated from the African continent who haven't been in schools for years and are now experiencing resettlement in the United States. A different level of support was needed and Dr. Burks sought to make sure such support was provided to these students.

Dr. Burks, through his leadership of site leaders and inclusive outreach to all stakeholders in his schools and their school communities, definitely demonstrated the essential role of district offices to support the journey of school sites toward practice of the 5 A's. Nevertheless, using the rationale of a need for massive cuts to district administrative staff, the board of education chose to reorganize the supervisorial structure of the district after less than a year of implementation. The board voted to reduce the number of area superintendents from 10 to 6.

Although Dr. Burks applied for one of the six positions, he was one of the four area superintendents whose services were terminated, even though he had given 3 years of exemplary service at the district level, which was documented in writing by the district superintendent. Currently, in addition to serving as the superintendent-in-residence at the National Center for Urban School Transformation (NCUST) at San

Diego State University, he recently assumed the position of transformation coach in the North Carolina department of public instruction, as part of the roll out of their federal government "race to the top" grant. However, he continues to serve as a consultant to school districts for NCUST, helping further its mission of working with urban school districts and their partners. The goals of NCUST are to transform urban schools into places where all students achieve academic proficiency, evidence a love of learning, and graduate well prepared to succeed in postsecondary education, the workplace, and their communities. Burks is working with both the North Carolina department of public instruction and the NCUST leadership team to accelerate and sustain school transformation.

Dr. Burks' layoff is an illustration of a major problem in urban school districts that terminate both teachers and administrators who demonstrate the commitment and skills to make significant progress in facilitating movement toward equitable educational outcomes. When people like Dr. Burks have done exemplary work as indicated by the statements of those they supervise, the public, and the district superintendent, it is critical that boards of education and district superintendents demonstrate the political courage and insight to do whatever is necessary to maintain as much continuity as possible in retaining proven winners.

MAKE IT PERSONAL

FN12–1 (SEE FACILITATOR NOTES IN APPENDIX 1)

1. From reading the two leadership profiles, describe three understandings you acquired about how culturally courageous leadership can be manifested in school communities.

2. What can you apply from the leadership profiles to your own work context?

જાન્જી

SIMILIARITIES AND DIFFERENCES

There are several similarities between the major players discussed in this chapter. Both Dr. Hollie and Dr. Burks strongly articulate a compelling vision, which is influenced by their knowledge of community, parent, staff, and student priorities/concerns. They also share what they envision to their entire school community, and demonstrate commitment to the vision through their priorities, modeling, and coaching of others. Both are very student-centered and knowledgeable of research-based best practices for administrators and teachers. In each of their situations, they experienced challenges related to district or school deficits and budget cuts, and in response, made a strong case to policymakers for more equitable approaches. In each case, their schools are populated primarily by poor, historically underserved students. They confront the politics head-on and relentlessly pursue greater political support on behalf of students. They each experience negative consequences from the cultural politics that occurs, in part because of their courageousness and commitments.

One of the major differences between Drs. Burks and Hollie is that Dr. Hollie created a school based on his educational philosophy and interpretation of how to implement culturally responsive instruction for his student population. He is the lead codirector of a small charter school populated by students of African descent. Dr. Burks was an area superintendent with responsibility for 27 very diverse schools, with a majority from limited-English-speaking backgrounds. Dr. Hollie is the lead person in developing and providing professional development for his teaching staff, while Dr. Burks took the initiative to facilitate professional development for his site administrators that is consistent with board of education priorities and the area vision that he crafted based on data from multiple sources.

Each of these educational leaders exemplify a commitment to supporting the conditions that reflect the 5 A's as documented by Johnson and Chenoweth. They also demonstrate a commitment to all four components of the culturally courageous leadership paradigm. More specifically, they actively promote and nurture collaborative leadership by all school community stakeholders. They practice many of the characteristics of culturally courageous leaders, and are committed to fostering both personal and organizational transformation within their sphere of influence. Finally, they constantly work to improve how they handle the politics associated with trying to improve cultural democracy, increase social justice, and achieve equitable educational outcomes.

REVIEW OF CHAPTER 12

- Additional examples of promising departures as exemplified in the "5 A's" discussed in Chapter 11 are briefly described in two leadership profiles. The first profile is the lead codirector totally committed to cultural and linguistic responsiveness in a K–8 charter school composed of a mostly Black student body. The second profile is the person who was an area superintendent with responsibility for 27 K–12 schools composed primarily of limited English-speaking students in the eighth largest school district in the United States.

- The context in each of these situations was briefly delineated, which contributed to the decisions and initiatives made by each leader, as demonstrated by their emphasis on the "5 A's," and on what is called culturally courageous leadership in this guide.

SECTION III

Making It Real

Keep in mind the following questions or tasks as you read this final section of the guide:

1. Describe how the attitudes and behaviors of those leaders discussed in this section are similar and/or different from those in your own work setting.

2. What can you do differently, one step at a time, to improve the "equity walk" in your work setting?

3. Identify the issues, do's, don'ts, and lame excuses that need priority attention by you and/or your school and district.

Defusing the   13
Political Land Mines

*Transcending personal and institutional norms that contribute to
inequitable educational outcomes requires crafting, participating in,
and sustaining a new political and social order.*

Pursuing equity transformation at a personal and organizational level in schools includes dealing with tenacious overt and covert resistance, some of which is based on conscious or unconscious fears. The resistance to both levels of change may come from various individual stakeholders who deny they are biased or racist, but passively participate in the ideology of White dominance as discussed in Chapter 1. They may also defend some treasured organizational norms and policies that are identified by equity proponents as a primary cause of inequitable educational outcomes, such as how students may be assigned to classes, commonly called tracking and discussed in Chapter 5. Confronting racially biased individual and school organizational practices must be a very strategic undertaking.

In several schools, I have been told by individual teachers or support staff in private interviews about specific policies or norms that were biased and discriminatory. Upon further investigation of other sources, I found merit in many of these allegations. However, there has often been little willingness to go public with such characterizations by those who blew the whistle, so to speak, or discuss questionable practices in staff meetings.

When it comes to confronting racism, ethnocentrism, sexism, classism, or biases related to primary language, disability, and so on, even when corroborating evidence is provided, there is often little willingness to "open up Pandora's box." Fear of retaliation or strong discomfort is ever-present in some school environments when such topics are put on the table. Persons advocating a need for changes in some attitudes, beliefs, practices, and identities (i.e., equity transformation) are viewed by some as "troublemakers" who only have a self-serving agenda.

To complicate matters, those attempting to make positive changes on behalf of students may demonstrate attitudes and behaviors toward their detractors, which are manipulated to negatively reflect on their cause. Just because one is an ardent advocate of equity doesn't mean she doesn't have her own biases, and her demonstration of them can be counterproductive to achieving her social justice goals. In other words, ardent equity advocates can unwittingly cause political land mines as well as have responsibility for defusing those caused by opponents.

Sometimes those on the front lines trying to achieve equity express themselves very passionately and may make sweeping generalizations. Opponents of the changes being advocated may try to increase opposition by attacking the "messenger." The bottom line is that culturally courageous leaders must be collectively willing and able to effectively defuse land mines, whatever their source or characteristics.

KWL EXERCISE

1. What are some of your personal rules for how to address the politics associated with trying to implement any equity initiative?

2. What would be helpful to know in order to improve how you personally navigate the politics of equity transformation in your district or school?

3. What are three or more ideas from the "5 A's" and the leadership profiles that you will add to your arsenal when providing leadership to equity initiatives?

ঌৎ

WHAT IS MEANT BY THE "POLITICS" OF EQUITY TRANSFORMATION?

In the discourse on how to achieve equity transformation in 21st century U.S. schools, there are very different educational philosophies. Those engaged in this effort often demonstrate a missionary zeal and experience a lot of political resistance.

Different school community stakeholders vie for shaping decisions about what changes should occur in who is taught, what is taught, how it is taught, and the relationships between students, parents, and teachers. This battle for power and authority may be based on very different visions about the purpose, process, and desired outcomes of education in the United States for the historically underserved. The strategies decided upon to influence the actions of others must be very carefully considered by those attempting to engineer improvements in social justice. The word "politics" has multiple meanings, as illustrated by the following definitions.

Definitions of Politics

a. Social relations involving intrigue to gain authority or power (WordNet, 2010).

b. A process by which groups of people make collective decisions . . . generally applied to the art or science of running governmental or state affairs. . . . It also refers to behavior within civil governments, but politics has been observed in other group interactions, including corporate, academic, and religious institutions. It consists of "social relations involving authority or power and refers to the regulation of public affairs within a political unit, and to the methods and tactics used to formulate and apply policy (TheFreeDictionary.com, 2011; Wikipedia, 2012).

c. Politics is the process and method of decision making for groups of human beings. Although it is generally applied to governments, politics is also observed in all human group interactions including corporate, academic, and religious (WordIQ.com, 2012).

d. Competition between competing interest groups or individuals for power and leadership (Merriam-Webster, 2012).

ঌৎঌ

HOW DEFINITIONS APPLY TO
THE TERM "POLITICS OF IMPLEMENTATION"

When trying to implement equity transformation, the skills, needs, perspectives, strengths, feelings, and concerns of those most directly affected should be considered. The relationships among the various school stakeholders will be impacted by whatever is done and how it is done. In school after school, all low performing and populated by families of low socioeconomic status, I have witnessed the prevalence of ethnic rivalries and perceived, as well as real, slights. The lack of trust and respect within and across racial and cultural boundaries still abounds in the 21st century. Such cultural dynamics and politics are counterproductive to the achievement of equitable educational outcomes and require leadership from all stakeholder groups that reflects a willingness to rise above the forces that help perpetuate deep-seated dissonance. Administrators and teachers must model such behavior.

For example, when board policies create program support for English language learners, or African Americans are selected for administrative positions in predominately Latino/a schools, or vice versa, such decisions must be implemented in ways that are a win-win for all constituencies in the school community, rather than in a way that exacerbates resentment. The decisions on any policy changes or personnel selections may impact how equity efforts are undertaken, if at all. Any equity initiative requires new working relationships and norms to be initiated, such as those between parents and teachers, teachers and administrators, teachers and teachers, students and students. University faculty in teacher and administrator preparation programs need to be involved, because they are preparing future teachers and administrators who must have the skills necessary to help schools be successful with all students.

With or without the involvement and preparation of all involved, efforts may be made to sabotage whatever directions are taken to achieve genuine equity. Some of the relationships needed that will enable the changes to work may not be willingly undertaken, if at all. Therefore, the *politics* of implementing equity transformation must be carefully navigated, but not at the expense of those for whom equity is sought.

The competition for power between various interest groups influences what decisions and how decisions are made. Without an effort to influence the psychological climate in which decisions occur, it is unlikely that equity efforts have a chance of succeeding. Such efforts must also be collectively undertaken by all stakeholder groups in the school community. This means those who experience inequitable outcomes must be involved, as well as those who would experience a change in some of their privileges and entitlements.

For example, if a proposal was being considered to stop sorting students into several academic levels, such as advanced placement, honors, general, and so on, students who are scheduled into various "tracks" should be involved in a discussion about the proposed change as well as their parents and other community representatives. A transformation is required in personal identities, such as how people view themselves in comparison with others on the socioeconomic and academic status continuum, and in use of available resources, such as how government funds are used. All those impacted in one way or another by the culture and structure of the school system and community in which schools reside should have chances to be involved in the change process used to foster equity transformation. Making such attempts requires a lot of political savvy by a core group of various stakeholders.

❧⟡☙

POLITICAL SAVVY

Political savvy includes having intuitive instincts and diagnostic skills when assessing people and situations to determine the course of action needed at a given time. This includes the ability to effectively motivate persons with very diverse cultural identities and agendas. They must work together rather than at cross-purposes. Effective cross-cultural communication involves using one's intimate knowledge about the organizational culture and organizational factors that most influence the identities of those within the organization.

It is important for administrator and teacher equity leaders to appropriately leverage their personal or formal power as a way of influencing others' motivation and behavior. Personal power is based on interpersonal relationships, referent power (e.g., degree of likability due to personal traits), and connection power (e.g., the "connections" a leader has with influential others). Formal power can be based on legitimate, expert, reward, or information power. Legitimate power is based on the position held by the leader. Expert power is based on the leader's possession of expertise to facilitate the work of others. Reward power is based on the leader's ability to provide rewards for people who comply, such as recognition. Information power is based on the leader's possession of or access to information considered valuable by others (Stimson, 2011). All of these forms of power must be utilized with respect for those one is trying to influence, which further induces receptivity. Everyone must see the equity transformation as something that will serve their personal self-interest as well as contribute to the common good.

One reason political savvy is imperative is that the job of improving the educational experience and outcomes of those who have been underserved involves helping nonbelievers (e.g., nonbelievers include those who do not believe most Black and Brown students can achieve at high levels) become believers, and helping everyone of all colors, ethnicities, language backgrounds, social, and economic status positively change their ways of interacting and working with each other.

$$\vartheta\!\!\sim\!\!\mathcal{E}$$

EQUITY TRANSFORMATION VS. EQUITY REFORM

Qualitatively different degrees of political savvy are needed based on whether equity transformation or equity reform is being attempted. Equity reforms are more like appendages to the existing institutional structure and culture whereas equity transformation efforts are aimed at changing the entire school community, meaning changing the school culture and structure. Changes in individual ways of being are required in equity transformation and not usually in equity reform. When equity reforms are undertaken, persons can continue to believe what they have always privately believed and make only minor modifications in the behaviors they have practiced as teachers, administrators, support staff, and so on. However, in most cases, new identities, roles, attitudes, beliefs, values, and behaviors are required when pursuing equity transformation.

Vignette 13–1 describes an initiative that is in the very early stages of attempts to achieve equity transformation, where the intentions were good but the political actions taken were counterproductive. Vignette 13–2 describes how a districtwide equity reform effort was being implemented in a particular school. Both vignettes emphasize the major impact that the politics and equity leadership can have on the success of any equity initiative.

MAKE IT PERSONAL

1. What is your opinion about the extent to which there continues to be a major lack of trust and respect across racial and cultural boundaries in the United States, and in your life?

2. How would you characterize your own level of political savvy when it comes to working with diverse constituencies with different, sometimes conflicting, agendas related to achieving equitable educational outcomes?

VIGNETTE 13–1: AN ATTEMPT AT EQUITY TRANSFORMATION–THE MOUNT VERNON SCHOOL DISTRICT

In the Mount Vernon school district, the equity transformation effort was a proposal by a community-based group to the Board of Education for a policy change that would grant all students, regardless of prior academic performance, greater access to college preparatory courses at the high school level. Students would also have greater access to "highly qualified" teachers, as redefined in the proposal. The impact of this policy would primarily affect students of African and Latino/a descent. This effort began when Latino/a and Black community organization leaders jointly invited a few district and school site administrators, teachers, parents, and students to join an ad hoc community group they were creating that would conduct a series of meetings. The purpose of the group was to discuss some potential solutions to the growing gap in educational outcomes being experienced by students of color at the high school level.

After those who accepted the invitation to join the group met on several occasions and heard presentations by various educational "experts" invited to the meetings, the group proposed two major policy changes to the board of education. The first proposal was for change in the policy determining criteria for student access to college preparatory courses, whose successful completion is a requirement for application to the state university system. The second proposal was for change in district policy determining teacher work assignments, that is, the school site where teachers work and the courses/academic levels they teach. These changes were based on the strong belief that students of color with the weakest academic backgrounds need equitable access to being taught at high academic levels and to the most experienced and accomplished teachers.

Equitable access was defined by the ad hoc group to mean that if 60% of White or Asian students have access to college preparatory courses and to the teachers with the most experience, then students of African and Latino/a descent should have comparable access. There were several complexities associated with this proposal that were acknowledged by the ad hoc group. For example, in Mount Vernon, providing equitable access to college preparation courses taught at high levels would require a major increase in the

number of such courses in high school schedules as well as changes in the teacher's con-
tract. Many teachers would not voluntarily agree to these changes in work assignment and
could not be required to do so because of their seniority. In previous contract negotiations,
the teachers union had expressed its very strong opposition to such changes. Another
complexity is that the ad hoc group proposed ongoing training on culturally responsive
pedagogy for existing teachers of college preparatory courses and any additional teachers
given such assignments. Their rationale was that all teachers assigned to such classes
should be prepared to effectively teach the curriculum to more culturally diverse students
in the district.

These proposals definitely have implications for the teacher contract and the district
budget. In addition, the ad hoc group is aware that many qualified students of color have
previously opted to not take such classes. Despite acknowledging these complexities, those
who voluntarily came together in this ad hoc community group are adamant in their
resolve to strongly lobby for a positive board response. They know they are challenging
well established norms and policies in the district. They argue that a sense of urgency is
needed, since the U.S. Department of Education has designated the entire district as low
performing. To further complicate things, there has been a lot of community reaction to
the proposals, both pro and con.

The creation of this group and their proposed changes have spurred a lot of debate
among those on different sides of the issue, increased racial tension in the community,
and legal threats by the teacher's bargaining unit. The conflicts have led to a broader
discussion of relevant issues, such as the quality of teaching experienced by historically
underserved students in general, the quality of instructional support provided by the dis-
trict to all teachers, and the nature of the curriculum in college preparatory classes com-
pared with all other classes.

To the Reader: Before continuing to read the rest of this vignette, think about what you would do if you were an administrator, teacher, or parent in the ad hoc group before a vote was taken by the Board of Education on these proposals.

After very contentious debates in the media on the recommendations, the assistant
superintendent for curriculum and instruction, in consultation with her superintendent,
created a district task force composed of teacher, parent, community, and student repre-
sentatives. The charge to the task force was to investigate what the potential effects would
be of making such changes, and listing the pros and cons of taking such action based on
evidence they had collected. The district task force was also asked to develop a list of
recommendations for what if any immediate courses of action should be taken in response
to the proposals.

Several proponents and opponents of what was being proposed are incensed by the
creation of this district task force, and want the Board of Education to get directly
involved, including the possibility of initiating their own investigation, and hiring their
own experts. There are rumors spread by the teachers union that the superintendent

privately encouraged the community ad hoc group to meet on their own and develop such proposals for presentation to the Board of Education. The district administration has refused to comment on the rumors.

One board member, a retired teacher, who was heavily supported by the teacher's union in his last campaign for a seat on the board, is furious over this entire series of events. He has publicly stated that he thinks there were ill-advised political decisions made by district and school site administrators to become involved with this community group. He claims this was a premeditated effort by the superintendent to put public pressure on the teacher's bargaining unit to change their opposition to contract language on teacher assignments.

‽‽

FACTORS CONTRIBUTING TO THE POLITICS ASSOCIATED WITH THE EQUITY TRANSFORMATION EFFORT

The attitudes and actions described in vignette 13–1 include some very controversial political decisions made by the ad hoc group. These decisions underscore the political dimensions of culturally courageous leadership discussed in Chapter 9. The vignette also illustrates how important it is to be politically savvy when trying to change any inequities. It is essential to identify and navigate any "political land mines." Attention to three dimensions of POI might have lessened the negative reaction to the ad hoc group proposal.

Engage in Problem Definition and Analysis (the process for defining problems)

From the information provided in the above vignette, it appears the "problem" has been identified as one of unequal access to being taught at high levels (i.e., access to academically rigorous instruction) and to what are considered "highly qualified" teachers, as redefined by the community leaders in the vignette. A major assumption is that college preparatory courses are taught at high levels, and that the most experienced teachers are the most "qualified" or competent. Other issues or problems related to the problem of limited access are not addressed in the proposal, such as student academic readiness level for participation in such courses, and the right of students, under current board policy, to not choose such courses. In other words, there is no default curriculum in the school district that requires all students to enroll in and pass college preparatory classes in order to graduate from high school.

Another problem not addressed in the proposal is the low pass rate of historically underserved students who are enrolled in such courses. In the proposal, there is no acknowledgement of the relationship between all of these associated problems or the assumptions undergirding these additional problems. The issue of there being a low pass rate by students of color in college preparatory courses is indirectly addressed by acknowledgement of the need to provide teacher training on culturally responsive pedagogy. However, when little attention is given to problem definition and problem analysis during the development of proposals for equity transformation, the likelihood of their success is greatly compromised.

Be Sensitive to the Psychology of Equity Transformation (the climate cultivated when actions are undertaken)

Equity transformation is usually not attempted in school districts, and even then, it is not often pursued in an open, direct, linear fashion, and may be the result of civic unrest, public protests, lawsuits, or court decisions. Equity transformation may also be initially undertaken because of elections that result in a new board of education majority that has the power to take a school district in a new direction. In vignette 13–1, it is unclear what motivated some community leaders to initiate a series of meetings about the condition of underachievement being experienced by students of color. The politics in the community and on the school board might have motivated the superintendent to encourage such actions by community leaders, especially given the district is designated a low-performing district by the federal department of education.

In addition, it is unlikely administrators in the school district would have agreed to participate if they didn't think such actions were approved by the superintendent. It is also unlikely these community organizations in the Black and Latino/a community would have taken the initiative to work together to form such an ad hoc group, since they have no history of having taken any joint actions before. This initiative suggests they received encouragement to do so from the superintendent or new board of education president, who happens to be of Latino/a descent. Rather than go directly to the Board of Education with their concerns or ideas, the community leaders chose to invite a group of individuals in the school district community to deliberate with them on what should be done about the situation.

Out of all the changes they could have advocated, they chose to identify two that are extremely contentious and difficult to achieve. Why? No doubt, they were making some assumptions based on their collective beliefs about what should have highest priority in order to turn around low student achievement. What were the opinions of students in the group? Did teachers in the group share some insider information about their colleagues that influenced the choices made? The administrators, parents, and community persons might have had their assumptions confirmed by what they heard from the teachers and students, who are at the heart of the teaching and learning process.

At some point in the deliberations of the ad hoc group, they seem to have reached consensus on what they needed to do. When that happened, there was a psychological break-through because persons with very different perspectives and in very different roles came to the position of having one mind about what they would propose. They might originally have had very diverse reasons for deciding to accept the invitation to be part of the group and different ideas of what the group should propose, if anything. The ad hoc group appears to have individually and collectively transcended their personal doubts or agendas to decide on direct confrontation and strong public advocacy. They do not seem to have any fears about what their actions could trigger or what the personal consequences might be. Their proposal stimulated a different kind of discourse in the school district community that may lead to an entirely new dynamic of communication between persons in diverse groups as well as potentially plant some seeds for new forms of collaboration among school community stakeholders. The psychology of this budding initiative is stimulating more openness and authenticity among different players in the school district community, whether that was intended or not. The psychology of equity transformation includes the degree of willingness to air strongly held feelings and values of all the players for and against such transformation as well as what people are open to accepting, respecting, or rejecting.

An Essential Strategy: Awareness, Team, and Trust Building

The equity proposal for greater access was developed by district administrators and community leaders without much dissemination of information in the school community about the conditions and circumstances that they thought necessitated such action. The results of having inadequate information may be pushback now being experienced from some teachers and others who resent, resist, or fear such equity initiatives. Building greater awareness of the need for certain changes is of paramount importance if there is an interest in building greater support within school communities for such efforts.

In addition to increased awareness building, there is a great need for team and trust building, all of which can be undertaken simultaneously. Persons from all stakeholder groups must be engaged in activities that improve the climate in which equity transformation is attempted, such as an increase in the communication between, and problem solving by, school community stakeholders in order to increase their cohesion, morale, and goal focus. Such activities can concurrently improve their willingness to trust each other and trust in the potential benefits of equity transformation. Increasing the acquisition by historically underserved students of 21st century skills cannot likely be achieved without simultaneous attention to improving relationships in school communities and relevance in classroom instruction (Partnership for 21st Century Skills, 2011).

How do you substantially improve rigor, relationships, and relevance? As stated throughout Section II of the guide, there must be the political will and political savvy among all adult stakeholder groups. A good starting point is to have a much more candid dialogue within school communities about how race, class, and culture impact educational environments and outcomes. There is usually a strong reticence within most stakeholder groups to engage in such dialogue. There is even more discomfort with trying to make the personal and organizational changes needed in the entire school community to achieve positive relationships, academic rigor, and curriculum relevance. The school is the major part, but not the only part of the school community that requires transformation. A major value often articulated by "privileged" parents and the community at large, and thus echoed by teachers and administrators in the dominant cultural group, is that *all* students must benefit from whatever is done for low-income historically underserved students of color. This is a constant refrain, or mantra, and reflects the willingness of those with power and authority to only consider improvements in equity for the underserved when those with privilege receive even greater benefits.

The reticence to avoid discussing the notion that "all students must benefit" cannot be allowed to inhibit such discussions from ever taking place. The psychology of equity transformation that culturally courageous leaders help to craft must include opportunities for ongoing dialogue and problem solving that is undertaken by all school community stakeholders within an environment where respect and trust are nurtured among the various players. Dialogue and problem-solving activities must include students, parents, other community members, and university faculty in teacher/administrator preparation programs who have helped prepare educators who work in the school community. These stakeholders are every bit as important as teachers, instructional support staff, and administrators. Without simultaneous attention to trust building, it is highly unlikely equity transformation will ever take place, much less that equitable outcomes will result.

It might be necessary to initially bring together ethnic-specific subgroups of various stakeholder groups, so that African, Latino/a, Asian and/or White students, teachers, administrators, parents, and so on, can first discuss their questions and concerns with each other. Such ethnic-specific activities can help improve the communication, problem-solving, and team/trust building within subgroups before trying to do it in cross-cultural groups. This decision should be based on an analysis of the context in specific locales.

MAKE IT PERSONAL

1. Describe the feelings, values, motivation, and openness of all parties when you were personally involved in an equity initiative.

2. How would you characterize the level of trust and team effort during the initiative you described?

Focus on Standards Categories Receiving Low Priority
(expand the accountability criteria)

The history of the standards-based movement in K–12 schools within the United States since the early 1990s reflects a focus almost exclusively on content and performance standards: what students should know and/or be able to do, to what extent, and how the expected degree of mastery should be ascertained. However, during the early years of the standards movement in some school districts, greater attention was also given to opportunity to learn (OTL) standards, which primarily meant whether students of all backgrounds had sufficient opportunity to learn the designated content standards (AERA, 1993; Elmore & Fuhrman, 1995).

Opportunity was defined initially as whether there were equitable financial resources provided to ensure all students had equal access to the requisite instructional resources for achieving the standards as well as sufficient time provided to teachers and students for mastery of the standards. The push for inclusion of OTL standards in national education legislation, that is, the federal elementary and secondary education act, was dropped due to opposition from both the left and right wings of the political spectrum. There was considerable concern over what this would cost and who would pay for it as well as the resistance in congress to the federal government having too much influence over education. This was and still is considered by many to primarily be the prerogative of individual states.

Since that time, in the last 15 to 20 years, the federal government has assumed a much larger footprint by requiring measurement of performance outcomes on high stakes tests, as specified in the No Child Left Behind legislation enacted into law in 2001. During the 1990s, the original concept of opportunity to learn standards was expanded as well as the creation of delivery standards that stood alone from OTL standards.

Finally, professional development standards, influenced by the National Staff Development Council, were also conceptualized to spell out all of the perceived requirements for significantly improving teacher and administrator professional development that would then impact the quality of education offered and learning outcomes experienced by all student subgroups. Examples of each category of standards are identified in Chapter 5 of this guide.

Despite the identification and development of five categories of standards, content and performance standards became the default standards to which all schools were held accountable, initially by some school districts, and finally by almost all state governments and the federal government. In my work with several school districts with high numbers of underachieving historically underserved students, there was less attention, if any at all, to delivery, OTL, and professional development standards by school boards and district-level executive administrators. Without more fidelity to the latter three categories of standards, it is not likely that educational opportunities and learning environments will be equitable for all racial, cultural, ethnic, and socioeconomic groups, much less equitable educational outcomes. There was a landmark superior court decision (California Department of Education, 2004) in the last decade that requires California to provide more financial resources to identified schools that did not provide student access to adequate facilities, instructional materials, and qualified teachers. These areas encompass some of the opportunity to learn standards as defined in this guide. However, that court decision is the exception and not the rule in educational policy throughout the United States.

Culturally courageous leadership, as stated above, includes confronting and changing organizational practices that help perpetuate inequitable educational outcomes of historically underserved students of color. The plaintiffs and their supporters in the Williams court decision mentioned above exemplified a degree of culturally courageous leadership (CCL), in their dedication to seeking implementation of some opportunity to learn standards in low-income schools, so there would be a better chance to achieve equitable educational outcomes.

In vignette 13–1, it appears the group of diverse stakeholders who were convened by community leaders came to the same conclusion. It is likely that they concluded underperforming students of color were definitely not experiencing fidelity to what is defined in this guide as opportunity to learn, delivery, and professional development standards.

Lawsuits that result in favorable court decisions are one way that state governments can be required to give higher priority to the implementation of some delivery and opportunity-to-learn standards. In addition, school boards can require district and school site administrators to give higher priority to establishing multiple benchmarks that the district and school sites must collaboratively achieve in the implementation of such standards. One benchmark could be greater access to courses taught at high levels.

MAKE IT PERSONAL

1. What would happen if your school board received a similar community-based proposal about improving student access?

2. Describe how you would attempt to use the above dimensions of POI as part of your implementation plan for achieving equitable educational outcomes in your work setting.

3. Based upon discussion of the difference between equity reform and equity transformation in Chapter 4 and in this chapter, describe equity "reforms" that have been attempted in your school district compared with equity "transformation," and what the results were.

VIGNETTE 13-2: AN ATTEMPT AT EQUITY REFORM— PIERSON ACADEMY FOR LEADERSHIP (PAL)

The equity reform (as opposed to equity transformation) attempted in the Pierson Academy for Leadership (PAL) was voluntary metropolitan busing. This would ostensibly increase desegregation and the quality of education provided to low-income underachieving students of color who were voluntarily bused from a much larger adjacent school district. PAL is the most culturally and socioeconomically diverse school in a suburban upscale small community adjacent to a large city. The suburb is composed primarily of homes occupied by middle- and upper-middle-class White families. However, there is a growing number of large apartment complexes, populated by culturally, linguistically, and socioeconomically diverse persons who live in the residential boundaries of PAL, which is the oldest K–8 school in the district but has the newest school facility.

The school district is part of a metropolitan voluntary busing program that brings native-born and immigrant students of color to PAL from the adjacent city school district, starting in the third grade. The bused students constitute about 10% of all students at PAL, and the total school population is 75% White and 25% students of color. Resident students of color are another 15% of the student population at PAL. There are two Black teachers and no Latino/a teachers out of 27 teachers on staff, most of whom are below the age of 40. There is a large achievement gap between most White students and most students of color, resident and bused, that hasn't substantially changed in the last 5 years. This is the case because even though the achievement by students of color on statewide tests has improved, the achievement of White students has improved much more.

One indicator of the school climate at PAL is the attitude of most teachers that the students of color, both resident students and those bused, are lucky to be attending such an innovative and accepting school as PAL, where the teachers say they really "care" about the students. The teachers are quick to point out they have been very receptive to the district's state-funded multicultural education program, even though they have resisted integrating most of the program's concepts into the district core curriculum. They also proudly proclaim they voted overwhelmingly for Pierson to participate in the metropolitan busing program. Based on these espoused forms of support for diversity, these teachers feel the students should appreciate being at PAL by practicing good citizenship, including making their best efforts to do well in school, as demonstrated by consistently completing homework and being on task during classroom instruction.

When students of color don't exhibit such appreciation and effort in the opinion of their teachers, some of the teachers get very frustrated with them and also with their parents when they don't respond to teachers' request for their help. Conversely, many of the parents of color, especially those whose children are bused from the adjacent city, complain about the attitude of several teachers, whom they accuse of pretending to respect and welcome them to the school but only on their terms.

Teachers at PAL have great discretion in instructional decisions, with the principal playing a low profile when it comes to observation of classroom instruction. He is receptive to teachers who seek his counsel or guidance, but usually only intervenes to influence class-room functioning for two reasons. Those reasons are when there are curriculum directives from the district office or when long-time resident White parents with political clout think teachers are spending inordinate time with the more academically needy students at the expense of their children's needs.

Some parents of color whose children have been frequently sent to the office for disciplinary reasons think the principal should be more visible in classrooms to monitor whether teachers are discriminating against their children. Their children tell them their teachers don't adequately explain what they are teaching and say that when they (the students) ask for help, the teacher moves on to something else or says they need to pay closer attention and stop engaging in off-task behavior. The same children complain that they don't get time on the computers in the classroom, only those students who finish their assignments early. Time on the computers is only used as a reward for finishing assignments before end of the designated time and having good citizenship grades (i.e., being compliant to all teacher directives).

The principal requires teachers to engage in some joint lesson planning but never attends these meetings nor does he initiate any problem-solving discussions about strained cross-cultural relations in the classroom. He also doesn't participate in quarterly staff reviews of progress by each student subgroup on school-wide formative assessments unless invited to do so.

Although Pierson teachers say they have a very cohesive staff, there is actually dissension among some of those with strong personality or educational philosophy differences. Most teachers see themselves as social liberals and will give the politically correct appearance of being very committed to changing any inequities. However, they will not engage in large- or small-group problem solving devoted to joint development of instructional strategies for "needy" students. This reticence by many staff to engage in such discussions is for diverse reasons, including the desire to avoid conflicts and maintain their autonomy over what instructional strategies to use, the differences among staff in their teaching styles and attitudes about the students, and their desire to avoid at all costs appearing to be biased. Furthermore, most of the teachers have strong doubts about the ability of bused-in students to perform at high levels, and they have some other negative attitudes about these students.

Several teachers want the principal to think they are courageously tackling major challenges experienced in their teaching of those they consider the "most needy." These same staff will sometimes take credit for student academic success more likely caused by after-school tutorial assistance provided by community volunteers and instructional support staff. A few teachers like to give the false impression they are working closely with one or more of their peers who are having great success in their classroom with very academically and culturally diverse students. However, their "collaboration "consists of "farming out" some of their students with whom they have difficulty to the room of the other teacher. They let their more successful teaching partner do most of the teaching with students of color they cannot handle.

ॐ॰॰ঔ

FACTORS CONTRIBUTING TO THE POLITICS ASSOCIATED WITH THE EQUITY REFORM EFFORT

The attitudes and actions of some teachers and the school principal described in vignette 13–2 demonstrate the need for more attention to the political dimensions of equity transformation and reform discussed in Chapter 9 and elaborated upon in this chapter. The vignette also illustrates the potential negative consequences of distributed instructional leadership. When instructional leadership is shared by the principal with several teacher leaders, all persons providing such leadership need to have very clear rules of engagement to which all agree. For example, they need to have protocols for investigating any parent allegations of discriminatory treatment by teachers, in such areas as discipline, monitoring of student engagement, and building on student interests, strengths, and prior knowledge.

Being politically savvy when making equity efforts includes taking the actions needed to improve capacity building and cohesion of persons in multiple stakeholder groups, so they more effectively work together. Actions needed include taking the initiative to increase personal awareness of and responsiveness to the needs and concerns of those one is attempting to lead. As indicated earlier, an example of such awareness and responsiveness may result in convening ethnic/race-specific groups for problem definition and problem-solving discussions before bringing them together for the same kind of discussion in culturally diverse groups. For example, in some schools there are community members, parents, teachers, students, and administrators who work at cross purposes with others in their cultural group or job category as well as across cultural or stakeholder groups. They even conspire against and/or malign each other to the detriment of success by all students. At PAL, there are some major philosophical, pedagogic, and personality differences between some teachers, even though it is kept under wraps. Skilled facilitation by the principal is needed to expose and resolve dysfunctional attitudes and behaviors between staff, but that is not happening at PAL.

Vignette 13–2 does not illustrate political savvy and instead illustrates the need for the following political dimensions to be strongly considered when trying to initiate any equity reform.

Learn From Observations During Other Equity Initiatives (make more informed decisions based on what has happened during other equity initiatives)

Most of the teachers at PAL are inclined to view some bused students and their parents as problematic, because they do not exhibit appropriate appreciation for being "allowed" to attend the school. The teachers didn't seem to see these persons as resources whose feedback and suggestions could help them improve school achievement. If pushed, most of these same teachers might acknowledge their belief that African and Latino/a American students cannot be taught at high academic levels if too much time is spent on multicultural education, especially if they are from low socioeconomic backgrounds. These attitudes of some teachers are never explicitly expressed to parents, but the parents intuit this attitude being prevalent among many staff, so they react accordingly.

Many districts and schools are implementing school choice programs or approving charter schools that result in a greater percentage of African and Latino/a American students in these educational settings. When they do so, they could benefit from acquiring information about the challenges experienced by choice or charter schools elsewhere with similar demographic profiles. In Chapter 4, I shared 10 major observations from my experience with equity initiatives and as an external evaluator in low-performing schools. I have already discussed how poor school climate contaminates and compromises efforts to achieve the goals of any equity "reform" or "transformation." Two examples of my observations relevant in vignette 13–2 are as follows:

1. "There is cultural dissonance within each stakeholder group, as well as within and between stakeholder groups, that contributes to the failure of some equity initiatives."

2. "There is little if any nurturing and utilization of students and parents, especially those of color, as resources in helping to develop, implement, and monitor equity plans."

In the above vignette, Pierson school has a lot of cultural dissonance, despite efforts by some to give the impression they have a very harmonious school community. Some teachers say they have a very cohesive staff but in private will admit there are major personality differences and differences in educational philosophy that contribute to avoidance of situations where such differences might have to be discussed. In addition, the Black and Latino/a parents are almost evenly divided between those who are residents of the school community and those whose children are bused to the school from the adjacent city. The resident parents of color and parents of bused students rarely have the opportunity to talk to each other, and some of them have incorrect assumptions about each other, based on hearsay. Cultural dissonance isn't always displayed, but that doesn't mean it doesn't exist. The tension in some settings can be a reflection of such dissonance between many diverse stakeholders.

Parents and teachers from what may seem to be very different backgrounds can often find they have a lot in common when they are helped to reach out to each other. In PAL, the culturally diverse parents and students of color in the busing program do not feel welcome at the school. This could be due to a variety of factors. From their perspective, the concerns they have shared with the principal fall on deaf ears. It is incumbent on principals to take the initiative to see that parents and teachers come together. Likewise, principals need to meet directly with students to elicit their thoughts, feelings, and any grievances they have about the school. This kind of relationship building is of critical importance. It is ironic that the Pierson school is named the Pierson Academy for Leadership, but there are no programmatic efforts to build student leadership across all cultural groups. There are also no cross-cultural teacher initiatives that reflect the acronym of the school that is PAL, so that those students bused to the school feel they have "pals" who warmly embrace them at Pierson and appreciate what they have to offer.

The issues described in vignette 13–2 are not uncommon and require a different kind of distributed leadership among the principal and teachers than what has been practiced. The teacher leaders probably need to be held to a higher level of accountability. There also seems to be a strong reticence of many staff to acknowledge school climate problems at Pierson. The conditions in schools described in Chapter 11 that have eliminated achievement gaps are examples that Pierson needs to follow. The distributed instructional leadership in those achieving schools is qualitatively different than that in Pierson. The prevailing tendency of PAL seems to be a proclivity to paper over any major problems with school climate, the work environment, and with equity reform efforts, and to give an impression to the Board of Education, district leadership, and general public that all is under control and being well managed.

PAL is in a school district that has a public image of being a beacon of educational innovation and quality education, albeit for mostly middle- to upper-middle-class White families. The desire to protect the school district's reputation may have inappropriately influenced the approaches taken or not taken at PAL to adapt to their more diverse student population.

The district administration must hold the principal to a higher standard, and he must do the same for all PAL teachers, starting with teacher leaders, regarding their response to students of color and bused students in particular. Sometimes school staff must be held to higher expectations and help provided for them to meet expectations that they responsibly collaborate with all stakeholders to improve the school climate. This expectation should require confronting and changing some personal and organizational norms at Pierson, but this may be unlikely if some district office organizational norms related to support for equity are not subject to critical examination. There appears to be a need for some hands-on supervision and coaching from district office staff or others they designate, and the district office may not have the capacity or disposition to provide such support.

Is There Transparent and Institutional Racism at PAL?

Does the learning environment at PAL reflect both transparent and institutional racism? There do seem to be covert and overt forms of resistance to initiatives for equity reform. Racism is when a given group of people, such as a racial/ethnic group, a religious group, or a group distinguished by other cultural characteristics, such as primary language, are kept in a subordinate position by government entities, organizational culture, and/or policies in the public or private sector. This is the raw use of political and/or economic power, and those targeted are usually not able to change that subservient position (Miles & Brown, 2003).

Transparent racism is when racist beliefs or practices are very easily seen but may not appear to be obviously racist, such as low teacher expectations. Institutional racism is when there are policies or regulations that legitimize social injustice and indefinitely keep a group or groups in a subservient role based on their racial/cultural/linguistic identity. Institutional racism is usually more overt. In PAL, the students' rebellious behaviors could be interpreted as reactions to or misunderstandings of some teacher's expressed attitudes, resulting in teacher referrals to the office. When school policy is used to support disciplinary actions that keep students and parents in a subservient role, the policies can arguably be construed as racist when the point of view of those targeted is given no consideration.

However, the district and school site administration, as well as PAL teachers, appear to be unconsciously incompetent in their ability to discern either institutional or transparent racism. In other words, they do not seem to know what they don't know, or pretend to not know what they don't know, and would vehemently deny such a characterization.

An entire group doesn't have to experience such treatment or oppression for racism to be present. At PAL, there are no policies requiring a watered-down curriculum and lower teacher expectations for Black and Brown students, but that is nevertheless what occurs, reflecting a clear case of de facto transparent racism. This is all the more solidified via an almost total absence of any instructional supervision. The classroom supervision that occurs does not include the use of observation rubrics for characterizing what is being taught and how it is being taught to any students. Likewise, there is no ongoing monitoring of what if any schoolwide instructional support systems are in place for those students needing them. Arguably, one consequence is perpetuation of inequitable educational outcomes for students of color. The racism is easily seen or transparent, but because there are no policies requiring such omissions in educational practice, they are not likely viewed as racist.

Students claim some teachers don't provide extra help in the classroom, saying they need to move on and complaining students need to pay closer attention and be less distracted during instruction. The teachers' posture is a part of the transparent racism, because even though their practices don't reflect school policy, they do contribute to denying access of some students to the curriculum and keep some students in a state of underachievement. The teacher attitudes display a total dismissal of student and parent concerns about their teaching practices and the Eurocentric curriculum.

Institutional racism at PAL is reflected in formal rules, and transparent racism is reflected in norms that keep bused students of color in a subservient role. These policies and norms are key barriers to achievement at high levels.

MAKE IT PERSONAL

1. Describe an example, if possible, of institutional and/or transparent racism in your school and/or school district.

2. If you described an example, what do you think should be done about it?

Reduce Some Key Barriers to Achievement at High Levels (work on major constraints that must be eliminated to remove gaps in educational outcomes)

Three of the major barriers to high achievement that were discussed in Chapter 6 are weak instructional leadership, toxic school and school community climate, and limited accountability. The toxic school climate and weak instructional leadership at Pierson were discussed above. The actions of the principal and some teachers are also examples of limited accountability, another major barrier to achievement at high levels by students of color.

Limited Accountability

In vignette 13–2, weak instructional leadership has led to limited accountability for the educational outcomes experienced by students of color. The vignette describes teacher resistance to collective problem solving on how to improve instruction for students of color, so there is no goal focus or instructional plan adopted by the entire staff for serving this student population. I have found the same schooling conditions in several low-performing schools to be major barriers to high achievement. In this vignette, the district leadership seems complicit in this lack of responsibility and accountability. The principal hasn't been directed to do anything about such conditions as long as achievement goals are met for the overwhelming number of resident White students.

One could infer that teachers are not giving the students of color who need it more assistance during the school day, because their marching orders may be to make sure they are not perceived as taking time away from other students to serve the most needy. There is a very deep-seated antipathy in some low-performing districts to differentiated instructional interventions that may be resented by the families of higher achieving students who don't want limited or dwindling resources disproportionately allocated to help historically underserved students. Another factor that may influence resistance to changing current practices is the end-of-year test scores by students of color bused to Pierson. These test results are better than what their test scores were in their home schools, even though a very large achievement gap continues to exist between the bused students and the resident White students. The old cliché that a rising tide raises all boats masks the embedded racism in such a rationalization for tolerating continuation of major gaps in educational outcomes, despite the espoused intent of the federal No Child Left Behind legislation.

Conditions Contributing to Limited Accountability

At Pierson Academy, there are several conditions that may be contributing to limited accountability, which are major barriers to all student groups achieving at high levels. The conditions fall into three broad categories, the first of which is an absence of the three R's: relationships, rigor, and relevance. Teacher relationships with some parents of color, relationships between some teachers, and relationships between the principal and some parents of color were characterized in the vignette as tense. The curriculum and instructional strategies for students of color were also described as less rigorous than for other students, and students of color probably do not find the Eurocentric curriculum relevant or the instruction motivating.

Another relationship issue in PAL and the district at large is the intense competitiveness between adults, whether they are teachers, administrators, or parents. Most staff have a strong motivation to work in this district because of its reputation. There is a strong preoccupation with one's "status" in the school community at large and in their stakeholder group in particular. This proclivity leads to constant efforts to improve both one's position power and personal power within the district, and this same inclination is true to varying degrees in different schools. This dynamic is part of the back story helping to explain the principal's style and the teacher's relationships with each other and with students.

The second category of conditions is the absence of the three A's: accountability, assessment, and access. It is my view that school districts should vigilantly hold all stakeholders accountable, especially principals and teachers. As an assistant superintendent in charge of all instructional programs as well as the supervision and evaluation of all principals in a secondary school district, I used multiple assessments during the instructional supervision process to monitor the quality of leadership, teaching, and student educational outcomes. I also monitored the extent to which the district was able to give priority to opportunity to learn, delivery, and professional development standards. Vignette 13–2 describes supervision of the principal as limited and focuses primarily on whether achievement targets for the White student population are met. It should be no surprise that accountability, assessment, and access issues addressed by the principal mirrored the district's priority and went no further. Accountability, assessment, and access experienced by students of color, especially those bused in, did not receive the same level of scrutiny and urgency by the principal or instructional staff.

The third category of conditions contributing to limited accountability at Pierson is the absence of several communication behaviors: facilitation, mediation, and candor. The vignette provides no evidence of any attempts to facilitate better communication and team building among all staff. During such discussions, the principal, teacher leaders, or university faculty engaged for that purpose could help surface any conflicts and attempt mediation between those with differing perspectives, at the same time that candor, that is, open honest dialogue, would be encouraged and supported. In PAL, the teachers avoid candid conversations about school problems, especially those involving race and culture, and the principal does not take the initiative to convene meetings for that purpose.

Who should be engaged in addressing the above conditions? District and site administrators, as well as teacher and community leaders, should all be working collaboratively to address the conditions described. For example, the principal should be helped if necessary to develop a work plan that calls for collaboration with "other stakeholders" and helped, if needed, to carry out the plan. "Other stakeholders" include parent and upper grade level student representatives whose perspectives on the causes and barriers to high achievement should be solicited and not discarded once received. In addition, principals need their own professional learning community where they can candidly share and receive feedback and suggestions from colleagues in a synergistic fashion.

I have found an effective strategy can be the creation of a network of schools within a district or a network of districts within a geographic region who focus primarily on increasing the expertise of principals to improve and expand instructional leadership and accountability for equitable educational outcomes. Such a network should engage as often as possible in electronic and live synergistic activities, where they learn from sharing personal challenges and build upon each other's successes. I facilitated such face-to-face "synergy groups" of principals when I was director of leadership development in a county office of education. I found principals more comfortable in being open and candid when such groups were composed of people from different districts, because they felt a greater sense of confidentiality was possible.

The Role of Culturally Courageous Leaders in Reducing Barriers

Improving the three R's, the three A's, and several communication behaviors in PAL requires CCL. For all of the above barriers to achievement at high levels to be reduced or eliminated, the appropriate district administrators, site administrator(s), and teachers must be willing to work collaboratively in addressing their day-to-day challenges.

Culturally courageous leaders are willing to critically examine and transcend personal influences that may significantly contribute to prejudicial beliefs, discriminatory actions, avoidance behavior, and cultural incompetence.

Culturally courageous leaders are more open and honest about human difference biases, their own and others, as well as biased organizational norms in their work setting. Through more critical self-reflection, cultural consciousness is raised, and also the comfort to openly and candidly discuss what has been happening compared with what needs to happen. As discussed in Chapters 7 through 12, culturally courageous leaders consciously take the initiative to think and act in ways that help all students achieve at high levels. That is not happening at PAL.

The focus of problem solving must include collective strategizing on how to deal with *barriers* to creating culturally democratic learning environments, where all voices are legitimized and priority is given to the needs of all students. Culturally democratic learning environments are those where teachers are in a constant state of "learning," enabling them to stay motivated to effectively teach culturally diverse students.

An example of a barrier to creating culturally democratic learning environments would be teachers not having the knowledge or comfort to integrate content about societal conditions negatively impacting cultural and ethnic minorities in the United States. Some of the political constraints to successfully implementing the three R's, three A's, and communication behaviors include the interpersonal and philosophical differences within and between ethnic-specific and stakeholder groups about whether students should learn about the negative dynamics between groups and individuals in their neighborhoods and larger communities. Some equity advocates would assert that if children live in environments where they experience such conflicts on a day-to-day basis, then schools should help them develop the capacity to make things better.

There is a lack of collaborative effort and trust within groups (e.g., teachers, parents, racial groups) as well as across groups. Some ethnic specific community-based organizations have their internal conflicts and trust issues as well as their difficulties in establishing trust and collaboration with other community-based organizations. Likewise, when it comes to equity reforms or equity transformation, school administrator and teacher organizations each have their conflicting priorities and trust issues within their groups and between their groups. Many parents from each cultural/ethnic group experience the same problem within their peer groups and across their groups. All of these conflicts among the stakeholder groups make it very difficult, but not impossible, to reduce the key barriers to achievement at high levels for historically underserved students of color.

The political priorities of culturally courageous leaders must be to improve social relations within and among all constituencies, expand collective decision making so that there is more investment and ownership in the decisions made and willingness to implement them, more equity in power and authority relationships, and less competition between stakeholder groups. These are overlapping priorities complementary to each other. It is not possible to improve power and authority relationships, personal investment, ownership, political will, and savvy unless social relations are dramatically changed across all boundaries. Elizabeth Martinez discusses the need for multiethnic coalitions to join forces in their struggle for social justice in her book *De Colores Means All of Us: Latina Views for a Multi-Colored Century* (1998).

MAKE IT PERSONAL

FN13-1 (SEE FACILITATOR NOTES IN APPENDIX 1)

1. Which of the above conditions, such as absence of the three R's, three A's, or communication behaviors, contribute the most to weak instructional leadership and limited accountability in your work setting?

2. What is one thing you would do if you were engaged in direct efforts to correct the absence of any conditions identified in response to the previous question?

Prevent "Equity Hustlers" From Compromising Equity Efforts (be able to identify and eliminate any negative impact of those who want others to think of them as equity leaders even though they are not)

Based on information provided in the vignette, there may be some equity hustlers at PAL, and the school district itself may be an equity hustler. Social relations within and between groups are exacerbated by wanksters, gangsters, and riders.

Wanksters can be identified based on the gap between what they say and do. They talk a good game but never follow through. Although they pretend to embrace the need to improve the achievement of bused students, thus "talking the talk," they do not "walk the talk" of the equity reform undertaken in the school. Although they seem committed to nurturing relationships with their bused students or their parents, they do not defend the right of students and parents to feel the way they do about how they are treated. They say there is staff cohesion in the school when actually there are major philosophical and pedagogical differences among staff causing resistance to teacher collaboration on problem solving and joint lesson planning. There are many wanksters at PAL. However, as already mentioned, school districts as a whole can be "wanksters" when it comes to a commitment to equity transformation, and the district in which PAL is one school could be considered a wankster in some regards, unwittingly or consciously contributing to such attitudes and behaviors among the principal and staff at PAL.

Gangsters take credit without attribution for the work and accomplishments of others. They also take credit for what others do for them (i.e., taking credit for the academic successes and/or improved behavior of students one cannot handle by "farming" them out to other teachers who work better with the "farmed out" students). PAL has a few teachers who meet the definition of a gangster.

Riders need to be helped, mentored, or coached so they can over time become more self-secure and motivated to make efforts at the next level of functioning, instead of hiding behind the high visibility role of others committed to social justice. Riders may value culturally responsive teaching, but they don't have the psychological readiness or skills to promote the implementation of culturally responsive teaching in the face of resistance. They prefer to stay in the background and let others provide all of the visible leadership, take all of the risks and do the heavy lifting when it comes to actually confronting biased attitudes, or trying to change biased school policies. They must ride other's coattails. There are also a few riders at PAL; a few of the teachers are very successful with their bused students, but don't assume an aggressive public role of advocacy within the school or district on behalf of their historically underserved students .

It is the duty of the principal to work with his expanded leadership team to raise everyone's consciousness about the phenomenon of "equity hustlers" that can be counterproductive to equity initiatives, followed by vigilant efforts to identify and correct any instances when there is evidence of such attitudes and behaviors, or even the appearance thereof. This should include the courage to self-identify and model the willingness to change, and will probably require a critical self-examination of whether the ideologies of White dominance and color-blindness discussed in Chapter 1 are embraced by the district and school.

MAKE IT PERSONAL

FN13-2 (SEE FACILITATOR NOTES IN APPENDIX 1)

1. Identify either an equity transformation or equity reform initiative undertaken in your school district, school, or program in the recent past, and then describe the politics (i.e., the dynamics between people based on their competing interests, beliefs, values, and priorities) during roll out of the initiative.

2. Given the politics you have just described in response to #1 above, identify one of the six political strategies discussed after vignette 13-1 or 13-2 that was NOT used in your situation but should have been. Explain your reasoning.

❧❧

WHAT WAS HAPPENING IN THE VIGNETTES

In vignette 13-1, the community leaders who convened the meetings to discuss lack of student access were attempting to achieve *equity transformation* by getting leaders from all stakeholder groups to collectively identify causes of the achievement gap and develop a proposal for how to begin correcting the problem. The proposal was directed at transforming both the culture and structure at the school that perpetuated some school conditions contributing to low student achievement. Personal and organizational identities, beliefs, values, and norms would be transformed during the course of this equity initiative if it had been successful.

In vignette 13-2, however, the district was attempting to implement an *equity reform*, that is, metropolitan desegregation, that would ostensibly improve student achievement of the target students, but there was no hint of leadership at the district level or at the receiving school level to transform personal and organizational identities, school norms, and policies that contributed to maintenance of the achievement gap. The parent complaints about the classroom actions of some teachers and the principal's lack of response to their concerns illustrate the inadequacy of the school's response at the end of the bus ride.

Given the above vignettes about equity initiatives and analysis of how the politics in each case was inadequately handled, it is important to remember some key points about what culturally courageous leaders do when undertaking such goals.

ôôôõ

POLITICAL STRATEGY REMINDERS

Culturally courageous leaders must do the following:

- Demonstrate the insight, will, and savvy to rise above personal cultural influences (that is, beliefs, values, priorities, norms) that are divisive, as they simultaneously work with other stakeholders to change individual behaviors, organizational priorities, and norms that work against equitable educational outcomes. They must be able to withstand and push back against prevailing winds, without succumbing to demonstrating disrespect or destructive behaviors.
- Forge broader and more in-depth coalitions to develop common agendas and goals, both within racial/cultural/stakeholder groups and across such groups. For example, there is a need for ongoing discourse between and joint strategic planning by several types of organizations. These include churches or other community-based organizations that primarily serve particular communities of color, ethnic studies departments and schools/colleges of education at a university, and educational organizations that focus on serving and advocating for particular ethnic communities. There is a critical need for joint efforts by these entities to advocate for and help achieve equitable outcomes for historically underserved students. There is not enough of this going on. These organizations tend to be very insular.
- Reach out to persons who seem indifferent or are diametrically opposed to what you want to achieve. For example, concerted efforts are needed to educate and increase understanding about cultural democracy and equitable outcomes by persons of European backgrounds. They may mistakenly consider issues of social justice, race, and culture as minority issues that have no relevance for them and cannot benefit them. There are White scholars, politicians, and community activists (as well as persons from other racial/ethnic/cultural backgrounds) who have a very strong commitment to cultural democracy and social justice, but in any particular school or school district, there may be no connection between such persons and those of the same racial background who steadfastly oppose such initiatives.

- Have an unswerving commitment to assist the disenfranchised and alienated who may strongly resist and distrust the motives, sincerity, and expertise of those trying to help.

- Exhibit patience, and they might initially need to work on establishing two-way communication, building relationships and establishing trust with a small number of people in one stakeholder group. This may be necessary before trying to work with multiple stakeholder groups to tackle the major causes of social injustice and inequitable educational outcomes.

- Not attempt equity transformation initiatives on a predetermined timeline. In many cases, the initiatives must be allowed to evolve with the initial work focusing on developing new norms of communication, collaboration, and commitment within particular cultural, ethnic, and stakeholder groups. One of the ultimate goals should be for each group to develop greater capacity to work effectively across stakeholder groups on common interests.

MAKE IT PERSONAL

FN13–3 (SEE FACILITATOR NOTES IN APPENDIX 1)

1. Which of the political strategy reminders would you find most difficult to do? Explain your reasoning.

2. What is your experience that confirms or contradicts the statement about how equity transformation initiatives cannot always be attempted on a predetermined timeline?

REVIEW OF CHAPTER 13

- The term "politics" is defined and personalized in terms of how it relates to the phenomenon of attempting "equity transformation" and "equity reform."

- The differences between equity transformation and equity reform are discussed.

- Two vignettes are provided, one describing the politics of implementation (POI) during an attempt at equity transformation and the other the POI during an equity reform effort.

- Each vignette is followed by an analysis of how using three POI dimensions could have minimized the political land mines associated with each equity initiative, and political strategy reminders are provided to emphasize the importance of practicing CCL.

৵৵৻৶

Three
Equity Warriors

14

Cultural courageousness is not for the faint of heart.

The three equity warriors discussed in this chapter each have very unique personalities and consistently demonstrate strong congruence between their sense of self, life purpose, and the walk behind their talk. The descriptions of these three personalities and some of their work-related situational contexts are a natural sequel to every topic, condition, and challenge discussed in this guide. The primary goal is to provide examples of how to model as well as lead equity transformation and navigate the political land mines which may get in the way.

Personal information is provided on each "warrior," their equity interventions, and some of the politics each has successfully navigated. The stories of the equity warriors should serve as a stimulus to greater self-reflection and assist you in making decisions about your next steps in working with others to provide equity leadership.

KWL EXERCISE

1. What is your vision for how you want to help teachers and/or administrators when it comes to the educational outcomes of historically underserved students?

2. If you could personally interview each of the "equity warriors" in this chapter, describe what you would be most interested in learning.

3. What did you learn from the last chapter on defusing political land mines that you can apply to your own work context?

LEADING BY MAKING THE INVISIBLE VISIBLE

Jean Richardson, Principal

Personal Background

Jean Richardson, a White elementary principal in a small very culturally and linguistically diverse K–12 northern California school district, has been an elementary principal in two different schools over a 20-year period, and both schools are populated primarily by low-income ethnically diverse students. She asserts she has a transparent leadership style and puts herself on the line by publicly acknowledging that as a White person she is a racist and participates in White privilege. Jean says her journey began at her place of birth, "Where I had no awareness of diversity as I grew up in middle-class Midland, Michigan, a white community where the Dow Chemical Company seemed to control the lives of those who lived there." Jean went on to say that "when I was 16, my sister married an African American man and I became a godmother to their daughter. In my travels with my sister's family, for the first time in my life I experienced a totally different reception from the world that was hostile and questioning. As I further branched out into the "real" world, attending Michigan State University, where I was in the minority, I woke up to my responsibilities and vision of equity as a White woman of privilege. I made an agreement with myself to live and work in diverse communities throughout my life and serve children and their families by becoming an antiracist leader. I had to start by facing my own fears about race and racism."

To work through her fears, Jean made a commitment during her early years as a school site administrator to immerse herself for a whole year in a non-White world, through the books, movies, music, lectures, performances, and shows she chose to experience. She reports that as she held herself more accountable for stepping into a world totally unfamiliar, she got in touch with the sense of entitlement she had always held and came to appreciate and then enjoy the perspective, thought, expression, and values of Black and Brown artists, performers, and politicians.

Jean periodically tells her staff there is a need to examine White privilege in order to effectively serve in a culturally diverse community. She also makes clear to her staff that if they want to be "in this boat," they need to participate in an ongoing examination of institutional and transparent racism. Jean is attracted to working in diverse and complex communities that she says have a vibrancy and reality not found in more homogeneous communities of privilege. She has always believed it takes both will and skill to teach, and heart, heads, and hands to lead. In her words, "To build a responsive cultural democracy in schools we must address White privilege and step forward into each other's cultural realities."

Some of the conditions that have helped Jean experience some success in her equity leadership include involvement in community and professional organizations as well as the support of two very strong female superintendents, one Asian and one White. Conversely, some factors she says have hindered success are an employee bargaining unit that protects teachers who don't believe in the potential of all students to learn at high levels, and some teachers who don't implement instructional best practices in their classrooms.

Nevertheless, Jean has steadfastly worked with bargaining units and all teachers, including those who are marginal, to improve the quality of teaching and learning, always within the parameters of the teacher's contract.

A major multiyear leadership intervention of Jean since the early 1990s in two different schools has been the institutionalization of antiracism.

MAKE IT PERSONAL

1. What do you have in common with Jean, based on what you have learned?

2. What are your immediate thoughts about Jean deciding to focus on the institutionalization of antiracism?

Interventions

In Jean's current school, there are 17 languages spoken, and there are immigrants from Asia, Africa, Europe, and South America. The ethnic breakdown is 43% Latino/a, with about 13% each for African American, Asian, Filipino, and White. Jean has forthrightly addressed many vestiges of institutional racism without hesitation. Examples are changing the dress code so it is more culturally responsive, changing the school rules that required students who were fasting for religious reasons to stay in the cafeteria during lunchtime, and changing the makeup of parent leadership in the school so leadership positions are shared by culturally diverse parents.

Jean has organized groups of staff, parents, and community members to support culturally responsive teaching, including classroom discussions about race. In order to do all of this, Jean made sure her staff and parent representatives participated in professional development on diversity, and she helped diverse parents increase their comfort with and respect for each other and their belief that they have rights and power. She firmly believes equity transformation has to start with self, then one on one, followed by group efforts and culminating in efforts within the larger community. From the very beginning of her tenure as an administrator, Jean has worked within her school communities to develop ways to address negative attitudes, develop capacity, establish norms for behavior, and support cultural democracy for all students and adult members.

Jean foresaw the need to increase awareness of factors and conditions that contribute to personal and institutional racism. She involved staff and parent representatives in Beyond Diversity training by Glenn Singleton and contracted with Sharroky

Hollie, who is discussed in Chapter 12, to train all staff in using culturally responsive teaching (CRT) strategies. Jean used high-priority schools grant funds to secure a year of CRT training and coaching for all staff. CRT and Explicit Direct Instruction (EDI) by Data Works are integrated and comprise the school's major instructional interventions for lessening the achievement gap experienced by Brown and Black students at the school. EDI, in conjunction with CRT, facilitates implementation of scaffolding instruction, instead of watered-down curriculum for students of color, and helps teach to more rigorous, grade-level standards.

A major tool to assist implementation of the instructional intervention was creating a group called the "Dream Keepers," after the Gloria Ladson-Billings text of the same name and a major function of this group is to serve as coaches in helping institutionalize antiracism. The Dream Keepers, above all, is a race-relations focus group that Jean established when she first became a principal in 1990. At the beginning, there was only one non-White teacher on staff. Since teachers did not reflect the ethnic makeup of students, the Dream Keepers also drew members from parents and nonteaching classified employees who were racially similar to the students.

The Dream Keepers began as a core group with eight members. They volunteered their time and resources to discuss racism in schools by meeting during the evening hours for dinner in each of their homes. The perspective and fervor of small-group discussions naturally entered the halls and classrooms of the school when they returned. The same ground rules for courageous conversation by the Dream Keepers were used at school and included the following: "We will . . . experience discomfort . . . stay engaged . . . speak our truth . . . and not reach closure (Singleton & Linton, 2006).

Jean's leadership is very holistic. She has developed a strong infrastructure of support for translating an antiracist philosophy into educational practice. This is evident in her purposeful recruitment of participation by staff and parents in multiple "teams" and professional development activities. For example, in addition to the Dream Keepers, Jean created, with help from her superintendent, school site CARE teams (collaborative action research for equity), ETOT leaders (equity trainers of trainers), and PASS committees (parents advocating for successful students).

Jean's theory of action was to initially work on increasing awareness of and willingness to change discriminatory attitudes, expectations, and policies. This was followed by involving all staff in training that led to new rules, that is, rubrics of practice, called standards-based instruction that is culturally responsive. She topped it off by adding a system for standards-based formative assessments with the results used to drive subsequent instruction. However, realizing that the desired changes would not take hold without redefining what it meant to be an effective teacher, Jean engaged staff in the creation of professional learning communities (PLCs) that help establish new norms in how staff work together to meet the needs of all students.

Jean realized during PLC meetings that all teachers were not at the same place regarding their understanding of how racism is manifested in schools. Just like teachers were doing with students in classrooms, Jean began to differentiate professional development by creating heterogeneous groups of teachers with varying levels of understanding and also on occasion created some homogeneous groups for training, whose members were at approximately the same level of awareness. They were called affinity groups. Some staff members in homogeneous groups were grateful to be in such a group because the leveling process facilitated greater focus, and others in some heterogeneous groups were uncomfortable exposing their own "gaps" in learning.

Jean pointed out that this system of differentiating is what we do continuously to children. It increased her credibility to further suggest that permanent tracking/ grouping of adults or students is not in the best interest of any participant. As PLC members demonstrated the capacity to use instructional strategies, they moved to the level of mentor for new teachers. Shared leadership and transparent learning became an integral part of all training for cultural consciousness.

Simultaneously, Jean has demonstrated a warm, nurturing, people-oriented style of communicating with all students and adults. She models what she expects from others, provides a lot of positive feedback and has a humane way of holding people accountable. She is fearless in her approach to emotionally laden issues. Her conscious use of self to influence greater social justice is very indicative of her personal and professional goals.

"When discussing race with my staff, I compare it to a light switch that goes on and off when you enter a room. For people of color, the light is always on. For White people, it can be turned off or on, depending on the situation. I am extremely clear that, as a White woman, I must keep the switch 'on' at all times. When I speak to other White people, they often see themselves in my own journey. It has been essential for me to begin any training with literature, such as Tim Wise's article 'White Like Me' or the video of Chimamanda Ngozi Adichie talking about the "Danger of a Single Story." Jean's intent is to bring into conversations about school functioning the power of White racism or any human difference bias. She strongly believes in helping her staff develop a common language to discuss the evolution of racism in everyone's lives. The staff is then able to connect these conversations when talking about curriculum, instruction, staffing, scheduling, parent education, procedures, plans, and programs that touch children's lives.

One of the most poignant experiences during my several visits to Jean's school was reading the "I Am From" student poems that are written and posted around the school. They are a spinoff of teachers, parents, and students doing racial autobiographies, which were introduced in the Beyond Diversity training. In addition, when Jean interacts with students having conflicts on the playground or when referred to her office for some disciplinary reason, her way of engaging students in the use of

"I" statements demonstrates her use of each incident as a teaching moment. She is consistent in her efforts to improve student problem-solving and conflict-management skills related to human differences.

Jean's classroom observations for instructional supervision include use of culturally and linguistically responsive rubrics developed by Sharroky Hollie to ascertain whether and how culturally responsive teaching is being integrated into classroom instruction.

Jean has a strong expectation that teachers practice CRT skills and a commitment to provide them with ongoing coaching and feedback, including her modeling what is expected by teaching CRT lessons in every classroom. She also initiates an instructional performance improvement plan in the area of CRT for a staff member when necessary.

MAKE IT PERSONAL

1. What are three interventions that Jean initiated that most resonate with you and why?

2. Describe your experience, if any, with similar equity interventions as those initiated by Jean and what you learned as a result of your efforts.

Obstacles and Politics

Some obstacles and politics Jean experienced during her effort to institutionalize antiracism fall into three broad categories: instructional challenges, challenges in dealing with institutionalized racism, and personal challenges.

Instructional Challenges

• The demographics in the community of Jean's school district have dramatically changed since she became a school principal. The district was three-fourths White when she became a site administrator 20 years ago, and for some years has been three-fourths students of color, mostly poor. However, the decision makers in the community and school district, as well as the teachers, have remained overwhelmingly White, and many are resistant to the necessity for academically rigorous culturally responsive instruction. Some still verbally express the nostalgic desire for "returning to the way it was." The students in the district are primarily English language learners, especially at the K–8 level, and are the recipients of very low teacher expectations.

• There are differences between how many teachers teach and how students learn (i.e., their learning styles). Major challenges are being experienced in student academic engagement and student learning. Jean reports that 20% of the problem may be student attitudes and behavior, and 80% adult attitudes and behavior, with many adults not recognizing student differences as strengths. For example, she thinks there is a need to build on the home language of students as a bridge to mainstream English.

• Grouping practices have mixed results, especially during English language development instruction and instruction for students performing at the far below and below basic performance level on statewide end-of-year tests. Differentiated instruction as practiced is not working for many underperforming students.

• Student growth is not being sustained over time in some ethnic groups, and some teachers are not implementing the curriculum with full fidelity, due in part to inadequate time to teach all of the essential standards on standards-based benchmark and end-of-year tests. In addition, some teachers do not utilize benchmark assessment data to drive subsequent instruction on a consistent basis.

• Translation is not available for some home languages of students.

Challenges in Dealing With Institutional Racism

• Individual teachers or the district teachers union have alleged violations of the teacher's contract as a way of protesting instructional changes or expectations for staff performance. An example is when Jean asks teachers to give more instructional time to students scoring on statewide end-of-year tests at the far below and below basic performance levels. When Jean asked teachers to begin implementing the elements of EDI in lesson planning and delivery because she knew these strategies were particularly helpful with Latino/a students and English Learners, union representatives insisted there could be no expectation of EDI use during the teacher evaluation process.

Jean says, "I knew if I gave teachers time to learn the strategies and experiment with them without the worry of evaluation documentation, they would see them as essential to their instruction. During the first year of EDI training, all feedback was given on a school-wide basis. By the second year, grade-level feedback was given and some teachers were asking for individual feedback. I had agreed not to refer to EDI in my evaluation until all training was complete, but 80% of the faculty was so adept at using the strategies that it would have been impossible not to mention them in their evaluations. Though using a differentiated system of professional development, by the end of the fourth year all veteran and even new teachers were using EDI strategies proficiently."

Personal Challenges

• The fact that it is almost impossible to get rid of or transfer teachers who don't support the school's vision.

Although it is difficult to transfer out teachers who don't support antiracist work, Jean has always made sure the notion of equity is in the school's vision statement. Then, when a pattern of avoidance occurs with an employee, she is able to make it very clear that their participation in antiracist work at this school, at this time, with our students, is mandatory. As a consequence, she has noticed staff members leave when the opportunity arises, rather than endure her insistence that they need to be a part of the solution, not a part of the problem.

• It has been very difficult to get White members of the school community to habitually identify the critical nature of this work.

Jean has observed CRT (i.e., culturally responsive teaching) training participants engage in side conversations, grade papers, fall asleep, or get up and walk out, saying, "This is not the work for me." Whether it has been parents, teachers, Board members, or other administrators, Jean follows up this observation with a direct and private conversation that usually begins with, "I noticed that you checked out during the equity training. Why is that? We all have the moral obligation to stay the course if we work with children."

• It is very stressful when having to make impromptu decisions on whether "to fold or to hold" when advocating for students or confronting questionable performance related to internalized racism.

Over the 12 years Jean has been at her present school, she has sometimes shifted from noticing racist remarks or actions and walking away, to using "I statements" to address such remarks. She reports that an Asian teacher noticed that a White teacher was using the book *Five Chinese Brothers* in her classroom. Instead of letting it go, this courageous teacher said, "I see that you are using that book in class. As an Asian woman, I feel stereotyped when children hear the story and look at me. I want them to know that Chinese people do not all look alike and aren't comedic in their characteristics." The White teacher had never thought that using the book would be prejudicial. Everyone walked away from this courageous conversation having learned more about themselves and others. Jean acknowledges "not all conversations go so well, but we have worked together to practice in mixed-race groups how to say sensitive things to parents, peers, and students themselves. As a White woman, I have made mistakes and sometimes feel embarrassed or angry that this work is so hard. If I don't remain open to learning and considering that I don't know it all, I should not be in this business."

Sometimes it is necessary to make spontaneous decisions on when and how to confront those who are making prejudicial remarks reflecting cultural biases and lack of awareness or concern about what is offensive to others. There have been cultural slurs made by some teachers when asked to assign students to write about their cultural experiences. An example is the comment, "What will they write about, going to Wal-Mart?"

• Achieving a level playing field for historically underserved students, when some staff and even board members seem to have no sense of urgency.

Jean feels the larger community must be called upon to join in the care for underserved students. She has written dozens of grants and received 90% of them, securing more than $3.6 million over her administrative career. Her school currently has reduced class sizes and secured on-site coaches and student leadership projects that most schools have eliminated. To connect with the community power brokers and business leaders, she established a Guest Speaker Bureau. Judges, business owners, lawyers, doctors, politicians, superintendents, nurses, counselors, city managers, real estate managers, sports figures, and mayors have come to answer the question, "What do you do? How was school important to become what you are? Did racism impact your life and how did you overcome the barriers?" Jean says, "Children see themselves in others who look like them and the individuals who visited us as guest speaker bureau members reflect the race and language of our students."

- The difficulty of deciding what strategy to employ when trying to increase support for guarding the rights of students over the needs of adults in the schools, when some look at every initiative to improve what is done for kids in terms of whether it is convenient for them.

A hot and heavy topic in every school is student suspension. Jean insists she cannot and will not ignore policies and rules, expectations, and consequences. Yet when she and some of her staff noticed the pattern that Black and Brown students were suspended far more frequently than others, they took a look at what was behind each action that resulted in suspension. When examining the type of events that typically led up to a serious infraction, they built in interventions that resulted in diminishing the most serious offenses.

For example, Jean developed "Talking Tickets" that specific students could use to come into her office, with teacher permission, to talk out their feelings. She and some staff developed the training and use of "I statements" so students could identify their feelings in conflicts and ask for what they need. Midyear they identified students who had been referred for discipline repeatedly and met with them regularly, to check in on ways their leadership could shift from negative to positive.

Additional Priorities of the Principal Based on the Above Challenges and Politics

Over the course of her 20 years as a principal and ardent equity advocate, Jean says she has tried to consistently adhere to the following seven priorities:

1. Meet regularly with union representatives to discuss contractual concerns ahead of time, troubleshoot with them when new agreements or expectations occur, and always meet with any employees who do not feel their rights are being honored. Adhere to the motto that an ounce of prevention is worth a pound of cure.

2. Always plan staff development sessions with teacher leaders and share the responsibility with them for implementing such sessions.
3. Use the same CRT strategies when working with teachers that teachers are expected to use with students. In other words, *practice what she preaches.*
4. Post the norms for courageous conversations in her office and refer to them often.
5. Reach out to the business and civic community for city and private sector resources that are needed but not affordable within the school budget.
6. Find ways to make connections with community power brokers and key business leaders to make sure they are aware of service learning projects in the community.
7. Fight against the reality that schools and school systems are not set up for children of color, in such areas as language, cultural democracy, transportation, the school calendar, and schedule.

Jean has demonstrated both the political will and savvy necessary for equitable inputs and higher educational outcomes to be experienced by historically underserved students of color, through her no-excuses instructional leadership, engagement of the entire school community in equity work, and modeling what is expected. She emphatically and persistently walks the equity talk.

DEMONSTRATING LEADERSHIP BY COACHING AND FACILITATION

Kathryn Haywood, Principal

Personal Background

Kathryn Haywood, an African American principal in one of the ten largest school districts in the United States, has been a principal in two large low-income ethnically diverse schools for 8 years. Her current school's student population is composed of approximately 65% Latino/a students and 25% African American (the campus has a preK–2 building and a Grades 3–5 building). She is viewed by her staff, peers, and supervisors as a strong instructional leader. She facilitates school improvement more by example than by directive and is able over time to get culturally, linguistically diverse parents and racially diverse staff to work together on what is best for students.

Kathryn began her professional career in education as a special education resource teacher before becoming a vice principal and then a principal, and has been an educator almost 30 years. She initially worked in the private sector before entering the public education profession. During her tenure as a special educator, Kathryn says she increased her awareness of the many conditions and circumstances faced daily by many culturally diverse special needs students. She also increased her expertise in helping facilitate collaborative decisions about the best educational plans, based on cutting edge research to meet the needs of individual students.

Principal Haywood has always been a prolific student of the research and literature on improving the literacy of historically underserved students, whatever their cultural background, primary language, or academic readiness. She stays abreast of documented best practices by both administrators and teachers for eradicating major gaps in educational outcomes. Kathryn challenges doubts about student potential that may be reflected in the viewpoints, expectations, and behaviors of teachers and parents. She is also vigilant in monitoring the expectations demonstrated by educators during the teaching and learning process.

In the short time since she became principal of her current school, she has given a lot of attention to improving academic rigor through frequently monitoring student academic progress, doing instructional rounds focused on a "problem of practice," and implementing a lot of professional development on teaching strategies and team/trust building. She has also focused on increasing parent involvement tenfold, and creating 19 school/community partnerships.

When asked what is one intervention she has consistently employed to improve student educational outcomes, her response was that she is always trying to improve her pedagogy and her teachers pedagogy, which is to say she is constantly trying to improve her methods used to facilitate capacity building, and improve the methods teachers use to improve student achievement.

MAKE IT PERSONAL

1. Compared with Kathryn, what is your major approach to facilitating school improvement?

2. What documented best practices are used by you and others in your school setting to improve the literacy of historically underserved students, whatever their cultural background, primary language, or academic readiness?

Interventions

When Ms. Haywood arrived at her current school as principal, many teachers were used to grading papers, having side conversations, and even using their cell phones at staff meetings. There was also very little follow-through on decisions made at meetings or what was learned regarding the improvement of instructional practice.

In a total staff meeting early in her tenure, she stopped in the middle of a discussion on an important agenda topic related to improving student achievement.

She confronted a small group of teachers in the back who were having their own conversation and totally ignoring the staff discussion. One of those in the small group confronted by Kathryn was a long-time teacher at the school and a union representative, who protested she wasn't guilty. Ms. Haywood's immediate response was to say she apologized if that was the case, but the noise was coming from that direction. Such behavior by teachers has never occurred in subsequent meetings.

On another occasion, the principal called a meeting with third-grade teachers because of her concern about below basic and far below basic students not meeting benchmark targets in word analysis, reading fluency, and comprehension. The school has a Grades K–2 and Grades 3–5 language arts intervention program that teachers use with appropriate students who need extra instructional support above and beyond the regular curriculum.

Ms. Haywood asked the third-grade teachers to reflect on how the Sorpis-West reading program intervention is working or not working with small groups. Prior to the meeting, the vice principal suggested the third-grade teachers consider using the Grade K–2 Super Readers intervention model since some of the teachers said the Grade 3–5 program was not working with students. The third-grade teachers eagerly agreed. Ms. Haywood intervened by reminding the third-grade teachers they needed to consider what worked and did not work the previous school year. One of the third-grade teachers tried to rationalize why there has been limited success with the Sorpis-West program, by saying Ms. Haywood had mandated them to use it and they didn't know they could stop using it even though the students were failing. She went on to say that speaking for herself, she was scared to say anything because she was afraid of Ms. Haywood.

Ms. Haywood immediately responded she had not mandated anything, but did indicate she expected better academic progress this year with whatever was used. She further said it is not about the program, but the pedagogy, and whether teachers have the necessary pedagogical skills. She also indicated teachers needed the courage to stand up and say when a program they are using is not working. A couple of teachers then shared they had no problems with the Sorpis-West program, and had been able to rotate many of their students out of the program successfully. After this exchange, the teacher who had offered a rationalization recanted her statement and said she needed to reexamine her work further. Teachers are no longer refusing to take responsibility for their own learning.

How Kathryn goes about doing this is very tongue-in-cheek, with little exhortation and a lot of hands-on small group planning, problem solving, and coaching of her staff, helping them recognize when their behaviors are counterproductive to what is best for kids. The equity interventions of the principal also include the following:

- Increasing the academic rigor of preK and K–1 instruction, with emphasis on securing a dramatic improvement in grade-level readiness at first and second grades.

- Helping students of all backgrounds in the primary grades to become lovers of books and of learning in general.
- Initiating professional development activities on literacy, vocabulary building, writing, critical thinking, mathematics, collaboration, and culturally responsive teaching, at all grade levels, with follow-up peer/administrative observation and coaching on a regular basis.
- Making sure all adults are on the same page, through using readings on a toxic environment, on core beliefs, and on building relationships. Teachers began to see themselves in the readings, and engaged in very open conversations with each other that led to subgroups/cliques starting to pull together and establish new norms (i.e., what the staff agreed to live by) for how to work together and be accountable to each other.
- Demonstrating to teachers and support staff that she is there to support them by modeling ethics, respect, openness, and collaboration in working relationships.
- Not mandating or telling, but modeling and showing, that is, coaching, and instilling in her coadministrator and resource staff the need for them to do likewise in areas of need.
- Helping teachers be able to engage in modeling for and coaching of their students.
- Helping the staff focus on what is best for the children, by discussing "what we are about and what we need to be doing to help the children."
- Creating a series of principal awards in both the upper and lower grade schools for academic improvement and achievement, with meetings for parents to see their children receive such awards, resulting in a dramatic improvement in parent attendance at school events.
- Working with teachers to revise their attitudes/beliefs about parents, and parent attitudes about their role in working with the school and their power.
- Holding teachers accountable for changing course when needed.
- Engaging in risk-taking advocacy with staff, community, peers, and superiors regarding what is needed to improve student achievement.

Ms. Haywood provided an example of working with teachers to revise their attitudes/beliefs about parents, and parent attitudes about working with the school. An African American parent met with the principal soon after Ms. Haywood came to the school. This parent had a history of very little trust with teachers in the school and not allowing special services for her two children in a timely manner. Ms. Haywood promised to initiate preliminary informal assessments by the Student Study Team, including use of a psychologist and speech therapist. The preliminary results revealed a need for more formal assessments to be done. The ultimate result was providing additional special education services for the two children, and glasses. Prior to this change in services, both the boy and girl were presenting discipline problems; they said they couldn't see and couldn't keep up with the work. The instruction was modified and there have been no more behavioral problems caused by the children.

Kathryn has given priority to securing greater parent involvement, such as work on developing and implementing the school vision, and increased membership on the governance team. She also gives priority to improving community involvement, and has more than 40 persons working with students on a weekly basis in such areas as mock trial, science, theater, reading, and writing. These priorities help create a school environment supportive of higher student achievement.

More precisely related to her high priority on closing gaps in educational outcomes is principal Haywood's establishment of precise improvement targets in core curriculum areas on formative assessments for individual students and subgroups in each classroom. These targets are accompanied by monitoring progress in meeting them and more timely instructional interventions when improvement targets aren't met.

Part of the monitoring is accomplished by doing instructional rounds. Ms. Haywood uses a research-based rubric during instructional rounds and shares with the whole staff any problems identified. All staff know what academic areas and which student groups are the focus of school improvement and classroom observations, which are based on formative and end-of-year assessment results. After the principal does individual observations, she identifies a "problem of practice." She also has the school's governance team, composed of both certificated and classified staff, in addition to parents, doing instructional rounds. Once, when the principal announced in a staff meeting that the school's governance team would be doing instructional rounds to identify any problems of practice related to the three areas of concern in the school site plan (i.e., student engagement, teaching practices, and room environment that supports teaching and learning), a union representative immediately interrupted the principal to say that would be in conflict with the teachers' contract.

The principal immediately responded by saying, "I could care less about your union at this moment. I highly respect the union. My goal is to do nothing against your union. My ultimate goal is to ensure the rigorous work we committed to doing in our classrooms is happening on a daily basis. The only way to ensure this is for the governance body to monitor this work by getting into the classrooms to see if it is being done." Based on past history under a previous superintendent, the main concerns of the teachers were that evaluative notes would be taken and used against them. The principal further explained that no notes would be taken during observations and "a full review, with emphasis on the 'problem of practice,' not on individual teachers, will be written and shared with the staff." No additional concerns were subsequently voiced.

Principal Haywood is willing to risk standing up to staff resistance, and asking hard questions of her staff, other principals, district board members, or executive administrators when she feels it is necessary to clearly advocate for and be more critical about the work being done by all teachers, counselors, students, and parents to improve academic success.

MAKE IT PERSONAL

1. What are some of your experiences related to teacher professionalism that are similar or different from what Ms. Haywood experienced?

2. To what extent have you been a part of the problem or a part of the solution related to improving teacher professionalism in addressing student underachievement?

3. What are the similarities and differences in the approach of principal Haywood and your approach or that of someone you know, when it comes to improving instructional effectiveness?

Obstacles and Politics

Some of the variables in the work context that were obstacles to improving student outcomes when Kathryn became principal were no goal focus, poor communication and problem-solving adequacy, low trust, little school-wide collaboration, no staff cohesion, and low student expectations. Kathryn has successfully worked with staff to improve these conditions.

Ms. Haywood inherited a very divisive staff largely along racial lines when she became principal of her current school. There was also a great deal of parent apathy. Kathryn described the staff conflicts in the previous school year as very toxic, with very negative consequences for the school environment and for student academic outcomes. Many of the federal government annual yearly progress targets in recent years had not been met.

For example, she discovered teachers who didn't know each other and didn't want to know each other. The African American teachers, who had been at the school the longest, made very disparaging remarks about some non-African American (White and Hispanic) teachers, in some cases to their face. Some of the Black teachers said the other teachers didn't belong here in "our community," that they just came through here on their way to somewhere else, and didn't know how to teach "our kids," often pointing to the test scores to justify their attitudes.

The end-of-year test scores of African American students with African American teachers were higher than in other classrooms. The principal called a meeting with the two union representatives (both African American) and basically said, "No, it's not about [calling out or blaming other teachers], we need to take ownership of all our students. Since you say you are doing such great things you should be willing to share with others." Per the direction of Ms. Haywood, in staff meetings each staff member is expected to choose two to three other staff members they don't know and write two to three new facts about the person they didn't know before they met.

To follow up on the expectation of shared ownership, Ms. Haywood attends grade-level meetings to monitor new communication and collaboration norms that she encouraged them to develop. Grade-level groups also have to submit to the principal at the end of each meeting a summary of their meeting that includes a "problem of practice" they will be focusing on until they meet the next time, what they will be doing about the problem of practice, and assessments to be used.

On another note, several African American parents, because of not trusting the recommendation of their school or of their pediatrician, wouldn't give their children the prescribed medicines. The principal helped change this situation by building trusting relationships with the parents and students, and by citing positive examples of how other students on the medication had excelled. She also assured the parents the medication would not have to be used on a permanent basis. As the children learned behavioral modification strategies that resulted in greater academic growth, they were weaned off the medication.

The principal has also confronted some teachers about how they yell at students and asked them to refrain from doing so. She has said to some teachers about the way they talk to students: "You kill the kids, leave them there to rake the dirt over themselves, and you wonder why they are defiant?" When she arrived at the school, there were more than 200 school suspensions the previous year, many directly from the classroom. This has been reduced to only 13 by stopping teacher-initiated suspension, requiring that all suspensions be personally approved by her.

All of the above actions that are part of Kathryn Haywood's equity intervention have political implications, because of changes she is advocating or implementing that represent different ideas of how schools should be run and what they should be doing about particular issues. Kathryn identified four categories of obstacles she has addressed and how she deals with these obstacles.

School Climate

There have been major demographic changes in the student population of Kathryn's school within the last 10 years. What was once a school populated primarily by students of African American descent, and then a school with a plurality of African American students, is now and has been for some time a school populated primarily by English language learner students of Latino/a descent from low-income families. The racial/ethnic makeup of the staff has also changed over the years, and African American teachers are in larger numbers. As discussed above, there was considerable racial tension between the teachers before the arrival of Ms. Haywood and during her first year at this school. Part of these intergroup dynamics may be attributed to some remaining resentments since the makeup of the student population has changed.

Even as Ms. Haywood has worked with teachers to let go of their prejudices that kept all teachers within grade levels and across the entire school from working together on behalf of the students, the tension hasn't entirely dissipated. It has gotten better, and so some would like to pretend such conflict never happened, but that hasn't worked. The overall school climate has significantly improved within the last school year, but there are still occasional conflicts.

Instruction

Ms. Haywood has pursued an ambitious agenda of curricula and instructional improvements to improve the performance of all student groups on state wide end-of-year assessments. Issues requiring immediate attention have included the delivery of special education services, the resistance of some parents of color to allowing their children to receive such services, and the low expectations of students in general. There is also less than rigorous instruction in some classrooms and inadequate support services for special needs students not assigned to special education.

Administration

The counterproductive racial dynamics also extend to school discipline and conflict management practices, which result in all problems with Black students being referred by White staff to the principal, and all problems of the White vice principal with Black staff being referred to the principal. In addition, teacher work assignments, student class assignments, and implementation of the district benchmark assessments resulted in some mismatches between teachers and students, and some teacher lack of accountability in meeting benchmark assessment timelines and providing quality instruction. Ms. Haywood has not hesitated to reassign staff within her school and make scheduling changes when needed and provides close monitoring of staff follow-through.

Parents

Ms. Haywood has addressed a host of challenges related to parent apathy, low self-esteem, and involvement. Parents reported that in the past they were subjected to many perceived slights and disrespect, such as not being allowed to visit their children's classrooms. Kathryn strives to channel parent anger and upset into positive ways of communicating with staff when necessary. She has also improved the capacity of staff to work with parents as partners. She astutely confronts parents and strongly advocates for children's rights when there is evidence of problems in the home.

In summary, Kathryn exemplifies many aspects of culturally courageous leadership in her day-to-day work, including the skill and tenacity to focus everyone on what is best for the children by bringing together a school community where there had been a lot of animosity and hard feelings. She has tirelessly engaged in capacity building, team building, and trust building within and across all stakeholder groups, drawing upon resources from within the school and the larger school community to accomplish this feat. Her persona and priorities illustrate an unwavering commitment to relationships, rigor, and relevance. She is straightforward and unrelenting in walking the equity talk.

⋔⋕

MENTORING FOR SOCIAL JUSTICE

Robert Montoya, University Professor

Personal Background

Robert Montoya, a Latino, is a university professor who teaches graduate courses on "educational leadership for equity" to current and aspiring school administrators in one of the largest state university systems in the United States. He has been in this role for more than 6 years. Dr. Montoya has also been a mentor for principals and district office administrators over the same period of time. Prior to his work at the university level, he was a middle and high school teacher as well as a high school counselor before becoming an elementary principal. He then became an assistant principal and principal at the middle school level. Earlier in his career, he served as a program improvement coach, and a coach for football, basketball, and soccer teams. He is totally dedicated to enhancing the effectiveness of leadership and instructional systems designed to achieve equity and excellence, especially but not exclusively in school districts populated largely by Latino/a students.

Montoya's commitment to social justice is demonstrated by the vision and fortitude he has shown in creating and directing a network of statewide mentors to develop and increase the numbers of Latino/a administrators as well as support current Latino/a education administrators in his state. An indication of the mentoring program's success is that enrollment has more than tripled in the last 2 years.

Dr. Montoya walks the equity talk for all historically underserved students. This is demonstrated by his research, actions, and forcefully stated values and beliefs. The leadership intervention he has given the most attention to throughout his educational career is the capacity building of educational leaders that results in their having the skills to foster more equitable educational inputs and outcomes. Regardless of the racial/ethnic background of those with whom he is working, or whether they are students, parents, public school teachers, and administrators, Robert's goal is to inspire and strengthen individuals as well as organizations so their efforts result in greater social justice for historically underserved groups.

Recently, he decided to transition from being Director of the mentoring network for Latino/a administrators to Executive Director of a new organization he created that has an expanded vision, including a dedication to stopping many Brown and Black children from being lost to the penal system. One very small part of addressing this crisis will be ensuring that those charged with caring for foster youth have the cultural competency to better understand and positively respond to the children in their charge. This is just one of the many issues and areas to be addressed by his new organization, which include leadership development, mentoring, equity, and research, as he becomes even more of a major "voice" for historically underserved students.

Dr. Montoya's motivation to focus on equity issues is influenced by his personal life experiences, including living in a foster home, being subjected to low expectations in school, working on farms, and his time in the military. Montoya is also influenced by his job experiences in both the private and public sectors before going back to community college and ultimately to a distinguished university to complete his doctorate. He knows firsthand what discrimination and racism is all about, and consciously uses his personhood and his current position to teach others so inclined how to confront social injustice and institutional racism.

A major leadership intervention of Dr. Montoya over the last 6 years has been equipping his graduate students with the knowledge, skills, and savvy to become educational leaders who will deeply implant a culture of equity and social justice wherever they work.

MAKE IT PERSONAL

1. Based on what you know about the background of Dr. Montoya, describe how he is similar and different from other university professors you know who teach educational administration courses.

2. If you had a chance, what are one or two personal concerns related to your work that you would like to discuss with Dr. Montoya?

Interventions

Focusing on leadership for equity is not a common practice among university professors who teach graduate-level courses in educational administration. Dr. Montoya has embraced such an emphasis because of his personal and professional experiences, and his strong belief that "it is necessary to address issues of race, culture, and equity because they greatly affect student learning." Earlier in his career, Dr. Montoya was the only Latino teacher in different settings and was often called upon to be the voice for the large Latino/a student population. He wanted to improve his skills as an advocate. As he moved from being a teacher to a counselor to an administrator, he became more confident and stronger as an advocate. He felt an obligation to use his voice for all kids, but specifically for students of color. Asked how he felt about being a spokesperson for Latino/a students, he responded that he was glad to be a spokesperson for all students so all could see that Latinos were capable of effective leadership. Dr. Montoya consciously and purposefully serves as an ardent advocate for all historically underserved students, modeling the need for equity activist scholars to steadfastly walk the talk.

Dr. Montoya concluded that educational systems are not designed to meet the needs of historically underserved students. They are designed to meet the needs of mainstream White students and teachers. Based on his personal experiences of racism on many occasions, Montoya knows firsthand the difficulty of maintaining one's self-respect when constantly subjected to such discrimination. He talks about his own experiences and reminds his mostly White students as well as people of color to not be quiet about the need for social justice. His goal is to equip them to become actively involved in this struggle related to power, authority, and control. A few examples of the emphases in Dr. Montoya's courses are as follows:

- Learning activities that require students to grapple with the complexity of views and perceptions about what to do about cultural diversity.
- Explicit attention to individual and organizational norms in schools that reflect racism, sexism, classism, disability bias, homophobia, and so on, with the requirement that students come up with ways to successfully combat such norms.
- Based on what is happening in the student's work setting related to the "isms," develop a plan for how to address what is observed or develop a plan for a staff workshop, including what you will do and how you will do it.
- Engage students in educational praxis, where they have to apply what they learn, conduct action research, and learn how to strategically get things done that are in the best interests of students when people don't agree with you.
- Engage students in critical reflection of their practices and share their insights during class.
- Develop trust and create a safe place to do all of the above.
- Complete readings and class assignments that require digesting and utilizing a variety of interdisciplinary, diverse ethnic perspectives when performing job-related tasks.

Some items in recent final exams given by Dr. Montoya also reflect the emphases in his courses:

- Given the power and influence of school leaders, what factors should they consider when exercising authority and when empowering others in the areas of diversity, equity, and culture? What is the school leader's role in establishing educational equity so all students have the resources they need to learn? Provide examples from the assigned articles for each of these questions.

- As an educator who is now more conscious of the need for multicultural awareness in the educational system, what steps would you take to promote this awareness in others? How do concepts such as personal and group histories, privilege, cultural value, equitable educational systems, and so on, play a role in the development of this awareness? Please cite course reading materials to support your answer.
- Charles V. Willie (Charles V. Willie is the Charles William Eliot Professor of Education, Emeritus, at the Harvard Graduate School of Education) defined educational equity in the following manner:

> We, in education, should be discovering creative ways of putting together different people with different talents, intelligences, and experiences so that one can do for another what the other cannot do for him- or herself. Education, therefore, should focus neither on cultivating excellence at the expense of equity nor on cultivating equity at the expense of excellence. In a well-ordered society, the goal of education is to seek both excellence and equity because they are complementary. One without the other is incomplete.

Provide your well thought-out response to his definition, how you might develop it at your school site, and cite course readings to substantiate your point of view.

One student said to Dr. Montoya, "You challenged everything I thought I knew and it pissed me off at first but then I started challenging everything I had done."

Dr. Montoya has a very strong commitment to engaging his graduate students in synthesizing new info with existing beliefs and experiences, and sharing perspectives on issues/topics that are politically sensitive. An environment is created which helps students feel a level of comfort and trust so they can do these things.

The new statewide research and advocacy organization created by Dr. Montoya is a very political decision by him to take his work for social justice to the next level. As stated above, the focus will be on "at-risk" youth in all student subgroups. The rationale for this move includes a recognition of how many foster youth often end up in the juvenile justice system. He has written that "too often, the support needed in schools and communities to ensure that foster youth have an equal chance at successfully transitioning into successful adults is not present. . . . An overwhelming number of these students are African American and Latino." He feels there is an urgent need for Browns and Blacks to develop their own power structure, their own leaders and constituencies, and their own support systems, that need to be interrelated to advance the cause.

MAKE IT PERSONAL

1. How is the approach used by Dr. Montoya in his teaching and professional activities similar or different from what you have personally experienced?

2. What would you most like to discuss with Dr. Montoya regarding how he teaches his classes on educational leadership for equity?

Obstacles Experienced

Dr. Montoya does not like to give any energy to "obstacles" because he is determined to proceed as if they don't exist and carry on with complete optimism and determination. Nevertheless, he does address every obstacle in his own unique way, but not how others might expect him to. Some of the frustrations (his preferred word) he acknowledges are as follows:

- Being unable to address issues of race, culture, and equity with the verve and intensity he desires, but addressing them anyway in such a manner that the listener can hear them.
- Getting faculty or students to feel comfortable in explaining why they feel the way they do, when cultural biases are unwittingly and blithely expressed by them.
- Very few at the university or school district level demonstrating the passion and sense of urgency to address issues of institutional racism, causing him to feel "ambushed" whether he addresses the issues or not, because of negative reaction either way. He always decides to address the issues, but how he does it is based on the context.
- Very few educational leaders at all levels: school site, district, or university level, having the courage to speak up on behalf of equity issues. This motivates Robert to better prepare the next generation of educational leaders from all walks of life, but there are very few willing to join in preparing future leaders for advancing the cause of equity.
- The racial divide and complaints of racial groups about each other (e.g., Blacks, Browns, Whites), and the resistance of those professing to be equity advocates to admitting being our own worst enemies.
- The discomfort some students have when focusing on the issue of White privilege, and helping them resolve any problems with what is happening in the course.
- Teaching/research by colleagues that reflects support of the existing power structure, including teaching and research done by persons of color who reflect internalized racism.

- The complacency by persons of color in general to take action against racism and cultural ignorance; most seem to just be living day to day, accepting their circumstances because they have become used to institutional racism as a norm and fact of life.
- The struggle to maintain a healthy personal identity in the face of being treated with indifference, ridicule, abuse, disrespect, and oppression.
- The difficulty in finding personal support groups for some that need help in acquiring new knowledge and skills, inspiration, and maintenance of high self-esteem. Robert works constantly to provide access to such support groups.
- The price that is paid, mentally, physically, and professionally, including ostracism and being deemed a troublemaker, when your values and beliefs are out there for opponents to see and use against you.

Dr. Montoya deals with all of the above "frustrations" by digging deeper to find the energy to confront, challenge, and coach, negotiate, mediate, and strategize, but above all expand the networks and support systems for advancing the cause of social justice. He is a model for how to use research, advocacy, and organizing as tools to diminish social inequities. He is unyielding in his total commitment to working for equity at all levels of the educational enterprise, preK through graduate school. He is always aggressively trying to increase the support for historically underserved students who face dire out-of-school factors impacting their school success. He lives, breathes, and indefatigably walks the equity talk.

శ్రీ

SIMILARITIES IN THE THREE EQUITY WARRIORS

Jean, Kathryn, and Robert are totally committed to walking the equity talk. They practice what they preach, so to speak, although their approach is not to literally "preach," but to model what they expect of others. But when necessary, they directly confront biased attitudes about "different" others. Each of them has a persona and affect of high regard for everyone's humanness. People with whom they work know to not display pettiness or let anything get in the way when it comes to making social justice for all students a high priority. All three of these "equity warriors" demonstrate daily how they are consciously attending to several of the needed actions described in Chapter 7.

For example, they don't adhere to any unstated rules about how to play the cultural politics usually emanating from human fears. They also give a lot of ongoing attention to what I call the toxic hidden curriculum, which include adult dysfunctional relationships in the work environment. They are persistently trying to increase the expectations and efficacy of those under their charge, whether they are classroom teachers or graduate students, regarding the ability of historically underserved students of color to achieve at high levels. But none of the three naively think it is simply a matter of improved attitudes. They are steadfast in building capacity, when it comes to the knowledge, skills, and savvy needed to make a lasting difference in the lives of historically underserved students. Each of them personally facilitate frequent problem-solving dialogue about some of the most intractable barriers encountered when trying to significantly improve student educational outcomes.

All three have each dealt successfully with some potential land mines. Jean has always been very upfront and in the face of teachers about White racism and privilege, but not in a way that teachers can call "foul" when it comes to their contract. Over the years, she has been successful in turning her staff around or helping them transfer elsewhere, except for a couple of teachers.

In Kathryn's case, she was appointed principal of the school where she taught many years ago, but in the interim the school's student and staff population drastically changed. Her mantra is that teachers, whatever their identity or previous enmity, will be held equally accountable for collaboratively doing all they can that will best meet all students' needs, with no excuses.

Robert has to deal almost daily with the unconscious incompetence of his colleagues at the university level, including their aversive and dysconscious racism (see Chapter 8), manifested in total uncritical acceptance of White privilege, power, and authority. Some of these persons who are in charge of developing the next generation of educational leaders support policies and values that perpetuate cultural hegemony.

All three equity warriors have had experience in successfully defusing what could have been volatile political issues. The institutional biases and barriers discussed in this guide are at the top of their agenda. They are committed to empowering the disenfranchised.

Each have a strong sense of personal and professional identity, including their racial identity, which they have drawn upon in tackling the narrow mindedness of some who consciously or unconsciously support cultural hegemony in American society. They make trust and team building a hallmark of their day-to-day work and know you can never put aside the need to build on what you have already achieved in that regard. The three equity warriors are masters at discerning the character and intent of those with whom they work, especially their biases and priorities.

Even when equity leaders like Jean, Kathryn, and Robert acquire more personal and position power in their respective jobs, they must constantly deal with the cultural blindness and indifference of their colleagues, which exacts a toll. The phrase "only the strong survive" is very relevant in describing what is required of them to practice culturally courageous leadership.

MAKE IT PERSONAL

FN14–1 (SEE FACILITATOR NOTES IN APPENDIX 1)

1. Given the three warriors' backgrounds and equity interventions, if they were in your school district, what are the political obstacles they would likely face?

2. Describe the conditions, circumstances, attitudes, and/or behaviors in your school or district that require interventions by "equity warriors," such as those described in this chapter, and also describe the special knowledge, skills, dispositions, and priorities you would want "equity warriors" to have in your work setting.

REVIEW OF CHAPTER 14

The following topics were discussed in this chapter:

- The personal background and equity interventions of each "equity warrior" are described in some detail as well as some of the politics and obstacles experienced when being an unswerving voice and force for social justice.

- A description of similarities in the character, priorities, and types of challenges experienced by the three equity warriors.

૭ન~ઈ

Practicing the "Equity Walk"

15

There is nothing as humbling as realizing that for all of your sound and fury on behalf of equity, you are part of the problem and not part of the solution.

SETTING THE STAGE: INTRODUCTION TO TWO CULTURALLY COURAGEOUS LEADERSHIP DIAGNOSTIC QUESTIONNAIRES

In this guide, six chapters are devoted to a description of many conditions and circumstances contributing to large gaps in the educational outcomes of historically underserved students. This is followed by six chapters devoted to describing the culturally courageous leadership (CCL) paradigm, including examples.

The major activity in this chapter is a role-playing exercise that requires use of several concepts discussed in earlier chapters. In addition, to further facilitate your practice of the equity walk, there are two diagnostic instruments in Appendix 2. The first is the Culturally Courageous Leadership Diagnostic Questionnaire, for individuals (CCLDQ/I), which engages the respondent in exploring how their equity concerns and perceived needs in their work setting compare with their personal beliefs, priorities, and behaviors. This is followed by a discussion of some beliefs, priorities, and behaviors that may be necessary for a good match with certain concerns and perceived organizational needs.

The second questionnaire is the CCLDQ, school learning environment (CCLDQ/SLE), which enables school leaders to engage representatives of their entire school community in sharing perceptions about what is happening or not happening in a given school related to laying the foundation for achieving equitable educational outcomes. Directions are provided for computing the collective score of the CCLDQ/SLE, and what the score means in terms of where the school stands in the practice of CCL.

Both versions of the CCLDQ are *diagnostic* questionnaires, meaning they are designed to engage the respondents in looking at self and then looking with others at the school's learning environment through the prism of what may be contributing to inequitable educational inputs and educational outcomes. Each CCLDQ will help individuals acquire a better sense of where they and their school need to begin or where they can refine their existing equity work.

I have found many ardent equity advocates aren't aware of the inconsistencies between their personal concerns, perceived organizational needs, personal beliefs, priorities, and behaviors. They may need to engage in some critical self-examination before undertaking equity initiatives. You need to have as much insight as possible about your personal inconsistencies in order to improve your effectiveness in walking the equity talk. These diagnostic questionnaires should *not be used* before there has been some attention given to creating a safe environment for respondents to be truthful and forthcoming when responding to all categories and items in the instrument. In addition, respondents who have not read the guide will need an in-depth briefing on the major concepts and understandings addressed in the guide. Unless those taking one or both of the instruments have a clear understanding of the terminology used, the results of respondents will not be valid because they probably won't understand what is being asked. The items require respondents to be very open and honest in their responses, and it is likely that will not occur unless some preparation for responding to the questionnaires is given, including the promise of anonymity, and a discussion of how the results can be helpful.

KWL EXERCISE

1. Write three to five phrases that in essence capture your top priorities when it comes to what you consider prerequisites for effectively doing the "equity walk."

2. What will help you master the prerequisites identified in response to the first question and help make the concept of culturally courageous leadership more real for you in terms of specific steps to take?

3. How did the three equity warriors discussed in Chapter 14 broaden your understanding of culturally courageous leadership?

ళుడ్

INTRODUCTION TO THE ROLE-PLAYING EXERCISE

This chapter is titled "Practicing the 'Equity Walk'" to give you some practice in addressing some issues requiring culturally courageous leadership. If possible, before reading and participating in this role-playing exercise, complete the CCLDQ for individuals (in Appendix 2) and follow the subsequent directions for interpretation of your results, including the commentary on select items within each category.

That should help you gain more insight into who you are and what if any discrepancies there are between what you espouse and what you do when it comes to the crisis being experienced daily by historically underserved students. However, it is okay to still engage in this role-play without taking the CCLDQ for individuals.

The role-playing exercise requires you to assume the role of an executive decision maker, an area superintendent at the school district level, who must make decisions about what to do in the situation presented.

కావా

BACKGROUND INFORMATION ON THE HARBOR VIEW UNIFIED SCHOOL DISTRICT

As a new area superintendent in the Harbor View Unified school district, you supervise and evaluate all principals in the Bethune-Chavez high school (BCHS) cluster, including principals of the elementary and middle schools that feed into BCHS. You also have administrative responsibility for two other high school clusters. The district has 12 high school clusters and has just become a No Child Left Behind (NCLB) program improvement district because it has not met the annual yearly progress (AYP) targets for all subgroups, as directed by the U.S. Department of Education. As one of four area superintendents in the new district reorganization, each of you also oversee all support services and instructional program operations in your schools, due to massive district budget cuts in the last school year totaling more than $80 million dollars.

You have been charged by your deputy superintendent to give priority to dealing with a problem situation at BCHS, which has escalated to a lawsuit being filed against the school district.

When responding to this situation, remember that as an area superintendent, you have direct access to all district personnel who can assist you in a myriad of ways, such as providing you with information or analyses you request, related to budget, board policies and administrative regulations, staffing, practices in other schools dealing with similar situations, and so on. You can request meetings with appropriate persons to make inquiries, you can launch investigations, and you could choose to take a hands-on approach and go to the school to find out things for yourself. You could seek advice from those to whom you report, the deputy superintendent, superintendent, and even the board of education member in whose area this school is located.

When you were appointed area superintendent, you were given four directives by the Board of Education and Superintendent:

1. Improve the accountability of school site administrators for instructional performance, as determined by meeting end-of-year adequate yearly progress and state performance targets

2. Improve home/school relations

3. Increase community input into school site decision-making processes

4. Seek ways to consolidate instructional program initiatives, in light of the projected need for the district to cut at least another $60 million dollars in the budget for the coming fiscal year due to the state deficit

෨෧

DIRECTIONS FOR THE ROLE-PLAY

1. Read the brief history of BCHS, and a description of the problem situation, school climate, and learning environment at the school, as well as additional background information.

2. Respond to five items in your in-basket, all related to the problem situation at BCHS. Follow the directions for how to respond to each item, being mindful that your responses will illustrate the extent to which you demonstrate management skills in six areas* as well as the extent to which you display culturally courageous leadership.

3. Determine which of 16 questions related to CCL that you choose to answer, and then provide written answers, with the stipulation that your answers to any of these questions will constitute a draft action plan for how you intend to address the problem situation at BCHS.

Definition of Skills* You Should Display in Response to the In-Basket Items:

*ADAPTED FROM: problem analysis, judgment, decision making, organization, stress tolerance, and sensitivity skills, which were some of the management skills assessed via experiential activities in the original assessment center of the National Association of Secondary School Principals (Hersey, 1982).

Problem Analysis

Know what questions to ask, what information to collect, how to analyze what is collected, and how to define problems based on both empirical and intuitive data; identify relationships and conflicting interpretations of relationships between related problems; investigate the context of each identified problem and the assumptions undergirding the definition of each problem; discern different political perspectives and underlying beliefs of diverse advocates for each definition of the same problem.

Judgment

Discern when caution should be exercised when taking action, or whether caution dictates taking no action at the present time; ability to discern when top priority should be given to an issue; ability to discern the intent and achievement motivation of others and whether any personal counterproductive agendas exist among persons involved; having the insight to know when to change directions and take an entirely different course of action in any given moment by paying attention to subtle but telltale signs of possible failure, and knowing when to take risks and not to take major risks.

Decision Making

Discern when an immediate decision is needed and what the process should be for making a decision, in terms of data needed, persons that should be involved, criteria that should be employed, the ethics required, and the potential consequences of decisions made.

Organization

Exercise good time management and delegate properly, based on diagnosis of whether those to whom tasks are delegated have the requisite skills, interest, willingness, creativity, motivation, resilience, experience, and self-confidence; ability to develop thorough action plans that take into consideration an incisive and comprehensive environmental scan as well as assessment of strengths and weakness, pros and cons of alternative courses of action; always have a plan B and plan C as contingencies if needed.

Stress Tolerance

Withstand any work-related psychological, emotional, budgetary, or physical pressures, as well as setbacks, allegations, character assassination, duplicity or treachery, and whatever Murphy's law might cause (i.e., whatever can go wrong will go wrong), and still prevail with laserlike focus, decorum, sense of humor, respect for others, and empathy.

Sensitivity

Respond to the stated and unstated needs or requests of others in a timely fashion; having the presence of mind to not always have to be right, based on the circumstances; ability to discern other's strengths and virtues even if they oppose your course of action and personally attack you; ability to be authentic, open, and honest, knowing when to display genuine positive interpersonal communication behaviors that may entice opponents to reverse their opposition and support your goals.

කංක

BRIEF HISTORY OF BETHUNE-CHAVEZ HIGH SCHOOL (BCHS)

BCHS is one of the oldest high schools in the school district. Bethune-Chavez "tipped" several years ago from a majority of African American students to a majority of Latino/a students, because the residential makeup within the school's boundaries changed drastically.

Bethune-Chavez is also the newest high school facility in the school district. When it closed so construction could begin on the new facilities, it was one third the size it is currently and a plurality of the students were African American. Since it reopened, Latino/a families who are recent immigrants have become the majority by a slim margin. Eighty percent of all students' families qualify for free or reduced-price lunch, so BCHS is a total Title I school. BCHS is in its third year of program improvement since the new school facility opened.

❧

SALIENT FACTS RELATED TO THE "PROBLEM" AT BCHS

The Situation

- Latino/a family files lawsuit against school district alleging discrimination based on requested tutoring not provided to son, and his being removed from football team for academic reasons without due process.
- Enrique Rodriquez is a star on the team, and his low grades caused school to warn family he was in danger of losing his eligibility status.
- Enrique's parents paid for private tutoring until the previous year, but are no longer able to do so. BCHS recently reduced budget for afterschool academic support services.

❧

SCHOOL CLIMATE AND LEARNING ENVIRONMENT AT BCHS

Recent History of School	Evidence Related to Extent of Cultural Democracy, Institutional Biases, and Barriers to High Achievement
In the last 4 years, school population has changed to 52% Latino/a American, 35% African American, and 10% Asian American	Most Latino/a students are first or second generation Americans and resent being treated with disrespect. Some are erroneously labeled as illegal immigrants.
	Most Black community members feel if you are American you should learn how to speak English on your own and resent any special help provided to "immigrants" to learn English, especially when it takes money away from meeting the instructional needs of African American students.

(Continued)

(Continued)

Recent History of School	Evidence Related to Extent of Cultural Democracy, Institutional Biases, and Barriers to High Achievement
Major cultural/racial conflicts have occurred among students, parents, and teachers since new high school facility opened 4 years ago	Two-thirds of the high school teachers are White and almost all do not speak Spanish; most teachers of all backgrounds expect all students to adapt to how they teach, and resist adapting to how some students best learn.
	There are low teacher expectations, the district curriculum is largely Eurocentric, instructional practices are not culturally responsive; discipline as well as special education referrals are overwhelmingly given to African and Latino males; no academic support services are provided during the school day.
Many Latino/a's feel even though they now have the largest school population, there is strong resistance to including curriculum content, instructional strategies, sports, and student clubs reflecting their cultural heritage and learning styles	There is a centralized decision-making process, with a history of little input solicited from parents at the district- and school-site level.
	There is limited instructional supervision in classrooms, and teachers are not held accountable for student academic outcomes. The teachers' bargaining unit has successfully kept any language out of the teachers' contract that would include student academic performance as one of many criteria for evaluation of teacher performance.

ॐ

ADDITIONAL BACKGROUND INFORMATION ON "PROBLEM" AT BCHS

1. The parents of Enrique have never allowed him to receive English Language Development (ELD) assistance in pull-out classes or be assigned to ELD classes for his regular instruction.

2. Parents requested the student study team (SST) to do a formal assessment, which resulted in the finding that Enrique has a moderate delay in ELD.

3. La Raza community organization and La Raza student union both support lawsuit against district.

4. Black community organization supports district not giving additional tutoring that isn't given to Black students with documented needs.

5. Black student union supports Enrique's need for tutoring, and says Blacks, not just ELD students, should receive "extra help" when needed.

6. Enrique's teachers say he needs tutoring but they can't do it in the evening when he would be available after football practice.

7. Parent's priest alleges BCHS has provided same level of tutoring requested by them to other ELD students in his parish.

8. BCHS special education specialist thinks Enrique should have ELD pull-out instruction and daily afterschool help; psychologist who did assessments reports that no funding is available for 10 hours of weekly tutoring, that only 5 hours is provided to qualified students, and major factor contributing to Enrique being moderately delayed is his never having had ELD instruction.

9. Principal says teachers report they have done all they can do, and Enrique was told he would lose eligibility status on team if grades didn't improve.

10. Latina community leader has called for an investigation into district policies and funding practices related to tutorial services.

11. African American PTO president supports the school's position, and Latino school site committee chair says site plan includes provision for tutoring without it having to be provided right after school.

MAKE IT PERSONAL

1. How are BCHS and the situation/background information similar to circumstances and conditions in any schools with which you are familiar?

2. Based on what you know about BCHS and the problem situation in the role play, what are your questions of clarification that need to be answered?

૭-૭

IN-BASKET ITEMS OF AREA SUPERINTENDENT RELATED TO BCHS

In-basket items are forms of communication sent to the area superintendent by various players in the BCHS school community, and each communication requires a response or responses of some kind from the area superintendent.

Directions for Responding to In-Basket Items and Sixteen Questions

1. Respond to each item based on your role as area superintendent, which means you supervise and evaluate the school principal, and have administrative responsibility for general oversight (not direct supervision) of all operations at your assigned schools as well as all instructional programs. Make note of all the support services and instructional programs you oversee in your administrative area because you may want to be in touch with some of them in response to specific in-basket items. Operations include support services such as federal and state program funding, counseling, attendance, afterschool tutoring, security, library, instructional materials, custodial and office staff; facilities; personnel; community relations; business partnerships; race/human relations; athletic programs; and business functions. Instructional programs include curriculum, instruction, technology, evaluation, and assessment/testing,

professional development, special needs and academic enrichment, including special education, English language development, gifted, advanced placement, magnet and other special career or theme-based programs, and alternative education programs.

2. At the end of each in-basket item, place a check (√) next to each action listed that you would take, and write any brief notes in response to the item, indicating to whom the note would go or if it is only a note/reminder to you of action to be taken.

3. Use chart 15a to place a check (√) in the box of particular CCL actions and in-basket items to signify your interest in taking actions related to that item and with what priority.

4. There are 16 questions you should consider addressing when drafting your action plan for how to work with BCHS, taking into consideration major ideas in this guide. Choose the questions you consider most relevant and answer those questions, followed by comparing your answers with those of the author provided later in the chapter. Write down your answers to chosen questions before reviewing the author's answers to the same questions.

In-Basket Item #1

Dear Area Superintendent: I am writing at the request of the Rodriquez family in my parish to request your attention to a matter causing great concern. The family has a son attending Bethune-Chavez high school. Enrique is a fine young man, active in the parish, and a star football player at BCHS until recently. The parents have been unsuccessful in getting the school district to provide evening tutoring for Enrique, who is having a very hard time with his studies this year. When Enrique received a warning from the school that he would lose his academic eligibility for remaining on the team unless his grades improved within 1 month, the parents started requesting 10 hours of weekly tutoring for him to no avail. He was subsequently removed from the team's roster until his grades in each subject are a C or higher. I know of two other youngsters in our parish who also attend BCHS and have received the level of tutoring requested by Enrique's parents. Can you do something to correct this injustice? His parents do not feel they are receiving the respect and fairness they deserve from school officials and have asked a lawyer in our church to file a discrimination suit against the district. I am hoping that won't have to be the way this issue is resolved. I can be reached at 321-4567. Respectfully, Father Mendez

RESPONSE: ___ call Father Mendez; ___ call Rodriquez family; ___ call Principal; ___ call football coach; ___ check on district policies regarding afterschool tutoring; ___ check on budget for afterschool tutoring at BCHS; **ADDITIONAL NOTES: (state who recipients will be, if any):**

OTHER ACTIONS TO BE TAKEN:

In-Basket Item #2

Dear Area Superintendent, attached is a petition signed by more than 200 students who belong to the La Raza student union at BCHS. We strongly support the request of the Rodriquez family for the district to provide 10 hours of weekly tutoring for Enrique, starting immediately, and also for Enrique to be reinstated to the football team within 1 week after he starts getting additional tutoring. There is a lot of discrimination going on at BCHS, and all Latino/a (La Raza) students here are not being treated fairly in classrooms by most teachers, especially if we don't speak English that well. Some of the teachers and other students don't want us here and treat us like dirt. The new principal is trying to deal with the problem, but she just got here. We asked a lawyer in our community to write this letter for us to send you, and hope you will investigate this situation and make it right.

RESPONSE: ___ visit BCHS and meet with LaRaza student union students; ___ call Principal; ___ schedule joint classroom visits with principal at BCHS; ___ get records of Enrique's grades since entering BCHS and any tutoring or extra help he has received to date; **ADDITIONAL NOTES: (state who recipients will be, if any):**

OTHER ACTIONS TO BE TAKEN:

In-Basket Item #3

Dear Area Superintendent: You might not remember me, but I was the Black student among the three students on the community interview committee when you applied for your current job, and the only student from BCHS. I am glad you got the job. I am writing because we got a real problem here at BCHS. There were already a lot of conflicts between various factions at the school, teachers vs. teachers, students vs. students, parents vs. teachers and vice versa, etc., but it has really gotten out of hand since Enrique Rodriquez was thrown off the football team because of his grades. When Black students on the team had this happen in the past, no one created a stink, because the students were warned just like Enrique was. But now that Latino/a students are in the majority, they think they should control everything and get away with it when breaking the rules. Some of us don't want to see Enrique stay off the team, especially since he is a good player and we are having our best season in years, but we want the same rules to apply to everybody. If he gets 10 hours of tutoring a week, when 5 hours is the standard amount given, we should, too. A lot of the teaching here is terrible, because teachers cannot explain anything, and also cannot control their classes. Thank goodness we also got some real good ones, but they are in the minority. You got to check out what is happening here; we need help bad!

RESPONSE: ___ go to BCHS and randomly visit some classrooms; ___ check records of all students removed from football team for low grades in last 5 years, and what was done to correct problems; ___ have principal set up joint meeting with football coach; ___ investigate whether athletic coaches are required to conduct study halls with their teams, and be accountable for helping to keep their team members eligible; ___ schedule meeting with the district's chief legal counsel to get particulars related to the suit filed against the district by the Rodriquez family, and to solicit his advice.

ADDITIONAL NOTES: (state who recipients will be, if any):

OTHER ACTIONS TO BE TAKEN:

In-Basket Item #4

Dear Area Superintendent: I thought I should take the initiative to provide you with some background information about the recent suit brought against the district by the Rodriquez family from BCHS. I am one of two special education resource specialists at BCHS and have responded to teacher requests for assistance with Enrique over the last 2 years. I served as chair of the student study team that recently did a formal assessment of Enrique. I will also share a couple of key findings of the district psychologist who participated in the formal assessment.

I feel it imperative to let you know that every effort was taken to persuade Mr. and Mrs. Rodriquez of the need for Enrique to receive ELD instruction since his arrival at BCHS. Such instruction was refused by the parents throughout his K–8 schooling. This probably contributed to his scoring 3 years below grade level in

English language arts and 2 years below grade level in math upon his arrival at BCHS. The family has been adamant that they did not want ELD instruction, because they feared he would be unfairly labeled, and his academic progress would be hindered by any pull-out instruction.

Pull-out instruction is the model we use at BCHS since we don't have academic courses specifically designed for ELD students, or the teachers with the necessary credentials to teach them. It wasn't until his junior year at BCHS (this school year) that Enrique hasn't been able to keep up with any of his assignments. The family provided some private tutoring for him in the ninth grade and beginning of the 10th grade, but couldn't continue because of some economic hardships and the cost of the tutoring.

Enrique received two F grades and one D grade on the first progress report that just came out recently, but the teachers warned him a month ago that he needed to have at least C grades in each subject to remain eligible for the football team. Since the warning, Enrique's parents have been trying to get the district to provide 10 hours of weekly tutoring, 2 hours four nights a week and 2 hours on Saturday. This is 5 hours more than we usually provide, except in exceptional circumstances when students qualify. But Enrique isn't available after school when tutoring is available because of his being on the football team and also because with the budget cutbacks, there is no funding for 10 hours of weekly tutoring, even if he were available.

The district psychologist concluded that Enrique is moderately delayed in his English language processing but feels that could be greatly improved with intensive support for the remainder of his high school career. Another conclusion was that Enrique is very self-conscious of his academic challenges and tries at all costs to keep others from knowing about his problems. I have been told almost all communication with Enrique in the football program is in Spanish, so they say they weren't aware of his problem. I doubt that claim.

I strongly recommend a new effort be made with Enrique's parents and with Enrique to coax him to receive tutoring right after school, but he needs to start that assistance immediately rather than at the end of the football season, in order for him to pass his current courses. Please let me know if you have any questions.

RESPONSE: ___ set up appointment with special education specialist and psychologist to discuss memo sent by special education specialist; ___ call district special education administrator; ___ investigate district and school site special education budgets, as well as any board policies related to afterschool academic support; ___ call principal to discuss the school's ELD program. **ADDITIONAL NOTES (state who recipients will be, if any):**

OTHER ACTIONS TO BE TAKEN:

In-Basket Item #5

Dear Dr. _____, As the executive director of the Harbor View Alliance of African American Parents (AAAP), I am writing to strongly lobby for an equitable response to the recent lawsuit filed by a Spanish-speaking family with a son at BCHS. As the area superintendent in charge of BCHS, we assume your input will be of critical importance when the district decides whether to respond affirmatively to the parent's requests for 10 hours of weekly tutoring, which would constitute "extra tutoring" for their son. We are of the opinion, based on our past experience when African American parents have requested afterschool academic support for their children, that any "regular" or "extra" tutoring should be based on whether the student has met certain eligibility criteria, and then whether the student's family is willing to sign a contract agreeing to make the student available when tutoring is normally provided. I think I am correct in saying that Enrique Rodriquez has not met any eligibility criteria established by the district (such as his participating in whatever instructional assistance programs are offered during the school day), and his parents have also not signed a contract as specified above, and that in fact, they want an "exception" to the rule about availability and participation of the student on a regular basis in the tutoring program when it is normally offered. We cannot support the granting of such exceptions about meeting eligibility criteria, or the signing of the contract, because that would be flagrant favoritism if it is allowed. We are not opposed to any student receiving extra tutoring if the rules are consistently followed for *all* students. Please respond to this letter in writing at your earliest convenience.

RESPONSE: ___ investigate whether the statements about eligibility criteria and contract are correct; ___ contact principal and other appropriate personnel to secure records of all students receiving afterschool help at BCHS in the last 3 years, and whether there was consistency in enforcing whatever rules exist for such support to be given; ___ find out if AAAP has taken prior actions in support of equitable support for African American students, and what, if any, problems occurred regarding African American students receiving equitable afterschool academic support; ___ write a response to the executive director of AAAP. **ADDITIONAL NOTES (state who recipients will be, if any):**

OTHER ACTIONS TO BE TAKEN:

SOME SUGGESTED RESPONSES TO EACH IN-BASKET ITEM

In-Basket Item #1

The suggested skills to be displayed when responding to this item are problem analysis, judgment, decision making, organization, and sensitivity. It is suggested that the notes include the intention to ask the priest for additional information about the other students in his parish that supposedly have received the amount of tutorial assistance the Rodriquez family requested. Also, some questions to be considered are why Enrique isn't currently receiving extra help during the school day; who teaches in the afterschool tutorial program, regular BCHS teachers or a contracted agency, and if the help is provided by a contracted agency, to what degree is there articulation between what is taught in the regular classroom and in the tutorial program. In addition, additional information that may be helpful is whether other students have received 10 hours of weekly school tutoring, since the most recent district budget cuts, and if so, why this has occurred. Additional suggested actions are visiting an afterschool tutoring session and talking to the tutor; determining the process used for students to be approved for afterschool tutorial help; and what the contract language is, if any, for regular BCHS teachers to provide afterschool tutoring. For example, is there any restriction on teachers or another provider conducting tutorial sessions in the early evening as opposed to right after school. CCL actions in chart 15a that you should consider are numbers 5, 6, 10, 11, 16, 18, 20, and 21.

In-Basket Item #2

The suggested skills to be displayed are problem analysis, judgment, organization, decision making, and sensitivity. Suggested notes are to send a written response to the student La Raza organization, work with the principal to find a way to get help for Enrique during the school day, and find out if the new principal had any direct contact with the Rodriquez family before the lawsuit was initiated, and if not, to request that the principal call Enrique's parents to offer an alternative to afterschool tutoring. You should request more specific documentation from La Raza and other community sources regarding the claims of discrimination against Latino/a students at BCHS, and try to meet with (or request the principal to do so) a small group of La Raza students to get more specific documentation of their allegations as well as their personal perspectives. Also do some unannounced observations in BCHS classrooms as soon as possible. CCL actions in chart 15a that you should consider are numbers 4–8, 10, 11, 13–15, 17, 18.

Chart 15a CCL Actions Response Sheet for In-Basket Activity

Some Specific Actions of CCL (see Chapters 7–10 for explanation of items)	In-Basket Item #1	In-Basket Item #2	In-Basket Item #3	In-Basket Item #4	In-Basket Item #5	Priority: 1 = High 2 = Medium 3 = Low
1. Facilitate collaborative leadership by all school community stakeholders.						
2. Foster personal transformation.						
3. Lead organizational transformation.						
4. Be a committed caregiver.						
5. Be a cultural consumer.						
6. Be a consummate conciliator, especially when dealing with the cultural politics.						
7. Be a conscientious coach.						
8. Be a courageous change master in confronting institutional biases and barriers to equitable outcomes.						
9. Be a community organizer.						
10. Be a communication guru.						
11. Engage in problem definition.						
12. Attend to the psychology of equity transformation.						

Some Specific Actions of CCL (see Chapters 7–10 for explanation of items)	In-Basket Item #1	In-Basket Item #2	In-Basket Item #3	In-Basket Item #4	In-Basket Item #5	Priority: 1 = High 2 = Medium 3 = Low
13. Utilize delivery standards that foster culturally responsive teaching.						
14. Utilize opportunity to learn standards.						
15. Utilize professional development standards.						
16. Review school district policies/practices regarding resource allocation.						
17. Lessen cultural dissonance within and across ethnic and stakeholder groups.						
18. Increase use of students and parents as resources in helping implement school improvement.						
19. Expand distributed instructional leadership to include investigation of all alleged cultural bias.						
20. Improve toxic school climate.						
21. Improve limited accountability.						
22. Finesse wanksters, gangsters, and riders.						

In-Basket Item #3

The suggested skills to be displayed are problem analysis, judgment, organization, decision making, and sensitivity. Suggested notes are to send a note to the student, after getting input from the principal, inviting the student to identify a small group of five to seven students that you or the principal could meet with to discuss their perspectives on what needs to improve at the school. Ask the principal to do some investigation of whether the student's comments about conflicts going on at the school have any merit, and get back to you as soon as possible with a report on what is happening, who is involved, and the course of action the principal plans to take regarding any conflicts found. Another suggested action is to ask the principal to investigate the purported double standard regarding what happens when Black students on the football team are academically ineligible versus what is now going on because a Latino student on the team is having the same problem. A final suggestion is to find out what the BCHS athletic department is doing about providing academic support for their student athletes. CCL actions in chart 15a that you should consider are numbers 2–4, 6, 8, 10–12, 16–20.

In-Basket Item #4

The suggested skills to be displayed are problem analysis, judgment, organization, decision making, sensitivity, and stress tolerance. Suggested notes are to privately seek third-party confirmation of the claims about the Rodriquez family, Enrique's educational history, and his showing evidence of moderate delay in ELD. Furthermore, it is suggested you also try to talk with "neutral" persons about how BCHS evolved from being the "Black" school to becoming a "Latino/a" school and what the reverberations have been as a consequence. You also need to find out if Enrique's failing grades are primarily a function of his never having had ELD instruction, or if there are other factors contributing to his academic problems. Other problems could include the norms in the athletic department regarding academic support for athletes, teacher's level of instructional expertise or attitudes about ELD students, and no funding for evening tutorial support. These statements by the special education resource specialist might be exaggerated or based on hearsay. The accuracy of the analysis and recommendation of the district psychologist also needs to be verified. It is suggested you exercise extreme caution in accepting without further investigation the conclusions and recommendations of school and district level personnel in this instance. Although it will be time consuming, it is suggested you try to conduct your own inquiry. CCL actions in chart 15a that you should consider are numbers 1–8, 9–18, 21, and 22.

In-Basket Item #5

The suggested skills to be displayed are problem analysis, judgment, organization, decision making, sensitivity, and stress tolerance. Suggested notes are to call the person sending this letter, express appreciation for it, and request a meeting to discuss several points made in the letter, such as "equitable response," "eligibility criteria," "contracts" to be signed by parents before student enrollment in after-school programs, "exceptions," and "favoritism." This organization could be a valuable community resource, so inquiries are likely needed about their history, track record, and disposition to work with the district in tacking some challenging issues related to student success and collaboration among various school community stakeholder groups. A follow-up in writing after the call would be an important gesture. Additional suggestions are to immediately make inquiries about whether several points in the letter are accurate, such as whether there are currently district or school-specific eligibility criteria and contracts for student participation in academic support programs. It these statements are accurate, it would be helpful to know if the procedures are the result of board of education policy, if the procedures are consistently used, and with whom, as well as whether other high schools follow the same process. Since the letter may also be suggesting that the district is not always consistent in application of policies and procedures, it is suggested that efforts be made to find out if this is true, who has usually been favored in the past if any, and whether there are some changes taking place in the recipients of "favoritism." CCL actions in chart 15a that you should consider are numbers 1–3, 6–12, 16–22.

કર્જા

QUESTIONS TO BE CONSIDERED IN DRAFT ACTION PLAN FOR WORKING WITH BCHS AS THE NEW AREA SUPERINTENDENT

Given the emphases in this guide, choose the items below you find most relevant, answer in writing, and only after writing your answers, examine how the author answers the same 16 questions related to use of the CCL paradigm in this role-play:

1. How will you attempt to positively influence the racial attitudes of any of the following persons in the BCHS community: teachers, administrators, Latino/a parents and students, African American students and parents?

2. What are some of the racial/cultural conflicts that seem to exist?

3. What actions will you take to attempt lessening the conflicts at BCHS?

4. Based on what you know at this point, does there seem to be any indication of cultural democracy at BCHS?

5. How will you attempt to improve cultural democracy at BCHS?

6. What seem to be some examples of the cultural politics at the school?

7. How will you work with the new principal to deal with the cultural politics?

8. What seem to be some examples of cultural hegemony at the school?

9. What are your ideas about how to address any cultural hegemony you find at BCHS?

10. What appear to be institutional biases and/or barriers to achievement at high levels?

11. How will you attempt to eliminate any biases and barriers?

12. How will you model what you expect of others at BCHS?

13. Given the four directives you have from the board and superintendent, how will you address these board directives while working with the BCHS school community?

14. How will you use any of the 10 observations, discussed in Chapter 4, and implement one of the needed actions, discussed in Chapter 7?

15. Of the five categories of standards in chart 5a, which will you give greater priority at BCHS, and how will you do it?

16. Given the four components of CCL discussed in this guide, what are three specific things within any of the components that you think should be the focus of capacity building in the coming year within the BCHS school community?

కిం

HOW THE SIXTEEN QUESTIONS RELATE TO THE CULTURALLY COURAGEOUS LEADERSHIP PARADIGM

1. How will you attempt to positively influence the racial attitudes of any of the following persons in the BCHS community: teachers, administrators, Latino/a parents and students, African American students and parents?

Adherents to the CCL paradigm confront and transcend personal fears, human difference biases, and discriminatory behaviors. Any of these feelings or actions may be influenced by their cultural and racial identities, ideas and actions of significant others, perceived pressure by subgroups with which they most identify, and/or how they react to the way they are treated by others.

Share your personal journey as a means of trying to influence the racial attitudes of others. Also help create an emotionally safe trusting environment where people feel safe and more receptive to taking risks, when engaged in what Singleton and Linton call "courageous conversations about race" (2006). Both the Latino/a and Black communities at BCHS seem to strongly feel there has been or will be discriminatory treatment regarding access to school-based tutorial practices. Through problem-solving dialogue with relevant parties, engage them in discovering any differences between their perceptions and the realities and also the basis for their perceptions. Sometimes persons have a strong investment in adhering to their perceptions or biases, and they need to first acknowledge if that is true.

A complication is that some Latino/a and Black parents are very hesitant to allow their children to either be pulled out of regular classes for English language development instruction or assigned to receive special education services, even when formal assessments suggest that is the best course of action. There is a strong distrust some parents have about the wisdom of allowing their children to participate in such programs, that is deep-seated and long-standing, because they feel there is more harm than good their children experience from being "labeled," and they may have some historical memory to justify their distrust.

2. What are some of the racial/cultural conflicts that seem to exist?

The CCL paradigm includes a commitment to engaging in problem analysis (adapted from the national association of secondary school principals original assessment center), and to seven CCL principles, two of which are being a committed caregiver and a consummate conciliator. When identifying any conflicts that appear to exist, keep in mind that appearances are often deceiving. It may appear that Latino/a and African American parents, as well as students, have conflicts with each other over whether the Rodriquez lawsuit is justified, and whether there has actually been discrimination against the Rodriquez family practiced by the school district.

Whether there has been or not, there could still be conflicts. You must decide if any conflicts are racial in nature. The information in the background information and in the in-basket items includes strong feelings and conclusions about the attitudes and behaviors of authority figures and other stakeholder or ethnic groups. Being a committed caregiver and conciliator, you might want to be cautious in how you characterize the evident conflicts before collecting additional information.

3. What actions will you take to attempt lessening the conflicts at BCHS?

A practitioner of CCL is also a conscientious coach and communication guru, who facilitates both personal and organizational transformation. BCHS conflicts appear to be long standing and strongly felt by all parties. Coaching is one avenue that could be used to facilitate capacity building in conflict management over time, but it cannot be successful without all parties willingly and totally committed to achieving whatever growth is desired. The CCL must often motivate the person(s) to be helped to willingly and enthusiastically participate in such coaching. Transformational blended coaching, also called CLASS (Coaching Leaders to Achieve Student Success) was developed by the New Teacher Center at the

University of California, Santa Clara, and the Association of California School Administrators, to support growth and change in both what principals do and who they are (Bloom, Castagna, & Warren, 2003).

The CLASS model involves a very interactive inquiry-oriented exchange between coach and person coached, with the coach guiding his or her mentee toward developing objectives, observable, measurable benchmarks, and specific action steps. This is followed by regular meetings to collectively examine the thinking, problem-solving, and decision-making processes used during efforts to achieve benchmark targets. The coach asks questions that exhibit a range of interpersonal communication skills to facilitate the mentee's metacognitive processing, assessment of what has or has not been accomplished, and deciding on corrective actions or next steps to be taken. Whether formal coaching occurs or not, the practitioner of CCL must be able to help all parties practice respectful protocols during conflicts being experienced, through the modeling of strong interpersonal communication and conflict management skills.

4. Based on what you know at this point, does there seem to be any indication of cultural democracy at BCHS?

When answering this question, reflect on the definition of "cultural democracy" initially provided in Chapter 1, and then review the background information about the problem at BCHS, looking for examples of behaviors by various parties or situations that may illustrate whether there is some degree of cultural democracy. Regardless of whether there are certain policies or regulations in place at the school level, it is possible for some measure of cultural democracy to exist when any stakeholders are able to freely express their beliefs about what is contributing to social injustice and engage in advocacy for certain changes without negative consequence.

Culturally courageous leaders work to improve the school climate, which includes several dimensions, such as communication and problem-solving adequacy, cohesion, morale, goal focus, and opportunities for all to participate in the decision-making process. These climate dimensions and the others mentioned in Chapter 4 give you a lot to look for when deciding if there is any indication of cultural democracy.

5. How will you attempt to improve cultural democracy at BCHS?

There are references to concerns about what is taught and to whom as well as the school climate issues already mentioned. When attempting to improve cultural democracy, remember such efforts are inherently political and possibly pregnant with potential land mines. Therefore, be sure to think about which dimensions of the politics of implementation need to be addressed. Practitioners of CCL are courageous change masters, which is essential for cultural democracy to be improved, especially when there is a very Eurocentric curriculum and toxic school climate.

6. What seem to be some examples of the cultural politics at the school?

Refer to the definitions of "politics" in Chapter 9 and "cultural politics" discussed in Chapter 1. At BCHS, there are several suggestions of conflict in agendas and perspectives, so this question should not be difficult. However, be wary of jumping to the conclusion that every instance of "difference" between various persons in ethnic and stakeholder groups is an instance of "cultural" politics. As discussed in this guide, cultural politics has been associated with competing views and actions related to perpetuating or eliminating cultural hegemony. The CCL paradigm includes engaging in problem definition, and problem definition is necessary to identify examples of cultural politics at the school.

7. How will you work with the new principal to deal with the cultural politics?

Keep in mind that as stated in the background information on the problem at BCHS, both you and the BCHS principal are new in your respective roles. As the new area superintendent, you should be looking at the dynamics in BCHS as possibly representing some thorny issues you may have to deal with in the entire BCHS cluster of schools and their school communities. You need to closely collaborate with the new BCHS principal on identifying the cultural politics and in stepping up the degree of research-based instructional supervision.

However, in the final analysis, because of a lawsuit against the district, you as area superintendent may need to take the lead in trying to change any negative impact of the cultural politics on the school. The CCL paradigm includes attending to the psychology of equity transformation (e.g., the beliefs, values, assumptions, and strong feelings) when dealing with the politics of any equity initiative. The Rodriquez lawsuit has implications far beyond the specifics of the case. Each of the parties in the school community on either side of the lawsuit need to feel the district is addressing all relevant issues in a fair manner.

8. What seem to be some examples of cultural hegemony at the school?

Many persons who experience "White privilege" are very loathe to acknowledge the existence of cultural hegemony, are insulted by the statement that in the United States there is a dominant cultural group, and that the cultural experiences and priorities of the dominant cultural and socioeconomic group are given priority over the beliefs, experiences, and interests of other groups in the nation.

Review what is said about attitudes in the BCHS community about English language development, the Latino/a student population at BCHS, and student allegations about instructional practices. Then decide if there are reasons to conclude there seem to be examples of cultural hegemony. The CCL paradigm includes giving more attention to both delivery and opportunity to learn standards, which if done, would likely lessen the degree of cultural hegemony. Investigate the attention given to these standards categories.

9. What are your ideas about how to address any cultural hegemony you find at BCHS?

Depending on whatever instances of cultural hegemony one identifies at BCHS, there are many directions one could take to address any particular instance. For example, some might identify the English/language arts and history/social studies curricula as instances of cultural hegemony. This could be addressed by community organizing, one of the characteristics of culturally courageous leaders. Increasing public awareness of the problem and mobilizing the public to lobby school boards to not adopt any textbooks or other instructional materials/software that only reflect the dominant cultural group perspective would be one way to address what may be perceived as cultural hegemony. Community organizing can be a tool to work against hegemony as well as a tool to strongly lobby for positive approaches to improving cultural democracy in school settings. Refer to the discussion in Chapters 3 and 5 for ideas about how to address any cultural hegemony.

10. What appear to be institutional biases and/or barriers to achievement at high levels?

Chapter 5 on biases and Chapter 6 on barriers provide several examples that you can use as a point of departure when deciding which if any apply to BCHS. I have found most if not all of the biases and barriers discussed in those chapters to be prevalent in low-performing schools populated primarily by historically underserved students of color. In my experience, the degree to which they exist varies depending on a host of variables. A key phrase in the above question is "achievement at high levels." Achievement at *high levels* must be defined. Jackson operationalizes the concept of high intellectual performance (2011). Common criteria related to high levels are whether critical thinking skills are mastered and whether student performance on end-of-year statewide tests in core academic subjects are at the proficient or higher levels, as determined by the state.

But there are other measurable criteria that could be used to define what is meant by high levels. For example, *high levels* should be defined to include the acquisition of 21st century skills and "opportunities for students to use what they are learning in ways that directly impact their lives," such as learning how to address their material concerns and act upon these concerns in the service of their communities (Duncan-Andrade & Morrell, 2008). Culturally courageous leadership includes a focus on improving accountability of all stakeholders. Despite the NCLB legislative requirements, many teachers in low-performing schools are not held accountable for facilitating achievement at high levels by many historically underserved students who are considered special needs or limited English proficient, and are not sufficiently supported in developing the capacity to become more accountable. Board of education priorities, policies, and politics might be a major reason teachers are not adequately supported or held accountable.

11. How will you attempt to eliminate any biases and barriers?

The CCL paradigm includes an overarching commitment to facilitating collaborative leadership by all school community stakeholders, whether it is leadership to confront and collectively work on changing institutional biases and barriers or is a focus on organizational transformation. As you consider how you would work to eliminate any biases and barriers at BCHS, you need to make sure you have concrete data on the who, what, where, when, and how, which illustrate the biases and barriers being addressed. Bring representatives from all stakeholder groups together to investigate any alleged instances of biases and barriers, and then attempt to reach consensus on specific instances of bias and barriers, followed by identifying the kind of organizational changes needed in the school as a whole. I reiterate there needs to be consensus on some specific examples of institutional biases and barriers to high achievement at BCHS and some collaborative efforts by all stakeholder groups to lessen or eliminate these biases and barriers.

12. How will you model what you expect of others at BCHS?

Since BCHS seems to have some staff, students, and parents who have opposing and deeply held views on what the problems are at BCHS and what should be done about them, the leadership of the area superintendent must include fostering greater respect and civil dialogue between all parties, including students, parents, and community members. Team and trust building should be a first step when deciding how to model what is expected of others. As already mentioned, the CCL paradigm includes being a courageous change master and a communication guru. Definitions of these CCL characteristics are in Chapter 8 and need to be modeled.

13. Given the four directives you have from the board and superintendent, how will you address these board directives while working with the BCHS school community?

Culturally courageous leaders review school district policies/practices related to resource allocation as a first step toward seeking a change in them, especially when it comes to negative impacts on the educational experience of historically underserved student populations. Practitioners of CCL also work to lessen cultural dissonance within and across ethnic and stakeholder groups, increase use of students and parents as resources in helping implement school improvement, and expand distributed instructional leadership. All of these actions are part of chart 15a, and all apply to specific conditions evident at BCHS that require priority attention. It is very important to also use relevant information from other staff, school sites, or programs under your supervision. Refer to the second leadership profile in Chapter 12, and the discussion of three equity warriors in Chapter 14 for ideas on how you could simultaneously respond to the directives from the board of education and the issues being experienced by the BCHS school community.

14. How will you use one of the ten observations, discussed in Chapter 4, and implement one of the needed actions, discussed in Chapter 7?

Of the 10 observations in Chapter 4, at least half of them directly apply to BCHS, based on the information provided, and perhaps more apply indirectly if you as area superintendent worked with a representative group of others to engage in problem analysis of the conditions described. All of the needed actions discussed in Chapter 7 that reflect societal and educational conditions experienced by historically underserved students of color seem to be needed at BCHS. When deciding *how* you would use one of the observations and one of the needed actions, some strategies discussed in Chapter 9 should be considered. Each is suggested when dealing with the politics of equity transformation. They are all part of the CCL paradigm, such as a need for joint efforts in the confrontation of obstacles to equitable educational outcomes; more focus on culturally responsive academic rigor, more attention to improving human relationships and school being perceived by students as relevant to their everyday lives. Increasing access, assessment, and accountability, as discussed in Chapter 11, and improving the use of facilitation, mediation, and candor during problem-solving discussions, are essential. All of these should inform how you go about attempting to "walk the equity talk" at BCHS.

15. Of the five categories of standards in chart 5a, to which will you give greater priority and how will you do it?

The top three categories of standards needing priority at BCHS to address the "problem situation" involving Enrique are likely the delivery, opportunity to learn, and the professional development standards. Chapter 5 discusses how it is very hard to improve attention to delivery and professional development standards if the opportunity to learn standards haven't been adequately addressed. However, based on what is described or alleged in the problem situation at BCHS, and the accompanying in-basket items of the area superintendent, there is reason to believe that the content and performance standards also need attention as well, when it comes to the content needing to be more culturally relevant and responsive, and the performance criteria needing to be more vigorously utilized, so that no students are subject to low expectations. The use of rubrics and exemplars, referred to under performance standards in chart 5a, would likely help to improve greater consistency in application of high-performance standards to all student subgroups. Rubrics provide observable and measurable evidence/criteria to determine if an objective has been accomplished; exemplars provide concrete examples of what success would look like when a specific task is completed. Refer to the upcoming book of Dr. Joseph Johnson (2012) on *Teaching in America's Best Urban Schools*, to be published by Eye on Education, to acquire information on instructional practices in high-performing urban schools, to the book by Dr. Robyn Jackson (2011) titled

How to Plan Rigorous Instruction, and the book by Dr. Yvette Jackson, titled *The Pedagogy of Confidence* (2011), as well as to what is discussed in Chapters 11 through 14 of this guide. As indicated earlier, it is not possible to be an effective instructional leader without being a culturally courageous instructional leader. Without cultural courageousness, you are playing around the margins, a lot of sound and fury signifying nothing, when it comes to facilitating equitable educational outcomes of the historically underserved.

16. Given the four components of CCL discussed in this guide, what are three specific actions within any of the components that you think should be the focus of capacity building in the coming year within the BCHS school community?

When answering this question, take into consideration that you will likely identify more than three actions within the four CCL components that need urgent attention at BCHS. However, what three "building blocks" are most likely in your judgment to be those you can use as stepping stones to build over time the kind of culturally responsive district and schools desired? Also, if you are no longer in your district in another 2 or 3 years, or the philosophy and politics of your superintendent or board majority change sooner than you would like, what should you have tried to put in place?

I have found in my own work and study that increasing an equity consciousness and developing transformative relationships are critical, and more easily withstand the revolving door of policy and decision makers at the top. Acquiring a new cultural lens as well as qualitatively different kinds of relationships among and between students, parents, teachers, and community persons of all backgrounds are to a large extent both a cause and reflection of changed identities and changed beliefs about themselves, as well as their potential and power for good within the larger community. If you can help make a dent in the level of consciousness and quality of relationships, through your vision, perseverance, goodwill, and savvy, then nurturing the cultural courageousness of self and others to take the necessary steps toward social justice will not be in vain. We must wake up in order to stand up and truly engage in the equity walk.

MAKE IT PERSONAL

FN 15–1 (SEE FACILITATOR NOTES IN APPENDIX 1)

1. What have you learned from participating in the role-playing exercise?

2. How has your participation in the role playing exercise enhanced your understanding of the culturally courageous leadership paradigm?

REVIEW OF CHAPTER 15

- A role-playing exercise is provided, with salient facts about a problematic situation at a high school involving a lawsuit against the school district alleging discrimination. Background information on what led up to the situation as well as responses to the situation are provided. The person completing the exercise is asked to respond to five in-basket items that require the demonstration of up to six skills, and 16 questions to choose from when deciding how to intervene at the high school as a culturally courageous "area superintendent."

- Two diagnostic questionnaires in Appendix 2 are introduced as tools to assist CCL work. One is a questionnaire designed to diagnose the relationship between individual concerns, perceived organizational needs and personal beliefs, priorities, and behaviors related to culturally courageous leadership. The second is a 60-item questionnaire designed to assist schools in determining how staff and other school community stakeholders feel about how the school is doing in several areas critical for achieving equitable educational outcomes. Neither instrument should be completed by persons who have not read the text or been briefed on the text. Persons completing either of the questionnaires must be familiar with language used in the questionnaire.

&&

The Time Is Here, the Time Is Now

16

If not us, then who? If not now, then when?

Despite reform after reform, voluminous research studies, court decisions, legislative mandates, major funding allocations, and civil rights movements, social justice in the schools of the United States is still beyond reach for millions of people. As a national society, the United States continues to find many excuses for why there have been less than comprehensive efforts to address educational inequities. This guide makes the case that our present status in the area of educational equity is largely a function of a lack of will, a lack of skill, and more specifically, a lack of culturally courageous leadership (CCL) by all school community stakeholders.

The time is past due for concerted action, and we certainly cannot afford the luxury of further posturing, "perpetrating," and delay in attacking full force all of the many things we know are wrong about the way we educate all of our population. But public education cannot be separated from other public policy and practice in such areas as public health, law enforcement, social services, banking and financial services, employment opportunities, and postsecondary education. Discriminatory, and specifically racist, ethnocentric, or sexist practices, among others, in any area of public policy and practice will always have a harmful if not devastating effect on realizing equitable educational opportunities and outcomes in preK–12 learning environments.

The time is here, in every school, school district, university, hamlet, suburb, city, and state, and the time is now for us to stop all the sidestepping and truly begin to collaboratively walk the equity talk. To do that, we must be willing to acknowledge where we have been, where we are, and what we need to do individually and collectively in order to truly achieve a sea change in our social, political, and economic order that results in social justice for all.

Collaboration, repeatedly urged in this guide, is not promoted with rose-colored glasses, or naively suggested as the answer to all problems and challenges related to equity. There will be times when the culturally courageous leaders among board of education members, administrators, and teachers must take action, alone or in concert with only a few others, when they cannot secure widespread agreement for the kind of joint efforts preferred. Even when one thinks they have made their best effort and demonstrated their willingness to go more than halfway to secure consensus, others may resolutely oppose and even do everything possible to sabotage any kind of equity initiative. Meaningful collaboration across all school community stakeholder groups requires ongoing coalition building and community organizing. It is very labor-intensive work, which may ultimately have benefits for the stalwarts at heart who don't accept "no" as an acceptable answer and steadfastly persevere. However, equity initiatives must be authentic movements and not pseudo-movements, and Parker Palmer (1998) says it is essential for communities of congruence in education who develop a powerful common vision for educational reform. To be authentic though, he asserts such communities must go public and engage in give and take. Culturally courageous leaders must be disposed to initiate such public dialogue to persuade and attempt facilitating greater understanding and buy-in. In doing so, adherents of CCL need to model respect for divergent points of view and be transparent with historically underserved constituencies about the hurdles that keep the equity walk from occurring, rather than convey the impression that good intentions and inspiring rhetoric alone will carry the day. The equity walk is an uphill climb at best, and even when seeming to go well, can be ambushed.

KWL EXERCISE

1. Based on your completion of the role-play in Chapter 15, what do you know about yourself that you might not have known before?

2. Write a short list of three to five things that you consider prerequisites for you to wholeheartedly and enthusiastically begin to consistently practice CCL.

3. Draw something or create some visual that represents what you have responded to the most within this guide.

ॐॐ

ADDITIONAL ISSUES YOU *MUST* CONSIDER

CCL is conceptualized as a holistic, interdisciplinary, democratically inspired way of influencing the thoughts and behaviors of persons in all school community stakeholder groups. The major premise is that equitable educational opportunities/inputs/resources and outcomes for all student subgroups cannot be achieved and sustained without a sea change in our national culture, subcultures, personal cultures, and school organizational cultures. Culture is an operative word, which I simplistically define as including all that we think and do. Without changing how we think and act, most of us cannot be all that we need to be if we want to help ourselves and others achieve "life, liberty, and the pursuit of happiness." Courage is required, the kind of courage to transcend prejudicial beliefs about self and others, influenced by our peers, prevalent media-inspired attitudes in society, and sometimes what we learn in formal educational settings.

Seven issues briefly touched upon in this section are as follows:

1. "We have seen the enemies and they are us."

2. What can be learned and applied from private sector equity initiatives to urban culturally diverse schools?

3. Factors influencing research on the impact of holistic culturally responsive teaching and culturally relevant curriculum on student educational outcomes.

4. The "silent conspiracy?"

5. The absence of cross-cultural educational coalitions between historically underserved groups.

6. "Challenging the challenges or resisting the resistances."

7. "All that glitters is not gold."

We Have Seen the Enemies and They Are Us

The word *enemies* refers to worldview, human difference beliefs, concepts of self and others, and behaviors that reduce personal motivation, sense of efficacy (i.e., belief in one's ability), and self-discipline when it comes to achieving equity initiatives. Some school community stakeholders play the "victim" card very well and often, when it comes to being challenged on why they aren't able to make more of a difference with historically underserved students of color. The finger is pointed at others when they blame student attitudes and behaviors, students' families, class size, budget cuts, or any other educational conditions as the sole reasons for student underachievement. In addition, when any courageous educators, teachers or otherwise, overcome personal and organizational norms that are counterproductive to facilitating equitable educational outcomes, the crab barrel mentality will sometimes be demonstrated by unfair peer pressure because they dare to be more responsive to the characteristics of their students.

Both the victim syndrome among some educators and the crab barrel mentality in some school environments are examples of power/control dramas in schools.

In such situations, competing constituencies with different educational philosophies results in a standstill when it comes to doing what is necessary to increase the life chances of underserved students.

What Can Be Learned and Applied From Successful Private Sector Equity Initiatives to Urban Culturally Diverse Schools?

Taylor Cox Jr. (1993, 2001) developed an interactional model of the impact of diversity on individual career outcomes and organizational effectiveness as well as a model for cultural change in response to the challenge of diversity. He emphasizes the need for managers to be coalition builders and the absolute need for the top executive of any enterprise to be directly involved (2001, p. 36). Cox's interactional model has individual level factors such as personal identity structures, prejudice and stereotyping, and intergroup factors, such as ethnocentrism and intergroup conflict. The model also includes organizational context factors, such as organizational culture and institutional bias (2001, p. 9).

Cox says that all of these factors collectively define the diversity climate of an organization. He is talking about much more than the diversity of the workforce. He is also talking about the way that the more diverse workforce goes about doing their work, and asserts that the amount of diversity in both formal and informal structures of organizations will impact creativity, problem solving, and intra-organizational communication (2001, p.10). There may be much that can be learned by public school district superintendents who are eager to pursue equity transformation, and are willing to reach out to the corporate community. Perhaps through closer communication and some joint endeavors, school districts can benefit from learning about the approach to diversity by some Fortune 500 corporations in areas such as capacity building and accountability.

Factors Influencing Research on the Impact of Holistic Culturally Responsive Teaching and Culturally Relevant Curriculum on Student Educational Outcomes

There is a growing body of empirical and qualitative research on how culturally diverse students benefit from culturally relevant curricula (CRC) and culturally responsive teaching (CRT) that are multidimensional, including attention to the creative and performing arts from a cultural perspective, with the spoken word being part of the performing arts. CRC and CRT have been too narrowly defined in most schools and most studies. CRT must also include respect for the multiple identities of students, and to how they choose to express these identities. How educators respond to students' expression of their identities at any given moment must be the subject of critical inquiry and modified when the response is dehumanizing with a preoccupation solely on exercising authority and control. The outcomes of such research, curriculum and instruction may include improvements in the self-concept of both teachers and students, critical thinking and literacy, time on task, teacher attitudes about culturally diverse students, student attitudes about school, use of interactive instructional strategies, and more positive classroom learning environments. However, there may still be mixed results on improvements in scores on standards-based academic measures. One of the difficulties has been finding demographically and educationally comparable groups of students when trying to determine the impact of certain interventions. Another challenge is the logistics and politics associated with implementing large-scale studies.

There is a need for more political will and savvy, that is, CCL, by university faculty and by educators responsible for testing and evaluation. Even when positive results of studies undertaken are disseminated, there may be excuses, primarily of a cultural and political nature, for why large-scale implementation or integration of holistic CRC and CRT are not feasible. We must not allow limited funding and test scores to be the reasons for not making schools more joyful places for children to learn. If we have the will, we must find a way.

A Silent Conspiracy? How the Practices of Accreditation Agencies, University Administrator and Teacher Preparation Programs, and Status Reports on Foundation Funded Efforts to Improve Such Programs Are Tiptoeing Around Hegemony and Equity Issues

Earlier in this guide, comments were made about the failure of most teacher and administrator credential programs to adequately prepare students for effectively dealing with the "isms" and "institutional biases" when implementing equity efforts. A major issue receiving too little attention in the literature and research on achievement and other educational gaps in United States schools is the extent to which all of the "isms" and "biases" are still very prevalent in educational policy and practice, especially, but not exclusively, in urban low-income schools.

The "isms" include racism, ethnocentrism, sexism, classism, religious beliefs or lack thereof, as well as deep-seated personal and institutional prejudice and discrimination directed toward persons based on their size, weight, primary language, sexual orientation, and disability status. Despite a plethora of federal and state laws that prohibit some or all of the above "isms" or discrimination, the teaching and learning experience of the historically underserved demonstrates otherwise.

An issue needing more attention is whether there is a conscious or unconscious "silent conspiracy," as manifested in the protocols and practices of accreditation agencies for university colleges/schools of education, and for high schools. We must ask why most teacher education and administrator preparation programs are given a free pass if they fail to engage their students in assignments, classroom activities, and action research tasks related to manifestation of the "isms" and other bias. Such coursework could more effectively prepare them for working with others to ameliorate institutional biases and barriers to achievement at high levels by historically under-served students. If accreditation agencies do not give much attention to instructional leadership for equitable outcomes, accountability by all, and a school climate condu-cive to achieving such leadership and accountability, what role are they playing in supporting such negligence? Is this a silent conspiracy to consciously or unwittingly support perpetuation of the ideology of White dominance by avoiding such hot and politically volatile topics?

The recent well-funded study on teacher preparation programs undertaken by the Carnegie Corporation in conjunction with the Annenberg Foundation, Ford Foundation, and the Academy for Educational Development did not explicitly address that concern, as reflected in the research design and objectives. The report on school leadership preparation conducted by the Stanford Educational Leadership Institute and Finance Project funded by the Wallace Foundation was a more detailed summary of what is currently being done, not including what needs to be done based on a review of the sociocultural and achievement realities being experienced in many school districts. In both instances, there were no explicit references to the culture and structure of school districts that supports institutional racism and cul-tural hegemony that arguably significantly contribute to gross underachievement and other educational disparities experienced by historically underserved students. It seemed like those who conceptualized the teacher preparation study and leader-ship report did not perceive this crisis as relevant to their undertaking, or thought it politically expedient to not acknowledge the elephant in the room. It is likely not a conspiracy but is at the least blatant neglect.

The Scarcity of Cross-Cultural Educational Coalitions Between Historically Underserved Groups

The history of race/cultural/ethnic relations in the United States over the last 40 years has included a lot of prejudice, resentment, conflict, suspicion, and lack of respect between various historically underserved groups, including persons of Latino/a and African American background. In some cases, the dominant cul-tural group has adroitly manipulated competition and clashes between these two groups for dwindling resources. There is a great deal of diversity within each of these two population groups, and they have more in common than many would like to acknowledge.

Many residential areas within mostly urban communities across the country have become a majority Latino/a, when the population used to be primarily African American in makeup. This is consistent with the Latino/a national population being the second largest population group in the United States. Whenever I have referred in this guide to historically underserved students in the public schools, I am talking primarily, but not exclusively, about the African and Latino/a American populations, who comprise the overwhelming numerical majority of such students. However, this is not to imply that there aren't major injustices perpetrated against other histori-cally underserved groups, such as Native Americans, some Southeast Asian ethnic groups, Pacific Islanders, recent African immigrant groups, and Appalachian Whites. Unfortunately, there are far too few political, cultural, or educational coali-tions between these population groups even though they are all fighting for an end to cultural hegemony, more cultural democracy, and equitable educational inputs and outcomes, among other things.

Powell (2007), executive director of the Kirwan Institute for the study of race and ethnicity at Ohio State University, wrote a working policy paper for the National Black Latino summit on necessary coalitions. More recently (Powell, 2009), he authored a paper on "African American-Immigrant Alliance Building." Martinez (1998) talks about the great White origin myth, which includes a set of stories that are patently false and have no basis in historical fact. The genocide, enslavement, and imperialist expansion during the 19th century have been omitted or distorted in our nation's textbooks and folklore. There is very little if any attention in history or social studies textbooks to the exploitation of former slaves and other ethnic groups from Asia, the Caribbean, and elsewhere, whose labor helped build the country while the laborers were kept in their place by White supremacy.

Despite such economic exploitation, when it comes to the presence of all the "isms" in many of our schools, also referred to in this guide as institutional biases and barriers to achievement, Latinos/a's and Blacks do not sufficiently work together for the most part or with other historically underserved groups in addressing a common plight. Many other variables influencing the Black–Brown divide are discussed by Matt A. Barreto, Benjamin F. Gonzalez, and Gabriel R. Sanchez (2010), who focus on factors influencing Latino/a attitudes toward African Americans and see cause for optimism when it comes to Latino/a attitudes toward Blacks in California. CCL is urgently needed in both ethnic communities, and in all historically underserved communities, so there is more outreach to each other and collaboration to address common concerns.

Challenging the Challenges or Resisting the Resistances

In a major presentation on culturally responsive teaching at the professional devel-opment institute sponsored by the California Alliance of African American Educators at Stanford University, Geneva Gay (2011) spoke about the need for equity leaders to be critically conscious of their own and their students' cultural values and habits, and how these shape their teaching and learning behaviors. Sometimes equity warriors can become so engrossed in strategizing how to get more receptivity to their initiative that they fail to share the reasons for their motivation to do what they are doing. They may unconsciously share information, train or teach in ways that they themselves best learn, and not in the ways their target audience, be they staff, community members, or students best learn or internalize information. All information has an affective component, and sharing feelings may not be part of their "selling" strategy.

Gay also identified some alternative beliefs about the causes of "performance challenges" experienced by ethnically diverse students, such as an existential divide between students and teachers, transitional traumas, stress, and anxiety. My interpretation of her point in both cases was that equity warriors must always be aware of how they are coming across when engaged in capacity building or advocacy, and must also be vigilant in challenging traditional wisdom about the causes of inequitable educational outcomes. They can get caught up in their own hype and think others are "getting it," when actually they are not. They can also be working so hard to eradicate the most popular reasons for performance challenges, that they get caught up in the hype of those who are or aren't well meaning, and totally off track. The challenges to equitable educational outcomes may be very different than what we spend most of our time addressing. We can unwittingly contribute to our own failures and therefore must be open to the possibility of the challenges and resistances being quite different than what we think they are. For example, a major challenge can be the interpersonal cross-racial dynamics among multiethnic teams who are engaged in planning and implementing major equity initiatives. Although they may all be highly committed to achieving the equity goals, they still bring to the task personal racial perspectives, or "baggage," which may get in the way of being as open, honest, and supportive of each other as needed. When this happens, the equity work suffers because of the communication and trust issues being avoided by the equity leaders.

All That Glitters Is Not Gold

School districts whose boards of education want a master plan for dramatically improving the achievement of historically underserved students should be mindful that all that glitters is not gold. Processes used to develop plans, the scope of stakeholder involvement in developing plans, and the plans themselves may seem to cover all the right bases, but still end up being a dud. As indicated earlier in this guide, there are no magic bullets, and even when funding sources are identified and allocations approved, the proof is always in the pudding, so to speak. Boards of education like plans, and some evidence of community and staff involvement in the development of plans, but they may not want to upset anybody, especially in an election year. When plans are research-based and parallel what has happened elsewhere with great success, that doesn't mean they will work in another setting. The glitter of a good plan or a good conference to initiate the planning process may convey the impression there is a strong district commitment to achieving equitable outcomes, until reality sets in. "Feel-good" platitudes in districtwide forums or in plans may be window dressing with no substance or deep-seated commitment behind them. It is imperative for ongoing monitoring of plan implementation. Timelines and benchmark targets, as well as persons assigned to oversee specific tasks, may be more fiction than serious intent. Equity plans have a tendency to be put on the back shelf or left to do after the "regular work" is done, which may mean never. Even plans considered exemplary often avoid any attention to specific strategies for eradicating institutional biases and barriers (see Chapters 5 and 6), sometimes based on the rationale that such constraints in the past do not apply at the present time. Constraints also emanate from competing programs or priorities approved by the board, or a lack of support from some of the most influential families or special interests in the school district community. There might even be the equivalent of a conspiracy to avoid talking about such things, because key decision makers like to maintain the illusion of widespread support. The hidden game plan in such cases is to pretend the glitter is real gold and not fool's gold. Beware!

DO'S AND DON'TS

The intent of the "do's and don'ts" discussed in this section is to provide the reader with additional suggestions when "planning to plan" how to embrace the CCL paradigm as a vehicle to achieve equity. Each of the do's and don'ts are based on my personal experience and scholars whose work has focused on educational change; they may or may not be appropriate in your work context.

Do's

1. When planning an equity initiative, it is important to try engaging representatives of all stakeholders in a visioning process where they have opportunities to provide input on goals, activities, and desired outcomes. However, stakeholder input on the above topics should not occur until after there have been some team- and trust-building activities. Sometimes equity initiatives fail because everyone isn't on the same page before they are undertaken, and stakeholders aren't ready to work together to ensure success, mainly because they have never worked together.

2. Pilot and phase in large-scale equity initiatives rather than trying to implement comprehensive equity transformation all at once, especially in large school districts during economic downturns in an environment of major budget cuts and staffing uncertainties. Many equity initiatives are good ideas based on sound data about the match between the problem and the initiative, but too much is undertaken too soon and is too top down. If major budget cuts are occurring in the school or district, there may be staff reductions, reassignments, and higher class sizes. Equity programs already in place may be the first things cut under such circumstances. Therefore, it is important to consider "bottom up" or a dynamic mix of top-down and bottom-up piloting and phasing in initiatives to learn as much as possible without major system disruptions. In addition, the phase in of large-scale equity initiatives will provide time for pulling the weeds before planting the flowers, as articulated by Reeves (2009), who feels it is essential that any new educational initiatives be preceded by eliminating other practices that at the least severely limit the time and energy needed to pursue any new undertaking, and also may be having no impact whatsoever related to the reasons for their initial implementation.

3. Anticipate push back and be prepared to address it. Most equity initiatives, such as culturally democratic guidelines for disciplinary referrals, protocols for academic support to needy students, or incentives for school/home collaboration, could generate a lot of controversy and second guessing about the intent. The outward manifestation of any angst is what I call "push back." When engaged in trying to achieve any kind of equity, especially for the historically underserved, you could be the recipient of misplaced anger, and the change perceived as a threat. This is inevitable because the pursuit of equity (when there is little or none at the onset of your initiative) is revolutionary insofar as it represents an effort to alter existing power/authority/control relationships reflected in the allocation of resources. And no one cedes power willingly. Since push back as a reaction is a given, you should always anticipate it and be prepared to deal with it. You must calmly respond to any accusations, without panic or overthinking what to do. If you have brainstormed many kinds of wrong turns or mistakes or totally out of the blue occurrences and conducted simulations of what to do in those situations, then you can act instinctively if and when the time comes. Try never to be caught flatfooted, shocked, and unprepared when strong resistance occurs. If that happens, you haven't done your homework as a culturally courageous leader. Covey (2004) has said, "Listen far more than you talk: seek first to understand before trying to be understood." That trait is absolutely necessary to be ready for any "pushback" that occurs, and to have foreknowledge about the likely sources of major resistance.

4. Focus on winning the war, not as much on winning each battle when it comes to equity transformation. To win the war instead of fretting over losing some of the battles during equity transformation, you must know the difference between the two. Imagine your vision is to have within 3 school years 70% or more of your African and Latino/a American students scoring within 10 scale points of White and Asian student groups on statewide end-of-year achievement tests in English Language Arts and Math. You must identify some battles that must be undertaken along the way to achieve your vision.

Is the achievement of benchmark targets by all student subgroups during the 3-year period a battle to be undertaken? Are teacher reassignments one of your benchmark targets? Is the use of culturally responsive standards-based rubrics during classroom observation by peers or school administrators a battle or a war? Is mandatory participation of all staff in a new professional development sequence that interfaces culturally responsive teaching, rigorous standards-based lessons, and high expectations a battle or a war? These are just some examples of key interventions you might want to implement in your own work setting, but you must decide which if any are battles to be undertaken, and whether others are wars that must be won. Very few if any boards of education, superintendents, or principals will pursue all or even most of the items just mentioned without considerable political support and/or pressure to do so.

5. Use Vygotsky's zone of proximal development when implementing any professional development to enhance the capacity of teachers and administrators to be culturally courageous leaders.

Professional development has been a recurrent emphasis throughout this guide, in terms of what the culturally courageous leader must engage in as well as help to plan and implement. In addition, it has been stressed that it must be ongoing and embedded into the culture of the school, and not just a series of events. Ongoing culturally courageous professional development will in all likelihood be different than many current professional development practices in your school or district. A level of transparency is essential when it comes to issues of culture, and when it comes to the "isms" in thought and practice. In other words, you must be very up front in saying exactly how you define your terms, and you must provide relevant examples to those engaged in discussing such terms. But you must also be open to hearing other definitions of your terms from professional development participants.

Vygotsky's zone of proximal development (ZPD) has been a very popular concept in the field of cognitive psychology, used to advocate how teaching and learning should occur in order to maximize student learning (Chaiklin, 2003). Black psychologists who formed the conceptual framework of Black psychology also advocated the same concepts even though they don't get credit in the research literature for their contributions to what is necessary to improve the achievement of many historically underserved students (Lee, 2005). Scaffolding; building on the prior knowledge, life experiences, and interests of the student; differentiated instruction, cooperative learning; constructivist learning; and in all cases working with "more knowledgeable others" whether they be peers or teachers, are all outgrowths of Black psychology and Vygotsky's ZPD.

To ascertain one's ZPD in any area of learning, a lot of social interaction, diagnosis, problem solving, and "reciprocal teaching" is undertaken. It is unfortunate that some professional development associated with equity transformation has not utilized Vygotsky's ZPD when ostensibly engaging in capacity building. Not all adults are at the same level of awareness or motivation, and conducting some training in differentiated groups could be more effective if it is properly introduced and agreed to. The description of the equity interventions done by the equity warrior Jean Richardson in Chapter 14 is an example of when differentiated professional development was utilized to enhance capacity in culturally responsive teaching. However, I have not found this to be the norm in most professional development conducted in schools.

Don'ts

1. Do not delegate inappropriately or limit leadership of equity initiatives to those in traditional stakeholder groups. The success or failure of equity efforts is largely determined by whether the persons to whom equity initiatives are delegated have the requisite willingness, skills, and philosophical commitments. In Chapter 8, the description of a communication guru was provided. It includes having the skill to determine where persons one is considering for specific tasks fall on a continuum of task and relationship behaviors they need from their supervisor for a specific assignment. Depending on the task, some people need more of a task or relationship orientation from whomever is guiding them. This is one small aspect of "situational leadership" as conceptualized by Hersey and Blanchard (1993). Another is the "achievement ethic" of the person related to a specific task. If one does not have a high achievement ethic when it comes to what they are expected to do and have agreed to do in the area of equity initiatives, it doesn't matter how skilled they are.

A different combination of what Hersey and Blanchard call task and relationship behaviors are required by the supervisor based on the "psychological" and "job" maturity of each employee or volunteer given an equity task. In other words, persons being considered for a specific leadership role related to equity may be very committed, organized, and articulate advocates, but not be at all comfortable with resistance, conflict, or what I have earlier called "push back."

Also, when trying to achieve equity transformation, some persons in positions of leadership appear to have the skills, willingness, and psychological strength needed, but grossly underestimate what is involved and the time required to do a good job. They may already be very busy with other commitments. It is possible for a superintendent, assistant superintendent, or executive director of a community-based organization to delegate critical assignments to others without adequate consideration of whether the person assigned a new task actually has the time to do it well. There are often multiple layers of complexity involved when implementing equity activities such as classroom protocols on high expectations, training activities on teacher and parent efficacy, culturally courageous instructional supervision, or culturally responsive pedagogy across the curriculum. Inappropriate delegation of such tasks can result in failure of equity efforts.

Historically underserved students and parents cannot be overlooked or underutilized when it comes to the planning and implementation of equity initiatives. Their voice must be empowered, listened to, and respected. For example, the knowledge and perspectives of communities of color must be solicited when grappling with the complexities of secondary school improvements, given the staggering rates of high school dropouts in all of these communities. The campaign for high school equity (CHSE) (http://www.highschoolequity.org) is a coalition of national organizations representing communities of color. If feasible, the input of both CHSE and its constituent organizations should be sought when high school equity initiatives are conceptualized, planned, and implemented. African, Latino/a, Native American, and Southeast Asian American organizations are part of CHSE.

2. Do not limit attention to any one category of injustices experienced by historically underserved students in the mainstream population. You must deal with the interface of race, gender, socioeconomic status biases with language, ethnic, disability, sexual orientation, obesity, and foster care/homelessness issues as appropriate. This may require even more courage, skill, and savvy because of the severity of the need.

There is an enormous amount of societal discord over the rights of parents and students who require translation because they are not sufficiently fluent in English. Several school districts have a student population who collectively represent 30, 40, 50 or more primary languages spoken in the home. So the cultural/ethnic diversity within the limited English proficient population is tremendous, and there are likely conflicts and cultural politics within the group as a whole and within subgroups.

For example, in some districts, limited-English-speaking White ethnic groups who have immigrated from the Middle East or Eastern Europe may receive more service and support than Latino/a, African, and Southeastern Asian families who are limited English speaking. There might be a pecking order in terms of how districts address social justice issues for different immigrant populations. Although I have observed less variation in the level of service provided for students with major physical or cognitive disabilities, I have noted much more variation in the response to students characterized as emotionally disturbed (ED) or developmentally delayed. The percentage of Black and Latino males in the ED category is significantly higher than their numbers in the total student population.

In addition, the degree of educational neglect may be much more profound based on sexual identity, orientation, and lifestyle, or based on body weight. The emotional and physical abuse suffered by gay and obese students at the hands of other students is almost an epidemic in some places. Some adults act as if they are totally oblivious to what is happening. In addition, the number of homeless students has rapidly increased and has been a growing population throughout the 21st century. For many Black and Latino/a families, the number of students in foster homes has also exploded in recent years, and there is a direct correlation between the size of this population and the dropout rates. Partnerships with appropriate community organizations are essential.

3. Never stop making attempts to enhance your leadership influence. Stephen Covey (2004) talks about how modeling is the spirit and center of any leadership effort. He further says, "It is only when people actually experience for themselves how a conscience-driven person models pathfinding, aligning, and empowering, that leadership actually takes place . . . their opinions are sought, their input is respected, their unique experience valued (p. 127).

Modeling, according to Covey, is not the work of just an individual; it's the work of a complementary team. He refers to the Greek philosophy of influence called ethos (modeling trustworthiness, establishing credibility), pathos (seek first to understand, showing empathy), and logos (then to be understood through use of logic) as a very important sequence. Covey illustrates his ideas about leadership by talking about how to become a trim-tab leader, which means being able to be like the trim-tab, that is, the small rudder on a boat or plane that turns the big rudder that turns the entire ship. Covey says the trim-tab leader exercises initiative within his or her own circle of influence, however small it may be. Taking initiative is essential and requires situational sensitivity and judgment.

Covey's discussion of the trim-tab spirit includes the advice that one must be sensitive, wise, careful regarding timing, and always avoid complaining, criticizing, being negative, and absolving yourself of responsibility. He also says that taking initiative requires some vision, discipline, passion, and conscience. The culturally courageous leader must be able and willing to describe what educational injustices are occurring and offer alternative ways of thinking and acting by modeling the same. On occasion, this may be interpreted as critique, complaints, or negativity, especially if your ethos, that is, ethics nature, personal credibility, and trust or confidence others have in you, is in doubt. Covey asserts the choices made by leaders when responding to challenges and problems are critical. This also applies to culturally courageous leaders in all stakeholder groups.

4. Don't underestimate the scope and intensity of the resistance to the cultural, structural, and political changes needed to achieve and sustain equitable inputs and outcomes. Darling-Hammond and Baratz-Snowden (2005), Duncan-Andrade and Morrell (2008), Gause (2011), Gay (2010), Howard (2010), King (2005), Lee (2005), Nieto (2007), Noguera and Wing (2006), and Thompson (2007), among many others, have written extensively about the cultural and structural inequities in American schools as well as the politics involved in securing support for research that has the potential to challenge many racist paradigms about historically underserved students. These scholarly contributions are central to the premises underlying the concept of CCL.

In addition, the "habits of mind" (HOM) developed by Costa and Kallick (2008) are strongly related to what is needed to "walk the equity talk." Costa's concept of the term *habits of mind* includes a composite of many skills, attitudes, and proclivities that imply making choices and sensitivity to contextual cues. Costa goes on to say that after each experience in which these behaviors are used, the effects of their use should be reflected upon and modified as needed. Without "habits of mind" as described by Costa, the needed cultural and structural changes may never occur.

One structural change repeatedly emphasized by Darling-Hammond and Baratz-Snowden (2005) as critical to improving the achievement of historically under-served student groups is the necessity for "qualified teachers." However, the federal and state definitions of the term are woefully inadequate, not requiring any teacher expertise in topics discussed by Howard (2010), such as "adaptive unconsciousness," or the topics discussed by Gay (2010), such as ethnic learning styles and instructional bridging. No doubt for political reasons, there is a total lack of culturally specific content knowledge specified in federal and state requirements for a highly qualified teacher. In addition, changes in how teachers think and teach require ongoing support systems for the changes to be nurtured and sustained. The major work edited by King (2005) on a transformational research and action agenda for Black education, and the work by Gándara and Contreras (2009) on the Latino/a education crisis are examples of what must be studied and utilized to carry out in what will be needed in the foreseeable future.

❧

DEBUNKING LAME EXCUSES

There are three excuses commonly given by some who claim a commitment to equity but reject either the need for or the feasibility of embracing the leadership paradigm advanced in this guide. Each of the excuses is further described and then all are collectively debunked.

Excuse #1: The Timing Isn't Right

The rationale for this excuse includes the belief that persons in various stakeholder groups are not sufficiently disposed to work together and have very different, even conflicting ideas about what is needed to achieve major improvements in student achievement. A common example used is that when teachers of the same grade level or subject area can't even collaborate or agree on instructional strategies needing priority, it is obvious they aren't ready to collaborate with other stakeholders. Another reason for claiming that the CCL paradigm is ahead of its time is the claim that district offices are far from ready for more equitable power relationships because of board politics and the attitude to do as I say, not as I do.

Excuse #2: The Fear of Unacceptable Consequences

This excuse is similar to the first one but focuses more on what would happen if certain constituent groups in the school district no longer have the privileges they are accustomed to experiencing. Some associate a serious commitment to equitable inputs and outcomes with a lowering of "standards" and sacrificing the quality of education, if all students were expected to be taught and learn at high levels.

Currently, this is only experienced by some students of varying ethnic and socio-economic backgrounds, and any change is anticipated to necessitate a major shift in allocation of limited resources. One of the unacceptable consequences feared is White flight and/or middle-class flight to other school districts or private schools. A second fear is that there will be teacher flight to other school districts where there wouldn't be the anticipated requirements for changes in the teacher knowledge, skills, and attitudes that might be necessary if academic tracking and Eurocentric curricula were eliminated. A third fear is that if the first two fears actually happen, there will be a concomitant loss in school district reputation and revenue from such flight.

Excuse #3: The Effort Required and Politics Involved Would Be Too Stressful

This excuse is even more similar to the first but is distinguished by the focus on what additional efforts would likely be required. There is a strong suspicion that being culturally courageous could be very divisive, and some don't want to endure the conflicts they anticipate would occur, as well as not wanting to face the fear of the unknown. Some are also very worried that such a change would pressure people to have to take sides. They don't want to experience any social ostracism or alienation from culturally or philosophically different others with whom they currently have comfortable working relationships.

All of these excuses are very real and even palpable, and only represent a small sampling of why there could be a lot of resistance and resentment caused by embracing the CCL paradigm. The beliefs and feelings expressed in the excuses cannot be easily attributed only to persons of particular racial, ethnic, or cultural backgrounds, or particular stakeholder groups. But similar excuses could be used by those against any systemic educational reform. However, I find the depth of feeling and angst to be much more intense when any changes related to such major identity constructs as race, ethnicity, social class, primary language, gender, sexual orientation, and so on are involved, because we are talking about the very essence of people. And most people just want to "get along" without disturbing the fragile illusion of peace. This predisposition works to the advantage of the dominant groups in society.

The "timing" is never "right" for social justice goals to receive priority. There will always be a host of dysfunctional norms, fewer in some places, that must be confronted. Almost all district offices are very contradictory in what they require vs. what they do. In the second decade of the 21st century, when the very survival of public schooling as a means of leveling the playing field is in great peril, it is time to face our fears and publicly discuss them. This must be followed by collectively doing all we can to make schools populated by large numbers of historically underserved children places we would want to send our own children. We cannot afford the luxury of being hamstrung to our fears of what could happen if we do the right thing. That said, there are steps we can take to increase equity and excellence if we walk the talk.

The research of Carl Jung on psychological types (OD portal.com, n.d.) continues to be used to develop diagnostic assessment instruments that help individuals learn more about their work and communication styles, learning styles, leadership styles, ways of relating to and perceiving the world, and so on. As mentioned in Chapter 10, being a communications guru is one of the CCL characteristics, which includes using information from the DiSC self-assessment, also known as the Personal Profile, which has been used extensively throughout the United States and the world for many years. DiSC results can be used to improve leadership and influence by helping to adapt personal behaviors so that others' needs and expectations are met. Many persons are uncomfortable with or offended by the style of others who are simply focused on meeting their own needs. Conflict can be better managed or even avoided if there is greater consciousness of the different ways people perceive situations and ways they fulfill their needs and exercise their strengths.

Even when using such self-assessment instruments as the DiSC, there will likely be some degree of conflict in work and social environments; but the possible benefits of working through these conflicts can be enormous. The four agreements of courageous conversation (Singleton & Linton, 2006), which are "stay engaged, experience discomfort, speak your truth, and expect and accept non-closure," are important guideposts to use when having your "buttons pushed," and when having to experience the reactions of others whose "buttons" regarding their values and beliefs are pushed by you.

But again, using the excuse that this paradigm will cause too much stress is facetious at best, since all human differences in perspective or experience can cause dissonance or open conflict and are probably experienced on a daily basis by most persons. Courage, and cultural courageousness, can be learned, if the necessary support systems are put in place. It is a journey, not a destination, requiring one step at a time.

৯৩৬

WHAT NEXT?

Throughout this guide, the reader has been encouraged to rethink many things, among them the role that students must play in making schools and communities exemplars of social justice. The voice of all students must be empowered and respected during deliberations on how to make schools a place of joyful learners who are being prepared to create a different world than the one in which they were born. Adults who want to exercise CCL or are already doing so for the purpose of achieving equitable educational inputs and outcomes should strongly consider networking with each other for information sharing, problem solving, and mutual support. Electronic networks with live interactive streaming would be an ideal way to develop support groups for those wanting the CCL paradigm to take root in their school community. In the tradition of the league for cooperating schools at the University of California, Los Angeles, initiated by John Goodlad (1975), and the National Coalition for Equality In Learning, facilitated by Sinclair and Ghory (1997), I propose an electronic network for culturally courageous schools (NCCS). NCCS should not be bound by any geographical location, and all schools in the network would be expected to serve as resources to each other in a collective synergistic effort to utilize research-based practices to nurture culturally courageous leaders among all school community stakeholder groups. The broad purpose of NCCS would be to improve cultural democracy and achieve equitable educational inputs and outcomes for historically underserved students of color. To obtain information about the network and also share your ideas, e-mail the author at NCCSJRBII@gmail.com.

To achieve the kind of changes needed in individual and collective consciousness, communities, organizations, and structures, a cultural tsunami must occur that overwhelms the negative beliefs, values, and practices that have kept citizens of the United States alienated from each other. We must engage entire school communities, and students above all, in creating the conditions that make possible this "wave" of human freedom. They must also, along with well-meaning culturally courageous adults from all walks of life, be mutually accountable in rolling out and monitoring whatever is attempted and making adjustments as needed. It's time to truly "walk the equity talk."

REVIEW OF CHAPTER 16

The following topics were discussed in this chapter:

- Seven issues, five do's, four don'ts, and three lame excuses were discussed to complete the suggestions for the reader on how to get ready for and then practice CCL in order to walk the equity talk.

- The role of meaningful student involvement and CCL networking was advocated to help all stakeholders stay honest during the "transformational journey" of pursuing greater social justice through alternative ways of thinking and being.

Appendix 1

Facilitator Notes for
Chapters 1 Through 15

In order to assist those readers who may wish to use this text as an integral part of classes, book study groups, or other forms of professional development they might be facilitating, I am providing facilitator notes for select items. In each case, the facilitator notes will briefly share additional background or contextual information and/or my experience/suggestions related to points and group activities the facilitator might want to take into consideration.

❧❧

Chapter 1 Facilitator Notes

Make It Personal: FN1–1

1. What are some ways your personal identity, including race, ethnicity, religion, gender, primary language, occupation, socioeconomic status, and sexual orientation, has been a major influence in your life? For example, have you made choices or developed life priorities based on your personal identity/identities?

When addressing this question, be mindful that some will be threatened by inquiries about their identity because of their self-consciousness or painful memories that have seared them emotionally, and others won't have ever thought much about their identity beyond being an "American. " Persons of color might be more comfortable in answering the question, but it may depend on the trust level in the group.

Caution must be exercised in how discussion is pursued. Pair sharing might be easier for some than large group sharing. An introduction to having participants answer the question should include self-revelation, including personal examples of ways your personal identity has influenced your life at different times. Also be very clear of why this question is being asked and what it has to do with improving cultural democracy and achieving equitable educational outcomes.

2. How has your self-identity influenced what you think about your life chances or potential, and what you think about others with identities very different than your own?

Again, use anecdotes from your personal experience if possible of how self-identity has influenced one's personal notions about what they can achieve or what their strengths are. After discussing the first half of this question, attempt to transition to what participants think about those with identities very different than their own. Participants might be uncomfortable with responding to this query because of not wanting to reveal any of their stereotypes, assumptions, or biases. Again, sharing an example or two of ways you have thought about others with different identities may make it easier for others to do so, and also lead to the group discovering that their assumptions about others' identities and life chances may have been way off base.

3. In what contexts (e.g., playing a specific sport, as a student of a particular subject, singing, performing, or public speaking) do you feel very confident and in what contexts do you have less confidence?

Like the first question, this question has the potential to be threatening to some. One's level of confidence about anything may be a function of what is happening in one's life at the time the question is asked. Providing participants with sample items to be confident about, such as school subjects, hobbies, or the subject of compliments received, can be helpful. The major purpose of this discussion should quickly lead to the relationship between personal confidence and school success, and the role of educators in building students' self-confidence.

4. Name some examples of contemporary cultural bias/prejudice against immigrant groups that are held by various native-born economic and cultural groups in the United States and influence what happens in your schools.

Unless there has been some team and trust building beforehand, there may be resistance by participants to sharing biases they know exist against immigrant groups. Again, you might want to model sharing some answers to the question, or ask everyone to discuss his or her responses in dyads or triads followed by report out by volunteers. Another approach could be asking about the consequences experienced by American citizens when illegal immigration occurs, followed by brainstorming the causes of such immigration. This might make it easier for some to then discuss the biases experienced by all immigrants and how biases vary based on their ethnic/cultural background (e.g., biases against immigrants of Mexican background compared with immigrants of Russian or other Slavic backgrounds). The major purpose of this conversation is to discuss how societal biases impact the dynamics in schools, and what can be done about the negative consequences experienced by immigrant students.

5. What do you think you should be doing, if anything, to counteract the cultural biases you thought of in response to #4 above?

Hopefully, participants will indicate that the response should be the same when biases are directed toward any group, namely immediate confrontation of the behavior without condemnation of the person, and a discussion of the causes and consequences of such behavior. You should also guide participants to brainstorm what preemptive instructional interventions can be initiated to create a more accepting environment in classrooms that includes skill development in respectful communication. Examples of such an intervention are role playing when reading particular pieces of ethnically inspired literature, or when studying historical conflicts between particular groups in the United States.

Make It Personal: FN1–2

1. At the end of each scenario, identify what you think are the major influences on the identities of persons described in the situation.

Refer to items in the identities chart for persons to respond to the question. Be willing to accept responses that may seem to you to be atypical. Ask participants whether they have ever experienced incidents like the ones described, and what they think were influences on similar persons or incidents in their life. Explain that the characters and situations described are based on real incidents.

2. Identify the conflicts (i.e., dynamics of difference) and reasons for the conflict in each of the four scenarios in this chapter; describe how you think each scenario could contribute to inequitable student outcomes.

Don't be surprised if some persons don't see anything wrong with the actions taken in each incident, or don't think they are anything to make a big deal over. The purpose of the incidents is to highlight some human difference situations that may negatively impact student achievement, and emphasize that the response to such situations can be worse than the fact that they happen. Attempt to engage participants in focusing on what they think would be in the best interest of all students, given each scenario.

3. What could be done to minimize the conflicts in each situation?

There are no right or wrong answers to any of these questions. If no answers are offered for how the conflicts can be minimized it may be because the situations are not perceived as major conflicts. Encourage respondents to think beyond what can be done in the specific context of the "conflict," and more about what could possibly have been done to prevent the persons in the conflict from manifesting the predispositions they have that are described.

For example, engage the participants in discussing what activities could have occurred in school in general and in limited English proficiency (LEP) classrooms in particular that might minimize the conflicts between students that are described. Use these discussions as the basis for a transition to engaging participants in discussing how schools can improve respectful attitudes toward and communication between adults, adults and students, and students and students.

4. What does the personal identity, including the racial identity, of students and educators have to do with student educational outcomes?

Review the discussion in Chapter 1 about the relationship between identity and achievement, and between race and identity. Make sure participants understand the meaning of cultural democracy and its relationship to achievement. Ask for volunteers to share a personal story about how their personal identity and other factors have influenced their achievement motivation. If you consider it appropriate, encourage those who volunteer to include in their stories the major relationships, conditions, or incidents that helped shape their personal identity. Don't avoid the topic of racial identity and be willing to share how you personally have experienced or observed a relationship between racial identity and achievement motivation. Be mindful though that whenever you share it should be for the purpose of stimulating like sharing by group participants.

৵৽৹

Chapter 2 Facilitator Notes

Make It Personal: FN2–1

1. Given the definition of cultural democracy in this guide, describe specific ways that one of the schools with which you are familiar is *not* culturally democratic.

Given the examples of cultural democracy provided in the text, most educators or lay persons do not tend to think of those things if asked to define cultural democracy. It might be best to first ask for a definition of cultural democracy or a guess of what it means, so the perspective of the audience can be ascertained and respect can be shown for their ideas on the subject. Additional examples of cultural democracy should be considered if necessary. Many elementary educators and persons with children under the age of 10 do not tend to be comfortable with teaching about how racial and cultural oppression has been and continues to be perpetrated in the United States. Anticipate this possibility. Some may also feel children are not as self-conscious about racial identity at younger ages. However, there are studies documenting how children as young as the age of four or five are very conscious of racial differences and how people are treated differentially based on their racial characteristics, especially when combined with their socioeconomic status (Derman-Sparks, Higa, & Sparks, 1980). The question behind the question above is whether your group thinks it is desirable and necessary for schools to be culturally democratic, and what that would mean in terms of such things as teacher behavior, parent involvement in decision making, curriculum and instruction, school celebrations, and problem-solving norms.

2. What is your opinion about the quantity and nature of conflicts in very culturally diverse schools?

Audiences tend to have a lot to say in response to this question, from the perspective as a school employee, or as a parent/caregiver. However, the underlying factors contributing to conflicts are not as quick to be openly discussed. Such factors may include family dynamics and life circumstances, teacher biases, or class "favorites" as perceived by students, and status issues in the classroom and school, that is, who gets the most attention, respect or favors, and who is considered more smart or talented. My research suggests more racially/culturally mixed schools may have more overt conflict upon initial exposure of students to each other, but even in more segregated schools, there is a lot of conflict over some of the same issues. In both kinds of schools, there is also a lot of covert conflict between students, between adults, and between adults and students, which rarely gets put on the table for examination and problem solving (Browne, 1975).

The facilitator may wish to elicit examples of both overt and covert conflict, their causes and consequences, especially in culturally diverse schools. Also, schools perceived as segregated tend to be as diverse as racially diverse schools. The variable often used to determine whether a school is "integrated" or "segregated" is how many white students attend, and not the ethnic, nationality, religious, socioeconomic, academic, gender, and linguistic characteristics of students. The facilitator should attempt to help the audience realize there is a lot of diversity other than Black/White diversity being used as the norm for how schools are characterized.

3. In schools you know well, what is done to minimize any racial/cultural conflicts?

The answers to this question can get very long winded and involved. It is suggested that attention initially be focused on developing a laundry list of activities that don't require a lot of explanation, and then have the audience prioritize the top three to five items they want to discuss in greater depth. The responses of the audience should not be evaluated, but compared with the kinds of things suggested in the text. Participants should be asked to weigh which kinds of responses tend to work the best in the situations they mention and to identify the criteria they use to determine what works best.

In this text, the term racial/cultural conflict is used interchangeably with "dynamics of difference." The intent of the above question is to ascertain whether participants acknowledge any relationship between human conflicts and student educational outcomes, and if so, what is done on a regular basis to keep conflicts from having such impact, including adult/adult conflicts.

4. How do you react to the statement that "adults and students' perceptions of each other are both a result and a cause of their behaviors toward each other"?

One objective of this question is to inquire about the impact of both adults' perceptions of other adults, as well as adults' perceptions of students and vice versa. I have found during my work in low-performing schools that quite often adult/adult conflict is a major factor impacting school climate, the quality of teaching and learning, and student educational outcomes. Students also tend to mimic both negative and positive adult attitudes and behaviors to which they are exposed. The facilitator might want to initially brainstorm with the audience a list of teacher perceptions about students and other adults that are manifested in things they say to students and how those teacher perceptions cause a similar response by their students toward the people about whom they were speaking.

This exercise could be followed by a discussion of the negative consequences experienced by all as a result of negative perceptions and behaviors by all parties, and then some courageous work could be done on identifying the causes of the initial perceptions. A logical next step is to brainstorm how to positively impact students' perceptions of each other as well as their perceptions of adults. Discuss ways to increase awareness of how positive or negative perceptions influence personal behaviors, causing a like response from the other. The intent is to facilitate problem-solving discussions about how to stop the vicious cycle that may occur between students and teachers as well as between students and students, and adults and adults.

5. What is one example of how your lived realities cause conflict between the way you prefer to be as a teacher or administrator versus how you feel compelled to be?

"Lived realities" may include human difference conflicts, misrepresentation of intent, false allegations, or malfeasance of colleagues, that may cause you to engage in corrective actions and/or escalate conflict, versus your preference to be open and collaborative with specific persons if they were not conspiring against you.

Cultural democracy includes respect for those of all cultural backgrounds in all stakeholder groups, but sometimes a disposition toward fostering such democracy is compromised by all-out attacks against those who threaten the privileges of persons benefitting from the lack of cultural democracy. The facilitator should attempt to engage participants in discussing how the push back against those advocating cultural democracy can sometimes involve personal attacks or political efforts to undermine your efforts, including getting the board to remove you from your position or direct you to stop your equity initiatives. That is why developing a strong political base of support for your actions is imperative. When discussing this question, it is critical that you model empathy for the conflicts between lived realities and preferred ways of being and sensitively probe to get more information about perceived realities and preferences. I have found that sometimes what are identified as "realities" and "preferences" are not consistent with the data provided to substantiate one's statements. Many educators at all levels need support in determining how to reconcile perceived conflicts between their "realities" and "preferences," and may need even more help to determine if their perceived conflicts are actually based on fact.

Make It Personal: FN2–2

1. To what extent are the cultural groups to which you strongly relate a major influence on your personal identity and perceptions of others?

I have found it helpful to pass out a list of diverse cultural groups or have participants brainstorm a list of cultural groups to which various people belong, before asking them to name the groups having a strong influence on their personal identity. Be open to groups you might not expect to be identified that are based on physical attributes or disabilities, hobbies, social affiliations, occupations, sports, the arts, geographical areas, and sexual orientation. The follow-up questions should focus on how one's perceptions of others translate into specific behaviors and what this has to do with the teaching and learning process in any educational setting.

2. What is your opinion about the relationship between cultural background, cultural conditioning, and cultural biases?

The three terms *cultural background, cultural conditioning,* and *cultural biases* may need to be defined as well as the term *culture,* with specific examples of each term, such as cultural background including religious beliefs or religious sect (e.g., Protestant, Catholic, Buddhist, Jewish, Muslim, or Hindu). Cultural conditioning includes the teaching or customs one has been exposed to and practiced. Cultural biases including beliefs, prejudices, stereotypes, and discriminatory practices at the policy or personal level. The purpose of this question is to help readers increase their understanding of how deep seated are variables that contribute to cultural hegemony as well as to stimulate thinking about the role of schools in response to the cultural background, conditioning, and biases of its participants.

3. What can *you* do to challenge the cultural biases of persons with whom you work who oppose one or more equity initiatives in your schools?

Again, it may be helpful to engage your group in brainstorming examples of how cultural bias is manifested in the day-to-day functioning of schools. Chapters 1 and 2 discuss some examples of bias in such areas as curriculum omissions and distortions, school staff assignments, disciplinary practices, and teacher expectations. Help participants critically reflect on what more they could have done in the past and what more they can do in the present or future to positively influence those who oppose specific equity initiatives in their work setting. Try to keep the dialogue focused on what is best for all students in the long run.

Make It Personal: FN2–3

1. Why does racial/cultural bias continue unabated in many school communities (or in your school community)?

There is no one correct answer; elicit personal stories from participants that don't rely on excuses to explain why students don't do well, such as family values about education and low socioeconomic status. Also encourage group participants who take exception to the question about racial/cultural bias being unabated to share their perspectives, and reasoning. This should be a healthy give-and-take dialogue. Be prepared to share a definition of racial/cultural bias.

2. What needs to happen so that implementation of changes proposed in this chapter will indeed result in meaningful societal change for the "have-nots"?

Try to focus discussion on what participants can individually and collectively do for the have-nots. Model what you expect from them by sharing examples of what more you can do, why you haven't done it, and what you will do differently in future efforts. Remind participants of suggested changes in the chapter, such as the response to academically at-risk students, bullying by students or teachers, intergroup and interpersonal relations, and positive impacts on school norms.

Chapter 3 Facilitator Notes

Make It Personal: FN3–1

1. In your opinion, what is the responsibility of teachers to build on students' life experiences to teach about prejudice and discrimination, including the oppression experienced by persons of diverse cultural/racial/ ethnic backgrounds?

The intent of the question is two-fold. The first purpose is to elicit thoughts about including more substantive curriculum content about prejudice and discrimination in the United States. The second intent is to have the reader think about how to utilize students' life experiences related to prejudice and discrimination when teaching on the topic. In my experience, many if not most teachers are loathe to address this topic, perhaps because of their discomfort in doing so, little if any experience in participating in such discussions, and not wanting to ignite any student conflicts from such discussions. Because some parents might react negatively to readings and lessons of this nature, the plans for such teaching should be shared beforehand with supervisors, parents, and students and be preceded by attention to enhancing student discussion skills. This kind of content should be considered as early as upper elementary school as part of the social studies and English language arts curriculum.

2. What are some of the consequences when students of all backgrounds don't learn about how much the political and economic fabric of society in the United States has been influenced by historical and contemporary discrimination, such as racism, ethnocentrism, sexism, classism, and homophobia?

Students are recipients of and engage in biased treatment of others from early elementary school but may not be helped to develop a broader understanding of human difference bias in its many forms. The postulate behind this question is that student identities and racial/cultural conflicts are intertwined, possibly resulting in dysfunctional dynamics between diverse students. Those discussing this question should be encouraged to reflect on when they ignored "teachable moments" because of some incidents that have occurred in classrooms or other adult work settings. The consequence of avoiding some topics because they might be volatile is to leave students ill prepared for effectively communicating with diverse persons. Discussing this question should not be allowed in an atmosphere of blaming or judging persons, but getting group participants to describe what has occurred and is occurring from multiple perspectives of those who represent all walks of life.

3. If you were the teacher in the eighth-grade English classroom of Jimmy and Josephina and were aware of their attitudes about what is taught in the class, how would you respond?

This scenario could be used as a stimulus to engage participants in making some informal inquiries about whether other Black and Hispanic students at the same grade level feel similarly about what they have to read in their English and social studies classes. Another exercise could be exploring how White participants would feel if they were in a class where they only learned about the life experiences, feats, or heroes of persons they considered culturally and racially different from themselves. Such terms as ethnocentric content and culturally responsive teaching can be introduced during such discussions and what the role of the middle school educator should be in humanities classes.

4. Describe an example of where the customs, history, or common culture in the United States is being taught in your elementary or secondary school with very little if any attention to inclusion of the positive contributions of various historically underserved students' cultures/races/religions represented in the school.

This discussion should be undertaken within the larger context of what textbook publishers include in their classroom materials and the forces that influence their decisions, including the content standards of state governments, and the historical purpose of public schooling in the United States. Participants should be encouraged to share other resources they might use to address the omissions and distortions in the adopted texts, such as trade books and alternative texts that are available. The consequences of using Eurocentric texts in both culturally/racially homogeneous and in racially/culturally diverse schools should also be explored, especially when it comes to the pervasiveness of cultural hegemony in the United States.

5. Hypothetically, if all or most students attending a school in your community were from Asian, Black, Latino/a, and Native American cultural groups, how might history/social studies curriculum/instruction be different or the same as in schools where Whites are in the majority?

OR

Briefly describe what your English language arts and history/social studies curriculum would include if you were teaching in a school where a majority of students were from African and Latino/a American backgrounds and whether it would be any different if your class included all major racial/ethnic groups.

There are several avenues one can take when addressing either of these questions, such as whether texts should be the same for all students regardless of the student composition, whether there should be standard texts at all, whether the choice of instructional materials should affect the assessment tools and/or strategies used and what if any common core knowledge should be taught to all students, regardless of their demographic makeup. Participants should be engaged in examining the extent of attention to cultural pluralism in a variety of history/social science texts, by using rubrics influenced by multicultural education scholars.

Make It Personal: FN3–2

1. Based on your experience, what are some examples of how cultural hegemony is being practiced in schools or in teacher/administrator preparation programs with which you are familiar?

Cultural hegemony is not likely to be a familiar concept to most, since it may not be found in the research, literature, or course syllabi used in teacher or administrator preparation programs. Anticipate the need to discuss why the examples provided in the text are labeled as cultural hegemony and also try to share information about school practices or preparation programs with which you are familiar where there are examples of cultural hegemony. This will be good modeling for how your audience can do the same thing. There may be resistance to suggestions in the text that there is a dominant cultural group in the United States with inordinate power, authority, and influence over other groups, and that preparation programs for teachers and administrators should help them learn how to create culturally democratic learning environments.

Finn (2009) documents some practices supporting hegemony, such as the differential kinds of instruction and educational opportunities provided to students based on their families' socioeconomic status. Oakes, Wells, Datnow, and Jones (1997) also document how tracking practices in schools help perpetuate a permanent educational underclass in America. These practices are a result of the cultural politics that occur at all levels of government when it comes to educational policy. The major reason for addressing the issue of cultural hegemony in the United States is to make the point that it is one of the major factors negatively impacting student educational outcomes. Kozol's book on savage inequalities (1991) does not use the term, but he strongly implies that it is a major reason for the horrible schooling conditions he describes being experienced by poor historically underserved students of color.

This can be a sensitive topic depending on the perspective of any participant who may feel somewhat defensive if they really liked their preparation program and did well. When people don't know what they don't know and have been led to believe they are well prepared, they may have difficulties identifying deficiencies in their teacher or administrative preparation. This topic should not be discussed until participants have first been exposed to readings or presentations on programs that do give high priority to cultural responsiveness. This information will give participants a base of comparison when discussing their preparation programs. The purpose of the discussion should be to identify any gaps in preparation that may be based on what participants have experienced compared to the challenges they face on a day-to-day basis in the culturally diverse classroom and school.

2. What is your opinion of whether schools should help teachers and students learn about and collectively combat institutionalized racism?

Don't assume that the audience will have a firm grasp on what institutional racism is and how it is manifested. It might be appropriate to begin the discussion of this question by defining the terms and providing examples. Beverly Daniel Tatum's book titled *Why Are All the Black Kids Sitting Together in the Cafeteria?* is a good resource on the definition of racism and institutionalized racism. The role of cultural politics in whether there will be a serious effort to combat racism also needs to be part of the discussion, and how the differential self-interests and priorities of various constituencies in a school community will help determine whether combating racism, including racism in education, is something they would support. Racism almost always is a hot topic that can generate a lot of emotion, accusations, defensiveness, or avoidance. Some preparation of the audience, such as developing trust and team building, should also occur. Adults or students who are led in discussions of racism need to receive and/or share information about actions that can help eliminate racism and improve the quality of life in their communities. It is also important to avoid any unintended consequences, such as vicious teasing or retaliation by some students because of what is learned about past and present discriminatory practices. In addition, discourage adults from making quick conclusions about the bias or prejudice of other group members based solely on what happened in the past or based on what is said during the discussions. Preparation of the group to avoid such occurrences is essential.

3. To ensure that such instruction occurs, what support is needed by teachers and school site administrators?

Depending on the cultural and political climate in the school district and school community where such instructional efforts are made, it is quite possible that at the very least, the principal needs to be informed of what is being done, and it may also be appropriate for the site administrator to inform his or her supervisors in the district office, so they are not caught unaware if complaints are subsequently made, and also request their active support, even if that requires providing them with a script of what they can say when or if complaints are registered. In addition, principals might want the teacher to inform parents beforehand and actually engage some parents in the planning process. Note that communication and involvement of parents is suggested, not seeking parent permission of whether such activities should occur. Be prepared to explain why such activities are occurring, including how they are consistent with the school's vision and mission, even if there are no content standards that explicitly call for such learning. It is likely there won't be any content standards that can be used as a point of reference when it comes to social action learning and activity that focuses on combating institutional racism. Support should also be sought from appropriate community organizations and agencies that have social justice as one of their major goals.

Make It Personal: FN3–3

1. What are some of the cultural politics practiced in your school community or school district?

While most may be used to using the term *politics* when referring to conflicting agendas or perspectives on particular issues, the term *cultural politics* may not have common usage. Even though the term is discussed in the chapter, the reader might not find it easy to acknowledge actually practicing cultural politics or to using the term *cultural dissonance* to describe what they may experience on occasion with culturally diverse students. Therefore, it may be necessary to share some personal experiences of how you have witnessed or participated in cultural politics in your school district or any social setting. This should assist participants to think of examples from their experience, and then to discuss the consequences of such politics.

2. To what extent is cultural hegemony a cause and/or consequence of the cultural politics you described in response to the above question?

Just as White persons may react strongly against being characterized as racists, many may also find it very difficult to agree they participate in helping to perpetuate cultural hegemony in the United States. It may be necessary to provide some historical context on the racial, cultural, and political oppression that has occurred and how it still occurs in the United States. The information on White racial identity development in Chapter 1 should be of assistance in this regard. You should also engage participants in discussing how some persons in groups that have experienced this oppression may unwittingly or consciously help perpetuate such hegemony by the dominant group. The quick answer to the question is that cultural politics, among other factors, may contribute to or be the consequence of cultural hegemony, and it is a phenomenon throughout the world, not just in the United States. Don't be surprised if someone rationalizes that if cultural hegemony is widespread throughout the world, then why should we make a big deal about it in the United States. You should be prepared to explain why the United States is not like other nations in the world in terms of its history and espoused political and moral values. Elicit responses from those in your group about whether any of them feel they have been negatively impacted by cultural hegemony.

Once cultural hegemony is in place to cement power, control, and authority in the hands of a particular group, cultural politics takes on a new life and mutates into other forms to help maintain the status quo. Depending on how the discussion progresses, you might want to transition to speculating about the conditions under which it would be possible to weaken such hegemony. Discuss whether it is possible to increase access to equal opportunities and outcomes for some underserved persons without really altering cultural hegemony.

On another note, there are some key prerequisites for facilitating book study group or professional learning community discussion of the "Make It Personal" questions throughout the guide. One is that the facilitator should be totally committed to the *journey* of becoming a culturally courageous leader as defined in this guide and model same; it is not a destination but a life-long journey where constant growth is necessary. Another prerequisite is that discussion groups should not collectively delve into the issues prompted by this guide without prior or simultaneous attention to becoming adept in developing and manifesting what I call "next level" communication skills. When such skills are practiced, the level of openness, trust, candor, empathy, and courage should be palpable during discussion of what can be very sensitive issues. It should not be just a social or intellectual undertaking, but an opportunity seized by all for the kind of growth and fervor needed to transcend any fears getting in the way of seeking deep seated social justice for all demographic groups.

3. What would be the reaction of culturally diverse students and school communities where you live if all students were required to learn about how oppression has been historically experienced by many groups in the United States, and also learn how discrimination against some groups continues to the present day?

The purpose of this question is to help participants discern a relationship between cultural and racial oppression in the larger community and in their schools, and also to increase sensitivity to the schooling experience students of color might have when exposed exclusively to a Eurocentric curriculum.

4. How do school organizational cultures with which you are familiar influence whether teachers include instruction about societal biases toward some cultural/ethnic groups?

Facilitators should acquaint participants with the characteristics of school organizational cultures, such as the beliefs, policies, rituals, ceremonies, heroes, celebrations, informal leadership, and norms, as discussed by Deal and Peterson (2009). Attempts should also be made to engage participants in drawing relationships between societal biases (e.g., toward persons based on race, ethnicity, appearance, dress, socioeconomic background, primary language, physical and mental abilities, size, being homeless) and the ways some children treat other children in school or in their neighborhood. Participants should discuss how they could teach such content if there were no ready-made instructional materials and the absence of content standards that require such information to be taught. The issue to then explore is whether influences in individual school cultures result in such information having a low priority, and what those influences are.

5. In your opinion, what are some of the prerequisites that must be met for improving the response to new students in a school community when the new students *seem* very different from the majority?

I suggest the facilitator initially engage participants in discussing recent demographic changes in their schools, especially if there has been a major growth in the population of immigrant groups with inadequate response to their unique needs, resulting in low academic performance in core academic courses. Explore the reasons for there being an inadequate response to these student needs and whether other long-time resident students also experience the same level of education. After these preliminary discussions, it will probably be easier for participants to identify some prerequisites that must be met for improving the response to new students in a school community, such as change in what are perceived as best instructional practices and best instructional supervision practices. Deep-seated biases in a school community toward families of particular religious, ethnic, or language backgrounds also need to be surfaced if they exist. Without acknowledgement of a problem, it is very difficult to identify remedies.

6. What are some of the human fears in a school community that may inhibit equitable treatment and equitable outcomes?

I have found most teachers find it very difficult to acknowledge having any of the fears mentioned in the guide, probably because of their own embarrassment. They must usually be in a very emotionally safe environment without major concerns about being judged, if they are going to discuss personal fears. Try to elicit authentic responses that are based on personal feelings and not political correctness. To avoid targeting any stakeholder group, make sure to seek examples of unique fears that may be held by different stakeholder groups, such as teachers, students, parents, support staff, community persons, district staff, and so on, before asking for "I" statements from group participants.

❧❦

Chapter 4 Facilitator Notes

Make It Personal: FN4–1

1. In your opinion, what instructional supervision strategies should be used by school administrators when working with teachers in the school attended by Jimmy?

This question requires participants to identify what their priorities would be if they were a site administrator in Jimmy's school. The facilitator should refer participants to the vignette to answer the question. Vignette specifics deserving attention include monitoring follow-through on the school site plan, focus during classroom observations and feedback, clarifications provided in staff meetings, and monitoring of progress on benchmark targets. Be prepared to assist participants' identification of supervision strategies they would use, through asking them to first name the categories a supervisor should pay attention to in a culturally diverse school like Jimmy's.

2. If you were a teacher or administrator in the middle school attended by Jimmy, how would you attempt to improve the personal motivation and academic success of Jimmy and his school friends?

Ask participants to share what they do to try motivating students to do their best, especially African and Latino/a Americans, and how they capitalize on students' life experiences and cultural background. If necessary, ask them what motivated them to try harder in middle school, especially when they couldn't relate to the content. This should help them to answer the question. It might be helpful for the facilitator to conduct some research on popular interests of African and Latino/a American middle school students. In addition, get participants to think about students they know like Jimmy, and talk about some of the best middle school administrative practices they have ever witnessed, heard, or read about, when it comes to increasing the motivation of culturally and socioeconomically diverse students.

3. Identify some examples, if any, of how education administrators with whom you are familiar are not holding staff accountable for taking actions related to equity objectives in school site improvement plans, and describe the role you are playing to foster collaborative efforts to improve accountability for equity.

My experience is that school improvement plans seldom have the level of specificity on equity objectives that is necessary for a school administrator to hold staff accountable for the results. Nevertheless, the facilitator should encourage participants to come up with some examples of items in their own school improvement plan, equity based on not, that have not been implemented at all or as stated. This exercise should increase awareness of the norms at participants' schools when it comes to being accountable for what is in the plan. You should also discuss what determines whether it is the sole role of school administrators to enforce follow-through on implementation of action statements related to equity reform that are in the plan. Equity plans are sometimes the lowest priority, and excuses are accepted for not following through. Attempt to ascertain if this is true in the schools of participants.

Make It Personal: FN4–2

1. What three items from the list of ten observations require top priority in your work context?

You should encourage participants to first consider which of the 10 observations they think would have the greatest teacher support in their work setting. After that is decided by each person, they can then think about which of the issues identified in each observation will likely need top priority, based on their knowledge of the specific personalities who would be involved. Don't let participants get off the hook by saying all of the observations, or none of them, need attention. Push the group to agree upon their top three priorities from the list of 10. Every school has its own unique chemistry. The more important issue is what to do after deciding which of the 10 observations are most relevant in a particular work setting.

Encourage participants to never "assume," without doing perception checks, that others will agree with their ideas about the observations that need to be addressed. Additional data collection is likely necessary to help decide how to address the identified priority issues.

2. Explain the extent to which the statement "There is a yawning gap between the rhetoric and reality of equity initiatives" is consistent or inconsistent with your personal experience.

There are several issues you should discuss with participants in addressing this item. First, make sure everyone understands what is being asked, including what is meant by "yawning gap" and "equity initiative." Yawning gap refers to an ever growing gap between the equity rhetoric (i.e., the "equity talk," which is what people say needs to be done and what they will do about it) and the "equity walk," which is what actually happens, that is, the reality, when equity initiatives are undertaken and in many cases, unsuccessfully implemented. In addition, participants should be encouraged to use their personal work experience as a basis for critical reflection when comparing the rhetoric to the reality.

Most important is having everyone share what factors they think have contributed to a lack of follow-through, so that there is a gap between what was desired and what actually happened. Participants might not have adequate information on the causes of the gap, necessitating some investigation and data collection. Once some of the reasons are ascertained, it is important for some collective problem solving on what could be done to reduce the gap or decide if the initial plans need refinement, complete overhaul, or should be discarded altogether.

Chapter 5 Facilitator Notes

Make It Personal: FN5–1

1. How does your experience support or refute the claim that personnel selection practices are largely devoid of any attention to whether job candidates are knowledgeable about or have experience with culturally diverse students?

The facilitator should remind participants about a major purpose of the six chapters in Section I of the guide, which is to provide the reader with a review of possible schooling conditions necessitating culturally courageous leadership (CCL). This chapter discusses several biases impacting achievement at high levels by historically underserved students of color. Personnel and professional development practices are critical variables that can contribute significantly to achievement gaps in educational outcomes.

The facilitator needs to engage participants in exploring whether this is true in their work settings by doing some investigation of district practices and select interviews of persons recently hired. If personnel selection does not include such criteria, encourage participants to identify what kind of support systems need to be put in place for staff.

2. To what extent have your preservice teacher or administrator training and on the job professional development given attention to developing cultural proficiency and culturally responsive standards based instruction?

Engage participants in discussing the possible relationship between their experiences during on-the-job professional development activities and the perpetuation of systemic incapacity to eradicate achievement discrepancies. Ask them to identify what kinds of training are especially needed to improve their effectiveness in teaching historically underserved students. If they don't mention training on cultural proficiency and cultural responsiveness, ask them why. Participants also need to brainstorm what other kinds of training are needed to improve their effectiveness in teaching all students, followed by your facilitating a comparison of their answers to the two questions. Explore with them their concept of leadership and the degree of importance they place on teacher leadership.

3. In your opinion, how should preservice or on-the-job professional development needs be identified and addressed?

I suggest the facilitator start by having a brief discussion about how participants feel in general about the way professional development needs are determined and addressed compared with the way they think their needs should be addressed. My experience is that teachers say they want more modeling and coaching than is provided. However, when it is provided, I find some make excuses why they cannot do what they see others doing successfully or cannot see the wisdom of the guidance received concerning needed changes. Sometimes, participants just don't agree with the knowledge or perspectives they receive in courses or during capacity building activities. This may be even truer when the content is on cultural diversity issues, including biases and barriers impeding improved achievement. I have had a few students in my teacher education courses who strongly disagreed with some of the cultural content. The purpose of discussing how to identify and address professional development needs is to discover what if any resistance participants have to theories, methods, and research discussed in courses or professional development that are divergent from what they have come to embrace as part of their identity and educational philosophy. Such dissonance, expressed or withheld, can have negative consequences for the students in their classrooms. You might want to engage participants in reviewing the information in Chapter 1 about White racial identity development, and how some of the attitudes and beliefs associated with certain levels of White racial identity might help to explain resistance to certain kinds of professional development.

4. Discuss the extent to which there are conflicts in your school community that are similar to those in the McClelland secondary school district, and what your school district is doing about it.

I suggest chart 5b be used to review the particulars in the McClelland secondary school district, and to also discuss how participants have responded to the task in the chart asking them to identify what leadership is needed to address the issues listed. The core of the discussion should be on comparing the McClelland school community conflicts to those they are currently experiencing in their school district, and whether the conflicts at McClelland or conflicts in participant districts/schools are related to the institutional biases and the five categories of standards introduced at the beginning of the chapter. In all likelihood they are somewhat related, so the discussion should also focus on current leadership efforts in participant districts/schools to deal with the conflicts, and what their efforts reveal about the leadership paradigm being utilized. A major thesis of this guide is that current educational leadership paradigms are antiquated, given the current challenges faced by educators in schools within the United States.

Make It Personal: FN5–2

1. What changes are needed in your school community for supervision and evaluation practices to more effectively address the low achievement of historically underserved students?

Participants should address this question based on their own personal experience. I suggest you elicit responses in the following categories which may not be mentioned: use of classroom observation rubrics that require focus on specific students (e.g., boys in general, or African American or Latino boys in particular); use of a classroom observation protocol that includes asking a few students (one on one or in a very small group) questions to elicit their understanding of what they are supposed to be doing, whether they know how to do it, and what their product will look like if they do it well; facilitating a discussion of grade-level or subject area teachers about samples of student work related to a key content standard; use of formative assessment results as a basis for discussion with a small group of teachers about how they are responding to the results, especially the kinds of instructional interventions being employed; and use of parent volunteers to observe in classrooms, after being trained to do so, so they can help identify any "problems of instructional practice," without focusing on the specific teachers but the problems observed. I have found in my work that when doing joint observations with principals, most do not notice things I notice, such as how teachers don't have methods to check for understanding equitably across all students, and don't notice or intervene in a culturally responsive manner when they do notice student off-task behavior, especially that of African American and Latino boys. Also engage participants in discussing the degree of success their schools have in getting students to attend afterschool tutorial assistance; I have found most low-performing schools have a poor track record in getting those students with the greatest need to participate in such programs. Schools need much more support from parents on this issue.

2. What should be done when or if site administrators don't know how to identify explicit or implicit cultural biases during their classroom observations or don't have the political will and/or savvy to address what they do identify?

Administrators respond best to help when they are involved in deciding the focus of assistance or evaluation. For example, if a state has performance standards for education administrators, those can be collaboratively used to decide what the focus of coaching or evaluation should be. The facilitator should be prepared to acquaint participants with some alternative strategies for helping administrators improve their competencies if that is needed. Participants might already have some ideas on the subject. Joint classroom observations by the site administrator and their supervisor or coach, followed by discussions on what they observed, could be a way to acquire initial impressions of areas for improvement. The issue of "political will" should be defined and discussed, followed by brainstorming what some reasons might be for a lack of political will and how political will can be improved. This conversation can go in several different directions, such as the quality of supervision and coaching given to site administrators and the sociopolitical dynamics between some parents or some teachers and the site administrator, when the parent or teacher has some political clout.

3. What successful leadership practices are being used in your school community so the above problems in #2 are minimized?

Again, the facilitator might want to ascertain if joint observations followed by debriefing sessions are ever done. I have found it very important to precede any observations by preliminary discussions with the teachers to be observed, and at that time to acquaint them with the observation tool to be utilized. The observation tool should be based on research, on an area where the teacher wants feedback, and/or a solid rationale. If persons to be observed haven't had any professional development or participated in any discussions on "cultural biases" in the classroom, it will exacerbate any tensions that may already exist about being observed on that subject. Engage participants in discussing what activities should occur between principal and teacher before any classroom observations/supervision.

4. Describe actions taken by a school board member, district administrator, or principal in your school community who has actively and publicly been an advocate for historically underserved student groups receiving an equitable education.

The facilitator should refer to the section in Chapter 5 on "supervision/evaluation practices," and ask participants whether in their opinion the situations described there have ever happened in participants' schools/school districts (e.g., coaching and facilitation of small group problem solving related to the academic performance of Black and Latino/a students in specific skill or content areas, or the manifestation of low expectations and double standards by teachers). This prompt can be followed by eliciting information on what positive actions were taken at board, district, and school site levels. I have found that participants need very concrete examples of what actions can be taken by persons in the above three roles. Also be mindful that board and district actions, pro or con, are usually not transparent.

Make It Personal: FN5–3

1. What would be the reaction in your No Child Left Behind program improvement schools if they were required by the state to participate in a program of culturally relevant and responsive professional development for all school staff?

Anticipate participants challenging whether there is any relationship between such training and improved student achievement as well as wanting more specifics on the content, number, and scheduling of sessions, whether compensation would be provided for participants, whether college credits will be offered and count for advancement on the salary schedule, whether participation would be necessary if they have already completed courses or training on the topics, who would be the presenters, and what kind of activities would occur during the training. Try to redirect any such challenges or questions to the issue of what the reaction would be if there was such a mandate. Then engage participants in discussing what it would take to pull it off.

2. What are the major needs in the quality of education provided to low-income students of color in your district/school, and what leadership is being exercised at all levels to correct educational disparities?

Attempt to get a candid assessment from participants of the needs and the leadership being provided in their schools and districts. Also elicit reactions to comments in the text about gaps in legislative policy, educational research, scholarly publications, and in teacher credential requirements. The major issue in this question to be addressed is the difference between local needs regarding race and culture and the response of school community leaders as well as researchers and politicians.

Make It Personal: FN5–4

1. In your school community, to what extent are various student subgroups capable of code switching to mainstream academic English, and to

what extent do they have grade-level writing skills? Do most entry-level teachers have the requisite skills to help such students code switch when appropriate to mainstream English in their speaking and writing? What is the implication for what professional development is needed by teachers, as well as what success can be achieved with the students they teach if insufficient support is provided?

These three interrelated questions are all focused on what schools and teachers need to do about students whose primary language is nonmainstream English. Caution participants that the assumption cannot be made that this applies only to students of African descent and/or English language learners. Many students of almost all demographic groups do not speak mainstream English. Facilitators should try to engage participants in discussing the cultural politics influencing the educational response to students' primary discourse and what needs to change. In the second question above, based on my experience teaching future teachers, I am suggesting that a growing number of entry level teachers do not themselves speak and write mainstream English, and very little is being done about it by the administrators of teacher education programs. Most nontenured teacher education faculty may be reticent to take on the issue, since their continued employment may be heavily influenced by student evaluations. If there is insufficient support at the university level for such students and faculty, and no professional development at the school district level regarding teachers' speaking and writing skills, then historically underserved students of color will ultimately pay the greatest cost.

2. What are your ideas about how to build upon the nonmainstream English home language of all your students as a bridge to mainstream academic English?

This question is a continuation of the line of thought raised above. The facilitator should try to focus participants on what kind of leadership is needed to improve cultural democracy when it comes to attitudes about students' primary language and skills of educators to use it as a bridge to developing bilingual capacity in mainstream English. The work of Dr. Noma LeMoine (1999) and Dr. Susana Dutro (2005) should be two of the primary sources used to assist a seashift change in how schools go about improving the equal opportunity and literacy of Black and Brown students.

Make it Personal: FN5–5

1. Describe the difference between the school/home connection in high- and low-performing schools with which you are personally familiar. What are schools and what are parents doing differently in each type of school?

The terms "high- and low-performing schools" and "school/home connection" require definition, and I suggest the litmus test between the two types of schools include three criteria:

a. the extent to which the achievement disparities between various student subgroups based on end of year statewide tests have been eliminated,

b. the degree of progress in achieving equitable outcomes on other measures such as suspensions, expulsions, disciplinary referrals, referrals to special education, dropouts, enrollment in/successful completion of higher level courses, such as AP and honors courses, SAT scores, college-going rates, and

c. whether there is a large or small amount of discrepancy between end-of-year test scores, course grades, and student performance that meets the school criteria for standards-based work.

The school/home connection should include attention to the stimulus for teacher and parent initiated communication with the other, teacher/parent partnerships, and parent participation in the school-improvement and decision-making processes.

The second question about what schools and parents are doing differently in high- and low-performing schools should include but not focus exclusively on the nature of classroom instruction and parent involvement. Whether teachers in high- and low-performing schools are given different amounts of support in using some principles of learning is also worthy of investigation; four principles of learning I have found very important when implementing K–12 instruction are motivation, transfer, retention, and reinforcement, as originally conceptualized by Madeline Hunter. More recent principles of learning discussed in the online Wikipedia free encyclopedia are readiness, exercise, effect, primacy, intensity, and freedom.

2. What do you think are some of the additional roles parents can play in the schools of their children, other than what is usually done?

Engage participants in brainstorming answers to this question. Encourage them to consider parents as teachers of children and teachers of teachers; as decision makers, via serving on such committees as the school site team, governance team, fund-raising committee, public relations committee, and so on; parents as students; parents as school volunteers in critical places like the classroom, library, computer lab, playground, and cafeteria; and parents as mediators. The purpose of this question is to stimulate participants to think of how to take greater advantage of parents/guardians as a critical stakeholder group whose leadership, talents, and commitment are a vital necessity for maximizing school effectiveness in meeting the needs of all students.

3. Based on the information about parent involvement and how schools may treat parents differently based on income level, identify the points in this section with which you strongly agree or strongly disagree.

This question is based on the reference to Finn's work in the guide, wherein he reports on a study where there were four types of education being taught in a New Jersey school district. Participants should be encouraged to reflect on whether there are multiple kinds of schooling provided in their school or district, based on the income and social status of the students, and if so, what should be done about it. Again, the purpose is to get participants to consider whether the leadership paradigm in place is serving all students, and to speculate on what kind of new leadership priorities are needed to improve the school/home connection, especially with the families of historically underserved students of color.

Chapter 6 Facilitator Notes

Make It Personal: FN6–1

1. When no meaningful support is forthcoming from the district office, what initiatives should principals take to increase the support they and their staff need in order to effectively address challenging conditions at the school site?

Make sure the discussion of this question includes attention to the various roles that university faculty, college students, and parents can play in schools if adequate attention is given to recruiting, selecting, preparing, and supporting them for roles they are uniquely suited to play. Principals must develop stronger relationships with and outreach to human resources in their school communities. Making presentations to community leaders and organizations about the good things the school is attempting to do as well as inviting community leaders to be guest speakers for students are two practices being successfully used in many schools by enterprising principals. Refer group participants to the description of "Three Equity Warriors" in Chapter 14.

2. Given the limited resources available to school sites in the area of staff support, what in your opinion are some strategies site staff should consider to increase support within the building?

Some of the limited staff support to school sites is in such areas as qualified substitutes, instructional assistants to work with limited English speaking (LES) and special needs (not special education) students, and teacher coaches who can mentor and help build teacher capacity in instructional effectiveness. In addition, most principals do not get sufficient on-site coaching to help them effectively address leadership challenges they are experiencing. It is a myth that only new site administrators need such assistance. Principals should seek trained coaching assistance of retired administrators who have the requisite expertise given the needs of the site administrator. Principals should also reassess how they spend their time and possibly give more time to conducting capacity building for teachers who can be recruited to assume leadership roles for specific tasks. Engage participants in discussing specific areas where teachers can serve as coaches where they have demonstrated expertise, including the coordination of schoolwide programs for special needs and LES students. Along these lines, discuss sources of funding for stipends to teacher leaders within budgetary parameters. Principals must be willing to implement "distributed leadership" and develop more diverse and larger leadership teams. This requires cultural courageousness.

Make It Personal: FN6–2

1. What additional support is needed in your school(s) in order to effectively address some of your student, parent, and staff needs?

Group participants should first be engaged in discussing the student and staff needs they have at their school sites that require an increase in the level of support. Some new challenges they may be experiencing include major budget cuts, loss of staff, increase in the number of students with major learning needs, increased class size, and/or a mismatch between staff competencies and student needs. Attempt to get participants thinking less about district support to address their challenging conditions and more about what they can collectively do together within their school sites and communities. Redefining how teaching and learning takes place is one example, and the multiple responsibilities/roles that each staff member can assume if they are all working together. External support from universities needing access for research projects might also be bartered if they are committed to fostering equity and can help improve principal competencies and the quality of teaching to achieve greater equity. New forms of partnerships with community-based organizations might also be an avenue to explore, and participation in electronic networks or webinars with other educators can be a great source of new ideas. New ways of training and engaging select students to work with other students might also help improve the tutoring and mentoring needed. Discuss how principals and teachers need to have their own support system beyond their work environment, and how they can utilize their support system to secure information on best practices in the area of collaboration amongst all school community stakeholders.

2. What are the common explanations given in your school(s) for why it is not possible to improve staff support?

The most common explanation will likely be a lack of funding/budgetary cuts. Pushback when this excuse is given by challenging group participants to identify the ways existing funds, if any, are currently used, and exploring whether new needs can be combined with the current needs being addressed, or whether any ineffective programs can be eliminated and those funds reallocated elsewhere. In addition, engage participants in critically analyzing what their school priorities should be at this time in terms of staff responsibilities and use of limited funds available. Sometimes schools continue to fund efforts that are not achieving their intended purpose simply because there is a constituency that strongly lobbies to continue past practice out of loyalty to those making the futile effort.

Make It Personal: FN6–3

1. What are some of the work conditions that most affect some of the indicators of toxic school climate mentioned in chart 6a?

Most of the indicators of school climate mentioned in the chart are related to the social and psychological environment as opposed to the physical environment. Participants should be asked what they think causes the negative factors mentioned in the chart, such as competing educational philosophies, values, communication styles, or any racial/cultural issues. The facilitator should also attempt to engage participants in discussing how poor school climate negatively impacts student achievement. Participants should then be asked to brainstorm what each stakeholder group, including students, could do to improve school climate, and whether they think personal courage is needed to do the things they came up with on their list. Another major issue is what can be done to improve personal courage. It is also important to acknowledge that in some cases major improvements in the physical environment can improve the morale and motivation of staff and students.

2. Prioritize the three work conditions that you think have the greatest negative impact on school climate in your work setting.

Make sure participants have shared their perspective on all the indicators of school climate they can think of before prioritizing their top three. Acquaint them with the following 10 dimensions of school climate: staff morale and cohesion, goal focus, all staff feeling they have fair opportunities to influence the decision-making process, sometimes called optimal power equalization, utilization of resources, allocation of resources, communication, problem solving, and conflict management adequacy, and respect for human differences. After the group has determined the three conditions that contribute the most to a toxic work climate in their respective work environments, engage the group in brainstorming what actions can be taken to lessen or eliminate the identified conditions, including what they can personally do.

Make It Personal: FN6–4

1. Of the ten barriers to high achievement in chart 6a, which three do you think most apply to schools with which you are familiar, especially low-performing schools?

I have found that the ten barriers can be found in any schools, whether they are characterized by the state or district as low performing or not. When I have asked staff in schools where I served as an external evaluator to prioritize the five barrier categories, the top three are usually weak instructional leadership, insufficient support for instructional staff, and toxic school and school/community climate. Teachers, perhaps understandably, seldom acknowledge teaching problems are a category needing priority attention. However, when asked to prioritize the top three barriers in the five categories, insufficient time spent on classroom observation, and few efforts to address instructional areas needing improvement were at the top of the list. Low time on task and student engagement was also identified as one of the top three barriers. Whatever the ranking of your group, facilitators should focus participant discussion on why they came up with their top three barriers, based on sharing "personal stories," and what they think they can personally and collectively do to lessen these barriers.

2. In your opinion, which of the institutional biases discussed in Chapter 5 most contribute to the identified barriers to equitable outcomes?

The extent to which participants can engage in a very open, candid, and honest discussion on this question will usually depend on the extent to which the facilitator has previously worked with them on some team and trust building, because even persons who have known each other a long time can discover some major differences in perspectives. The six biases introduced in Chapter 5 and then tied to barriers in Chapter 6 are hard pills to swallow for many teachers, especially if they haven't been exposed to much equity literature, training, or coursework. The facilitator should help participants get into a problem-solving "zone" and focused first and foremost on how they can individually and collaboratively facilitate the kind of transformation that will result in more equitable educational outcomes for all student groups. That said, there isn't any one correct answer to which institutional biases contribute most to the identified barriers. Participants might not even agree that any of the identified institutional biases in Chapter 5, or identified barriers I found in a sample of schools apply to their own schools. That is no excuse for not addressing the question. The purpose of the question is to get the reader or the book study group focused on critically looking at their own educational environment and grappling with what applies to them. This should be followed by figuring out what they are going to do about it. Everyone's experience and cultural lens may be different in what they see and what they apply from the guide, and I have found the goal of educational equity and excellence can be approached from any of the angles mentioned in Chapters 5 and 6, as long as all of the angles are seriously considered, from curricula to supervision to professional development, socioeconomic status, language discourse, and parent involvement. In the sample of schools used as the basis for identification of the barriers discussed in the chapter, there was no one bias or two or three that always contributed the most to the barriers. The biases are all very interrelated, but a paucity of leadership across *all stakeholder groups* was a major contributing factor to the barriers, and most school leaders, whether they were principals or teachers, were working very hard but not very smart. They didn't know what they didn't know and weren't very open to finding out. The facilitator needs to help the group along that journey of discovery.

3. Select any *two* of the five *barrier categories* in chart 6a and describe what administrators and/or teachers can do to lessen or eliminate these barriers.

Facilitators should encourage participants to talk about what is happening in their own work settings as an approach to completing this task, and I encourage you to break your group up into dyads or triads and have each group talk about different barrier categories.

4. Select any *one* of the five barrier categories and describe what support staff, students, and/or community persons can do to lessen this barrier category.

The same strategy should be used when addressing this item. Participants should be broken into dyads or triads to complete the assignment, and cautioned to not be conservative when thinking of possible strategies. They need to think out of the box.

5. What actions are being taken by the school board and/or higher education faculty to eliminate any of the stated barriers?

I suggest some field assignments be given to answer this question, such as a subgroup interviewing a board member or two, and also another subgroup interviewing one or more university faculty members who teach courses that ostensibly would engage their students in studying these barriers. Make sure to include faculty members in both teacher preparation and administrator preparation programs.

6. What are *you* personally interested in doing, or are currently trying to do, related to any of the barriers you experience that are mentioned in chart 6a?

To avoid putting any group members on the defensive, you might make this a writing prompt during a group session, or an assignment to complete outside of the group setting, followed by volunteers sharing what they have written. Those who share in the group should be encouraged to also give highlights of their 'journey,' with such specifics as what they have read, actions taken, disappointments experienced, insights obtained, learning experienced, and confidence gained. The emphasis should be "road stops" or "bumps" on the journey, not necessarily the destination.

Chapter 7 Faciliator Notes

Make It Personal: FN 7–1

1. In your work setting, what are the major constraints working against meaningful sustained collaboration for equity by all school community stakeholders?

It might be easier for a group to answer this question by discussing the constraints to working collaboratively with one stakeholder group at a time, but it really depends on the school and subdivisions within a school. Teachers in some schools and within schools in some departments have less difficulty in working together but may have difficulty in working collaboratively with those in another department or with peers throughout the school from all departments or grade levels. When people have had prior successful experience in working collaboratively, within or across subject areas and grade levels, it is likely easier to work collaboratively on equity issues. But it may depend on the equity issue being addressed, such as suspensions, grades, access to higher level courses, or test scores. A good starting place is to facilitate collaboration by all persons, regardless of role, who work directly with students, and it might be helpful if these persons have a variety of cultural perspectives and awareness or skill levels. The biggest challenge might be facilitating meaningful collaboration between teachers, parents/community persons, and students. The facilitator needs to find out all stakeholders' previous level of experience and expertise during the course of their answering the question of what the major constraints are to collaboration in general, and to collaboration of representatives from all stakeholder groups for achieving equity in educational outcomes. It is important to remember that collaboration, like many things, requires practice, and learning from prior experience.

2. What is your experience in collaborating on achieving equity with at least two stakeholder groups other than your own?

Before discussion of the question, the facilitator should have all participants write down what other stakeholder groups they have worked with, on what equity needs or issues, and with what results. It is also important to find out how participants are defining what they mean by collaboration.

3. What are some small victories or major defeats you have experienced when collaborating with any other stakeholder groups to achieve equity?

The facilitator needs to model answering this question before expecting others to do so, and then encourage volunteers to share their answers. Beforehand, the facilitator might meet one on one with select members of the group to help them practice their answers before the meeting where the question will be discussed. It is important to also have participants share what they learned from their victories or defeats.

4. On reflection, what would you do differently in prior efforts to achieve equity reform/transformation?

Again, the facilitator should guide this discussion through example, by sharing what they personally would do differently, such as their recruitment of others involvement, their delegation of tasks, their choice of equity focus, their response to problems or constraints encountered along the way, and/or their definition of the equity problem(s).

$\gtrsim\ll$

Chapter 8 Facilitator Notes

Make It Personal: FN 8–1

1. What do you consider your most important personal qualities when it comes to being a committed caregiver?

Encourage participants to reflect on times when they might have chosen to ignore disrespectful or hurtful actions of students with students, adults with adults, or adults with students, or when they have engaged in such actions themselves. Publicly modeling a willingness to do this yourself will help others to disclose. Use this as a way of engaging participants in sharing how or whether they do see themselves as caregivers in a school community, and ways they can improve this behavior, not just on a personal level, but on schoolwide and district levels as well. The relationship between the level of genuine caring, staff effectiveness, and student achievement can then be fruitfully explored. Some might even share instances when they were mistreated or disrespected by work colleagues or supervisors, and how that impacted their work with students or disposition toward supporting equity initiatives.

2. What additional cultural knowledge do you need in order to improve student receptivity to and respect for what others share about their cultural heritage or family traditions?

Examples of cultural knowledge one may need to have to improve student receptivity and respect are the following: awareness of major factors influencing students' identities, knowledge of students' personal ethics (ideas about right and wrong), student's hobbies and interests, what vocabulary or communication styles are most popular with students, and what students' prior knowledge and experiences are when it comes to knowledge about cultural diversity, and when it comes to sharing information with others about their cultural heritage or family traditions. Some students may know very little about their cultural heritage or family traditions, and that can greatly influence how they react to others sharing about their heritage. Students' racial identity and stage of racial identity development can also have a large bearing on how they respond to others' sense of self.

Sources related to possible stages of racial identity development of different races in the United States are mentioned in Chapter 1.

Make It Personal: FN 8–2

1. What is the relationship between conflict and low achievement in your school community?

In this guide conflict is described as differing ideas and priorities among diverse school community stakeholders about what should happen in school, whether it is the curriculum, instruction, and disciplinary practices, support services, working relationships, or allocation of resources. All of these "conflicting" perspectives revolve around power, control, and authority, also described as the implicit battle over whether cultural hegemony or cultural democracy will prevail. The facilitator should engage participants in reviewing the kinds of conflicts they see and experience in schools, followed by having them share personal stories that illustrate how conflicts negatively impact student educational outcomes, particularly the outcomes of historically underserved students. The categories of potential conflict could be illustrated on your Smart Board or chalkboard, or via overhead transparency to stimulate participant response to as many of the conflict categories as possible perceived as impacting student educational outcomes. For example, student–student, student–adult, adult–adult, school–home categories should be considered as well as conflicts between and within different ethnic/cultural/language/socioeconomic/job category stakeholders within each of those categories.

2. What are two of the conflicts experienced in your school(s) that contribute the most to inequitable student outcomes?

In my experience, school–home and teacher–student conflicts are very popular to mention, and teacher–teacher conflicts are least mentioned but actually have a lot of impact in some educational settings on student educational outcomes.

Vignette 2–2 describes conflicts in Jimmy's middle school, so just discussing whether any of those conflicts are experienced in participants' schools could be used as a point of departure. Most of the discussion should focus on how to attempt resolving these conflicts, and whether the characteristics of consummate conciliators in the text will make any difference, or where they have made a difference.

Make It Personal: FN 8–3

1. What are some fears and/or prevailing beliefs in your school community that drive the resistance to changes you consider necessary for equitable educational outcomes?

Participants must first be engaged in identifying changes necessary for equitable educational outcomes. The discussion in Chapter 4 about 10 observations during leadership of equity initiatives as well as biases and barriers (see chart 6b) discussed in Chapter 6 are good starting points for the identification of needed changes. Once the needed changes are identified, participants can be asked to think about any fears or beliefs in their school community that may cause resistance to making the changes needed. The facilitator can ascertain if the fears mentioned in Chapter 3 of the guide resonate with participants' own experience and whether they think these fears contribute to inequitable educational outcomes.

2. On a scale of 1–5, with 1 being very low and 5 being excellent, how would you assess your effectiveness as a conscientious coach?

Encourage your group participants to do a self-assessment of the extent to which they see themselves reflecting any of the examples of a conscientious coach in the guide, followed by asking for feedback from at least one other person they know outside of the group about whether they reflect any of the examples. The point to be made is not how high or low they see themselves in this regard, but what are they doing or need to do so they might become a more effective equity coach with peers or others.

Make It Personal: FN 8–4

1. What, if any, changes related to equity have been most difficult to implement in your district or school, and what support was provided to administrators or teachers to help them embrace the changes and implement them with fidelity?

Your group may have difficulty identifying changes most difficult to implement that are related to achieving equitable educational inputs/opportunities to learn. Be prepared to share with them some examples, such as grouping practices, access to higher level courses, schedule changes facilitating longer instructional periods, and so on. Professional development required of all staff could also be a major change difficult for many to swallow, especially if such training deals with staff attitudes and predispositions toward certain students. A major point to discuss is the level of support provided to assist with the implementation of such changes, not the merit of the changes. Engage your group in identifying how such support can be improved within the limited resources available.

2. Describe the role you are playing to foster courageous change efforts related to equity.

Engage participants in discussing any of the indicators for courageous change masters that they may have demonstrated to some extent. The point is not how many they may exhibit, but whether they have done any, and also which indicators they would be interested in doing to increase the likelihood of an equity initiative they support being better received and implemented. This discussion could also be an opportunity to engage in a general discussion about educational change and how the district or school can improve how it is undertaken. The topic of why change requires courage is also worthy of consideration, as well as what is meant by courage.

৵৽৵

Chapter 9 Facilitator Notes

Make It Personal: FN 9–1

1. What are some of the "sacred cows" in your school district or school that seem impossible to change when trying to foster equity transformation?

Sacred cows can be policies, norms, persons, or whatever is untouchable (i.e., not open to question or critique) when examining schooling conditions that negatively impact equitable educational outcomes. Some examples of sacred cows in my experience as an educator and an external evaluator are some criteria for suspension, some school informal or formal teacher leaders with a lot of personal popularity/ personal power in the school; some funding sources such as local or national foundations, and some norms around teacher prerogatives, such as whether they participate in certain professional development activities and being able to pick the students assigned to their classes or remove them from their classes. After giving participants some examples, ask them to write down what they think are the sacred cows in their school, and share out if comfortable in doing so. The point of this discussion is to explore how to reduce the inordinate power and invulnerability of some sacred cows.

2. Describe the current politics in your school(s) when it comes to seeking equity, including some of the land mines that must be circumvented in order to achieve equity transformation.

Participants will likely not have any difficulty in answering this question, but I suggest you still emphasize the need to be totally open in mentioning all of the political issues that would likely get in the way of seeking equity. A political land mine that may not be shared is when one doesn't know about the out of school social networks/relationships among opponents of particular equity programs. In some situations, it is important to be careful of what you share with whom, because you might be giving confidential information to an opponent of the desired equity initiative who hasn't revealed their position. Another political land mine could be the absence of support for the equity initiative from the very persons it is supposed to most benefit. Unfortunately, some equity initiatives are undertaken without soliciting the input or support of any target recipients. This is also called liberal arrogance and culturally condescending behavior.

Make It Personal: FN9–2

1. Compare the process for equity problem definition and analysis utilized in your school or district with the process suggested in this chapter.

If possible, engage participants in an exercise of equity problem analysis and definition as described in this chapter after they come up with a short list of equity problems needing attention. Then discuss the extent to which the process just experienced is similar or different from what is done in participants' schools, and how they think the process actually used in their work settings needs to be improved.

2. What are the steps in the problem analysis process which you feel are in greatest need of being implemented right away within your work setting?

The steps include information collection, analyzing the information collected, defining problems based on the data, identifying relationships between the problems, studying the context of each problem, and assumptions underlying each problem. Attempt to determine if any of these steps are used by participants when negotiating the conflicts between those for and against particular equity initiatives. Finally, engage participants in identifying which of these steps need to be implemented right away in their work setting.

Make It Personal: FN9–3

1. What, if any, anxiety or discomfort have you felt or know about related to explicitly discussing race, culture, and the "isms" and biases in staff meetings, professional development activities, parent forums, classroom instruction, and teacher preparation classes?

In some cases with which I am familiar, some staff of various racial backgrounds have chosen to not attend staff meetings that were going to focus on race and culture or institutionalized racism. Sexism or disability bias are easier to discuss. But the issue of race scares off a lot of people, for different reasons. Explore with participants whether they or others have experienced anxiety or discomfort if ever participating in such discussions, and why some people have such feelings. Focus primarily on what can be done to significantly lessen such feelings of avoidance or anxiety, recognizing the winning formula may be different in every situation. Break the group into three or more small groups, and ask each group to come up with what they think the "psychology of equity transformation" is in a specific situation that they choose from their collective work experiences. Another option is to give all groups an equity initiative related to one of the "isms" that theoretically will be implemented in their work setting, and ask them to come up with what the psychology of equity transformation will be, given that initiative.

2. Describe the actions you have taken or avoided if feeling such anxiety or discomfort, and the underlying causes of your feelings.

This task may be a very difficult one for some in your group. I suggest you gauge the tension, that is, discomfort, with the nature of this task. If you consider it appropriate, focus participants on why they feel some tension about the request to describe their actions or avoidance related to discussing the "isms" and biases. Ask how they would feel and what actions they would take or avoid if asked to participate in such an activity during a professional development session. If they have been in such a situation before, ask what happened. The purpose of the task is to try engaging participants in metacognitive activities about their feelings, thoughts, and prior actions when or if they were ever asked to participate in discussions about the "isms" or biases in their work setting. Discussions about race, culture, the "ism's," etc. are not uncommon if a school is seriously trying to engage in equity transformation. They are part of what is called the psychology of equity transformation in this guide because there may be a lot of assumptions, attitudes, feelings, beliefs, values, and behaviors that come up during discussions of this nature. The guidelines of Singleton and Linton (2006) are very helpful in such discussions.

Make It Personal: FN9–4

1. Describe the extent to which delivery, opportunity to learn, and professional development standards as described in chart 5a are implemented in schools populated primarily by historically underserved students of color.

When engaging participants in discussing this question, be wary of glowing claims being made about the extent to which the above standards categories are actually being practiced, especially in schools populated by low-income historically underserved students of color. Elicit specific examples of how the standards are being implemented. If the reverse happens, discuss why the standards aren't being implemented, and in either case, what participants' beliefs are about a relationship between consistent implementation of these standards and equitable educational outcomes. In an era of ever decreasing school budgets, talk about which standard categories experience the blunt of budget cuts and what can be done to maintain fidelity to opportunity to learn standards without previous funding levels. For example, opportunity to learn standards have a very mixed record of implementation even in the best of financial times, so ask participants what can culturally courageous leaders collectively do to improve this situation.

2. If you had the power to cause an instant improvement to a standards category currently receiving the lowest priority in your work setting, what would that standards category be and the improvement needed?

Before this question is addressed, engage participants in identifying why any standards categories receive low priority in their work setting. Have them "unpack" the major obstacles to higher priority for some standards categories, followed by some problem-solving activities on how to reduce these obstacles, even with very austere budgets. After these discussions, the question to each participant about the lowest standards category in their work setting might be more comfortably addressed.

Make It Personal: FN 9–5

1. Describe how limited accountability for equitable educational outcomes is currently manifested in your school or district.

Refer to vignette 9–1 in Chapter 9 about the Oak Canyon elementary district and facilitate a discussion about specific strategies used in that district to foster greater accountability. Then compare what happens there compared with what happens in the districts of participants. More importantly, discuss what participants think is required to improve accountability. As an assistant superintendent, I negotiated with the teacher's bargaining unit new contract language on formal expectations for instructional performance and the quid pro quo was also increasing teacher participation in each school's decision-making process about curriculum initiatives and school functioning. Department chairs and others in each school site were given training as instructional leaders and paid to serve as peer leaders in monitoring classroom instruction and instructional improvement. Elicit examples from participants of where they have experienced success in increasing accountability for instructional performance and student outcomes, and the politics that was experienced to achieve such improvements in accountability.

2. How do you try to navigate the politics of implementation when attempting to improve accountability for equitable educational outcomes?

Engage participants in discussing what the concept of accountability means to them. Also ask them to share their definition of the "politics of implementation" based on what they have read so far. If they do not seem to have a complete understanding of the concept, plan B could be to review the appropriate section of Chapter 9 on the third and fourth components of CCL. Once everyone is on the same page, divide the participants into triads and have them answer this question, followed by report-outs in large groups. Once the triads have reported, identify the similarities and differences in their experiences, and then collectively discuss how to improve navigating the politics of implementing an equity initiative that all participants agree to utilize for the exercise.

Make It Personal: FN 9–6

1. Assume you are going to start practicing CCL by joining others leading an effort to implement a particular equity initiative. Based on your assessment of the politics in your school community when it comes to the equity initiative you are about to undertake, describe at least two actions or strategies in your work plan in each of the next three years.

Participants in the group must be very clear about the six dimensions discussed in Chapter 9. Once you have confirmed everyone is very clear, assign all in the group to dyads. Have each dyad apply their understanding of the six dimensions to how they would attempt to implement an equity initiative of their choice. Some of the dimensions may not apply, but ask each dyad to consider collecting data before concluding which dimensions most apply and which, if any, do not. Once making that determination, participants should consider, but not be limited to, the observations discussed in Chapter 4 and the needed actions discussed in Chapter 7. This should be done before deciding which two actions or strategies will be included in their work plan in each of the next 3 years. I have found it is very difficult to seriously undertake a CCL agenda without simultaneous efforts to initially engage in some personal and organizational transformation efforts. This requires embracing at least some of the CCL characteristics/principles, and not trying to do solo efforts, but working collaboratively with at least one or two others, if not more. You need others working with you so you will each be more accountable to yourself and others.

As the group facilitator, you should practice or model what you espouse, and also engage in developing a work plan. You should also help participants think about what contingency plans they will develop (i.e., plan B and plan C) if their initial actions or strategies don't pan out.

2. What are your greatest fears/concerns about taking the initiative to co-lead an equity initiative, and what will you do to alleviate your concerns?

Model for the participants the courage to answer this question and allow them to interview you about what you have said about your fears and concerns. Ask participants to reflect on how they have overcome any fears or concerns about anything from their personal or work life that they have successfully attempted in the past, before they answer the assigned question. For example, a major fear some have is public speaking.

Have each participant write on the chalkboard or Smart Board his or her answers to the question, and have the group discuss each response. An alternative approach is to have everyone anonymously type his or her answers on a piece of paper, and then have the group discuss responses without knowing who wrote each one. Again, utilizing the guidelines provided by Singleton and Linton in *Courageous Conversations About Race* (2006) can probably be of major assistance when facilitating the group discussion.

Chapter 10 Facilitator Notes

Make It Personal: FN 10–1

1. Identify those behaviors listed for your stakeholder group with which you agree, those you have implemented, and those listed for other stakeholder groups you consider most important.

Completing this task will stimulate participants' thinking about what they need to do in support of those in other stakeholder groups, especially students, parents, and community members. It is incumbent upon district and school site stakeholder groups to take responsibility for helping nurture the development of CCL by culturally and ethnically diverse persons in the above three groups. Don't underestimate the value of doing this with some upper elementary students as well, because they can contribute a lot to providing perspectives needed by all of the adult stakeholders.

2. Identify other CCL behaviors you think would be equally important for any stakeholder group.

The CCL behaviors listed for each stakeholder group are *examples* and are not at all inclusive. Participants should use these examples as a point of departure to come up with other examples of what behaviors and attitudes are needed by culturally courageous leaders. Several of the vignettes in the guide might stimulate thinking about additional CCL behaviors that are equally important for any stakeholder group. Encourage participants to also discuss any CCL behaviors listed in this chapter that they find troubling, and why that is the case.

Chapter 11 Faciliator Notes

Make It Personal: FN 11–1

1. As you reflect on successful collaborative efforts regarding student achievement in which you have been involved, what were some of the major conditions and/or activities that led to all participants feeling supported and valued?

In discussing this question, encourage participants to think beyond what they might do with each other in grade level, department or interdisciplinary teams, student study teams, or other efforts with school staff. Successful collaborative efforts discussed, if any, should include those which involved students, parents, and community persons, including university faculty. Participants should also be encouraged to identify some prerequisites for collaboration to occur, and whether collaboration is key to increasing mutual feelings of respect and support. Attitude is everything.

My experience is that there is no clear consensus on what is necessary for collaboration to occur, and some may claim collaboration can be counterproductive when trying to increase mutual respect and support. Collaboration is sometimes mandated, including collaborative efforts to improve student achievement, and has succeeded in some instances, while failing in others. Voluntary efforts to collaborate are not necessarily the only way to go. What is critical is that collaboration, however initiated, must include the development of certain attitudes and behaviors, and depending on those so engaged, be closely monitored and facilitated. Also, collaboration to improve the achievement of Brown and Black students is sometimes not undertaken with the same amount of zeal and perseverance as collaboration for achievement gains in general. Personal biases and life circumstances of persons in all stakeholder groups may contaminate such efforts,whether they are parents, students, teachers, support staff, or administrators.

2. What is your pattern of behavior when you personally experience interpersonal conflict in a work setting, whether it is the classroom, staff meeting, or one-on-one with a colleague?

When discussing this question, it might be helpful to start by engaging participants in a discussion of what causes interpersonal conflicts to occur in the educational work setting. They might not have anything to do with the work. Professional disagreements can morph into interpersonal conflicts, but it is not inevitable. The goal of discussing this question is to get participants thinking about how interpersonal conflicts, if allowed to fester, can contaminate the work climate and negatively impact student educational outcomes. Some teachers trash their colleagues in front of their students when they are experiencing dissonance. If teachers are collectively responsible for the success of their students, and they cannot get along, then any conflict can result in the involved parties not benefitting from the insights and perspective of their colleagues. Teacher interpersonal conflict also has a negative impact on students when the students aren't the collective responsibility of a group of teachers. When teachers who work alone in isolation from each other experience interpersonal conflicts, the students may pick up on the tension, especially if teachers emit negative vibes or worse toward their colleagues. Students will sometimes mimic behaviors of the teachers around them in their interaction with peers. I have seen this happen without either the teachers or students being aware of the symbiotic relationship between them. Teacher attitudes are a critical variable influencing their disposition toward productive, respectful working relationships that enable them to be supportive of each other. When they cannot do that, it negatively impacts their students. Cultural courageousness is essential for dysfunctional behaviors to be minimized or eliminated.

Make It Personal: FN 11–2

1. What is necessary for teachers in most situations to provide all of their students with challenging academic instruction?

Remind participants "challenging academic instruction" is ideally grade-level work or higher, but not necessarily if students are initially 2 or more years below grade level in particular subject or skill areas. Instructional activities that focus on acceleration rather than remediation are preferable, but not always possible. Accelerated remediation is sometimes more practical in the short term. Teachers' beliefs in their students' ability is of critical importance, as is the need for students to be exposed to challenging instruction on a consistent basis. The sequence of instructional strategies is also of paramount importance. The book by Robyn Jackson on *How to Plan Rigorous Instruction* (2011) is a valuable resource that can assist teachers as well as those working with teachers to improve instructional interventions. She discusses four stages of rigor in ways that reflect cultural responsiveness even though she doesn't use that terminology.

2. What should be done to enable more challenging academic instruction for all students to be more widespread and feasible?

From my experience, this requires a work environment which provides a support system for the teacher equivalent to the support system needed by many students. In Chapter 5, five standards categories were introduced and three of those standards categories (delivery, opportunity to learn, and professional development) were mentioned as woefully lacking the priority they should have, especially when trying to achieve equitable educational outcomes. Jackson's well-crafted strategies for how teachers can plan and implement rigorous instruction can be adapted for use in how to develop more effective instructional support systems for teachers, if the biases and barriers discussed in Chapters 5 and 6 can be mitigated. The facilitator should engage participants in discussing what support they think teachers need for them to consistently provide challenging academic instruction for all students. My observation is that use of community volunteers and student mentors in the classroom, creative use of technology, and hands-on learning stations can be very helpful.

Make It Personal: FN 11–3

1. What should be done to increase teacher receptivity to professional development that focuses on cultural responsiveness, cultural proficiency, and race-specific training,when student assessment results consistently show a need for new instructional approaches?

In response to English/language arts assessment results, the reading recovery (RR) (www. readingrecovery. org) program was initiated by the superintendent during my tenure as the district instructional team leader (i.e., director) for the humanities in a very large school district. This program experienced tremendous results for students in Grades K–2 who were significantly behind their peers in the acquisition of decoding, fluency, and comprehension skills. The delivery system was one of the keys to the program's effectiveness as well as the degree of articulation between what was happening during the one-on-one instruction provided by the RR teacher and by the language arts teacher in the regular classroom. A major challenge was trying to expand the number of students a RR teacher could work with at any one time and still achieve the same results, because so much was based on the teacher's close scrutiny of how students learned and responding accordingly with great patience and positive affect. RR instruction was very culturally responsive, and teachers' cultural competencies as well as their racial attitudes definitely impacted how they interacted with students in such intimate settings.

In addition, because the program was so labor intensive and therefore expensive, RR teachers were constantly required to teach behind one-way glass for evaluation of their performance and so other persons could be trained as RR teachers. The consequence was they always had to be at the top of their game when doing their job. In order for teachers at large to become more receptive to professional development that focuses on cultural responsiveness, cultural proficiency and race-specific training, they have to be "sold" on the relationship between having such skills and significant improvements in student educational outcomes, and also convinced they will not be out on a limb without sufficient support when they need it. There is limited research to document the benefits of such program prerequisites, and also most school districts do not think they can afford such a support system.

2. What are some other strategies needed in order to facilitate greater teacher receptivity to professional development on cultural responsiveness, cultural proficiency, and race-specific training?

The facilitator needs to encourage participants' "venting" about whatever professional development they have previously had on these topics, and the quality of follow-up. Even when participants may have had no training on the topics, they will usually have opinions or attitudes about what it would be like. Facilitators need to have a very keen "crap" detector so they can comfortably confront any lame excuses they think they are hearing when participants answer the question. Teacher assessments of or preconceptions about such training are important sources of data that require higher priority in order to customize the efforts needed to increase teacher buy-in.

Make It Personal: FN 11–4

1. Based on your experience, what kinds of efforts are needed in your school or district to facilitate greater leadership by students and parents?

A major tenet of this guide is that nurturing CCL by students and parents is one of the essential ingredients necessary for equitable educational outcomes. Discuss that idea with participants in your group. Elicit any skepticism, as well as their ideas about how such leadership can be achieved, and what student and parent leadership would look like in participants' schools.

2. What has your school or district done to ensure student safety nets are culturally responsive interventions?

As an external evaluator for some low-performing schools in different districts whose historically underserved students of color were experiencing large achievement gaps, I consistently found the schools either had no safety nets in place (i.e., in-school and afterschool academic tutoring above and beyond regular instruction), or had academic tutoring programs that were not culturally responsive interventions. The input of target students and their parents was not solicited before such programs were put in place. The result was that many of the students in greatest need of afterschool services either did not participate or participated on an irregular basis. In some cases, parents would agree to their participation and then consistently come midway during such sessions to pickup their children. If they were approached about the negative consequences of doing this and agreed to stop the practice, they still continued to interrupt the extra help being provided to their children. The parents seemed to have no investment in their children getting the extra help, but appearances do not always accurately reflect what is happening.

Engage participants in defining what a "safety net" is, and the process used in their schools or districts to determine what should be offered and how these safety nets are implemented. Attempt to ascertain if school governance teams or school site councils had community advisory committees to provide them with recommendations on how to go about implementing safety nets. Some schools feel it is their job and prerogative to decide what should be done, who should participate, and how it should be done, without needing to solicit any input during the planning process from parents, students, or community persons. Other schools make every effort to secure input before making decisions on safety nets, and still have problems in getting consistent participation.

A larger issue is the feasibility of attempting to implement collaborative leadership by all school community stakeholders, when it comes to trying to achieve equitable educational outcomes. In some places, there is a need for prior capacity-building activities that facilitate the development of stronger cohesion, accountability, and leadership in each demographic subgroup of each stakeholder group, before they can meaningfully collaborate on major schoolwide goals. My experience is that educators often complain about the lack of follow-through by other stakeholders, but never consider the need for spending time on some capacity, team, and trust building before they arbitrarily decide what will be done to help those students in danger of being left behind.

Most educators strongly resent or are frustrated by what they perceive as a lack of appreciation or responsibility on the part of those they are trying to help. The educators may never consider the day-to-day reality of those they are trying to help or that their approach may be perceived as very condescending. CCL requires a different way of seeing and doing things.

Make It Personal: FN 11–5

1. How do schools with which you are familiar motivate elementary and secondary students to share a sense of responsibility for eliminating the achievement gap?

In the book *Effort and Excellence in Urban Classrooms: Expecting—and Getting—Success With All Students*, by Corbett, Wilson, and Williams (2002), the authors talk about teachers being responsible for student learning, in such ways as insisting that students complete every assignment, expecting students to do high-quality work, making sure all students understand, and providing extra help. They discuss at length what each of these instructional tasks requires the teacher to do, and also document low-income inner city students' positive response to such expectations and support.

Help participants explore the notion that students will increase their sense of responsibility for eliminating the achievement gap they may experience when teachers demonstrate their commitment to do whatever it takes to help them achieve at high levels. Ask participants whether they think most teachers use examples from students' experience to help them clearly understand the work. Encourage participants to "speak their truth," when discussing the sometimes contentious issue of checking for understanding. Pacing schedules sometimes drive teachers to move on to other content even though they know all students have not mastered the previous content. Encourage participants to share stories from their own experience.

In addition, ascertain if participants have engaged students at the high school level in their school's decision-making process. In the book by Dana L Mitra titled *Student*

Voice in School Reform (2008), the author describes "student voice" initiatives across the United States that focus on the benefits of student participation for schools. Mitra advocates a broadened conception of professional collaboration and distributed leadership to include students. Schools and students benefit. Alienated students have been shown to reengage with a stronger sense of ownership in their schools when they work with adults to actively shape their own learning environments. Meaningful student involvement in the decision-making process is very consistent with the CCL paradigm.

2. What are some strategies you feel should be implemented to improve collective accountability for equitable educational outcomes?

Collective responsibility is defined as all stakeholders in a school community. This would include students, parents, community members, and select university faculty in teacher and administrator preparation programs who serve as resources to schools. Teachers, administrators, and support staff as well as representatives from each of the above groups should share their perspectives before deciding upon research-based actions to improve the educational outcomes of historically underserved students. Their goal should be to achieve significant improvement leading to equitable educational outcomes over time.

Engage participants in discussing what it would take to achieve collective responsibility in their school or district, including the role each of them must be willing to play. Strategies suggested in the text include an advisory committee established and convened by the board of education. Another suggested strategy is creating a representative group of stakeholders to investigate any alleged instances of documented discrimination, as well as oversee how efforts to achieve equity are implemented throughout the school district. Solicit reactions of your participants to these suggested strategies, and to also react to the proposals of each other.

❧❧

Chapter 12 Facilitator Notes

Make It Personal: FN 12–1

1. From reading the two leadership profiles, describe three understandings you acquired about how culturally courageous leadership can be manifested in school communities.

Be prepared for the possibility of a wide range of reactions to the two leadership profiles. Some may be inspired and others may think the actions of the two leaders were ill informed or naïve. Whatever the reactions of your participants, explore with them why they reacted whatever way they did, and how their reaction reflects some of their own values, assumptions, and theories of action. Make sure to ascertain whether they consider the actions of the two as examples of CCL. They may need help in that regard, by your pointing out relationships between what is said about them, the seven needed actions discussed in Chapter 7, the seven characteristics of CCL described in Chapter 8, and the 5 A's listed in charts 12a and 12b of Chapter 12. Also, if no one else brings it up, raise the issue of how culturally courageous leaders must be prepared for the negative reactions (i.e., "push back") of others to their valuing cultural democracy and the pursuit of personal as well as organizational transformation.

2. What can you apply from the leadership profiles to your own work context?

Areas of application you might want to make sure participants consider are the sense of urgency, the need to be responsible, the engagement of others, the emphasis on capacity building and shared leadership, and the willingness to confront dysfunctional norms that work against achieving equitable educational outcomes. Each of the leaders demonstrates these qualities.

Chapter 13 Facilitator Notes

Make it Personal: FN 13–1

1. Which of the above conditions, such as absence of the three R's, three A's, or communication behaviors, contribute the most to weak instructional leadership and limited accountability in your work setting?

In all likelihood, some participants will think that all of the choices in the question contribute a lot to weak instructional leadership. There is obviously no one correct answer. However, I have found most school site administrators with whom I have worked are not effective when tackling the three A's if they haven't mastered the three R's, and they don't adequately address the three R's if they are weak in their communication behaviors: facilitation, mediation, and candor. Keep in mind that facilitation and candor are not polar opposites. Candor, when appropriately and sensitively used, can set the stage for facilitation and mediation. Some site administrators don't need much guidance, monitoring, or coaching to master all three of these areas. But most do. When there is little equity at the classroom level, it is usually a function of weak instructional leadership at the school site and district levels, which may be due to little pressure from the community and board of education in this area.

2. What is one thing you would do if you were engaged in direct efforts to correct the absence of any conditions identified in response to the previous question?

The generic answer to the question is to collect data, work on building community support, and cultivate some strong relationships within the work setting that will help in deciding when to make a big move toward correcting any of the areas mentioned: the three R's, three A's, or the communication behaviors. However, what I suggest is to practice and refine personal skills in each of the areas yourself before working on others or the school as an organization. Engage your participants in discussing the pros and cons of whatever they come up with in response to this question, and then publicly compare what they have said to your ideas and mine. Make sure you discuss participants' attitudes and self-assessment regarding their communication behaviors: facilitation, mediation, and candor.

Make It Personal: FN 13–2

1. Identify either an equity transformation or equity reform initiative undertaken in your school district, school, or program in the recent past, and then describe the politics (i.e., the dynamics between people based on their competing interests, beliefs, values, and priorities) during roll out of the initiative.

Remind participants about the difference between equity reform and equity transformation as discussed in the beginning of Chapter 13. If participants have not personally experienced either type of equity initiative, then engage them in creating a theoretical example of equity transformation, referring them to vignette 13–1 for ideas. Then divide your group into two small groups, each charged with the task of deciding what strategies will be used to roll out the initiative in a particular context they have chosen from the diverse work contexts represented in their small group, and what politics they would anticipate. When each group reports out their action plan, the other group should play the role of critical friend by asking questions of clarification and otherwise scrutinize the plan to ascertain the extent to which the plan takes into consideration political realities they could anticipate.

If some participants have experienced an equity transformation initiative or equity reform effort, then remind participants to be thorough when describing the "politics" that occurred. Encourage them to share as much as possible about the competing interests and priorities, and the personalities on different sides of the fence, so to speak. For example, they should be able to talk about whether there was cultural dissonance between some of the major players, whether there were examples of institutional or transparent racism, the kind of instructional leadership practiced, the degree of accountability shown for achieving equity goals, and whether there were any wanksters, gangsters, or riders. Participants should have some data to back up their assertions, so it is not based on hearsay, assumptions, or conjecture.

2. Given the politics you have just described in response to #1 above, identify one of the six political dimensions discussed after vignette 13–1 or 13–2 that was NOT used in your situation but should have been. Explain your reasoning.

Remind participants of the six political dimensions: problem definition and analysis, psychology of equity reform, standards categories receiving low priority, observations during other equity initiatives, reduce key barriers to high achievement, and prevent equity hustlers from compromising equity efforts. The sharing required in this activity as well as in response to the previous question could take a lot of time, so it would be best to divide the group into triads or small groups, for each question to be answered. It is likely that more than one of the six dimensions was not used, but encourage participants to talk about only one that they think should have been used in their particular situation. They should have data and some logic to back up their choice of whichever dimension is identified.

Most participants may have little experience in dealing with the politics of educational change, so be prepared to share some of your ideas about how they might proceed. Allen G. Johnson, author of *Privilege, Power, and Difference* (2005), has several ideas about how systems of privilege work and how to deal with various forms of resistance or denial, especially when people don't want to talk about it. I have found all of the POI dimensions I discuss after vignettes 13–1 and 13–2 have received scant attention during equity reform or transformation initiatives. However, in my experience, any dissonance between those leading equity efforts, any transparent racism, any weak instructional leadership, and any "wanksters" among equity leaders (see Chapter 9 under "Politics of Implementation") are usually political constraints easily overlooked because the tendency is to focus on more obvious obstacles to achieving equitable educational outcomes. People who strongly espouse a commitment to equity (they talk the talk but don't walk the talk) can be some of the biggest constraints to success of an equity initiative, and petty differences or rivalries between equity advocates can be a form of dissonance that poisons equity initiatives. Furthermore, principals who talk equity but are unwilling or unable to provide the supervision and coaching for teachers who may not be meeting the needs of all students in their classrooms are a major constraint to achieving equity. When I have closely examined some of the causes for such leadership inadequacies, school district leaders, university credential programs, informal social and/or professional networks, accreditation agency practices, and professional association norms have had a lot of influence, if not the most influence, on how principals define themselves and the ways they go about doing their jobs.

Make It Personal: FN13–3

1. Which of the political strategy reminders would you find most difficult to do? Explain your reasoning.

I have found two of the five strategy reminders to be most difficult for equity leaders: #3, which says one must reach out to persons diametrically opposed to what you want to achieve, and #5, which says one must have a lot of patience and may need to start slow. In each case, what I discovered was that those who are very strong advocates of equity may be very intolerant of those who don't see things the way they do or don't march to the same drummer, so to speak. Explore with participants the reasons why one or more of the strategy reminders is most difficult for them, and what the implications are for their effectiveness and credibility as an equity advocate. Sometimes being culturally courageous has more to do with conquering personal demons first before working on those which we think are possessed by others or by toxic organizations.

2. What is your experience that confirms or contradicts the statement about how equity transformation initiatives cannot always be attempted on a predetermined timeline?

From my perspective, one of the major anomalies in equity work is the contradictory need to be very focused, specific, driven to achieve specific outcomes, and vigilant in monitoring progress toward achieving them, while at the same time capable of being very existential, flexible, patient, and civil to those who do not embrace an equity vision or the same equity vision as you. In many instances, I have discovered a host of needs that had to be addressed prior to continuing the equity initiative that had begun. Capacity building, especially trust building, has often been a prerequisite that couldn't be slighted. Engage participants in reflecting on "a-ha" moments they have had that woke them up to the need to slow down and be willing to take longer (and work both hard and smart) by adding benchmark targets needing to be achieved during the journey toward greater cultural democracy and equitable educational outcomes in a particular setting. It is extremely important to remember that a change in power and authority is never relinquished. Some will never agree with you and fight you every step of the way, often surreptitiously, and will work even harder against you after you seem to have succeeded. One can never be complacent after achieving your objectives. There is a constant need to build stronger constituencies of support, empowering ever more previously disenfranchised people along the way.

అౢఆ

Chapter 14 Facilitator Notes

Make It Personal: FN14–1

1. Given the three warriors' backgrounds and equity interventions, if they were in your school district, what are the political obstacles they would likely face?

Use this question as a prompt for reviewing the interventions of the three equity warriors. Then encourage volunteers from your group to share obstacles each of the "warriors" would experience if working either in your school district, or working with teachers or administrators in your district who were enrolled in a graduate degree program in educational administration. If the participants would be more comfortable, have them submit anonymous written answers to the question which you can read to the group. Have the participants collectively discuss how to deal with the obstacles read.

Other obstacles faced by equity leaders may be based on the gender or race/cultural background of the leader, because some staff have a more difficult time being receptive when the equity leader is of a different racial/cultural background or when it is a female who is providing direction. In addition, the circumstances surrounding the equity initiative can affect receptivity. If the intervention is being made by an untenured university faculty member, or a new administrator of any background who is seen as someone brought in to turn a school around or get rid of marginal staff, then that dynamic can affect staff receptivity. Some will mask their true feelings to save their jobs. You should discuss these other possible obstacles with your participants for their reaction.

2. Describe the conditions, circumstances, attitudes, and/or behaviors in your school or district that require interventions by "equity warriors," such as those described in this chapter, and also describe the special knowledge, skills, dispositions, and priorities you would want "equity warriors" to have in your work setting.

This question will probably be easy for participants to answer. However, most participants might not mention the need for equity warriors in their school or district who will make interventions to change board of education policies that prevent greater student access to higher level courses, programs, and culturally responsive teaching. Some administrators and teacher bargaining units use board policy as the excuse for not addressing the needs of historically underserved students. Equity warriors might be needed to galvanize community support and lobbying for a change in such board policies. The disposition required for such work would include close connections and high credibility with the community, strong community organizing skills, as well as a close knowledge of all relevant board policies.

෨ඏ෴

Chapter 15 Facilitator Notes

Make It Personal: FN 15–1

1. What have you learned from participating in the role-playing exercise?

There are several parts to the role-playing exercise:

- Directions for participating in the exercise
- Background information on Bethune-Chavez high school
- Salient facts about the school and the situation role players are asked to address

- In-basket items of the "area superintendent," requiring a response
- Skills to be demonstrated when responding to the in-basket items
- Sixteen questions to consider answering when developing your draft action plan for working with BCHS
- Suggested responses to the five in-basket items as well as any of the 16 questions

Engage participants in discussing each part of the exercise, or let them choose the parts to discuss, making sure that at the least the in-basket items and 16 questions are the subject of discussion regarding what they have learned from the role play and how they may be able to use what they have learned in their real job.

2. How has your participation in the role-playing exercise enhanced your understanding of the culturally courageous leadership paradigm?

Encourage participants to feel very free to be as open and honest when answering this question. They may not feel the role play enhanced their understanding at all and may think it further confused them about the paradigm. If that is the case, or not, refer to each component of the paradigm discussed in Chapters 7 through 10 to review how the circumstances in the role play require use of some suggestions in each of those chapters, or you can refer to the suggested responses to any of the 16 questions in Chapter 15. Those suggestions are also designed to show the relevance of the CCL paradigm to the situation in the role play. You might also discuss how all of the background information provided was very purposeful in giving the reader some avenues they could use when responding to the in-basket items or to any of the 16 questions. As before in this facilitator guide, the bottom line is to facilitate participants' openness to "trying on" some of the suggested behaviors of a CCL in their school community, regardless of their role.

Appendix 2

*Culturally Courageous Leadership
Diagnostic Questionnaire for Individuals*

CAUTION! The CCLDQ is for use by persons who have read the text *Walking the Equity Talk: A Guide for Culturally Courageous Leadership in School Communities* by John Robert Browne. **Do not** complete this questionnaire without first reading the text so there is a familiarity with the terms and language used in the diagnostic questionnaire. Persons completing this questionnaire must be totally honest in all responses for the questionnaire to have value.

കൟ

COMPARING YOUR CONCERNS AND PERCEIVED ORGANIZATIONAL NEEDS WITH PERSONAL BELIEFS, PRIORITIES, AND BEHAVIORS

I. From the list of examples below, place a plus (+) beside your *TOP FIVE CONCERNS* about your work setting that you think significantly contribute to *no support* for historically underserved students of color experiencing equitable inputs and outcomes.

EXAMPLES:

A. Little Supervision of Instruction or Coaching of Teachers When Needed

B. Instructional Planning, Instructional Delivery, and Classroom Discipline

C. Inadequate Assessment Practices and Timely Use of Results

D. Biased or Major Omissions in Educational Policies Related To Equity

E. Poor Professional Growth Opportunities and Follow-Up Support

F. Little Adult Accountability for Student Outcomes

G. Relationship Between One's Racial Identity and Achievement, Prejudice, Bias, Discrimination, Stereotyping, Racism, Ethnocentrism, or Other Isms

H. Poor Adult/Adult Relationships, Including Lack of Collaboration and Interpersonal Conflict

I. Poor Adult/Student Relationships, Including Little Trust and Respect, Poor Communication, and Low Expectations

J. Inadequate or Biased Instructional Materials/Technology

K. Poor Allocation and Use of Resources

L. Discriminatory Decision-Making Processes, Power, and Authority Relationships

M. Low Student Motivation, Engagement, and Resilience

N. Poor Problem Definition and Problem-Solving Practices

O. Poor School Climate

P. Unsafe and/or Dirty Physical Environment

Q. Low Student Attendance and High Rates Of Truancy

R. Little Parent Involvement/School–Home Communication/Parent Support

❧◦❦

ORGANIZATIONAL NEEDS IN YOUR WORK ENVIRONMENT RELATED TO ABOVE CONCERNS

II. Place a plus (+) beside the *top three* TOPICS THAT NEED HIGHER PRIORITY in your situation/work environment:

1. Open, honest discussion and problem solving related to eradicating practice of any "isms" in the school.

2. Changing organizational climate in the school that is very negative when it comes to respect for and valuing all human differences and points of view.

3. Collaboration by parents of color and educators on major achievement problems.

4. Minimizing chaos and constant change in schools that are due to major social problems in the community (e.g., illegal drug use, gang warfare, and/or extremely low income), budget cuts, and/or stalemates among board of education members over district priorities.

5. Change in the norms of administrators/teachers who do not effectively work together to address achievement problems or other problems.

6. Increasing awareness and interest in knowing more about how to implement academically rigorous culturally responsive instruction for all students.

7. Giving higher priority to honoring/building on student cultures when trying to improve student outcomes.

8. Providing more support for teachers who need help in effectively addressing the needs of all their students.

9. Participation in cultural politics that supports greater power equalization and respect for human differences.

10. Successfully securing greater community-wide support for equity transformation, including district-level, university faculty, and parent support.

III. Put a plus (+) next to your *top three items* in each category: beliefs/attitudes, priorities, and behaviors, that honestly *describe you* in your current role, and at the end of each plus (+) item assign a rating between 1–10 of the strength you give to each choice, with 1 meaning very low strength, and 10 meaning very high strength:

Your Beliefs/Attitudes: (Select your top three and rate the strength of each.)

1. I have a no-excuses philosophy when it comes to being responsible for student academic success.

2. I am willing to do whatever is necessary to help students in all groups enjoy school and do their best.

3. School administrators must monitor and facilitate improvement in instructional performance as needed.

4. The major reason for low achievement is the failure of educational leaders in schools and school districts.

5. Cultural biases, including racism, ethnocentrism, sexism, and classism, are alive and well in schools.

6. Most causes for the unequal outcomes experienced by many students are based more on what happens in the school, rather than being primarily based on out-of-school factors.

7. There is a lot of cultural dissonance between many parents of color and their children's teachers.

8. Some teachers and school administrators working with Black and Brown students require personal transformation.

9. The historical purpose of schooling in the United States must change for all students to learn at high levels.

10. All teachers and administrators must have better preparation and ongoing support if they are going to provide equity and excellence in the teaching and treatment of historically underserved students.

Your Priorities: (Select your top three and rate the strength of each.)

11. Actively work for more equitable power/authority relationships in school communities.

12. Eliminate cultural dissonance between student racial or socioeconomic subgroups and adult racial or socioeconomic subgroups.

13. Eliminate gaps in any educational outcomes between various racial/ethnic/socioeconomic groups.

14. Work to reduce school and school community violence, including emotional or cultural violence.

15. Contribute to a positive school climate, including goal focus, equitable allocation of resources, good communication, and effective problem solving.

16. Support all future/current educators in becoming culturally courageous instructional leaders.

17. Strongly advocate for culturally responsive and culturally relevant pedagogy in all classrooms.

18. Facilitate the acquisition of 21st century skills by all students at all academic levels in Grades preK–12.

19. Help create a multicultural environment in schools that focuses on the knowledge, skills, and attitudes necessary for effectively communicating with all persons in a culturally diverse global society.

20. Improve open and honest communication, collaboration, and effective conflict management within and across all adult subgroups within the work setting.

Your Behaviors: (Select your top three and rate the strength of each.)

21. Raise questions and concerns and provide examples in large and/or small group settings about policies or poor instructional performance that negatively impact historically underserved students of color.

22. Initiate new courses, programs, or professional development that will help reduce achievement gaps.

23. Publicly disclose and attempt to change my own attitudes, fears, failures, and actions that have contributed to low achievement, either before or simultaneously while trying to influence change in others.

24. Make sure the issue of race is "on the table," and efforts are made to avoid negative consequences for historically underserved students when decisions are made about any area of school and/or district functioning.

25. Engage in meaningful collaboration with persons in other stakeholder groups on an ongoing basis.

26. Privately confront overt bias, prejudice, and/or stereotyping when demonstrated by colleagues.

27. Model the attitudes, behaviors, and teacher or administrative practices desired in others regarding support for achievement at high levels by all student groups.

28. Regularly conduct non-evaluative classroom observations and do follow-up analysis, discussion, and coaching.

29. Demonstrate high expectations for self and all school community stakeholders regarding the academic potential of all students, and express the need for all to support others' display of such expectations.

30. Hold self and others accountable for implementing rigorous and responsive content, performance, delivery, opportunity to learn, and professional development standards in the service of all students.

❧❧

HOW TO INTERPRET THE RESULTS FROM COMPLETING THE CCLDQ FOR INDIVIDUALS

There are four categories into which the eighteen items under CCLDQ "Concerns" fall; the categories and items in each category are as follows:

1. Instructional Leadership: items a, d, f, k, l, n, o

2. Instructional Support: items c, e, j

3. Classroom Instruction: items b, m, q

4. School Climate: items g, h, i, p, r

Each of the 10 items under CCLDQ "Organizational Needs" is listed below as a best match for one or more of the four "concerns" categories.

1. Instructional Leadership: best matched with "Organizational Needs" items 1, 5, 6, 8, 10

2. Instructional Support: best matched with "Organizational Needs" items 2, 3, 6, 7, 8

3. Classroom Instruction: best matched with "Organizational Needs" items 3, 5, 6, 7, 8

4. School Climate: best matched with "Organizational Needs" items 1, 2, 4, 9, 10

Further Directions on How to Interpret Your Results

1. Based on the above information, determine whether there is a match between each of the top five items you selected from the "concerns" list and at least one of the "organizational needs" items listed as best matches.

2. If you selected items from the "concerns" list and "organizational needs" list that aren't best matches, it might suggest your choice of organizational needs should be reconsidered for you to be most effective in achieving your equity goals.

3. You have selected three items that represent your top "beliefs/attitudes" and have rated the degree of strength you give each of these. If your selections are any of the five items listed below, read the cautionary comments about these beliefs/attitudes.
BELIEF ITEMS #2, 4, 7, 8, 10

4. You have selected three items that represent your top "priorities" and have rated the degree of strength you give each of these. If your selections are any of the five items listed below, read the cautionary comments about having these priorities.
PRIORITY ITEMS #11, 12, 16, 19, 20

5. You have selected three items that represent your top "behaviors" and have rated the degree of strength you give each of these. If your selections are any of the five items listed below, read the cautionary comments about these behaviors.
BEHAVIOR ITEMS #23, 24, 26, 27, 30

6. If you gave a number of 7 or below as the strength of any of your top beliefs, priorities, and behaviors, that is a warning sign that your beliefs, priorities, and/or behaviors are not as strong as those needed by culturally courageous leaders.

7. A correlation exists between two examples of "concerns" ("a" and "o" in the above list) with select organizational needs, beliefs, priorities, and behaviors. See below for more information.

ȣȡ

CAUTIONARY COMMENTS ABOUT SELECT "BELIEF," "PRIORITY," AND "BEHAVIOR" ITEMS IN THE CCLDQ

All of the cautionary comments about the items below have a common thread among them, namely that select statements in each category are purposefully written as stereotypes, as generalizations, or have strong potential of exacerbating cultural tensions and contributing to toxic environments. A major assumption here is that to be cautious is a characteristic of exercising good judgment, especially given the history of race/cultural relations in the United States. The intent of the items being in the CCLDQ is to diagnose whether the person taking the CCLDQ will embrace loosely stated beliefs, priorities, or behaviors that might compromise their ability to help improve cultural democracy, social justice, and equitable educational outcomes by historically underserved students. Culturally courageous leaders should not model attitudes, behaviors, or thinking habits that are counterproductive to achieving commitment to the purpose of the paradigm. Equity opponents often look for examples of poor judgment by equity advocates, in order to solidify the power of their resistance to social justice efforts. The cautionary comments about an item are not meant to mean the item should not have been chosen, only that one should exercise caution when trying to act upon the statement as written. Many equity advocates embrace such statements or behaviors, but when questioned cannot define what the comment means to them or what they must do based on embracing the statement. After the reader selects these statements or others in the CCLDQ, he or she should rewrite them so they are more measureable and observable, with greater accountability being possible.

Belief Statements

Item #2

"I am willing to do whatever is necessary to help students in all groups enjoy school and do their best"

The phrases "whatever is necessary," "all groups," "enjoy school," and "do their best" are very general, lack specific focus, and are impossible to ascertain if achieved.

You also need to think about what you would mean by saying "whatever is necessary." That phrase could be interpreted by adversaries to mean you are willing to take actions that go well beyond the parameters of good decorum and respect for everyone's rights as well as actions that are not in the best interests of those you are attempting to help. In addition, if you are willing to help students in *all* groups enjoy school, you need to make sure you are conversant about the life experiences, strengths, interests, and needs of students in all demographic groups, and are willing to reconcile antidemocratic dynamics between those who appear to have competing interests, values and needs. "Enjoy school" can be interpreted in various ways, especially by persons of diverse cultural backgrounds. Much more specificity is needed.

Item #4

"The major reason for low achievement is the failure of educational leaders in schools and school districts."

As stated for the previous item, the phrases "low achievement," and "educational leaders" are very general, without specific focus, and impossible to ascertain if achieved. For example, do you mean school site and district-level administrators, or do you also include parent, teacher, community, and instructional support staff leaders? You also need to have thought through what you mean by "failure," and your specific reasons for characterizing educational leaders as "failures."In other words, what do you want educational leaders, however you define that term, to do differently than what they are doing at the present time? Also note that the statement does not say "low student achievement," and could also refer to the low achievement of teachers or other groups.

Item #7

"There is a lot of cultural dissonance between many parents of color and their children's teachers."

Although there are studies (see *Effort and Excellence in Urban Classrooms: Expecting—And Getting—Success With All Students* by Corbett, Wilson, & Williams, 2002) that support the germ of the thought in the above statement, as written it is a major stereotype and generalization, so if you strongly believe it, you need to revise the sentence so it is more specific to your experience. The words "parents of color" is much too broad a characterization that makes the sentence inaccurate on its face. Nevertheless, it is important to ascertain the perspectives of teachers and historically underserved parents about any tensions between them and the origins of the tensions wherever they exist.

Item #8

"Some teachers and school administrators working with Black and Brown students require personal transformation."

This is a generalization that may or may not be true in specific contexts. However, if a person embraces this belief without having a concrete definition of "personal transformation," such as the beliefs and/or behaviors that need to be 'transformed' because of the documented negative impact on students, then the statement can be a major stereotype. Standing alone, the statement also ignores whether some students and parents may also require personal transformation, however that is defined.

Item #10

"All teachers and administrators must have better preparation and ongoing support if they are going to provide equity and excellence in the teaching and treatment of historically underserved students of color."

Like the above statements, saying "*all* teachers and administrators" is a generalization, and the term "equity and excellence" is a very imprecise term even though the term is commonly used as code for a host of specific attitudes, behaviors, policies, and institutional norms. The term "ongoing support" is also very ambiguous, because what one person might consider as ongoing support would not be characterized that way by another.

Priority Statements

Item #11

"Actively work for more equitable power/authority relationships in school communities."

What does it mean to "actively work" for more "equitable power/authority" relationships? Again, the phrases are very ambiguous, unless they are backed up with specific observable measurable actions. Chart 6a in Chapter 6 identifies 10 barriers to equitable student outcomes, one of which is that the strengths of various school community stakeholders are not adequately utilized and staff input is not sought on major decisions affecting them. You need to be much more specific in your thinking when you say you will work for more equitable power/authority relationships. Culturally courageous leaders must be more precise in their language and laserlike in their needs assessment and actions taken if they are to model the level of accountability needed to achieve equitable educational outcomes.

Item #12

"Eliminate cultural dissonance between student racial or socioeconomic subgroups and adult racial or socioeconomic subgroups."

"Cultural dissonance" can mean many things. School leaders who tackle this condition must be as clear as possible about what kinds of dissonance they want to eliminate, and the collaborative efforts among all stakeholder groups that will be necessary to be even mildly successful. Cultural dissonance may also be a more polite term for much stronger deep-seated biases and even racist or ethnocentric practices. It is better to "call a spade a spade" when it comes to whether the cross-cultural dynamics reflect cultural dissonance or something much stronger. Only then will it be possible to develop the most appropriate strategies.

Item #16

"Support all future/current educators in becoming culturally courageous instructional leaders."

"Support" is a word that is usually more in the mind of the subject more than the eye of the beholder. Choosing this priority is again like motherhood and apple pie; in other words, almost all like the concept of support, but the devil is in the details. It is important to have priorities with explicit language, leaving less to chance and less ambiguity in terms used. Again, saying "all" future/current educators is a warning sign of not being serious or being totally unrealistic. Most of the examples provided in this guide for culturally courageous leadership have an instructional base because of the overarching purpose of the paradigm, which is equitable educational inputs and outcomes for historically underserved students. Again, equitable is not the same as equal. Equitable is based on what is needed, not everyone getting the same amount of attention to their needs. So the implication is that effective instructional leaders must exemplify cultural courageousness, which is a journey, not a destination. It is not possible to be an effective instructional leader without being culturally courageous, especially if the litmus test is based on what is happening for historically underserved students of color.

Item #19

"Help create a multicultural environment in schools that focuses on the knowledge, skills, and attitudes necessary for effectively communicating with all persons in a culturally diverse global society"

One caution, should one choose this priority, is that the impression is given there is consensus among cultural diversity scholars on what knowledge, skills, and attitudes are necessary for effectively communicating with all persons in a culturally diverse global society. The phrase "global society" is also a signal for caution, since that is infinitely more complex than effectively communicating with all persons in the United States, even though all citizens in the United States have national and ethnic roots from nations throughout the world. But it is not the same or as complex as effectively communicating with all persons in our global society. The phrase "creating a multicultural environment" should also give one pause unless one is prepared to work with all stakeholder groups in developing the learning, social, and psychological conditions that facilitate collective commitment to effective cross cultural communication becoming a major purpose of schooling. Many schools in the United States give lip service to this being a goal, but the follow-through varies considerably from school to school.

Item #20

"Improve open and honest communication, collaboration, and effective conflict management within and across all adult subgroups within the work setting."

If selecting this priority, one should be mindful that in some situations there will be differences or "biases" within subgroups, when it comes to educational philosophy and attitudes toward those perceived as "different" others. These differences within groups often end up with people just agreeing to disagree, because they strongly resist any efforts to be more respectful or open to other points of view. Therefore, any attempt to improve communication, collaboration, and conflict management within subgroups (e.g., racial, ethnic, age, religious, gender, job category groups) will likely require you to define what is meant by the terms, and also be prepared to engage in this effort over the long haul. For example, attitudes about what student behavior justifies a suspension from class can often cause major conflicts between students, teachers, administrators and parents. Adult fears, often unstated, or the absolute belief that some people have about what they think is "right," can cause verbal and even physical attacks on others, because of being entrenched in their perspectives. In many cases, it requires using both position and personal power to achieve this priority, and without adequate attention to strengthening one's leverage (i.e., influence) beforehand, success will be very difficult. Adult/adult value conflicts are one of the primary barriers to achievement at high levels by all student groups. When adults do not respect each other or get along, the students are the losers. Having said all of this, it doesn't mean the above priority statement is unwise to choose; it does mean that you need to have your eyes wide open when undertaking this task.

Personal Behaviors

Item #23

"Publicly disclose and attempt to change my own attitudes, fears, failures, actions that have contributed to low achievement, either before or simultaneously while trying to influence change in others."

It is important to model self-disclosure but do so prudently and appropriately. Another caution is to not attempt to prematurely influence biased attitudes and behaviors of others, before making sure sufficient "unfreezing" of deeply felt biases has occurred in group. For example, through frequent solicitation of reactions, concerns, and suggestions from those who are engaged in courageous conversations about race, and through drawing relationships between such conversations and specifics of the teaching and learning process, it is more likely you will be able to make more informed decisions about when people are ready to move to the next level.

Item #24

"Make sure the issue of race is 'on the table,' and efforts are made to avoid negative consequences for historically underserved students when decisions are made about any area of school and/or district functioning."

This equity initiative, while needed for cultural democracy and social justice to be advanced, is very rarely undertaken and if done correctly would be a signature example of culturally courageous leadership. Singleton and Linton (2006) discuss the need for keeping the focus on race in their book *Courageous Conversations About Race.* I am suggesting such focus needs to occur when very specific issues are addressed or decisions made, such as personnel decisions, staff assignments, student class assignments, scheduling, tracking, protocol development for student study teams and special education assignments, curriculum adoptions, professional development, student services, disciplinary practices, student assessments (i.e., testing and evaluation), facilities planning, maintenance and operations, performance supervision and evaluation, budgetary decisions, allocation of resources, academic enrichment and academic support programs, strategic planning, extracurricular activities, and so on. In other words, if a district is truly committed to equitable inputs and student outcomes, the impact on historically underserved students should be considered and influence the decision-making process for all areas of school and district functioning. However, one should be cautious before engaging in such behavior because doing so precipitously could cause a major political backlash, be a very risky undertaking, and be counterproductive if there hasn't been adequate preparation of all in the school community beforehand. Those who may need to have a chance to give their input on whether and how this (i.e., keeping "race" on the table) will occur include the board of education; executive administrators; middle management (e.g., program and site administrators); bargaining units; teachers; parents; student leaders; and key school community representatives.

Item #26

"Privately confront overt bias, prejudice, and/or stereotyping when demonstrated by colleagues."

This is similar to the above item in that it is a hallmark of being culturally courageous and could be instrumental in helping set an entirely new ethos around accountability for response to human differences of all kinds, but how it is done is of the utmost importance. Therefore, caution is essential, and this kind of feedback should likely occur only when sought, requested, or has already become a part of "the way things are done." New norms for desirable behavior need to be first put in place, or as indicated above, this behavior can cause a volatile reaction, even between supervisor and supervisee. Ideally this behavior should be practiced during professional development training before becoming a norm. "Privately confront" is a key phrase.

Item #27

"Model the attitudes, behaviors, and teacher or administrative practices desired in others regarding support for achievement at high levels by all student groups."

This behavior is more easily said than done. In the guide, I have previously stated that ardent equity advocates are sometimes their own worst enemy, in that they do not practice what they preach. However, one needs to come off as genuinely authentic when supposedly modeling practices desired in others. If they are not totally committed to the equity goals being espoused, then any attempt at modeling may be perceived as phony and duplicitous. That may be the case even when one is sincere, so caution should be exercised in not overdoing it and not allowing others who purposefully try to test your commitment to cause you to say or do things you will later regret. It is imperative that those trying to walk the equity talk not be sanctimonious or condescending in their interactions with others.

Item #30

"Hold self and others accountable for implementing rigorous and responsive content, performance, delivery, opportunity to learn, and professional development standards in the service of all students."

One should exercise caution in how the five categories of standards are discussed, advocated, or pursued, because there are lots of caveats regarding the validity and reliability of whether commitment to these standards categories will significantly contribute to equitable educational outcomes. Content standards, even the most recent national content standards for core academic subjects, are still basically very Eurocentric. If performance standards continue in large measure to be state determined, or even if national performance assessments are ultimately developed, the results of such assessments will likely be heavily influenced by how they are implemented at local levels. Also, the assessments in the humanities (i.e., English language arts and history/social studies) will probably not be culturally responsive, meaning students will not be assessed on knowledge that is based on the cultural funds of knowledge from various cultural/ethnic perspectives represented in the general population. If this is true, the likely result will be that European students will have advantages over other students, as is the current situation, because what is assessed will be content from their cultural heritage. There is no agreement on what the delivery and opportunity to learn standards should be, with the result that their use is very uneven across the United States. The same applies to professional development standards. In very hard economic times like the present, some of the first things cut are program supports that fall into the latter three standards categories. So although this behavior is also very important and characteristic of a culturally courageous leader, it must be undertaken with full awareness of the constraints, but it should still be a priority if one is fully committed to achieving equitable inputs and outcomes for historically underserved students.

❧

CORRELATION BETWEEN TWO "CONCERNS" ("A" AND "O" IN THE CCLDQ) WITH SELECT ORGANIZATIONAL NEEDS, BELIEFS, PRIORITIES, AND BEHAVIORS

Items "A" and item "O" under I. in the CCLDQ above (the list of 18 concerns, A–R, from which you selected your top five) are correlated with items you should have considered under II. in the CCLDQ (the list of 10 organizational needs in your work environment from which you selected your top three) and with items under III. in the CCLDQ (the lists of 10 beliefs/attitudes, 10 priorities, and 10 behaviors from which you selected your top three in each list). The purpose of showing you this correlation is because I have found items "A" and "O" to be two of the major barriers to high achievement in every low-performing school (see Chapter 6 of the guide) where I was a district administrator, education consultant, or external evaluator. The process I used to determine the correlations below included shadowing the principal, observing classroom instruction and staff meetings, examination of school records, confidential individual and small group interviews, and the results of surveys I developed and administered.

Item "A" states "LITTLE SUPERVISION OF INSTRUCTION OR COACHING OF TEACHERS WHEN NEEDED." This condition is highly correlated with ALL of the 10 items under II. in the CCLDQ, titled "Organizational Needs in Your Work Environment." In other words, in low-performing schools where I personally worked as an external evaluator, all of the topics listed under organizational needs needed to receive higher priority than they were receiving. In addition, of the 10 "Beliefs" listed under III. in the CCLDQ, I found numbers 1, 3, 6, and 9 to be the most important for improvement of the above condition "A." Of the 10 "Priorities" listed in the CCLDQ, I found numbers 13, 17, and 18 to be the most needed for improvement of the above condition "A." Finally, of the 10 "Behaviors" listed in the CCLDQ, I found numbers 27, 28, and 30 to be the most critical for improvement of the above condition "A."

Item "O" states "POOR SCHOOL CLIMATE." This condition is highly correlated with items 1, 2, 3, 5, 8, 9, and 10 under II. of the CCLDQ titled "Organizational Needs in Your Work Environment." Again, in low-performing schools where I personally worked as an external evaluator, the above numbered topics needed to receive higher priority than they were receiving. In addition, of the 10 "Beliefs" listed under III. in the CCLDQ, I found numbers 5, 7, and 10 to be the most important for improvement of the above condition "O." Of the 10 "Priorities" listed in the CCLDQ, I found numbers 12, 14, 15, 19, and 20 to be the most needed for improvement of the above condition "O." Finally, of the 10 "Behaviors" listed in the CCLDQ, I found numbers 23, 24, 25, 26, and 27 to be the most critical. If you selected either of these concerns, "A" or "O," as among your top five, you may or may not perceive the above mentioned organizational needs, beliefs, priorities, and behaviors to be the most needed in your work context. Keep in mind the cautionary statements I made about embracing several of these items. This information is only meant to provide you with some perspective on what may need to be addressed if instructional supervision and school climate are major concerns in your educational setting, given the inequitable educational outcomes of historically underserved students of color.

Culturally Courageous Leadership Diagnostic Questionnaire: School Learning Environment

CCLDQ/SLE

CAUTION!! The CCLDQ is for use by persons who have read the text *Walking the Equity Talk: A Guide for Culturally Courageous Leadership in School Communities*, by John Robert Browne. **Do not** complete this questionnaire without first reading the text or receiving a briefing on the meaning of major terms used, so there is a familiarity with the language used in the diagnostic questionnaire. In addition, persons completing the questionnaire must be totally honest in all responses for the questionnaire to have value.

෴

INTRODUCTION

The CCLDQ/SLE is a 60-item diagnostic instrument designed to assist schools in determining how staff, as well as representative parents and community persons, feel about how the school is doing in several areas that are critical for achieving equitable educational outcomes. The CCLDQ/SLE can also be used to determine where there is the greatest need for culturally courageous leadership in the school community. The items are all based on key topics addressed throughout the guide, either when discussing societal and schooling conditions that reflect cultural hegemony, institutional biases and barriers, or when discussing how culturally courageous leadership can help ameliorate these conditions. The CCLDQ/SLE is another form for determining the needs of your school. It is *strongly* recommended it only be used with persons who have read or been briefed on definitions of key terms in the guide.

   DIRECTIONS: Indicate with a √ in the appropriate column the extent to which you perceive each statement is highly accurate to not at all accurate for your school. You may only check *one* category for each item.

In my school,	Highly Accurate	Mostly Accurate	Do Not Know	Moderately Accurate	Not at All Accurate
1. There is little discussion with students and teachers about influences on their personal and racial identities/ self-esteem.					
2. We don't adequately help students or teachers to deal with peer pressure and racial/cultural conflict.					
3. Students are rarely helped to increase their understanding of relationships between life experiences, racial/cultural conflict, and personal identities.					
4. The hidden curriculum, including teacher expectations and discipline practices, has a negative impact on our low-achieving students.					
5. The increase in student diversity is a major challenge for many staff as well as a strain on limited resources.					
6. The prejudicial attitudes and biases in the larger community have major influence on what happens in school.					
7. We have major problems when it comes to the background and/or lifestyle of all students being respected.					
8. Meeting the learning needs and providing the support needed by all students and teachers sometimes seems like an overwhelming task impossible to achieve.					
9. There is almost exclusive emphasis in the curriculum on teaching the American Eurocentric culture and its origins.					
10. Most teachers have not been adequately prepared in their credential programs to identify and not fall prey to participating in transparent or institutionalized racism.					
11. There are no efforts to implement schoolwide transformation that is aimed at improving social justice in the community.					
12. The cultural politics is intense between different interest groups over what will be taught, to whom it will be taught, what support services will be provided, and how available funds will be spent.					
13. There are conflicting opinions on how to address the needs of African and Latino/a American students to be taught at high levels, and whether this can be achieved.					
14. Some teachers and some parents fear or distrust each other.					

In my school,	Highly Accurate	Mostly Accurate	Do Not Know	Moderately Accurate	Not at All Accurate
15. Some teachers fear some students.					
16. Some persons in two or more stakeholder groups fear losing their status and privilege.					
17. Delivery, opportunity to learn, and professional development standards are given less attention and resources than content and performance standards.					
18. Team and trust building to improve communication, collaboration, and conflict management occurs, and includes all administrators, instructional staff, and parent/community representatives.					
19. There is little attention in the curriculum to institutional racism or other forms of social injustice in the United States, past or present.					
20. Major criteria for selection of teachers include whether they possess cultural knowledge, culturally responsive teaching skills, and positive dispositions toward culturally/racially diverse students.					
21. Administrators engage in frequent classroom observation, during which they identify "problems of practice" related to achieving equitable educational outcomes.					
22. Classroom supervision is followed by one-on-one coaching, small group problem solving, or other forms of professional development on how to improve effectiveness with students at the lower end of the achievement continuum.					
23. Some teachers share in the distributed leadership for improving instructional effectiveness, resource allocation, and accountability for educational outcomes.					
24. Whenever there are concerns about or allegations of discriminatory practices being experienced by historically underserved students of color, parents are frequently dissatisfied with the response.					
25. There is no professional development on how to implement culturally responsive teaching or culturally relevant curriculum.					
26. The home language of students is used as a bridge for facilitating mastery of school language, that is, standard academic English.					

(Continued)

(Continued)

In my school,	Highly Accurate	Mostly Accurate	Do Not Know	Moderately Accurate	Not at All Accurate
27. Parent involvement is defined only in terms of what happens at school.					
28. Ongoing efforts are made to nurture strong communication with and respect for all parents, including opportunities for parent leadership in a variety of roles.					
29. Teachers use research-based best practices, such as academically rigorous culturally responsive teaching, standards-based culturally relevant curriculum, and frequent checking for understanding in a variety of ways.					
30. Inadequate help is given to teachers who demonstrate weak instructional and classroom management with their low-achieving students of color.					
31. Greater emphasis is given to teaching the prescribed curriculum to all students than is given to adapting the curriculum to meet student needs.					
32. The students who consistently have low time on task or are not successfully engaged in instruction are considered the problem more than the methods used by the teacher.					
33. Improving staff cohesion and goal focus related to equity is not a priority.					
34. There is little collaborative problem solving on the achievement of Black and Latino/a students.					
35. Teacher disciplinary referrals, special education referrals, suspensions, and dropouts are disproportionately African and Latino American male students.					
36. The attitudes about being accountable for the educational outcomes of students from low-income families need to be improved.					
37. There is a sense of urgency about the need to improve accountability for school–parent partnerships and achievement at high levels by all student subgroups.					

In my school,	Highly Accurate	Mostly Accurate	Do Not Know	Moderately Accurate	Not at All Accurate
38. The personal and collective beliefs of many school staff about Black and Latino/a students and parents/guardians are counterproductive to fostering achievement at high levels.					
39. There are norms in how some administrators and staff go about doing their job that serve as barriers to high achievement.					
40. There is shared leadership by all stakeholder groups on equity initiatives, including representative students, parents, and select higher education faculty in teacher and administrator preparation programs.					
41. School staff have a no-excuses attitude about facilitating the achievement of all students at high levels.					
42. There are only a few committed staff who see themselves as caregivers and consistently work on behalf of historically underserved students.					
43. Staff are always seeking to increase their personal knowledge about diverse cultures so they can apply their insights when working with students and other adults.					
44. Most teachers expect the administrators to handle all conflicts between adults, adults and students, or students with students.					
45. There are several persons who are always encouraging and helping others to work on behalf of social justice and equitable educational outcomes.					
46. The district leadership provides direction and support for our equity initiatives, and we are part of a plan for districtwide systemic equity transformation.					
47. There aren't any culturally diverse multi-ethnic coalitions that actively lobby community members and policymakers to support equity initiatives.					
48. No one publicly challenges/contradicts any mistruths or slanderous comments made about those who speak out about and encourage change in biased attitudes or practices.					

(Continued)

(Continued)

In my school,	Highly Accurate	Mostly Accurate	Do Not Know	Moderately Accurate	Not at All Accurate
49. There doesn't seem to be anyone who tries to improve poor interpersonal communication, especially when it comes to discussing what needs to be done to achieve equity in student outcomes.					
50. Sometimes the people who are most capable and motivated to develop and implement equity initiatives are not chosen for these roles.					
51. There is inadequate training for all staff and parent representatives on culturally responsive teaching, cultural proficiency, and courageous conversations about race.					
52. There are only cosmetic efforts to facilitate the personal transformation of staff so they have more cultural consciousness and commitment to student equitable outcomes.					
53. There have been initiatives to improve the use of data to drive instruction, but there is little or no follow-up support on how to adapt instruction based on the data.					
54. Proactive explorations of whether there are any biased practices related to cultural/racial differences are not done.					
55. Many staff do not demonstrate a sense of urgency about significantly reducing or eliminating student achievement gaps.					
56. Ongoing efforts are made to give all students equitable access to teaching at high levels.					
57. The performance evaluations of instructional staff do not include any reference to the need for improvement in student educational outcomes.					
58. Benchmark targets in school plans for improving student achievement are not specific enough to be rigorously monitored by a diverse group of stakeholders.					
59. School improvements related to equity focus on attitudes, values, biases, and barriers to high achievement as much as on new programs and support services.					
60. Students, parents, community persons, and higher education faculty in teacher or administrator preparation programs are seldom if ever involved in helping us achieve equitable educational outcomes.					

ॐ

INSTRUCTIONS ON HOW TO
COMPUTE THE SCHOOL SCORE FROM THE CCLDQ/SLE

1. Using the scoring sheet (below) for the CCLDQ/SLE, determine the assigned points for your responses to each of the 60 items, and compute the total number of points for all the 4's, 3's, 2's, and 1's.

2. The total for all of the 4's is your base score.

3. The totals for all of the 3's and 2's are your contingent scores, which must be added into one number and then divided by 2. That number should be added to the total for all of the 1's, and is your deficit score. Answers in the third column, titled "Do Not Know," are not assigned points.

4. The deficit score should be subtracted from the base score and that is your individual final score. The individual final score of each person in the same school community should be added, and then divided by the number of persons completing the diagnostic questionnaire. That score is your SCHOOL SCORE.

5. Interpretation of the School Score:
   - If the school score is 125 or higher, the school has an urgent need for implementing all components of CCL to discuss the 20 issues of greatest interest in the CCLDQ/SLE, starting with seven issues in priority order as determined by all respondents.
   - If the school score is 100 or higher, then the school should at the least use all components of CCL to discuss 10 or more issues in the CCLDQ/SLE, starting with five issues in priority order as determined by all respondents.
   - If the school score is between 50 and 99, the school should identify at least five issues in the CCLDQ/SLE to discuss what will improve cultural democracy and equitable outcomes, starting with three issues in priority order as determined by all respondents.
   - Do not try to address too many issues at the same time; prioritize your top 20, 10, or 5 issues.
   - The disaggregated scores of subgroups should also be compared (e.g., teachers, parents, race and cultural groups, grade-level or subject area teachers, community persons).
   - If more than 20% of those taking the CCLDQ/SLE have responded to 10 or more items as "do not know," then there should be discussions with all respondents about items that had this response.
   - All respondents should consider discussing the five items that received the largest number of "4's," since those items most likely represent topics that need the most attention.

CCLDQ Scoring Sheet In my school,	Highly Accurate	Mostly Accurate	Do Not Know	Moderately Accurate	Not at All Accurate
1. There is little discussion with students about influences on their personal and racial identities/self-esteem.	4	3	0	2	1
2. We don't adequately help students or teachers to deal with peer pressure and racial/cultural conflict.	4	3	0	2	1
3. Students are rarely helped to increase their understanding of relationships between life experiences, racial/cultural conflict, and personal identities.	4	3	0	2	1
4. The hidden curriculum, including teacher expectations and discipline practices, has a negative impact on low-achieving students.	4	3	0	2	1
5. The increase in student diversity is a major challenge for many staff, as well as a strain on limited resources.	4	3	0	2	1
6. The prejudicial attitudes and biases in the larger community have major influence on what happens in school.	4	3	0	2	1
7. We have major problems when it comes to the background and/or lifestyle of all students being respected.	4	3	0	2	1
8. Meeting the learning needs and providing the support needed by all students and teachers sometimes seems like an overwhelming task impossible to achieve.	4	3	0	2	1
9. There is almost exclusive emphasis in the curriculum on teaching the American Eurocentric culture and its origins.	4	3	0	2	1
10. Most teachers have not been adequately prepared in their credential programs to identify and not fall prey to participating in transparent or institutionalized racism.	4	3	0	2	1
11. There are no efforts to implement schoolwide transformation that is aimed at improving social justice in the community.	4	3	0	2	1
12. The cultural politics is intense between different interest groups over what will be taught, to whom it will be taught, what support services will be provided to which students, and how available funds will be spent.	4	3	0	2	1
13. There are conflicting opinions about how to address the needs of African and Latino/a American students to be taught at high levels, and whether this can be achieved.	4	3	0	2	1

CCLDQ Scoring Sheet In my school,	Highly Accurate	Mostly Accurate	Do Not Know	Moderately Accurate	Not at All Accurate
14. Some teachers and some parents fear or distrust each other.	4	3	0	2	1
15. Some teachers fear some students.	4	3	0	2	1
16. Some persons in two or more stakeholder groups fear losing their status and privilege.	4	3	0	2	1
17. Delivery, opportunity to learn, and professional development standards are given less attention and resources than content and performance standards.	4	3	0	2	1
18. Team and trust building to improve communication, collaboration, and conflict management occur, and include all administrators, instructional staff, and parent/community representatives.	1	2	0	3	4
19. There is little attention in the curriculum to institutional racism or other forms of social injustice in the United States, past or present.	4	3	0	2	1
20. Major criteria used for selection of teachers include whether they possess cultural knowledge, culturally responsive teaching skills, and positive dispositions toward culturally/racially diverse students.	1	2	0	3	4
21. Administrators engage in frequent classroom observation, during which they identify "problems of practice" related to achieving equitable educational outcomes.	1	2	0	3	4
22. Classroom supervision is followed by one-on-one coaching, small group problem solving, or other forms of professional development on how to improve effectiveness with students at the lower end of the achievement continuum.	1	2	0	3	4
23. Some teachers share in the distributed leadership for improving instructional effectiveness, resource allocation, and accountability for educational outcomes.	1	2	0	3	4
24. Whenever there are concerns about or allegations of discriminatory practices being experienced by historically underserved students of color, parents are frequently dissatisfied with the response.	4	3	0	2	1
25. There is no professional development on how to implement culturally responsive teaching or culturally relevant curriculum.	4	3	0	2	1

(Continued)

(Continued)

CCLDQ Scoring Sheet In my school,	Highly Accurate	Mostly Accurate	Do Not Know	Moderately Accurate	Not at All Accurate
26. The home language of students is used as a bridge for facilitating mastery of school language, that is, standard academic English.	1	2	0	3	4
27. Parent involvement is defined only in terms of what happens at school.	4	3	0	2	1
28. Ongoing efforts are made to nurture strong communication with and respect for all parents and guardians, including opportunities for leadership in a variety of roles.	1	2	0	3	4
29. Teachers use research-based best practices, such as academically rigorous culturally responsive teaching, standards-based culturally relevant curriculum, and frequent checking for understanding in a variety of ways.	1	2	0	3	4
30. Inadequate help is given to teachers who demonstrate weak instructional and classroom management with their low-achieving students of color.	4	3	0	2	1
31. Greater emphasis is given to teaching the prescribed curriculum to all students, than is given to adapting the curriculum to meet student needs.	4	3	0	2	1
32. The students who consistently have low time on task or are not successfully engaged in instruction are considered the problem more than the methods used by the teacher.	4	3	0	2	1
33. Improving staff cohesion and goal focus related to equity is not a priority.	4	3	0	2	1
34. There is little collaborative problem solving on the achievement of Black and Latino/a students.	4	3	0	2	1
35. Teacher disciplinary referrals, special education referrals, suspensions, and dropouts are disproportionately African and Latino American male students.	4	3	0	2	1
36. The attitudes about being accountable for the educational outcomes of students from low-income families need to be improved.	4	3	0	2	1
37. There is a sense of urgency about the need to improve accountability for school-home partnerships and achievement at high levels by all student subgroups.	1	2	0	3	4

CCLDQ Scoring Sheet In my school,	Highly Accurate	Mostly Accurate	Do Not Know	Moderately Accurate	Not at All Accurate
38. The personal and collective beliefs of many school staff about Black and Latino/a students and parents/guardians are counterproductive to fostering achievement at high levels.	4	3	0	2	1
39. There are norms in how some administrators and staff go about doing their job that serve as barriers to high achievement.	4	3	0	2	1
40. There is shared leadership by all stakeholder groups on equity initiatives, including representative students, parents, and select higher education faculty in teacher and administrator preparation programs.	1	2	0	3	4
41. School staff have a no-excuses attitude about facilitating the achievement of all students at high levels.	1	2	0	3	4
42. There are only a few committed staff who see themselves as caregivers and consistently work on behalf of historically underserved students.	4	3	0	2	1
43. Staff are always seeking to increase their personal knowledge about diverse cultures so they can apply their insights when working with students and other adults.	1	2	0	3	4
44. Most teachers expect the administrators to handle all conflicts between adults, adults and students, or students with students.	4	3	0	2	1
45. There are several persons who are always encouraging and helping others to work on behalf of social justice and equitable educational outcomes.	1	2	0	3	4
46. The district leadership provides direction and support for our equity initiatives, and we are part of a plan for districtwide systemic equity transformation.	1	2	0	3	4
47. There aren't any culturally diverse multi-ethnic coalitions that actively lobby community members and policymakers to support equity initiatives.	4	3	0	2	1
48. No one publicly challenges/contradicts any mistruths or slanderous comments made about those who speak out about or encourage change in biased attitudes or practices.	4	3	0	2	1
49. There doesn't seem to be anyone who tries to improve poor interpersonal communication, especially when it comes to discussing what needs to be done to achieve equity in student outcomes.	4	3	0	2	1

(Continued)

(Continued)

CCLDQ Scoring Sheet In my school,	Highly Accurate	Mostly Accurate	Do Not Know	Moderately Accurate	Not at All Accurate
50. Sometimes the people who are most capable and motivated to develop and implement equity initiatives are not chosen for these roles.	4	3	0	2	1
51. There is inadequate training for all staff and parent representatives on culturally responsive teaching, cultural proficiency, and courageous conversations about race.	4	3	0	2	1
52. There are only cosmetic efforts to facilitate the personal transformation of staff so they have more cultural consciousness and commitment to student equitable outcomes.	4	3	0	2	1
53. There have been initiatives to improve the use of data to drive instruction, but there is little or no follow-up support on how to adapt instruction based on the data.	4	3	0	2	1
54. Proactive explorations of whether there are any biased practices related to cultural/racial differences are not done.	4	3	0	2	1
55. Many staff don't demonstrate a sense of urgency about significantly reducing or eliminating student achievement gaps.	4	3	0	2	1
56. Ongoing efforts are made to give all students equitable access to teaching at high levels.	1	2	0	3	4
57. The performance evaluations of instructional staff do not include any reference to the need for improvement in student educational outcomes.	4	3	0	2	1
58. Benchmark targets in school plans for improving student achievement are not specific enough to be rigorously monitored by a diverse group of stakeholders.	4	3	0	2	1
59. School improvements related to equity focus on attitudes, values, biases, and barriers to high achievement as much as on new programs and support services.	1	2	0	3	4
60. Students, parents, community persons, and higher education faculty in teacher or administrator preparation programs are seldom if ever involved in helping us achieve equitable educational outcomes.	4	3	0	2	1

References

Introduction to the Guide

Achieving equity in special education: History, status, and current challenges, exceptional children (n.d). Retrieved from http://theapple.monster.com/benefits/articles/3615-achieving-equity-in-special-education-history-status-and-current-challenges?page=4.

Artz, L., & Murphy, B. A. (2000). *Cultural hegemony in the United States.* Thousand Oaks, CA: Sage.

Balfanz, R. (2009). Can the American high school become an avenue of advancement for all? *Future of Children, 19,* 1, 17–36.

Cataldi, E. F., & Kewal Ramani, A. (2009). *High school dropout and completion rates in the United States, 2007.* Washington, DC: National Center for Education Statistics. Retrieved from http://nces.ed.gov/pubs2009/2009064.pdf.

Dicker, S. J. (2008). U.S. immigrants and the dilemma of anglo-conformity, *Socialism and Democracy, 22*(3), 52–74.

Education Week. (2001). *Technology counts 2001: The new divides.* Bethesda, MD: Author.

Ferri, B. A., & Connor, D. J. (2005). Tools of exclusion: Race, disability, and (re) segregated education, *Teachers College Record, 107*(3), 453–474.

Gordon, R., Piana, L. D., & Keleher, T. (2000). *Tracking and other curriculum issues. Facing the consequences: An examination of racial discrimination in U.S. public schools.* Oakland, CA: Applied Research Center. Retrieved from http://www.arc.org/pdf/196apdf.pdf.

Greene, J. P., & Winters, M. A. (2006). *Leaving boys behind: Public high school graduation rates.* New York, NY: Manhattan Institute for Policy Research, Center for Civic Innovation.

Gregory, A., Skiba, R. J., & Noguera, P. A. (2010). The achievement gap and the discipline gap: Two sides of the same coin? *Educational Researcher, 39,* 59–68.

Harry, B., & Klingner, J. (2006). *Why are so many minority students in special education: Understanding race and disability in schools.* New York, NY: Teachers College Press.

Haycock, K., & Hanushek, E. A. (2010). An effective teacher in every classroom. *Education Next, 10*(3). Retrieved from http://educationnext.org/an-effective-teacher-in-every-classroom/.

Johnson, C., Lessem, A., Bergquist, C., Carmichael, D., & Whitten, G. (2000). *Disproportionate representation of minority children in special education.* College Station, TX. Public Policy Research Institute, Texas A & M University.

Knaus, C. (2007). *Still segregated, still unequal. The state of black America, 2007, portrait of the black male.* New York, NY: National Urban League.

Lewis, S., Simon, C., Uzzell, R., Horwitz, A., & Casserly, M. (2010). *A call for change: The social and educational contributions to outcomes of Black males in urban schools.* Washington, DC: Council of Great City Schools. Retrieved from http://graphics8.nytimes.com/packages/pdf/opinion/A-Call-For-Change.pdf.

Lipman, P. (1998). *Race, class and power in school restructuring.* Albany, NY: SUNY Press.

Mitra, D. L. (2008). *Student voice in school reform: Building youth-adult partnerships that strengthen schools.* San Francisco, CA: Jossey-Bass.

Noguera, P. A., & Wing, J. Y. (Eds.). (2006). *Unfinished business: Closing the racial achievement gap in our schools.* San Francisco, CA: Jossey-Bass.

Ramirez III, M., & Casteneda, A. (1974). *Cultural democracy, bicognitive development, and education.* New York, NY: Academic Press.

Rubin, B. C., & Noguera, P. A. (2004). Tracking detracking: Sorting through the dilemmas and possibilities of detracking in practice. *Equity and Excellence in Education, 37*(1), 92–101.

Valenzuela, A. (1999). *Subtractive schooling: US Mexican youth and the politics of caring.* Albany, NY: SUNY Press.

van Keulen, J. E., Weddington, E. R., & DuBose, C. E. (1998). *Speech, language, learning, & the African American child.* Boston, MA: Allyn & Bacon.

Chapter 1

Aguirre, A., & Turner, J. H. (2003). *American ethnicity: The dynamics and consequences of discrimination.* Boston: McGraw-Hill.

Akbar, N. (1998). *Know thyself.* Tallahassee, FL: Mind Productions and Associates.

Altschul, I., Oysterman, D., & Bybee, D. (September, 2008). Racial-ethnic self-schemas and segmented assimilation: Identity and the academic achievement of Hispanic youth. *Social Psychology Quarterly, 71*(3), 302–320.

Altschul, I., Oysterman, D., & Bybee, D. (2006). Racial-ethnic identity in mid adolescence: Content and change as predictors of academic achievement. *Child Development, 77*(5), 1155–1169.

Banks, J. A., Cookson, P., Gay, G., Hawley, W. D., Irvine, J. J., Nieto, S., Ward, J., & Stephan, W. G. (2001). Diversity within unity: Essential principles for teaching and learning in a multicultural society. *Phi Delta Kappan, 83,* 196–203.

Bankston, C. L., & Zhou, M. (Summer, 2002). Being well vs. doing well: Self-esteem and school performance among immigrant and nonimmigrant racial and ethnic groups. *International Migration Review, 36*(2), 389–415.

Bowles, S., & Gintus, H. (1976). *Schooling in capitalist America: Educational reform and the contradictions of economic life.* New York, NY: Basic Books.

Cross, W. E., & Vandiver, B. J. (2001). Nigrescence theory and measurement: Introducing the Cross racial identity scale. In J. G. Ponterotto, J. M. Casas, L. M. Suzuki, & C. M. Alexander (Eds.), *Handbook of multicultural counseling* (2nd ed., pp. 371–393). Thousand Oaks, CA: Sage.

Eisner, E. W. (1994). *The educational imagination: On the design and evaluation of school programs* (3rd ed.). New York, NY: Macmillan.

Freire, P. (1970). *Pedagogy of the oppressed.* New York, NY: Herder and Herder.

Gaertner, S. L., & Dovidio, J. F. (1986). The aversive form of racism. In J. F. Dovidio & S. L. Gaertner (Eds.), *Prejudice, discrimination, and racism: Theory and research* (pp. 61–89). Orlando, FL: Academic Press.

Glenn, D. (2003). Minority students with complex beliefs about ethnic identity are found to do better in school. *The Chronicle of Higher Education.* Retrieved from http://chronicle .com/article/Minority-Students-With-Complex/111085/.

Helms, J. E. (Ed.). (1990). *Black and White racial identity: Theory, research, and practice.* Westport, CT: Greenwood Press.

Helms, J. E., & Cook, D. A. (1999). *Using race and culture in counseling and psychotherapy.* Boston, MA: Allyn & Bacon.

Holcomb-McCoy, C. (2005). Ethnic identity development in early adolescence: Implications and recommendations for middle school counselors. *Professional School Counseling, 9*(2), 120–127.

Howard, G. (1999). *We can't teach what we don't know: White teachers, multiracial schools.* New York, NY: Teachers College Press.

Jackson, P. (1990). *Life in classrooms.* New York, NY: Teachers College Press.

Jackson, Y. (2011). *The pedagogy of confidence, inspiring high intellectual performance in urban schools.* New York, NY: Teachers College Press.

Jorgensen, K. L., & Brown, C. S. (1992). *New faces in our schools: Student-generated solutions to ethnic conflict.* San Francisco, CA: Zellerbach Family Fund.

Kirk, G., & Okazawa-Rey, M. (Eds.). (2004). *Women's lives: Multicultural perspectives.* New York, NY: McGraw-Hill.

Ladson-Billings, G. (Autumn, 1995). Toward a theory of culturally relevant pedagogy. *American Educational Research Journal, 32*(3), 465–491.

Marable, M. (1997). *Black liberation in conservative America.* Boston, MA: South End Press.

McHatton, P. A., Shaunessy, E., Hughes, C., Brice, A., & Ratliff, M. A. (2007). You gotta represent: Ethnic identity development among Hispanic adolescents. *Multicultural Perspectives, 9*(3), 12–20.

Mosselson, J. (December, 2006) Roots & routes: A re-imagining of refugee identity constructions and the implications for schooling. *Current Issues in Comparative Education, 9*(1), 20–29.

Murrell, P. C. (2008). *Race, culture, and schooling: identities of achievement in multicultural urban schools.* New York, NY: LEA/Taylor and Francis Group.

National Advisory Commission on Civil Disorders. (1968). Kerner commission report. Washington, DC: U.S. Government Printing Office.

Noguera, P. A., & Akom, A. (2000, June). The significance of race in the racial gap in academic achievement. *Motion Magazine.* Retrieved from http://www.inmotionmagazine .com/pnaa.html.

Noguera, P. A., & Wing, J. Y. (Eds.). (2006). *Unfinished business, closing the racial achievement gap in our schools.* San Francisco, CA: Jossey-Bass.

Ponterotto, J., Utsey, S., Pedersen, P. (2006). *Preventing prejudice: A guide for counselors, educators, and parents* (2nd ed.). Thousands Oaks, CA: Sage.

Ruiz, A. S. (1990). Ethnic identity: Crisis and resolution. *Journal of Multicultural Counseling and Development, 18,* 29–40.

Smith, E. P., Walker, K., Fields, L., Brookins, C., & Seay, R. (December, 1999). Ethnic identity and its relationship to self-esteem, perceived efficacy and prosocial attitudes in early adolescence. *Journal of Adolescence, 22* (6), 867–880.

Spring, J. (2009). *Deculturalization and struggle for equality: A brief history of the education of dominated cultures in the United States.* New York, NY: McGraw-Hill.

Sue, D. W. (2003). *Overcoming our racism: The journey to liberation.* New York, NY: Wiley.

Vigdor, J. L. (2008). *Measuring immigrant assimilation in the United States.* New York, NY: Manhattan Institute for Policy Research.

Zirkel, S. (2008). Creating more effective multiethnic schools. *Social Issues and Policy Review, 2,* 187–241.

Chapter 2

Berlinger, D. (2009). *Poverty and potential: Out-of-school factors and school success.* Tempe, AZ: Education and the Public Interest Center & Education Policy Research Unit. Retrieved from http://epicpolicy.org/publication/poverty-and-potential.

Corbett, D. (2002, September). What urban students say about good teaching. *Educational Leadership, 60,* 1, 18–22.

Corbett, D., Wilson, B., & Williams, B. (2002). *Effort and excellence in urban classrooms, Expecting—and getting—success with all students.* New York, NY: Teachers College, Columbia.

Deal, T. E., & Peterson, K. (2009). *Shaping school culture: Pitfalls, paradoxes, and promises* (2nd ed.). San Francisco, CA: Jossey-Bass.

Duncan-Andrade, J. (2007). Gangstas, wankstas, and ridas: Defining, developing, and supporting effective teachers in urban schools. *International Journal of Qualitative Studies in Education, 20,* 6, 617–638.

Elbertson, N. A., Brackett, M. A., & Weissberg, R. P. (2010). School-based social and emotional learning (SEL) programming: Current perspectives. In A. Hargreaves, M. Fullen, D. Hopkins, & A. Lieberman (Eds.), *The second international handbook of educational change* (pp. 1017–1032). New York, NY: Springer.

Jackson, Y. (2011). *The pedagogy of confidence, inspiring high intellectual performance in urban schools.* New York, NY: Teachers College Press.

Koenig, D., & Daniels, R. H. (Fall, 2011). Bully at the blackboard. *Teaching Tolerance, 40,* 58–61.

Ladson-Billings, G. (2003). New directions in multicultural education, complexities, boundaries, and critical race theory. In J. Banks & C. Banks (Eds.), *Handbook of research on multicultural education* (2nd ed., pp. 50–65). San Francisco, CA: Jossey-Bass.

Lowen, J. (2007). *Lies my teacher told me: Everything your American history textbook got wrong.* New York, NY: Touchstone.

Martinez, E. (1998). *De colores means all of us, Latina views for a multi-colored century.* Cambridge, MA: South End Press.

Murrell, P. C. (2008). *Race, culture, and schooling: Identities of achievement in multicultural urban schools.* New York, NY: Routledge.

Noguera, P. A., & Wing, J. Y. (Eds.). (2006). *Unfinished business: Closing the racial achievement gap in our schools.* San Francisco, CA: Jossey-Bass.

Sadowski, M. (2008). *Adolescents at school: Perspectives on youth, identity, and education* (2nd ed.). Cambridge, MA: Harvard Education Press.

Street, J., Harris-Britt, A., & Walker-Barnes, C. (2009, August). Examining relationships between ethnic identity, family environment, and psychological outcomes for African American adolescents. *Journal of Child and Family Studies, 18,* 412–420.

Thompson, G. L. (2007). *Up where we belong: Helping African American and Latino students rise in school and in life.* San Francisco, CA: Jossey-Bass.

UCLA School Mental Health Project, Center for Mental Health in Schools. (2011). *Hot topics, bullying: A major barrier to student learning.* Retrieved from http://smhp.psych.ucla.edu/hottopic/hottopic(bullying).htm.

Zehr, M. (2010). School discipline inequities a major problem. *Education Week, 31*(1), 17.

Zins, J. E., & Elias, M. J. (2006). Social and emotional learning. In G. G. Bear & K. M. Minke (Eds.), *Children's needs III: Development, prevention, and intervention* (pp. 1–13). Bethesda, MD: NASP Publications.

Chapter 3

Angus, L., & Jhally, S. (Eds.). (1989). *Cultural politics in contemporary America.* New York, NY: Routledge.

Bell-Jordan, K. (2008). Black, white, and a survivor of *The Real World*: Constructions of race on reality TV. *Critical Studies in Media Communication, 25*(4), 353–372.

Cochran-Smith, M. (2004). *Walking the road, race, diversity, and social justice in education.* New York, NY: Teachers College Press.

Covey, S. (2004). *Seven habits of highly effective people, powerful lessons in personal change.* New York, NY: Free Press.

Cross, B. E. (2005). New racism, reformed teacher education, and the same ole' oppression. *Educational Studies, 38*(3), 263–274.

Deal, T. E., & Peterson, K. D. (2009). *Shaping school culture: Pitfalls, paradoxes, and promises.* San Francisco, CA: Wiley.

Doubek, M. B., & Cooper, E. J. (2007). Closing the gap through professional development: Implications for reading research. *Reading Research Quarterly, 42*(3), 411–415.

Gause, C. P. (2011). *Diversity, equity, and inclusive education, A voice from the margins.* Boston, MA: Sense Publishers.

Gay, G. (2010). *Culturally responsive teaching, Theory, research, and practice* (2nd ed.). New York, NY: Teachers College Press.

Gusa, D. (2010). White institutional presence: The impact of whiteness on campus climate. *Harvard Educational Review, 80*(4), 464–489.

Hynds, A. (2010, October). Unpacking resistance to change within-school reform programs with a social justice orientation. *International Journal of Leadership in Education, 13*(4), 377–392.

Irizarry, J. G. (2007). Ethnic and urban intersections in the classroom: Latino students, hybrid identities, and culturally responsive pedagogy. *Multicultural Perspectives, 9*(3), 21–28.

Johnson, A. G. (2006) *Privilege, power, and difference.* New York, NY: McGraw-Hill.

Jordan, G., & Weedon, C. (1995). *Cultural politics, class, gender, race and the postmodern world.* Cambridge, MA: Blackwell.

Kellner, D., & Share, J. (2007). Critical media literacy, democracy, and the reconstruction of education. In D. Macedo & S. R. Steinberg (Eds.), *Media literacy: A reader* (pp. 3–23). New York, NY: Peter Lang Publishing.

King, J. (2005). A declaration of intellectual independence for human freedom. In J. E. King (Ed.), *Black education: A transformative research and action agenda for the new century* (pp. 19–42). Mahwah, NJ: Lawrence Erlbaum Associates.

King, J., & Hollins, E. (Eds.). (1997). *Preparing teachers for cultural diversity.* New York, NY: Teachers College Press.

Knaus, C. (2007). *Still segregated, still unequal. The state of Black America, 2007, portrait of the Black-male.* New York, NY: National Urban League.

Knight, S. L., & Wiseman, D. L. (2005). Professional development for teachers of diverse students: A summary of the research. *Journal of Education for Students Placed at Risk (JESPAR), 10*(4), 363–385.

Ladson-Billings, G. (2003). New directions in multicultural education, complexities, boundaries, and critical race theory. In J. Banks & C. Banks (Eds.), *Handbook of research on multicultural education* (2nd ed., pp. 50–65). San Francisco, CA: Jossey-Bass.

Lee, C. (2007). *Culture, literacy, and learning: Taking bloom in the midst of the whirlwind.* New York, NY: Teachers College Press.

Levine, A. (2005). *Educating school leaders.* Washington, DC: Carnegie Foundation. Retrieved from http://www.edschools.org/reports_leaders.htm.

Lin, M., Lake, V. E., & Rice, D. (2008). Teaching anti-bias curriculum in teacher education programs: What and how. *Teacher Education Quarterly, 35*(2), 187–200.

Mathis, W. J. (2005). The cost of implementing the federal No Child Left Behind Act: Different assumptions, different answers. *Peabody Journal of Education, 80*(2), 90–119.

Moll, L. C., Amanti, C., Neff, D., & Gonzalez, N. (1992). Funds of knowledge for teaching: Using a qualitative approach to connect homes and classrooms. *Theory into Practice, 31*(2), 132–141.

Montecel, M., & Cortez, A. (2002). Successful bilingual education programs. *Bilingual Research Journal, 26*(1), 1–21.

Murrell, P. C., Jr. (2006). Toward social justice in urban education: A model of collaborative cultural inquiry in urban schools. *Equity and Excellence in Education, 39*(1), 81–90.

No Child Left Behind Act of 2001, Pub. L. No. 107-110, 115 Stat. 1425 (2002). Retrieved from http://www.ed.gov/policy/elsec/leg/esea02/index.html.

Noguera, P. (2008). *The trouble with Black boys, and other reflections on race, equity, and the future of public education.* San Francisco, CA: Jossey-Bass.

Oakes, J., Wells, A., Datnow, A., & Jones, M. (1997). Detracking: The social construction of ability, cultural politics, and resistance to reform. *Teachers College Record, 98*(3), 482–511.

Omi, M. (1989). In living color: Race and popular culture. In L. Angus & S. Jhally (Eds.), *Cultural politics in contemporary America* (pp. 111–122). New York, NY: Routledge.

Omi, M., & Winant, H. (1994). Racial formation in the United States: From the 1960's to the 1980's (2nd ed.). New York, NY: Routledge.

Smith, D. L., & Smith, B. J. (2009). Urban educator's voices: Understanding culture in the classroom. *The Urban Review, 41*(4), 334–351.

Smith, S. E. (2012). *What are some criticisms of no child left behind?* Retrieved from http://r.wisegeek.com/what-are-some-criticisms-of-no-child-left-behind.htm.

Staples, J. (2010, Winter). Encouraging agitation: Teaching teacher candidates to confront words that wound. *Teacher Education Quarterly, 37*(1), 53–72.

Stroder, M. E. (2008). *Effects of culturally responsive teaching practices on the literacy learning of Latino students.* Master's thesis, Western Kentucky University. Retrieved from http://digital commons.wku.edu/theses/29.

Thompson, G. (2007). *Up where we belong: Helping African American and Latino students rise in school and in life.* San Francisco, CA: Jossey-Bass.

Zirkel, S. (2008). Creating more effective multiethnic schools. *Social Issues and Policy Review, 2,* 187–241.

Chapter 4

Duncan-Andrade, J. M. R. (2004). Toward teacher development for the urban in urban teaching. *Teaching Education, 15*(4), 339–350.

Futrell, M. (2010). Transforming teacher education to reform America's P-20 education system. *Journal of Teacher Education, 61*(5), 432–440.

Gay, G. (2010). *Culturally responsive teaching, Theory, research, and practice* (2nd ed.) New York, NY: Teachers College Press.

Ladson-Billings, G. (1995, Autumn). Toward a theory of culturally relevant pedagogy. *American Educational Research Journal, 31*(3), 465–491.

Lee, C. (2007). *Culture, literacy, and learning: Taking bloom in the midst of the whirlwind.* New York, NY: Teachers College Press.

Nieto, S. (2003) *What keeps teachers going?* New York, NY: Teachers College Press.

Noguera, P. A., & Wing, J. Y. (Eds.). (2006). *Unfinished business: Closing the racial achievement gap in our schools.* San Francisco, CA: Jossey-Bass.

Oakes, J., Rogers, J., & Lipton, M. (2006). *Learning power: Organizing for education and justice.* New York, NY: Teachers College Press.

Sleeter, C., Torres, M. N., & Laughlin, P. (2004). Scaffolding conscientization through inquiry in teacher education. *Teacher Education Quarterly, 31*(1),81–96.

Wells, A. S., Revilla, A. T., Holme, J. J., & Atanda, A. K. (2004). The space between school desegregation court orders and outcomes: The struggle to challenge white privilege. *Virginia Law Review, 90*(6), 1721–1750.

Zirkel, S. (2008). Creating more effective multiethnic schools. *Social Issues and Policy Review, 2,* 187–241.

Chapter 5

Abbate-Vaughn, J., Frechon, O., & Wright, B. L. (2010). Accomplished urban teaching. *Theory Into Practice, 49*(3), 185–192.

Berlinger, D. (2009). *Poverty and potential: Out-of-school factors and school success.* Tempe, AZ: Education and the Public Interest Center & Education Policy Research Unit. Retrieved fromhttp://epicpolicy.org/publication/poverty-and-potential.

Byrd-Blake, M. (2009). Operation 2014: Developing culturally competent teachers for a diverse society. *Florida Association of Teacher Educators Journal, 1*(9), 1–23.

Chandler, P., & McKnight, D. (2009). The failure of social education in the United States: A critique of teaching the national story from "White" colorblind eyes. *Journal for Critical Education Policy Studies, 7*(2), 217–248.

Corbett, D., Wilson, B., & Williams, B. (2002). *Effort and excellence in urban classrooms: Expecting—and getting—success with all students.* New York, NY: Teachers College Press.

Delpit, L. (1995). *Other people's children: Cultural conflict in the class room.* New York, NY: The New Press.

Frankenberg, E., Lee, C., & Orfield, G. (2003). A multiracial society with segregated schools: Are we losing the dream? Cambridge, MA: The Civil Rights project, Harvard University. Retrieved from http://www.civilrightsproject.harvard.edu.

Finn, P. J. (2009). *Literacy with an attitude, educating working-class children in their own self-interest* (2nd ed.). Albany, NY: SUNY Press.

Garcia, S. B., & Guerra, P. L. (2004). Deconstructing deficit thinking: Working with educators to create more equitable learning environments. *Education and Urban Society, 36*(2), 150–168.

Gay, G. (2010). *Culturally responsive teaching, Theory, research, and practice* (2nd ed.). New York, NY: Teachers College Press.

Gee, J. P. (1989). What is literacy? *Journal of Education, 171*(1), 18–25.

Hall, T., Strangman, N., & Meyer, A. (2011). *Differentiated instruction and implications for UDL implementation.* Wakefield, MA: National Center on Accessible Instructional Materials. Retrieved from http://aim.cast.org/learn/historyarchive/backgroundpapers/differentiated_instruction_udl.

Hilliard, A. (2003). The standards movement: Quality control or decoy? Retrieved from http://www.africawithin.com/hilliard/standards_movement.htm.

Hilliard, A., & Sizemore, B. A. (1984). *Saving the African American child: A report of the task force on Black academic and cultural excellence.* Washington, DC: National Alliance of Black School Educators.

Hollins, E. R. (2008). *Culture in school learning: Revealing the deep meaning* (2nd ed.). New York, NY: Routledge.

LeMoine, N. (2009, June 12). *Culturally and linguistically responsive instruction: A powerful pedagogy for advancing learning, in African American and other under achieving students.* PowerPoint presentation given at Cypress-Fairbanks ISD, Cypress, Texas.

Loveless, T. (1999). *The tracking wars: State reform meets school policy.* Washington, DC: Brookings Institution Press.

Melnick, S., & Zeichner, K. (1995). Teacher education for cultural diversity: Enhancing the capacity of teacher education institutes to address diversity issues (Research Rep. 95-4). East Lansing, MI: National Center for Research on Teacher Learning.

Miretzky, D. (2004). *Developing the teacher workforce.* Chicago, IL: National Society for the Study of Education.

Oakes, J. (2005). *Keeping track: How schools structure inequality* (2nd ed.). New Haven, CT: Yale University Press.

Orfield, G. (2008). *Race and schools: The need for action.* Washington, DC: National Education Association. Retrieved from http://www.nea.org/home/13054.htm.

Picower, B. (2009). The unexamined Whiteness of teaching: How White teachers maintain and enact dominant racial ideologies. *Race, Ethnicity and Education, 12*(2), 197–215.

Posey-Maddox, L. (2012). Middle- and upper-middle-class parent action for urban public schools: Promise or paradox? *Teachers College Record, 114*(1). Retrieved from https://www.tcrecord.org/library/Abstract.asp?ContentId=16213.

Roach, A. T., & Elliott, S. N. (2009). Consultation to support inclusive accountability and standards-based reform: Facilitating access, equity, and empowerment. *Journal of Educational and Psychological Consultation, 19*(1), 61–81.

Roschelle, J. (1995). Learning in interactive environments: Prior knowledge and new experience. In J. H. Falk & L. D. Dierking (Eds.), *Public institutions for personal learning: Establishing a research agenda* (pp. 37–51) Washington, DC: American Association of Museums.

Sleeter, C., & Stillman, J. (2005). Standardizing knowledge in a multicultural society. *Curriculum Inquiry, 35*(1), 27–46.

Spring, J. (2007). *The intersection of cultures: Multicultural education in the United States and the global economy* (4th ed.). New York, NY: Routledge.

Taylor, L. S., & Whittaker, C. R. (2003). *Bridging multiple worlds: Case studies of diverse educational communities.* Boston, MA: Allyn & Bacon.

Thompson, G. (2007). *Up where we belong: Helping African American and Latino students rise in school and in life.* San Francisco, CA: Jossey-Bass.

Valles, B., & Miller, D. M. (2010). How leadership and discipline policies color school-community relationships: A critical race theory analysis. *Journal of School Public Relations, 31*(4), 319–341.

Woodson, C. G. (1990). *The mis-education of the Negro.* Trenton, NJ: Africa World Press. (Original work published 1933)

Yosso, T. J. (2005). Whose culture has capital? A critical race theory discussion of community cultural wealth. *Race and Education, 8*(1), 69–91.

Zeichner, K. (2003). The adequacies and inadequacies to recruit, prepare, and retain the best teachers for all students. *Teachers College Record, 105*(3), 490–519.

Chapter 6

Sammons, P. (2007). School effectiveness and equity: Making connections. Berkshire, UK: CfBT Education Trust. Retrieved from http://www.cfbt.com/evidenceforeducation/PDF/School%20effectiveness%20Exec%20Summary%285%29.pdf.

Singleton, G., & Linton, C. (2006). *Courageous conversations about race.* Thousand Oaks, CA: Corwin.

Weitzenkorn, S. (2010, December 20). How Do You Define Who You Are?[Web log message]. Retrieved from http://findfulfillflourish.wordpress.com/2010/12/20/how-do-you-define-who-you-are/.

Chapter 7

Fullan, M., & Hargreaves, A. (1996). *What's worth fighting for in your school?* New York, NY: Teachers College Press.

Krovetz, M. L., & Arriaza, G. (2006). *Collaborative teacher leadership: How teachers can foster equitable schools.* Thousand Oaks, CA: Corwin.

Little, J. W. (1982). Norms of collegiality and experimentation: Workplace conditions of school success. *American Educational Research Journal, 19*(3), 325–340.

National Center for Culturally Responsive Educational Systems. (2005). *Professional learning principles.* Tempe, AZ: Arizona State University.

Chapter 8

Asante, M. K. (2003). *Erasing racism: the survival of the American nation*. Amherst, NY: Prometheus Books.

Chenoweth, K. (2009). *How it's being done, urgent lessons from unexpected schools*. Cambridge, MA: Harvard Education Press.

Cohen, E. G., & Lotan, R. A. (1995). Producing equal status interaction in the heterogeneous classroom. *American Educational Research Journal, 32*, 99–120.

Fullan, M. (1993). *Change forces, probing the depths of educational reform*. New York, NY: The Falmer Press.

Fullan, M., & Hargreaves, A. (1996). *What's worth fighting for in your school?* New York, NY: Teachers College Press.

Gay, G. (2010). *Culturally responsive teaching: Theory, research, and practice* (2nd ed.). New York, NY: Teachers College Press.

Grant, C., & Zwier, E. (2011). Intersectionality and student outcomes: Sharpening the struggle against racism, sexism, classism, ableism, heterosexism, nationalism, and linguistic, religious, and geographical discrimination in teaching and learning. *Multicultural Perspectives, 13*(4), 181–188.

Hersey, P., & Blanchard, K. (1993). *Management of organizational behavior, utilizing human resources*. Englewood Cliffs, NJ: Prentice Hall.

Howard, T. (2010). *Why race and culture matter in schools, closing the achievement gap in America's classrooms*. New York, NY: Teachers College Press.

Lindsey, R., Nuri Robins, K., & Terrell, R. (2003). *Cultural proficiency: A manual for school leaders* (2nd ed.). Thousand Oaks, CA: Corwin.

Luft, J. (1969). *Of human interaction*. Palo Alto, CA: National Press.

McIntosh, P. (1989, July/August). White privilege: Unpacking the invisible knapsack. *Peace and Freedom*, 10–12.

Nuri Robins, K., Lindsey, R., Lindsey, D., & Terrell, R. (2002). *Culturally proficient instruction: A guide for people who teach*. Thousand Oaks, CA: Corwin.

Ordonez, J. R., & Jasis, P. (2011). Mapping literacy, mapping lives: Teachers exploring the sociopolitical context of literacy and learning. *Multicultural Perspectives, 13*(4), 189–196.

Saifer, S., Edwards, K., Ellis, D., Ko, L., & Stuczynski, A. (2011). *Culturally responsive standards-based teaching, Classroom to community and back* (2nd ed.). Thousand Oaks, CA: Corwin.

Tough, P. (2008). *Whatever it takes: Geoffrey Canada's quest to change Harlem and America*. Boston, MA: Houghton Mifflin Harcourt.

Yen, D. H. (1999). *Johari window*. Retrieved from http://www.noogenesis.com/game_theory/johari/johari_window.html.

Chapter 9

Boykin, A. W., & Noguera, P. (2011). *Creating the opportunity to learn, moving from research to practice to close the achievement gap*. Alexandria, VA: ASCD.

Duncan-Andrade, J. (2007). Gangstas, wankstas, and ridas: Defining, developing, and supporting effective teachers in urban schools. *International Journal of Qualitative Studies in Education, 20*(6), 617–638.

The Efficacy Institute. (2011). *Mission: Academic proficiency & strong character for all students.* Retrieved from http://www.efficacy.org/strategy/tabid/246/default.aspx.

Hersey, P. W. (1982). The NASSP assessment center develops leadership talent. *Educational Leadership, 2,*370–371. Retrieved from http://www.ascd.org/ASCD/pdf/journals/ed_lead/el_198202_hersey.pdf.

Hilliard, A. (n.d.). *The standards movement: Quality control or decoy?* Retrieved from http://www.africawithin.com/hilliard/standards_movement.htm.

Lindsey, R., Nuri Robins, K., & Terrell, R. D. (1999). *Cultural proficiency: A manual for school leaders.* Thousand Oaks, CA: Corwin.

Marks, H. W., & Printy, S. M. (2003, August). Principal leadership and school performance: An integration of transformational and instructional leadership. *Educational Administration Quarterly, 39*(3), 370–397.

McWhorter, J. H. (2000). *Losing the race: Self-sabotage in Black America.* New York, NY: Simon & Schuster.

Murphy, J. F., Weil, M., Hallinger, P., & Mitman, A. (1982). Academic press: Translating high expectations into school policies and classroom practices. *Educational Leadership, 40*(3), 22–26.

Murphy, J. (2010). *Educational handbook for understanding and closing achievement gaps.* Thousand Oaks, CA: Corwin.

National Association of Secondary School Principals. (2004). *Developing the 21st century principal: Frequently asked questions.* Retrieved from http://www.nassp.org/portals/0/content/53524.pdf.

Singleton, G., & Linton, C. (2006). *Courageous conversations about race.* Thousand Oaks, CA: Corwin.

Southwest Educational Development Laboratory. (1992). *Leadership characteristics that facilitate school change.* Austin, TX: Author. Retrieved from http://www.sedl.org/change/leadership/character.html.

Chapter 10

Achinstein, B., & Barralt, A. (2004). (Re)framing classroom contexts: How new teachers and mentors view diverse learners and challenges of practice. *Teachers College Record, 106,* 716–746.

Achinstein, B., & Ogawa, R. (2006). (In)fidelity: What the resistance of new teachers reveals about professional principles and prescriptive educational policies. *Harvard Educational Review, 76*(1), 30–63.

Banks, J. A., & Banks, C. A. (Eds.). (2003). *Handbook of research on multicultural education* (2nd ed.). Hoboken, NJ: Wiley.

Cochran-Smith, M. (2004). *Walking the road, race, diversity, and social justice in teacher education.* New York, NY: Teachers College Press.

Corbett, D., & Wilson, B. (2002) What urban youth say about good teaching. *Educational Leadership, 60*(1), 18–22.

Duncan-Andrade, J. M., & Morrell, E. (2008). *The art of critical pedagogy: Possibilities for moving from theory to practice in urban schools.* New York, NY: Peter Lang Publishing.

Gaertner, S. L., & Davidio, J. F. (1986) The aversive form of racism. In J. F. Dovidio & S. L. Gaertner (Eds.), *Prejudice, discrimination, and racism: Theory and research* (pp. 61–89). Orlando, FL: Academic Press.

Gay, G. (2010). *Culturally responsive teaching: Theory, research, and practice* (2nd ed.). New York, NY: Teachers College Press.

Jimenez, R. T., Smith, P., & Teague, B. (2009). Transnational and community literacies for teachers. *Journal of Adolescent and Adult Literacy, 53*(1),16–26.

Kavanagh, K. (2010). *A dichotomy examined: Beginning teach for America educators navigate culturally relevant teaching and a scripted literacy program in their urban classrooms.* Published Childhood Education dissertation [Paper 12], Georgia State University. Retrieved from http://digitalarchive.gsu.edu/ece_diss/12.

King, J. (Spring, 1991). Dysconscious racism. *Journal of Negro Education, 60*(2), 133–146.

Krovetz, M. L., & Arriaza, G. (2006). *Collaborative teacher leadership: How teachers can foster equitable schools.* Thousand Oaks, CA: Corwin.

Murrell, P. C. (2000). Community teachers: A conceptual framework for preparing exemplary urban teachers. *The Journal of Negro Education, 69*(4), 338–348.

Murrell, P. C. (2008). *Race, culture, and schooling: Identities of achievement in multicultural urban schools.* New York, NY: LEA/Taylor and Francis Group.

Ponterotto, J., Utsey, S., & Pedersen, P. (2006). *Preventing prejudice: A guide for counselors, educators, and parents* (2nd ed.). Thousand Oaks, CA: Sage.

Chapter 11

Chenoweth, K. (2007). *It's being done, urgent lessons from unexpected schools.* Cambridge, MA: Harvard Education Press.

Denver Public Schools. (2011). *Overview: The multiple measures in LEAP.* Retrieved from http://leap.dpsk12.org/LEAP-Components/Overview.aspx.

Gladwell, M. (2008). *Outliers, the story of success.* New York, NY: Little Brown & Co.

Jackson, H. (2010). *Transforming school culture: Teachers' perspectives of professional learning communities as a reform initiative to close the achievement gap.* Doctoral dissertation, San Diego State University, California.

Jesse, D., Davis, A., & Pokorny, N. (2004). High-achieving middle schools for Latino students in poverty. *Journal of Education for Students Placed at Risk, 9,* 33–34.

Johnson, J. F. (2007, June 25). *Schools that serve African American children well.*[PowerPoint presentation]. San Diego, CA: National Center for Urban School Transformation. Retrieved from http://www.Edequity.com/images/Joe%20Johnson%20CAAAE.ppt.

Johnson, J. F. (2010, December 3). *Key characteristics of top-performing schools.*[PowerPoint presentation]. San Diego, CA: National Center for Urban School Transformation. Retrieved from http://www.ncust.org/docs/2010_12_03%20Key%20Characteristics%20of%20Top%20Performing%20Schools.pdf.

Nieto, S. (2007). *Affirming diversity: The sociopolitical context of multicultural education.* Boston, MA: Allyn & Bacon.

Chapter 13

AERA. (1993). School delivery standards. *Educational Researcher, 22* (5), 24–30.

California Department of Education. (2004). *The Williams case—An explanation.* Retrieved from http://www.cde.ca.gov/eo/ce/wc/wmslawsuit.asp.

Elmore, R. F., & Fuhrman, S. H. (1995). Opportunity to learn and the state role in education. *Teachers College Record, 96*(3), 432–457.

TheFreeDictionary.com. (2011). *Politics.* Retrieved from http://www.thefreedictionary.com/politics.

Martinez, E. (1998). *De colores means all of us: Latina views for a multi-colored century.* Cambridge, MA: South End Press.

Merriam-Webster. (2012). *Politics.* Retrieved from http://www.merriam-webster.com/dictionary/politics.

Miles, R., & Brown, M. (2003). *Racism* (2nd ed.). New York, NY: Routledge.

Partnership for 21st Century Skills. (2011). *Framework for 21st century learning.* Retrieved from http://www.p21.org/index.php?option=com_content&task=view&id=254&Itermid=120.

Stimson, T. (2011). *Sources of power.* Anchorage, AK: CLI. Retrieved fromhttp://www.consultcli.com/sourcespower.htm.

Wikipedia. (2010). *Politics.* Retrieved from http://en.wikipedia.org/wiki/Politics.

WordIQ.com. (2012). *Politics.* Retrieved from http://www.wordiq.com/definition/Politics.

WordNet. (2012). *Politics.* Retrieved from http://wordnetweb.princeton.edu/perl/webwn?s=politics&sub=Search+WordNet&o2=&o0=1&o8=1&o1=1&o7=&o5=&o9=&o6=&o3=&o4=&h=.

Chapter 14

Singleton, G., & Linton, C. (2006). *Courageous conversations about race.* Thousand Oaks, CA: Corwin.

Chapter 15

Bloom, G., Castagna, C., & Warren, B. (2003, May/June,). More than mentors: Principal coaching. *Leadership, 32*(5), 20–32.

Duncan-Andrade, J. M., & Morrell, E. (2008). *The art of critical pedagogy: Possibilities for moving from theory to practice in urban schools.* New York, NY: Peter Lang Publishing.

Hersey, P. W. (1982). The NASSP assessment center develops leadership talent. *Educational Leadership, 2,* 370–371. Retrieved from http://www.ascd.org/ASCD/pdf/journals/ed_lead/el_198202_hersey.pdf

Jackson, R. (2011). *How to plan rigorous instruction, mastering the principles of great teaching.* Alexandria, VA: ASCD.

Jackson, Y. (2011). *The pedagogy of confidence: Inspiring high intellectual performance in urban schools.* New York, NY: Teachers College Press.

Johnson, J. F. (2012). *Teaching in America's best urban schools.* Larchmont, NY: Eye on Education.

Singleton, G., & Linton, C. (2006). *Courageous conversations about race.* Thousand Oaks, CA: Corwin.

Chapter 16

Barreto, M. A., Gonzalez, B. F., & Sanchez, G. R. (2010). *Rainbow coalition in the goldenstate? Exposing myths, uncovering new realities in Latino attitudes towards Blacks.* Retrieved from http://faculty.washington.edu/mbarreto/papers/blackbrown_CA.pdf.

Chaiklin, S. (2003). The zone of proximal development in Vygotsky's analysis of learning and instruction. In A. Kozulin, B. Gindis, V. Ageyev, & S. Miller (Eds.), *Vygotsky's educational theory and practice in cultural context* (pp. 39–64). Cambridge, UK: Cambridge University Press.

Costa, A., & Kallick, B. (Eds.). (2008). *Learning and leading with habits of mind: 16 essential characteristics for success.* Alexandria, VA: ASCD.

Covey, S. (2004). *The 8th habit: From effectiveness to greatness.* New York, NY: Free Press.

Cox, Jr., T. (1993). *Cultural diversity in organizations: Theory, research, and practice.* San Francisco, CA: Berrett-Koehler.

Cox, Jr., T. (2001). *Creating the multicultural organization: A strategy for capturing the power of diversity.* San Francisco, CA: Jossey-Bass.

Darling-Hammond, L., & Baratz-Snowden. J. (2005). *A good teacher in every classroom: Preparing the highly qualified teachers our children deserve.* San Francisco, CA: Wiley.

Duncan-Andrade, J. M., & Morrell, E. (2008). *The art of critical pedagogy: Possibilities for moving from theory to practice in urban schools.* New York, NY: Peter Lang Publishing.

Gandara, P., & Contreras, F. (2009). *The Latino education crisis: The consequences of failed social policies.* Cambridge, MA: Harvard University Press.

Gause, C. P. (2011). *Diversity, equity, and inclusive education: A voice from the margins.* Boston, MA: Sense Publishers.

Gay, G. (2010). *Culturally responsive teaching: Theory, research, and practice* (2nd ed.). New York, NY: Teachers College Press.

Gay, G. (2011, June 29). *Keynote address.* Presentation given at the CA Alliance of African American Educators Professional Development Institute at Stanford University, Palo Alto, CA.

Goodlad, J. I. (1975). *The dynamics of educational change: Toward responsive schools.* New York, NY: McGraw-Hill.

Hersey, P., & Blanchard, K. (1993). *Management of organizational behavior: Utilizing human resources.* Englewood Cliffs, NJ: Prentice Hall.

Howard, T. (2010). *Why race and culture matter in schools: Closing the achievement gap in America's classrooms.* New York, NY: Teachers College Press.

King, J. (2005). A declaration of intellectual independence for human freedom. In J. King (Ed.), *Black education: A transformative research and action agenda for the new century* (pp. 19–42) Mahwah, NJ: Lawrence Erlbaum Associates.

Lee, C. (2005). The state of knowledge about the education of African Americans. In J. King (Ed.), *Black education: A transformative research and action agenda for the new century* (pp. 45–71) Mahwah, NJ: Lawrence Erlbaum Associates.

Martinez, E. (1998). *De colores means all of us: Latina views for a multi-colored century.* Cambridge, MA: South End Press.

Nieto, S. (2007). *Affirming diversity: The sociopolitical context of multicultural education.* Boston, MA: Allyn & Bacon.

Noguera, P. A., & Wing, J. Y. (Eds.). (2006). *Unfinished business: Closing the racial achievement gap in our schools.* San Francisco, CA: Jossey-Bass.

ODportal.com. (n.d.). *Carl Jung*. Retrieved from http://www.odportal.com/personality/carl-jung.htm.

Palmer, P. (1998). *The courage to teach: Exploring the inner landscape of a teacher's life*. San Francisco, CA: Jossey-Bass.

Powell, J. A. (2007). National Black Latino summit working policy paper on necessary coalitions by the Kirwan Institute for the study of race and ethnicity. Columbus, OH: Ohio State University.

Powell, J. A. (2009). *African American-immigrant alliance building*. Columbus, OH: Ohio State University Kirwan Institute for the Study of Race and Ethnicity. Retrieved from http://research.kirwaninstitute.org/publications/kirwan.african_american_immigrant_report.pdf.

Reeves, D. (2009). *Leading change in your school: How to conquer myths, build commitment, and get results*. Alexandria, VA: ASCD.

Sinclair, R. L., & Ghory, W. J. (Eds.). (1997). *Reaching and teaching all children: Grassroots efforts that work* (6th ed.). Thousand Oaks, CA: Corwin.

Singleton, G., & Linton, C. (2006). *Courageous conversations about race*. Thousand Oaks, CA: Corwin.

Thompson, G. (2007). *Up where we belong: Helping African American and Latino students rise in school and in life*. San Francisco, CA: Jossey-Bass.

Facilitator Notes

2–1

Browne, J. (1975). *Multicultural press in elementary school classrooms: A function of selected learning conditions*. Doctoral dissertation, University of Massachusetts, Amherst.

Derman-Sparks, L., Higa, C. T., & Sparks, B. (1980). Children, race, and racism: How race awareness develops. *Interracial Books for Children Bulletin, 11*(3&4), 3–9.

3–2

Finn, P. J. (2009). *Literacy with an attitude: Educating working-class children in their own self-interest* (2nd ed.). Albany, NY: SUNY Press.

Kozol, J. (1991). *Savage inequalities: Children in America's schools*. New York, NY: HarperCollins.

Oakes, J., Wells, A., Datnow, A., & Jones, M. (1997). Detracking: The social construction of ability, cultural politics, and resistance to reform. *Teachers College Record, 98*(3), 482–511.

Tatum, B. D. (1997). *Why are all the Black kids sitting together in the cafeteria? And other conversations about race*. New York, NY: Basic Books.

3–3

Deal, T. E., & Peterson, K. D. (2009). *Shaping school culture: Pitfalls, paradoxes, and promises*. San Francisco, CA: Wiley.

5–4

Dutro, S. (2005). Providing language instruction. *Aiming High, Aspirando a loMejor, Resource*. Retrieved from http://www.scoe.org/docs/ah/AH_dutro.pdf.

LeMoine, N. (1999). *English for your success: A handbook of successful strategies for educators*. Saddle Brook, NJ: The Peoples Publishing Group.

9–6

Singleton, G., & Linton, C. (2006). *Courageous conversations about race.* Thousand Oaks, CA: Corwin.

11–2

Jackson, R. (2011). *How to plan rigorous instruction: Mastering the principles of great teaching.* Alexandria, VA: ASCD.

11–3

Reading Recovery Council of North America. (2012). *Reading recovery: Basic facts.* Retrieved from http://www.readingrecovery.org/reading_recovery/facts/index.asp.

11–5

Corbett, W., Wilson, B., & Williams, B. (2002). *Effort and excellence in urban classrooms: Expecting—and getting—success with all students.* New York, NY: Teachers College Press.
Mitra, D. L. (2008). *Student voice in school reform.* Albany, NY: SUNY Press.

13–2

Johnson, A. G. (2005). *Privilege, power, and difference* (2nd ed.). New York, NY: McGraw-Hill Humanities/Social Sciences/Languages.

Index

Pages followed by f indicate figures or charts

Academic English, 87
Academic tracking, 75
Access condition, 169f, 170–172
Accountability
    as condition of achieving schools, 174, 175f
    cultural inclusiveness lacking in, 65
    increasing, 115, 228
    lack of as barrier to high achievement, 94f, 98
    at Pierson, 209–211
    politics of implementation and, 142–145
    victimology and, 144, 271–272
Accreditation, 48–49, 84–85, 273–274
Acculturation, cultural democracy as not, 5
Achievement disparities
    cultural democracy and, 28–29, 102
    5 A's and, 177
    personal beliefs and, 141
    racial identity and, 20–21
    racism in, 209–210
    reasons given for, 6–7
    See also Barriers to high achievement
Achievement ethic, 280
Achieving schools
    access condition at, 169f, 170–172
    accountability condition at, 174, 175f
    adaptation condition at, 173, 173f
    assessment condition at, 171f, 172–173
    attitude condition at, 163–164f, 164–168
    PLCs and, 165
    prerequisites for, 160f, 161–162
    research on, 159
Adaption condition, 173, 173f
Advocacy
    community-based advisory committees as, 61
    community organizers for, 128–129
    efforts towards, 139
    increasing, 87, 113–115
    leadership and, 83
    negative labeling of, 111–112
    support compared, 114–115
Affinity groups, 221
African Americans. See Black students
Afrocentric teaching, 181–182

Asian students. See Brown students
Assessment
    cultural politics and, 53, 65, 73–74
    DiSC profiles, 101, 285
Assessment condition, 171f, 172–173
Assimilation, 5, 14
Attitude condition, 163–164f, 164–168
Autonomy, 17
Aversive racism, 25
Awareness building, 199

Barriers to high achievement
    overview, 91–93, 94f
    accountability and, 94f, 98
    biases and norms and, 102–106, 103–104f
    conflicts and, 100–101
    cultural democracy and, 101–102
    culturally courageous leadership role in, 107
    identity and, 99–100
    instructional staff support insufficient, 94f, 95–96
    at Pierson, 209–212
    politics of implementation and, 140–146, 184–185
    teaching problems, 94f, 96–97
    toxic climate, 94f, 97–98, 142
    weak instructional leadership, 93–95, 94f
Behavior, perceptions by others and, 30
Beliefs, 105–106, 141, 194
Benchmarks, 115
Bethune-Chavez high school cluster.
        See Role play exercise
Biased beliefs, 105–106
Biased norms, 105–106
Biases. See Institutional biases; "Isms"
Biculturalists, 18–19
Black psychology, 279
Black students
    alienation of, 34–35
    at CLAS, 180–183, 181f
    cultural divide from other groups by, 275
    de facto segregation of, 84
    in low-performing schools, 96
    racial identity, 18–19
    Saving the African American Child report, 74–75

Blind selves, 129
Board members, 63, 151–152
Breakthrough Coach, 184
Bribes, 98
Bridging Multiple Worlds: Case Studies of Diverse Educational Communities (Taylor and Whittaker), 74
Brown students
    alienation of, 34–35
    characteristics of strong schools for, 176
    cultural divide from other groups by, 275
    de facto segregation of, 84
    in low-performing schools, 96
    racial identity, 19
Bucknor, Janis, 180
Bullying, cultural democracy and, 39–40
Burks, Tony Lamair, 183–188, 185f

California, opportunity to learn standards in, 202
Campaign for high school equity (CHSE), 281
Caretakers. *See* Parents
Castaneda, A., 4–5
CCLDQ. *See Culturally Courageous Leadership Diagnostic Questionnaire* headings
Center for Culturally Responsive Teaching and Learning, 180
Change masters, 127–128
Circles of Co-practice, 49
Civil Rights Act of 1964, 5
CLAS (Culture and Language Academy of Success), 180–183, 181f
Climate
    diversity climate, 272
    expectations to change, 207
    toxic, 94f, 97–98, 142
Closet skeletons, 144
Coaching, 81
Coalition of black student equity, 183
Cognitive processing, 155
Collaboration
    across stakeholder groups, 150–151, 277
    for culturally courageous leadership, 117–120
    politics and, 135–136
    public dialogue to create, 270
    trust and, 166–167
Collaborative leadership, for problem-solving discussions, xv–xvi
Color-blind ideology, 16–17
Committed caregivers, 122
Common culture, perpetuation of, 32–33
Communication, 193–194, 210–211, 278
Communication gurus, 129–131, 177
Community-based advisory committees, 61
Community members, xv, 155–156, 225.
    See also Stakeholders
Community organizers, 128–129, 177.
    See also Advocacy
Conflict
    avoidance of, 284–285
    barriers to high achievement and, 100–101

consummate conciliators, 124–125
    interracial, 14, 19–20, 23
    between teachers, how handled, 166–167
    See also Identity
Connection power, 194
Conscientious coaches, 125–126
Consummate conciliators, 124–125
Content standards
    overview, 72f
    input standards and, 138
    institutional biases and, 71–73, 72f
    lacking cultural oppression information, 45
    media literacy skills lacking, 53
    See also Curriculum
Cook, D. A., 17
Courageous change masters, 127–128
Courageous conversations, 285
Covey, Steven, 278, 281–282
Cox, Taylor, Jr., 272
Crab barrel mentality, 271–272
Credentials. *See* Preservice programs
Cross-cultural education coalitions, scarcity of, 274–275
Cross W. E., 18–19
Cultural biases, types of, 6
Cultural blindness, 143
Cultural competence, development of, 49
Cultural connectedness, 49
Cultural consumers, 123
Cultural democracy
    barriers to high achievement and, 28–29, 101–102
    bullying and, 39–40
    cultural hegemony compared, 3–5
    culturally courageous leadership role in, 42
    defined, xv, 4–5
    educator resistance to, 32–33
    as equity transformation, 28–29
    as needing social and emotional competence, 39–40
    as outcome of transformation, xv
    toxic school environments as limiting, 28–29
    See also Dynamics of difference
Cultural dissonance
    as limiting equity initiatives, 63, 66–67
    at Pierson, 206
    teacher education and, 51–52
    trust building to reduce, 113
Cultural funds of knowledge, 45, 84, 139–140
Cultural hegemony, 3–5, 46–47, 74
Cultural legacies, 167
Culturally courageous leadership (CCL)
    barriers to high achievement and, 107
    cultural democracy, role in creating, 42
    defined, 4
    equity initiatives and, 68
    grim continuities and, 57
    identity/conflict issues, role in, 25
    institutional bias elimination, 90
    major actions needed by, 111–115
    politics and, 215–216

Culturally courageous leadership (CCL) paradigm
overview, 116, 116f
collaborative leadership needed for, 117–120
committed caregivers, 122
communication gurus, 129–131
community organizers, 128–129
conscientious coaches, 125–126
consummate conciliators, 124–125
courageous change masters, 127–128
cultural consumers, 123
strands of, 157
Culturally Courageous Leadership Diagnostic
Questionnaire (CCLDQ/I) for individuals
overview, 172, 242–243
interpretation of, 341–350
text of, 337–341
Culturally Courageous Leadership Diagnostic
Questionnaire (CCLDQ/SLE) for school learning
environments
overview, 172, 242–243
scoring of, 357–362
text of, 351–356
Cultural politics
CLAS struggle with, 181–183
culturally courageous leadership and, 111
human fears and, 56
inequitable student outcomes and, 51–53
power competition and, 192–193
rhetoric versus reality of, 61
Culture, defined, 271
Culture and Language Academy of Success (CLAS),
180–183, 181f
Curriculum
accreditation and, 48–49
cross-curriculum integration, 170
cultural politics and, 52
Eurocentric materials in, 46–47, 52, 75, 102
exclusion from, 3, 28–29
institutional biases in, 73–75
scarcity mentality, 53–54

Dance of the lemons, 143
Data collection, politics and, 136
Davis, A., 176
Decision-making process, 29, 246
Deep-seated equity transformation, 114
Delegation, risk of, 280–281
Delivery standards, 72f, 86–88, 138–139
Demographics, xv, 13–14, 74
Desegregation, 61, 83–84
Differentiated instruction, 82, 209
Discipline, reducing need for, 225,
229–230, 232
Discourse, bias against, 86–88
DiSC profiles, 101, 285
Discrimination. See "Isms"; Specific "isms" and biases
Distributed instructional leadership, 205, 207
District administrative leaders, 152–153. See also
Culturally courageous leadership (CCL)
Diversity climate, 272

Dream Keepers, 220
Dynamics of difference
overview, 29–31
accountability issues, 144
actions to improve, 36, 37–38f
defined, 2
as racial/cultural conflict, 28
Dysconscious racism, 153, 240

EDI (Explicit Direct Instruction), 220, 223
Education, purposes of, 5, 15–16. See also
Preservice programs
Educators
bullying and, 39
civility issues with, 98
equitable student outcomes, responsibility
for, 31
instructional staff support insufficient, 94f, 95–96
new teacher placement, 97
practices of, 153–154
racial identity levels of, 19–20
resistance to cultural democracy by, 32–33
supervision and evaluation of, 80–83, 223
teacher/student relationship, 21–25, 22f
teaching problems by, 96–97
See also Personnel selection and assignment
Efficacy, 160f, 162
Efficacy Institute, 141
Elementary and Secondary Education Act, 83
Employee contracts, as limiting equity initiatives, 63
Enemies as us, 271–272
English language learners, 86–88
Equality, equity compared, 6, 16–17
Equitable student outcomes
cultural democracy as important for, 28
cultural politics and, 51–53
defined, xv, 6
human fears and, 53–56
instructional hegemony and, 46–47
preservice programs and, 48–50
requirements for, 62, 83
teacher responsibility for, 31
Equity, equality compared, 6, 16–17
Equity hustlers, 146–147, 213–214
Equity initiatives
accountability and, 65
board members support for, 63
cultural dissonance as limiting, 63, 66–67
culturally courageous leadership role in, 68
don'ts for, 280–283
do's for, 277–280
examples of, 58
excuses, debunking of, 283–285
false dichotomies and, 65–66
perception of as threats, 66
plans for, 275–276
support for, 60–62
Ethos, 282
Evaluation and supervision of educators, 80–83,
105–106, 223

Expectations
   to change school climate, 207
   examination of, xiii
   as lower for historically underserved students of
      color, 35, 78
   of shared ownership, 231–232
   student desire for, 35
   teacher beliefs and, 106
Expert power, 194
Explicit Direct Instruction (EDI), 220, 223

False dichotomies, 65–66
Favored status, 28
Fears, 53–56, 111, 125–126, 143
5 A's
   access condition, 169f, 170–172
   accountability condition, 174, 175f
   achievement disparities and, 177
   actions needed for, 177–178
   adaption condition, 173, 173f
   assessment condition, 171f, 172–173
   attitude condition, 163–164f, 164–168
   Burks, Tony and, 183–187, 185f
   at CLAS, 180–183, 181f
   priority of, 177
Formal power, 194
Fundamentalist orientation, 17
Funding
   at CLAS, 182
   false dichotomies and, 66
   institutional biases and, 83–84
   mandates without money, 44, 144
   politics of implementation and, 139

Gangsters, 147, 213
Grim continuities. *See* Equitable student outcomes

Habits, 105–106
Habits of mind (HOM), 282
Harbor View Unified School District. *See* Role play
   exercise
Haywood, Kathryn
   comparisons with other equity warriors, 239–240
   interventions by, 227–231
   obstacles and politics for, 231–234
   personal background of, 226–227
Helms, J. E., 17
Hidden curriculum, 21–25, 22f, 112
Hidden selves, 129
High Achieving Middle Schools for Latino Students in
   Poverty (Jesse, Davis, Pokorny), 176
High achieving schools. *See* Achieving schools
Highly qualified teachers, 45, 84, 283
Hilliard, Asa G., III, 75
Historically underserved students of color
   alienation of, 2
   defined, 3
   identity and achievement of, 15–17
   lower expectations for, 35, 78

Hollie, Sharroky, 180, 187–188
HOM (habits of mind), 282
Home languages, 86–88
Howard G., 17–18
Human fears, 53–56, 111, 125–126, 143

Identity
   achievement and, 15–17
   barriers to high achievement and, 99–100
   culturally courageous leadership role in, 25
   educators response to students,' 272–273
   effects of, 13
   factors influencing, 21, 22f
   hidden curriculum and, 21–25, 22f
   influences on development of, 12–14
   instruction and, 46–47
   perceptions by others and, 21
   race and, 17–21
   racial identity, 17–21, 30
Identity kits, 86–87
Immigrants, 13–14, 281
Improvement plans, involvement in, 64–65
Inequities, examples of, 5–6
Information power, 194
Institutional biases
   overview, 70–71
   barriers to high achievement and, 103–104f
   communication about, 165
   culturally courageous leadership role in, 90
   curriculum, 73–75
   low socioeconomic status students, 83–86
   parent involvement and, 88–89
   personnel selection, 76–80, 81f
   schedules, 73–75
   standards and, 71–73, 72f
   against student's primary discourse,
      86–88
   supervision and evaluation of educators, 80–83
Institutionalized antiracism, 219
Institutional racism, defined, 208
Instructional leadership
   Burks, Tony and, 185–186
   cultural politics and, 52
   distributed instructional leadership,
      205, 207
   lack of as barrier to high achievement, 93–95, 94f
   networks to increase, 211
   politics of implementation and, 140–142
Instructional rounds, 230
Integrationist orientation, 17–18
Interactional model of impact of diversity, 272
Interests-based negotiation, 118
Intergroup relations, 30, 37–38f
Internalization, 18–19
Interpersonal relations, 30, 37–38f, 100
Interstate School Leaders Licensure Consortium
   (ISLLC), 48–49
Intervention programs, 174
Intrapersonal conflict, 30, 100

"Isms"
consummate conciliators and, 124
defined, 273
as inhibiting transformation, 137
prevalence of, 273
racism, 7, 153, 207–208, 224, 240
See also Barriers to high achievement; Institutional biases
I statements, 222, 224, 225

Jackson, Anthony, 180
Jesse, D., 176
Judgment skill, 246

Language, 49, 86–88, 186, 281
Latino/a's. *See* Brown students
Leaders. *See* Culturally courageous leadership (CCL)
Leadership
enhancing of, 281–282
narrow paradigm for, 64–65
psychological and job maturity for, 280
weak instructional leadership, 93–95, 94f
Legitimate power, 194
Limited English proficient students (LEP), increases in numbers of, 13–14
Logos, 282
Low-performing schools, racial percentages in, 96
Loyalty versus effectiveness, 95

Mandates, unfunded, 44, 144
McWhorter, J. H., 144
Media, 52, 53
Mis-education of the Negro (Woodson), 74
Modeling, 281–282
Montoya, Robert
comparisons with other equity warriors, 239–240
interventions by, 235–237
obstacles experienced by, 238–239
personal background of, 234–235
Mount Vernon School District, 195–202
Multiculturalists, 18–19
Murrell, P. C., 16
Mutual interdependence, 143

National Alliance of Black School Educators (NABSE), 74
National Association of Secondary School Principals (NASSP) Principal Assessment Center, 135, 245–246
National Center for Urban School Transformation (NCUST), 186–187
National Council for Accreditation of Teacher Education (NCATE), 48–49
Nationalists, 18–19
National Urban Alliance for Effective Education, 49
Network for culturally courageous schools (NCCS), 286
Nigrescence theory, 18–19

No Child Left Behind (NCLB) Act
cultural inclusiveness lacking in, 65
gaps in, 44–45
specificity lacking, 85
standards and, 73–74
Norms, 105–106, 115

Observations, use of, 139–140, 205–208
Opportunity, defined, 201
Opportunity to learn standards, 72f, 138–139, 201–202
Organizational culture, impact of, 35–36
Organizational transformation, 133–134
Organization skill, 246

PAL. *See* Pierson Academy for Leadership (PAL)
Parents
bias against involvement of, 88–89
equity initiatives, role in, 64–65, 117–120
involvement by, 170, 173–174
leadership role for, 280–281
practices of, 155
professional development, involvement in, 77
Pathos, 282
Performance standards, 72f, 73–74
Personal power, 194
Personal Profiles (DiSC), 101, 285
Personal transformation, 133–134
Personnel selection and assignment
dance of the lemons, 143
encouraging uncooperative teachers to leave, 223–224
institutional biases in, 76–80, 81f
retention of exemplary staff, 187
special needs students and, 175–176
Pierson Academy for Leadership (PAL)
barriers to high achievement at, 209–212
distributed instructional leadership at, 205
equity hustlers and, 213–214
observations, use of, 205–208
vignette, 203–204
Pilot programs, 277–278
PLCs (professional learning communities), 165, 220–221
Pokorny, N., 176
Policies, xvi, 84
Political land mines
overview, 190–191
culturally courageous leadership role in, 215–216
at Mount Vernon School District, 195–202
politics, defined, 191–192
problem definition and analysis and, 197–198
psychology of transformation and, 198–200
reform versus transformation, 194
savvy and, 193–194
See also Pierson Academy for Leadership (PAL)
Political mobilization, 66
Political savvy, 193–194

Political will, 67
Politics, 191–193. *See also* Cultural politics
Politics of implementation
    accountability and, 142–145
    barrier reduction and, 140–146, 184–185
    educator resistance and, 32–33
    equity hustlers and, 146–147
    importance of addressing, xvi
    observations, use of, 139–140
    politics, definitions and, 192–193
    problem definition and analysis dimension, 134–136
    sensitivity to psychology of transformation
        and, 137
    standards getting low priority due to, 138–139
    transformation, relationship to, 132–134
    See also Cultural politics
Positionalities, 16
Power, types of, 194
Power-dominant bullies, 39
Power-lax bullies, 39
Pre-encounter stage, 18
Prejudice, persons of color experiencing the most, 14
Preservice programs
    discriminatory practices and, 112–113
    institutional biases and, 84
    institutional biases in, 76
    lacking cultural oppression information, 48–50,
        63–64
    practices of, 156
    See also Montoya, Robert
Principals, weak instructional leadership, 93–95, 94f
Prioritization, wars versus battles, 278–279
Privileged status, 61, 220–221
Problem analysis skill, 245
Problem definition and analysis dimension, 134–136,
    197–198
Professional development
    cultural politics and, 52
    discriminatory practices and, 112–113
    institutional biases in, 76–80, 81f
    to institutionalize advocacy, 60–61
    lacking cultural oppression information, 48–50,
        63–64
    student and parent involvement in, 77
Professional development standards, 72f,
    138–139, 201
Professional learning communities (PLCs),
    165, 220–221
Psychology of transformation, 137, 198–200
Push back. *See* Resistance

Racial/cultural conflicts. *See* Dynamics of difference
Racial identity, 17–21, 30
Racism
    courageous conversations about, 224
    cultural democracy and, 7
    defined, 207–208
    dysconscious racism, 153, 240

Ramirez, M., III, 4–5
Referent power, 194
Reforms, transformation compared, 62, 140, 194,
    214–215
Research, 50, 273, 274
Resistance
    to both levels of transformation, 190
    by educators, 32–33, 50
    to instructional rounds, 230
    preparation to address, 278
    strategies to overcome, 275–276
    underestimating of, 282–283
Responsibility, 160f, 161–162. *See also* Accountability
Retaliation, fear of, 143
Reward power, 194
Richardson, Jean
    comparisons with other equity warriors, 239–240
    interventions by, 219–222
    obstacles and politics for, 222–225
    personal background of, 218–219
    priorities of, 225–226
Riders, 147, 213–214
Rodriquez, Enrique. *See* Role play exercise
Role play exercise
    background information for, 244–245
    in-basket items, 249–259, 256–257f
    culturally courageous leadership paradigm and,
        260–267
    directions for, 245–246
    draft action plan considerations, 259–260
    prerequisites for, 243–244
    problem at school, 247–249
Ruiz, A. S., 19

Sacred cows, 133
San Diego Unified School District, 183–187, 185f
Saving the African American Child (Hilliard and
    Sizemore), 74–75
Scapegoating, 39–40
Scarcity mentality, 53–54
Schedules, 52, 65–66, 73–75, 170–171
School communities, defined, 6
School site administrators, 98, 152–153. *See also*
    Culturally courageous leadership (CCL)
Secondary discourse, 87
Segregation, within desegregated schools, 83–84
Self-identity. *See* Identity
Sensitivity skill, 246
Seven principles
    committed caregivers, 122
    communication gurus, 129–131
    community organizers, 128–129
    conscientious coaches, 125–126
    consummate conciliators, 124–125
    courageous change masters, 127–128
    cultural consumers, 123
Shared ownership, expectation of, 231–232
Shining lights, closet skeletons of, 144

Silent conspiracies, 273–274
Situated-mediated identity theory, 16
Sizemore, Barbara A., 75
Small group problem-solving, 81
Social justice, assumptions for, xiv
Social promotion, 35
Socioeconomic status, 83–86, 88–89
Special needs students, 175–176
Staff meetings, focus at, 227–228
Stakeholders
    administrators, practices of, 152–153
    board members, practices of, 151–152
    collaboration needed by, 150–151, 277
    community members, practices of, 155–156
    cultural dissonance, 63, 66–67
    defined, 4, 6
    equity initiatives, role in, 117–120
    parents, practices of, 155
    preservice programs, practices of, 156
    problem-solving involvement, 200
    psychology of transformation and, 137
    students, practices of, 156–157
    support staff, practices of, 155
    teachers, practices of, 153–154
    trust lacking by, 67–68
Standard English, 87
Standards
    delivery standards, 72f, 86–88, 138–139
    opportunity to learn standards, 72f, 138–139
    opportunity to learn standards as, 201–202
    performance standards, 72f, 73–74
    professional development standards, 72f,
        138–139
    professional development standards as, 201
    See also Content standards
Status quo, losing, 55–56
Stereotyping, 19, 51
Stress tolerance, 246
Structural biases, 6, 52. See also Institutional biases
Student motivation, perceptions by others and, 40–42
Students
    equity initiatives, role in, 64–65, 117–120
    fear of, 143
    input of, xv
    leadership by, 168
    leadership role for, 280–281, 285–286
    practices of, 156–157
    professional development, involvement in, 77
    special needs students, 175–176
    using prior knowledge of, 78
Students of color. See Historically underserved
        students of color
Supervision and evaluation of educators, 80–83,
        105–106, 223

Support, 63, 94f, 95–96, 114–115
Support staff, practices of, 155
Suspensions, 225, 232
Synergy groups, 211

Talking tickets, 225
Taylor and Whittaker, 74
Teacher preparation programs. See Preservice
        programs
Teachers. See Educators; Preservice programs
Teacher/student relationship, hidden curriculum and,
        21–25, 22f
Team building, 113, 199–200
Teamwork, 165–166, 220
Textbooks, 45–47, 53
Timing, 283–285. See also Schedules
Title I schools, 85–86
Toxic climate, 94f, 97–98, 142
Tracking, 75, 193, 220–221
Transformation
    personal versus organizational, 133–134
    reforms compared, 62, 140, 194, 214–215
Transformationist orientation, 18
Translations, 186, 281
Transparent racism, 208
Trim-tab leaders, 282
Truancy rates, 34
Trust building
    collaboration and, 166
    with parents, 232
    at Pierson, 212
    political land mines and need for, 199–200
    to reduce cultural dissonance, 113
    resistance to, 67–68

Unconscious incompetence, 144–145
Universities. See Preservice programs
University Council for Educational Administration
        (UCEA), 48–49
Urgency, 160f, 161–162

Victimology, 144, 271–272
Violence, 143
Vygotsky's zone of proximal development (ZPD),
        279–280

Wanksters, 146–147, 213
White privilege, 61, 220–221
White racial identity model (WRIM), 17–18
Willie, Charles V., 237
Woodson, Carter G., 74

Zone of proximal development (ZPD), 279–280
ZPD (zone of proximal development), 279–280

CORWIN
A SAGE Company

The Corwin logo—a raven striding across an open book—represents the union of courage and learning. Corwin is committed to improving education for all learners by publishing books and other professional development resources for those serving the field of PreK–12 education. By providing practical, hands-on materials, Corwin continues to carry out the promise of its motto: **"Helping Educators Do Their Work Better."**